東京

ロバート　スティルガー

七十一年　二月　六日

This is the first in a series of five volumes to be published by Princeton University Press for The Conference on Modern Japan of the Association for Asian Studies. The remaining four volumes in the series are:

The State and Economic Enterprise in Modern Japan, edited by William W. Lockwood

Aspects of Social Change in Modern Japan, edited by R. P. Dore

Political Development in Modern Japan, edited by Robert E. Ward

Tradition and Modernization in Japanese Culture, edited by Donald H. Shively

Changing
Japanese Attitudes
Toward Modernization

Edited by
MARIUS B. JANSEN

CONTRIBUTORS

ROBERT N. BELLAH	MARIUS B. JANSEN
ALBERT CRAIG	SHŪICHI KATŌ
R. P. DORE	MASAO MARUYAMA
ROGER F. HACKETT	HERBERT PASSIN
JOHN WHITNEY HALL	DONALD H. SHIVELY
STEPHEN N. HAY	HERSCHEL WEBB
JOHN F. HOWES	HELLMUT WILHELM

PRINCETON UNIVERSITY PRESS

PRINCETON, NEW JERSEY

Foreword

Scholarly studies of Japan have had a remarkable growth in the United States and other English-speaking countries since the end of World War II. To some extent this has been the natural result of the popular boom of interest in Japan stimulated by the war and its aftermath and by the increased opportunities which Westerners had to come in contact with the Japanese people. But it is more directly the result of the proliferation of academic programs devoted to Japan and particularly the appearance of a large number of scholarly specialists trained to handle the Japanese language.

In the fall of 1958 a group of scholars gathered at the University of Michigan to seek some means of bringing together in more systematic fashion the results of the variegated and intensive studies of Japan which had appeared in the years since the end of the war. The Conference on Modern Japan which resulted from this meeting was dedicated both to the pooling of recent scholarly findings and to the stimulation of new ideas and approaches to the study of modern Japan. Subsequently the Conference received a generous grant from the Ford Foundation for the support of a series of five annual seminars devoted to as many aspects of the problem of Japan's modern development.

The Conference on Modern Japan exists as a special project under the auspices of the Association for Asian Studies. The Conference is guided by an executive committee consisting of: Ronald P. Dore, Marius

B. Jansen, William W. Lockwood, Donald H. Shively, Robert E. Ward, and John W. Hall (chairman). Each member of the executive committee is responsible for the organization of a separate seminar devoted to his particular field of specialization, and the proceedings of the five major seminars are being published.

Although the subject of modernization *in the abstract* is not a major topic of interest to the Conference, conceptual problems are inevitably of concern for the entire series of seminars. Because of this, two less-formal discussions on the theory of modernization have also been planned as part of the Conference's program. The first of these was held in Japan slightly over a year preceding the seminar reported in this volume. The concluding conference will seek to review whatever contributions in theory the five major seminars may have made to a better understanding of the modernization of Japan in theoretical terms.

The present volume edited by Marius B. Jansen is thus the first in a series of five to be published by the Princeton University Press for the Conference on Modern Japan. The remaining four volumes are: *Social Change in Modern Japan*, edited by R. P. Dore; *The State and Economic Enterprise in Modern Japan*, edited by William W. Lockwood; *Political Development in Modern Japan*, edited by Robert E. Ward; *Tradition and Modernization in Japanese Culture*, edited by Donald H. Shively. As their titles reveal, the annual seminars have adopted broad themes in order to cast a wide net about the many scholars working within each of several major fields. Within these broad fields, however, the seminar chairmen have focused upon specific problems recommended either because they have received the greatest attention of Japanese specialists or because they seem most likely to contribute to a fuller understanding of the modernization of Japan. We trust, as a consequence, that the five volumes taken together will prove both representative of current scholarship on Japan and comprehensive in their coverage of one of the most fascinating stories of national development in recent history.

JOHN WHITNEY HALL

Contents

CONTENTS

PART ONE

The Genesis and Nature of the Inquiry

The papers which follow were prepared by the authors for a seminar held in Bermuda under the auspices of the Conference on Modern Japan of the Association for Asian Studies in January 1962. Although the first substantive meeting of the Conference on Modern Japan, the 1962 seminar was preceded by, and generically related to, a preliminary conference held in Hakone, Japan, from August 29 to September 2, 1960. This conference had a large proportion of Japanese scholars in attendance. Participants were as follows: E. S. Crawcour, Australian National University; Ronald P. Dore, London School of Economic Studies; Toshio Furushima, Tokyo University; Norton S. Ginsburg, University of Chicago; John W. Hall, Yale University; Roger Hackett, University of Michigan; Yasuzō Horie, Kyoto University; Chūzō Ichiko, Ochanomizu University; Marius B. Jansen, Princeton University; Madoka Kanai, Tokyo University; Shūichi Katō, University of British Columbia; Takeyoshi Kawashima, Tokyo University; Masaaki Kōsaka, Kyoto University; Hyman Kublin, Brooklyn College; Marion Levy, Jr., Princeton University; Robert Lifton, Yale University; Masao Maruyama, Tokyo University; Takashi Nakano, Tokyo University of Education; Jirō Numata, Tokyo University; Saburō Ōkita, Economic Planning Board, Japanese Government; Toshiaki Ōkubo, Rikkyō University; Tsutomu Ōuchi, Tokyo University; Richard W. Rabinowitz, Program Secretary, Japanese American Program for Cooperation in Legal Studies; (Ambassador) Edwin O. Reischauer, Harvard University; Henry Rosovsky, University of California at Berkeley; Yoshio Sakata, Kyoto University; Donald H. Shively, Harvard University; Shigeki Tōyama, Yokohama University; and Herschel Webb, Columbia University. In addition, A. Doak Barnett and John S. Everton of the Ford Foundation were present as observers, and T. Arima (Harvard University), S. Nakamura (University of California), and Tatsuo Tanabe of the International House of Japan, Inc., assisted with local arrangements and translation when needed.

The conference served to clarify conceptual problems (sometimes by highlighting disagreements) involved in the definition of modernization as a concept and in applying it to the case of Japan. The free and full discussion of those five days served two functions. It helped to sharpen awareness of conceptual problems common to all future seminars, and it served to focus the attention of social scientists in Japan upon the idea of approaching their country's modern transformation in this manner. The numerous summaries and commentaries on the concepts and methods aired in the conference that have appeared in Japanese journals showed the high degree of interest the Hakone meeting stimulated. It was also, to the best of our knowledge, the first truly international gathering in which Japanese served as the official language. John W. Hall, Chairman of the Conference on Modern Japan and principal organizer of the Hakone meeting, discusses its setting and significance in the paper which opens this volume.

With the Hakone meeting past, the Conference turned next to the preparation of the first of the five seminars. Planning and organization were the responsibility of the editor.[1] The theme selected as focus was "Changing Japanese Attitudes Toward Modernization." The reason for this is that at many points in Japan's recent century, and particularly in times of crisis, the responses of representative and leading Japanese were necessarily conditioned by the climate of opinion within which they moved and the picture of their world as it was known to them. It is therefore appropriate to investigate those areas at the outset, not so much in expectation of finding there the key to the Japanese response to the West, as to become freshly aware of the complexity of interrelationships between elements of "tradition," imported and indigenous, as they changed during the period of modernization. The second paper, "Changing Japanese Attitudes Toward Modernization," thus served as seminar focus and as survey of the larger problems which later chapters treat. In addition to authors of the chapters in this volume, the following participated in the seminar: E. Sydney Crawcour, Australian National University; Mitsusada Inoue,[2] Tokyo University; James W. Morley, Columbia University; Thomas C. Smith, Stanford University; and Robert E. Ward, University of Michigan.

[1] Assisted at various junctures by a committee which included W. Theodore de Bary, Roger F. Hackett, J. W. Hall, H. Passin, and E. O. Reischauer.

[2] Hereafter in the text only of this volume all Japanese names are given in Japanese manner with surname first.

CHAPTER I

Changing Conceptions of the Modernization of Japan[1]

JOHN WHITNEY HALL

> To have lived through the transition stage of
> modern Japan makes a man feel preternat-
> urally old; for here he is in modern times,
> . . . and yet he can himself distinctly remem-
> ber the Middle Ages.[2]
>
> —BASIL HALL CHAMBERLAIN

THE modernization of Japan is a phenomenon which cannot be viewed casually by any serious observer. Whether one looks upon it as some Westerners have done as the first phase in the rise of a new "peril from the East" or, on the contrary, as a miraculous example of progress from out of an Oriental Middle Ages; whether one sees it as the Japanese themselves have done as the triumph of their unique national will against great odds or as the dark story of autocratic domination leading to imperialist war, the observations are highly colored and strongly lined. For the observer who would maintain his impartiality, the facts of the last hundred years or so of Japanese history are available in great abundance and in rich detail. Yet the efforts to find meaning in these facts have been bafflingly varied. The contrasting popular stereotypes of Japan as a land of quaint exoticism or brutal militarism are no less extreme than the conflicting views of supposedly impartial academic observers. Inevitably the differing premises from which these observers have begun their studies and the varying degrees of involve-

[1] This paper is intended in part to summarize the discussion which took place at the 1960 Hakone Conference.

[2] Basil Hall Chamberlain, *Things Japanese* (London, 1891), p. 1.

ment which they have felt in the dramatic events of revolution, war, depression, or prosperity in Japan have colored their interpretations of Japan's modern development.

It is impossible to achieve any sort of dialogue on the subject of modern Japan unless some minimum agreement exists about what is being discussed. We need a common understanding of the meaning of modernization—that is our ideas about the nature of modern society and the process by which it came into being—if the recent history of Japan is to be discussed in terms other than a set of discrete monologues. For in a very fundamental way the scholar's conception of modernization sets the premises with which he approaches his data and frames the problems which he considers worthy of study. It is the glass through which he reads the events of Japanese history and judges their coloration. Although most scholarship on Japan is not consciously based on a particular conception of modernization, yet the hidden assumptions or the unconscious intellectual contexts which shape the organization of research and the setting of problems derive from some fundamental commitment to a view of the nature of modern society.

The idea of modernization as a technical term which can comprehend the essential features of the process of modern history is of relatively recent origin. As in all cases in which a technical term is created out of a word drawn from the vocabulary of common speech, we must expect that any technical usage will inevitably be confused with its more common meanings. The words "modern" and "modernization" have a fairly lengthy history, and there exists a wide variety of common assumptions about their meaning. From the technical point of view, of course, such ideas must be regarded as arbitrary or inadequate. And yet each generation has felt confident in its particular explanation of the modernizing process. And each generation has measured Japan's development against its own set of standards derived from such explanatory assumptions.

Most Westerners have assumed without much question that the standards of modernization against which Japan should be measured should be taken from the values inherent in the West's own experience of modernization. Western writers have tended to swing between hope and alarm, or between admiration and disparagement, depending upon the particular comparisons they have chosen, and especially upon the manner in which they have reacted to the Japanese impact upon the national interests of their respective countries. In the early decades after the opening of Japan, the British and American businessmen in Yokohama or the Western technical advisors in Japanese government saw Japan as a backward country nearly untouched by the technological progress of which the Westerners were so proud. Their early assessment was in terms of standards of living, miles of railroad track or telephone wires, or harbor facilities. But as Japan closed the technological gap and became a nation committed to the same goals toward which the West was striving, admiration for Japan's new achievements was tempered by a concern over her backwardness in such areas as social legislation or national morality. Material progress was not everything, the Westerner claimed. The essence of Western civilization must be looked for in the Christian ethic, or at least in the liberal tradition regarding the dignity of man and the democratic process in government. And so the missionary rued the lack of a Christian sense of sin or the wartime correspondent judged Japan as a country which had mastered the technology of modern warfare but had remained culturally and morally barbaric. "As Japan has had no adequate conception of God," wrote Sidney Gulick, "her conception of man has been of necessity defective."[3]

For those who observed Japan during and following the first and second world wars the main criteria for judging Japan's advance as a world power were the twin concepts of democracy and liberalism. Japan's failure to develop a stable party government and the drift toward militarism

[3] Sidney L. Gulick, *Evolution of the Japanese* (New York, London, 1903), pp. 312-313. The extreme expression of wartime hatred of the Japanese is expressed by Otto Tolischus, *Through Japanese Eyes* (New York, 1945), pp. 158-161.

and alliance with the Axis were looked at as aberrations, as signs of a malady which had infected a potentially safe member of the democratic community. But the chance to cure that malady was given. Seldom in world history has one group of nations had such an opportunity to reform an entire people according to their conception of proper domestic and international behavior. The Allied Occupation was in fact a massive attempt to put Japan on the right track as a modernizing country. As many SCAP publications so naïvely pointed out, Japan was to be rid of a disease, made safe for democracy, and inculcated with the values of the "free world." These assumptions still dominate our thinking on Japan today. And the friendliness of off-Ginza bar girls or the dexterity with which the Japanese government has stayed within the confines of Western policy has engendered the era of good will and optimism which characterizes our present relations with "Japan, the new far west."[4]

To be sure, these judgments and the premises upon which they have rested, have not gone unchallenged. There have been those who have refused to measure Japan against the Western conception of progress. But too often such counter judgments have come from persons who have succumbed to the "lure of the Orient." Their demands that the West slow down its clocks to the tempo of "old Japan" have rung hollow even to the Japanese. The voice of true objectivity has been rare indeed. Yet a turn of the century comment by a long-time missionary in Japan could express quite poignantly the dilemma of cross-cultural observation. "We ought to remember," said the Reverend Otis Cary, "that the besetting sins of a foreign people seem worse to us because they are not the ones that most tempt us; and that we may fail to appreciate another's virtues because they are not the ones that we make most prominent."[5]

The postwar world of Western scholarship has sought con-scientiously to find some objective ground from which to ap-

[4] See the special issue of *Show* Magazine for May 1963 entitled "Japan the New Far West."
[5] Otis Cary, *Japan and Its Regeneration* (New York, 1899), p. 25.

proach the problem of comparison. Anthropologists, developmental economists, and more recently political scientists and sociologists have attempted to push beneath the obvious levels of comparison which had been used by layman and scholar up to the present. Yet in the face of ideas proposed by the prominent generalists such as Marx, Weber, or Toynbee, the work of the modern social scientist has been confined pretty much to his limited disciplinary interest. The problem of creating a unified concept of modernization has received scant attention. The meaning of the modern world has remained, therefore, enclosed in such admittedly inadequate concepts as Westernization, democratization, or industrialization, or in the limited technical vocabulary of the social science disciplines. It is in this context that the concept of modernization has been brought into being as something more inclusive of the total range of changes affecting the world in modern times.

Conceptions of modernization and of Japan's place in modern history have been as varied in Japan as in the West. Cultural chauvinism has not been confined to the West. The wartime surge of ultra-nationalism and pride in "unique national qualities" was but the extreme expression of the Japanese counter-reaction to the impact of the West. Yet there has always seemed to be more fanaticism than certitude in the Japanese assertions of superiority. While Okakura was condemning the West for its materialism and calling for a return to the age-old inner truth which was the secret of Asia, the Japanese around him remained entranced by the example of the West. Even in that high pronouncement of traditional Japanese values, the *Kokutai no hongi*, Japan's role in the modern world was pictured as that of an amalgamator between the best of East and West.[6]

Despite fervent cries to "stay as you are" from Western Japanophiles, the Japanese have avidly looked to Europe and America for their inspiration. From the moment the Japanese gave up their voluntary seclusion from the world, comparison with the West has dominated their opinion of themselves. The Charter Oath linked the abandonment of "base customs

[6] R. K. Hall, ed., *Kokutai no hongi* (Cambridge, 1949), pp. 175-183.

of former times" and the securing of knowledge from abroad with the "strengthening of the foundation of the Imperial polity."[7] Except for some of the early Meiji enthusiasts such as Inoue, who suggested the need for miscegenation between the Japanese and the white race, or Mori, who proposed abandonment of the Japanese language, few Japanese have claimed the need for the complete remaking of the Japanese way of life. The desirability of selectivity and the inevitability of retaining cultural differences has generally softened the attitude with which Japanese have looked upon the success or failure of their efforts at modernization. "Modernization in Japan," writes the foremost educator Yanaihara Tadao, "involves Japan's importation and assimilation of the institutions, technology, and culture of Europe and the United States. Simply stated it is equivalent to the Westernization of Japan's society and culture . . . but it is not the way of the world that Japanese society should become exactly like that of the West. World culture is to be enriched by the peculiar characteristics and differences of the cultures of various peoples in the world."[8]

The assumption that modernization in Japan was equivalent to Westernization has tended to direct the search for definition of modernization among Japanese toward the task of finding "meaning" in Western civilization. What, in other words, were the essential features of the West which should be emulated? The early flirtation with Christianity, the vacillation between laissez-faire liberalism and militant statism, even the emulation of Hitlerian Germany were justified on the basis that each effort brought Japan closer to the secret of the West's success. Each generation of Japanese has had its particular sensitivities as to where Japan fell short of the Western ideal. Fukuzawa's advocacy of equality, Katō's re-

[7] These are phrases from the official translation. See Ishii Ryōsuke, ed., William J. Chambliss, trans., *Japanese Legislation in the Meiji Era* (Tokyo, 1958), p. 145.

[8] Yanaihara Tadao, *Kindai Nihon shoshi*, 2 vols., Tokyo, 1952, vol. 1, pp. 9-10. I am grateful to Mr. Motoyama Yukihiko for suggestions regarding the contemporary Japanese conception of modernization.

turn to nationalism, the militarist's dream of an Asiatic empire have seemed in successive eras the most essential goals for a Japan striving for identity in a new world. Since the Pacific war the goals have again changed. To Professor Yanaihara, continuing his previous statement, "Japan cannot be satisfied merely with the introduction of the externals of Western culture but must discover the essence, the basic spirit, of that culture and make this part of the flesh and blood of Japan. The spirit which stands at the center of Western civilization is indeed democracy."[9] To Professor Rōyama Masamichi the essentials appeared to be three: democracy, nationalism, and industrialization.[10] To the Left Socialist, the democratic ideal could only be achieved under socialist conditions.

Despite the popularity of the Western liberal ideal, for the Japanese intellectual, Marxism has seemed the most useful key to the discovery of the essentials of Western civilization and of the long range changes affecting the modern world. Few other concepts of modernization have appeared to the Japanese so comprehensive and so capable of application to the Japanese experience as that which sees the march of national history from feudalism through capitalism to socialism and which identifies two modern revolutions, bourgeois and proletariat, as the turning points in this march. The attractiveness of the system of economic determinism is that it seemed both inclusive and specific. It laid out the criteria for defining stages of development and critical points of analysis for determining the condition of a given society at a given time. The great prewar debates among Japanese historians and economists regarding the level which Japan had attained as a modern society were couched in terms of Marxist terminology and debated whether Japan had indeed experienced a bourgeois revolution or whether the oligarchic nature of Japanese government had imposed upon the country an absolutism which distorted the "normal course" of modernization. Arguments between the so-called Rōnō and Kōza groups in Japan

[9] *Ibid.*
[10] Rōyama Masamichi, "Atarashii kokka kan ni tsuite" in *Rekishi kyōiku*, vol. 6, no. 9 (1958.9), pp. 1-9.

have continued to the present day to divide the orthodox adherents of the Marxist interpretation.

The lack of dialogue in Japan between Marxists and non-Marxists has seemed to preclude the evaluation of Marxist theory on any empirical basis. Alternative points of view have generally been posed as competing systems based on entirely different premises. (Weber, in other words, is pitted against Marx.) For this reason it is all the more interesting to note a recent upsurge of skepticism among young historians who have heretofore been noted for their Marxian orthodoxy. Men such as Inoue Kiyoshi have claimed that time and place have made Japan's contemporary revolution inevitably different from the nineteenth century prototype revolutions; others like Eguchi Bokurō question the applicability of the traditional Marxist schema to contemporary Asian and African historical development. Though such skepticism stems less from a recognition of the limitations of deterministic theory than from a pan-Asian sense of revolt against subservience to the West, nonetheless it has questioned the acceptability of previously unchallenged Marxist concepts at the very time that scholars in the West have sought to work out a universal concept of modernization detached from familiar assumptions about Westernization or democratization.[11]

The attempt to devise a unified and objective conception of modernization is not a light task, for it calls upon the scholar first to detach himself from the actual flow of history around him and secondly to give up any preconceptions he may have had about the values upon which modern society might rest. An earlier generation of scholars could rest assured that Japan should be judged by comparison with the West, either in terms of the actual history of a country such as England, or against some ideal process such as that outlined by Marx. To the present generation of scholars these certainties are denied. The beauty of the older formulae was that they provided exact criteria for measurement. One could say with assurance

[11] Inoue Kiyoshi, *Nihon rekishi kenkyū nyūmon*, Tokyo, 1952. Eguchi Bokurō, "Gendaishi ni okeru burujyowa kakumei," in *Rekishigaku kenkyū*, vol. 234 (1959.10).

that the Japanese political party was "less modern" than the British or that Japan showed an "imbalance" in its economic development. Today we find such neat judgments harder to accept. But once one breaks with the old set of criteria, what judgments can one make? Is it possible to establish another set of universal measures, or are we to fall into a morass of relativity? The answer is, of course, *neither* in quite the same sense as these questions are asked. For our search turns these days less toward definitional certainties than to the working out of consistent methods of analysis which can lead to comparable results, an effort in other words to guide our inquiries by a consistent logic so that our dialogue may be continuous.

While it was not the intention of our Conference to devote its major effort to the formulation of some theory of modernization which might become the conceptual basis for the succession of substantive seminars which we had planned, we found ourselves drawn into the modernization controversy as the plans for seminars matured. And so it was that the Conference organized as its first meeting, a discussion among Western and Japanese scholars on the subject of modernization at Hakone in the summer of 1960.[12] This meeting, and the subsequent publications on the subject of modernization which appeared from the pens of several of those who attended the Hakone session, began an effort at revaluation of the concept of modernization around the Japanese example which will surely continue throughout the life of the Conference itself.[13]

[12] See above for participants at the Conference.
[13] Although no formal effort was made to elicit papers from the participants in the Conference a number of informal papers were written in response to a short statement on modernization circulated by the Conference chairman. After the meeting Messrs. Tōyama, Dore, and Reischauer wrote articles reporting on the Conference in the Tokyo press. Messrs. Hall and Kawashima had an exchange of viewpoints in *Shisō*; Mr. Reischauer wrote a piece which appeared in Japanese in *Chūō kōron* (March 1963) and later in English translation in *Japan Quarterly*, vol. x, no. 3 (July-Sept. 1963), pp. 298-307. And Messrs. Jansen and Bellah contributed essays on modernization to a special issue of *Asian Cultural Studies* published by International Christian University. Some of the above articles are cited below. A mimeo-

Whatever the success or failure of the Hakone meeting, it served as a milestone in bringing together a variety of viewpoints on the subject of Japan's modernization, and if nothing else it cast into relief the possible conflicts of interpretation which might emerge in the substantive discussions which were to follow.

Whatever it is that we are trying to name and comprehend by the term modernization, it is something that has happened in the real world within only the last few centuries; the conviction that these happenings can and should be named rests upon the premise that they constitute a new and distinct phenomenon in world development. As Mr. Reischauer put it, "When one compares the societies of most parts of the world in 1960 with those existing in these areas a few centuries (or in some places only a few decades) earlier, it becomes evident that great changes have taken place and are still under way. These changes appear to be far more fundamental than those that occurred in the same number of years at most other times in history. Moreover, they appear to be taking the same general direction all over the world and are not moving in different or opposite directions, as has sometimes been the case in the past. These changes are so profound and also so similar throughout the world that it seems possible that society is passing through a great transformation, comparable perhaps to those at the time when men made the transition from a hunting-gathering economy to agriculture or from the use of stone implements to those of bronze and iron. How great the present transformation may be we cannot yet determine, because we obviously are still in the midst of it, with no idea as to how far or where it will lead us. This is why it is difficult to grasp the essential features of this change and why it may be best to use a vague, unspecific term like 'modernization' to designate it."[14]

---

graphed record of the Conference was prepared by Mr. Kanai in Japanese. This is referred to below as *Gijiroku*.

[14] E. O. Reischauer, "An Approach to the Study of Modernization" (Hakone Conference Paper, mimeo.), pp. 1-2.

Perhaps "vague" and "unspecific" are not the words most appropriate to express the basically nominalist viewpoint which Mr. Reischauer was trying to advocate. Yet his remarks serve to expose a second problem, primarily epistemological, which must be confronted at the outset of any terminological discussion. Without agreement upon the kind of logic and reasoning which one proposes to utilize in dealing with historical data there can be no real meeting of minds. The deep difference between nominalists and realists in the handling of conceptual problems cannot readily be resolved. Any constructive give and take on the question of modernization as a general concept will have to be conducted in a nominalist atmosphere. In other words we should agree that such a concept is essentially a product of the scholar's system of classification; it is a conceptual formulation which derives from certain hypothetical judgments about history which themselves are subject to revision or refinement, and hence are open to discussion.[15]

Once one is willing to give up the established dogmas surrounding the idea of modernization, then it becomes obvious that there are many possible "definitions" depending upon the particular intellectual interests which one brings to the problem. Like the elephant, modernization may be described according to its several parts or by several classifying terms. Yet these may all be considered part of the truth about modernization so long as the relationships between the various "definitions" are clearly understood. Definitions of modernization can thus take several different forms. The most common style is descriptive and seeks to enumerate the many elements of the *modern condition*. Such descriptions, of course, may be phrased at many different levels of detail or generality. Another, and more taxing style seeks to identify the most essential modernizing changes and how they relate together as a *moving process*.

At Hakone our discussion began with the effort to phrase a descriptive definition in fairly general terms. We used as a

[15] This point was emphasized by R. P. Dore in his article "Mondai ishiki no sōi," *Mainichi shimbun*, Sept. 10, 1960.

starting point the following nine-point description of the essential features of modern society (the first seven points had been taken from the definition of modernization prepared by Professors Almond and Coleman in *The Politics of Developing Areas*) :

1. A comparatively high degree of urbanization
2. Widespread literacy
3. Comparatively high per capita income
4. Extensive geographical and social mobility
5. Relatively high degree of commercialization and industrialization within the economy
6. An extensive and penetrative network of mass communication media
7. Widespread participation and involvement by members of the society in modern social and economic processes[16]
8. A relatively highly organized bureaucratic form of government with widespread involvement by members of the society
9. An increasingly rational and secular orientation of the individual to his environment based on the growth of scientific knowledge

It was not our intention to leave this statement untouched. As it turned out the general categories of social change included in this preliminary statement were not placed under great attack. These were found generally adequate, though numerous changes in emphasis were suggested, and we eventually agreed that more stress should be placed upon the tendency toward secularization of society and on the national and international aspects of state interaction in the modern world. Our initial quarrel was chiefly with the descriptive expressions themselves, which, as Mr. Ōuchi pointed out, seemed heavily colored by capitalistic connotations. Words such as "urbanization" or "commercialization" or the phrase "high per capita income" were too specific in their reference to the

[16] Almond and Coleman, *The Politics of Developing Areas* (Princeton, 1960), p. 52.

18

advanced industrial societies of the West. Others such as "modern economic process" were tautological. Nor did the order seem particularly appropriate. As a result of considerable discussion and some contemplation in private (especially by Mr. Nakano) we arrived at a modified statement of the following order:

1. A comparatively high concentration of population in cities and the increasingly urban-centeredness of the total society
2. A relatively high degree of use of inanimate energy, the widespread circulation of commodities, and the growth of service facilities.
3. Extensive spatial interaction of members of a society and the widespread participation of such members in economic and political affairs
4. Widespread literacy accompanied by the spread of a secular, and increasingly scientific, orientation of the individual to his environment
5. An extensive and penetrative network of mass communication
6. The existence of large-scale social institutions such as government, business, industry, and the increasingly bureaucratic organization of such institutions
7. Increased unification of large bodies of population under one control (nations) and the growing interaction of such units (international relations)[17]

This revised statement, the result of one round of discussion, is offered with full realization that further modifications may be found desirable. (We shall in fact suggest one specific revision shortly.) But aside from refinements of this type, the statement can stand as a working summation of the "modern" elements of a society—given the limits of a descriptive method and at the particular level of conceptual vocabulary which we have adopted. Of course, it should be added that a descriptive definition of this type must be conceived

[17] Nakano Takashi, Communication of October 1960.

of as an interrelated whole. The separate elements of the description mean little in themselves unless combined with the other elements. As Mr. Katō put it, criteria of the sort we have just listed are like the symptoms of a disease in an individual. "In treating an illness we do not start with just any manifestation of disorder but consider the several symptoms and their relationships in a syndrome so as to obtain a complete picture. Such a unified approach to modernization recommends itself by its elegance."[18] The syndrome of symptoms described in our revised list of criteria serves then to isolate a process of change and a condition of society. It makes quite clear that our view of modernization is different from (or at least is more comprehensive than) such processes as Westernization or industrialization, or such systems of social organization as absolutism, capitalism, or socialism.

But we do not suggest that the matter of definition be left at this point. Our thoughts on modernization carried us further, both in the direction of greater specificity and of greater generality. Periodically as we discussed specific aspects of modern societies we found the descriptive criteria multiplying with no apparent limit. Prior to the Hakone meeting members of the Conference committee had been asked to prepare detailed statements on the characteristics of modernization, each from the point of view of a particular field. The resulting contributions on political, social, economic, and ideological modernization were helpful in providing bodies of detailed observation from which more generalized statements could be distilled.[19] But it was rather in the opposite direction, that of simplification, that our interests tended.

[18] *Gijiroku*, p. 3.

[19] Statements contributed by Robert Ward, Ronald Dore, William Lockwood, and C. E. Black are included somewhat hesitantly in this note. Many of these statements have been superseded in the thinking of the contributors. Mr. Ward's latest thoughts on political modernization will be found in the book *Political Modernization in Japan and Turkey* (Princeton, 1964).

POLITICAL MODERNIZATION

1. increasing allocation of political roles in accordance with standards of achievement rather than ascription

The effort to reduce the process of modernization to its simplest terms which proved most congenial to us at Hakone was the suggestion in Mr. Schwartz's conference paper that we make use of Max Weber's familiar concept of rationality. "It will be recalled," he pointed out, "that rationality in the Weberian sense has no necessary connection with rationalism

---

2. growing emphasis upon rational, scientific, and secular techniques of political decision-making

3. mass popular interest and involvement in the political system, though not necessarily in its decision-making process

4. predominance of functionally specific rather than generalized political roles organized in an elaborate and professionalized bureaucracy

5. broad and explicit governmental involvement in, responsibility for, and regulation of the economic and social aspects of individual and group life — *NO*

6. an increasing centralization of governmental functions

7. regulatory, control, and judicial techniques based increasingly upon a predominantly impersonal system of law

SOCIAL MODERNIZATION

1. a shifting composition of population as between town and country

2. a decline in the importance of social groups based on kinship or residence relative to that of groups created to perform certain specific functions (economic, political, religious, recreational, etc.) and joined by individual choice

3. a wider range of individual choice between alternative courses of action, relatively unrestrained by any social sanction — *NO*

4. a growing tendency for the sanctions which do limit that range of choice to take the form of impersonal laws rather than the pressure of group opinion

5. a lessening tendency for individuals to identify their interests with and feel loyalty toward small face-to-face groups (such as the family), with, consequently, a growing tendency for individuation, and/or identification with larger, impersonal groups (nation, class, etc.) *hmm*

6. an increasing specialization of roles in the economic, political, and intellectual spheres

7. explicit assignment of those roles and of social prestige on the basis of achievement

8. a tendency for relations between individuals to become (a) less often characterized by unbridgeable gaps of status, (b) more often contractually entered into rather than determined by birth or residence, (c) more often limited to contract in a specific functional sphere

in philosophy or world outlook. . . . It is *Zwecksrationalität* —the rationality of means and ends. It involves the creation of the appropriate means—the appropriate technology—for the achievement of certain ends. Ends which Weber seems to discern as dominant in the modern world are man's control of his physical environment (in economics and applied science)

(economic, political, recreational, etc.), (d) less often charged with emotion

ECONOMIC MODERNIZATION

1. increasing application of scientific technology, and of inanimate energy, to enlarge and diversify the production of goods and services per capita

2. a growing specialization of labor and subdivision of productive processes within and among firms, industries, occupations, and territories, and an increasing interdependence and mobility of individuals and groups within a network of widening impersonal markets

3. a concomitant improvement in human skills and economic efficiency, especially at the higher technical and managerial levels

4. an accumulation of capital goods in more productive forms and in growing amounts per worker, financed by a complex of financial institutions that characteristically divorce the savings from the investment process in order to pool liquid resources for the growing stream of investment

5. production, transport, marketing, and finance organized on an increasingly large scale, with concomitant tendencies to the concentration of decisions over economic life

6. as the dynamic force behind the above processes, a society increasingly oriented to the pursuit of economic opportunity, infused (especially within the elite) by a spirit of innovation and growth, and increasingly rational in its choice of techniques and allocation of resources to achieve its economic goals

7. as a result of these processes—and despite a characteristic increase in population—a rise in the level of material well-being, usually a widening of the range of personal choice, and sooner or later a reduction in the range of economic and social inequalities

8. as incomes rise, a shift in the balance of employment and production from the extractive industries to manufacturing and the services, with a concomitant urbanization of the labor force

9. the spread of wage labor as the chief form of gainful employment, and commonly the separation of ownership and management

10. the replacement of natural hazards (e.g., weather) as the main source of insecurity by technological change, the uncertainties of the

as well as his control and coordination of his social environment. If industrialism reflects rationality in the sphere of material technology, the modern state bureaucracy, military organization, police organization and industrialism itself reflect rationality in the sphere of social technology. The relationship between the two modes of technology is highly complex and varied. While Weber often discusses this process of rationalization or modernization under the rubric of capitalism (perhaps by force of habit) he by no means simply equates modernization with economic rationalization. He spends as much time discussing 'political modernization' (as well as military and legal modernization) as he does discussing the rise of industrialism. Nor does he attempt to establish a simple causal relationship between these various spheres of action. One could derive from Weber the view that military, political and legal rationalization had as much to do with creating the conditions for economic rationalization as vice versa.

"Following Weber it seems to me that one possible way of setting boundaries to the concept of modernization is as follows: Modernization involves the systematic, sustained and purposeful application of human energies to the 'rational' control of man's physical and social environment for various

---

market, and the bargaining disadvantages of the individual in relation to his employer and the state ~~11. The consumption-production spiral~~

INTELLECTUAL MODERNIZATION

1. the systematic accumulation of intellectually verifiable knowledge and the weakening of religious or cultural dogmas

2. acceptance of the concept of social change in human affairs

3. an increase in the value placed upon the individual

4. growing attention to the vocational, social, and intellectual training of the individual

5. secularization and emphasis on material goods

6. the creation through mass means of communication of new interest and belief groups with national, class, or occupational orientations

7. a constantly widening orbit of individual involvement in intellectual communities beyond the family, village, or province to the state and to supranational ideals

8. improvement of the means of dissemination of ideas to all members of the society

human purposes. I use the adjectives purposeful, systematic and sustained because it is quite obvious that the process of rationalization as such began long before the 'modern age' and is almost coextensive with recorded human history."[20]

The concept of rationality proved particularly durable in our subsequent discussion. Most other attempts at devising unitary explanations of the modernization process, in fact, seemed merely to be special cases of this principle, in other words they could be explained as manifestations of rationality operating in specific contexts. Aspects of the modern process such as bureaucratization, mechanization, secularization, industrialization, for instance, all could be subsumed under Weber's concept. The importance of rationality (or its "purposeful application" as Mr. Schwartz put it) is revealed in numerous ways, not the least of which is the existence of the belief in rationality itself. The idea of progress is itself a distinct manifestation of the modern spirit. In Mr. Reischauer's words, "modern men, as opposed to those of earlier periods, see themselves as not merely attempting to comprehend or rediscover truths already stated or revealed in the past, nor as simply trying to preserve an ideal tradition, or to recreate a 'golden age,' or even attempting to achieve an ideal that has been established in the past, whether or not by divine revelation. They assume that they are making progress in knowledge and believe that on the basis of this they can make social progress as well."[21]

One area in which the "purposeful application" of rationality to human affairs seemed most evident is in the sphere of economic and technological modernization. It was apropos of this that Mr. Levy was able to explain his variation on the theme of definition: "In seeking to define modernization I would prefer to hinge the definition on the smallest number of factors capable of yielding fruitful results. Such definitions are easier to use and easier to be precise about. In this case I would rest the definition on two types of measure, both

[20] Benjamin Schwartz, "Modernization and its Ambiguities" (Hakone Conference Paper, mimeo.), pp. 1-4.
[21] E. O. Reischauer, Conference Paper, p. 9.

24

technological in nature. One has to do with the extent to which tools are utilized to multiply or otherwise increase the effects of the application of energy to materials. The other has to do with the ratio of energy supplied from inanimate sources to that supplied from animate sources. There are of course no societies completely lacking in either of these factors. . . . In general the higher the multiplication of the applications of energy by tools the higher the level of modernization. The greater the ratio of energy from inanimate sources to that from animate sources the higher the level of modernization. Specifically, however, I would not consider modernization to be present at all in a society unless the ratio of inanimate to animate sources of energy had reached such a point that it was virtually inconceivable that the society would persist if the members of that society were forced to go back to a dependence on an animate source of energy. This definition does not imply any causative priority to these technological factors as opposed say to ideological ones. It is rather that I believe that no society can have these two characteristics without having many of the others variously named simultaneously."[22]

Mr. Levy's statement opened up a broad avenue of debate on the question of whether some sort of quantification of the process of modernization is possible. We were reminded that a few disciplines are actually at work on the problem: the economists for example with their attempts to define the transition point between traditional and modern economy, and the political scientists with their objective tests for what they call social mobilization.[23] Many lists of statistically compiled data adorn the literature on economic and political modernization. Comparative tables of literacy rates, life expectancy, urban population, GNP per capita, calories consumed per capita, utilization of electricity, circulation of newspapers and the like make fascinating reading. But we know

[22] Marion Levy, "On the Social Structures of Modernized Societies" (Hakone Conference Paper, mimeo.), pp. 2-3.

[23] Note particularly Karl W. Deutsch, "Social Mobilization and Political Development," in *The American Political Science Review*, vol. LV, no. 3 (September 1961).

too little as yet about how to interpret these figures as indices of "levels of modernization." For most of the elements of change which we put into our definition of modernization, we are still only able to suggest indefinite and intuitively judged calibrations of the scale of transition from traditional to modern.

It is interesting that the idea of rationality in the economy and its measurement as an index of the use of inanimate energy seemed to offer those accustomed to Marxist analysis the first reasonable alternative to the familiar concepts of capitalism and socialism. Mr. Kawashima was particularly attracted to the possibilities of measurement by a mechanical scale such as Mr. Levy had suggested. "On the point of whether there is no modernization without capitalism, if we think of Soviet Russia, although we note a number of differences [with capitalistic countries] they both use inanimate energy, they have a high level of industrialization, and they both have attained a high degree of urbanization and literacy. Nonetheless the [Soviet system] is different from capitalism. And since this vast productive power is influencing the development of contemporary world history, I believe we have to agree that there are certain commonalities in human society. If we try to grasp the meaning of modernization from this point of view, I would say that we certainly can agree upon the idea of efficiency."[24]

But no sooner had we begun to consider the objective and quantifiable measures of rationalization in the material life of modern society than our discussion was drawn off in the direction of less tangible subjects. Mr. Maruyama from the first considered our revised set of criteria too heavily weighted against the world of ideas and asked that the value system of the individual be given more consideration. Mr. Sakata, emphasizing the qualitative changes in Japanese values commented "What was considered good in Tokugawa Japan was considered bad in Meiji Japan. What was bad before was later made good. This is the crucial difference between Japan's traditional period and her modern age."[25] Mr. Kōsaka

[24] *Gijiroku*, p. 5.   [25] *Ibid.*, p. 7.

insisted that changes affecting the individual were most fundamental. "It is *modern man* who is of interest to us. I would like to add him to the theoretical definition of modern society."[26]

Unquestionably Mr. Maruyama and the others were right in insisting that greater recognition be given to the value changes affecting the individual in modern society. And although no specific recommendations were forthcoming at Hakone, much of the discussion of the first Bermuda Conference was to be directed to this problem. Mr. Maruyama himself in a subsequent visit to the United States was able to clarify his own thoughts on the role of the individual and of individual values. And to his work we should add the pertinent writings of Mr. Bellah, whose presence at the Bermuda Conference served to reinforce the emphasis on this feature of the modern process. If we return to our revised set of criteria of modernization, then, it seems essential that we add at least one statement drawn from this line of discussion. The statement which suggests itself is drawn out of the Weberian mode. It assumes, in other words, that modernization is accompanied by a movement in society from *Gemeinschaft* to *Gesellschaft* conditions. It might be stated as follows: "A widespread breakdown of communal and hereditary social groupings leading to greater individual social mobility and a more widely diversified range of individual performance in society."

Unfortunately the problem of ethos and value as it was discussed at Hakone took a different and more political turn, becoming associated with the question of whether or not democracy was an essential element of modernization. Whether in the tense political environment of the "summer of demonstrations" this subject could have been objectively discussed is open to question. In his subsequently published criticism of the Conference Mr. Kawashima made clear his dissatisfaction with the lack of discussion on this point. " 'Democracy' is as we all know a matter of greatest concern to Japanese. Granted that 'political discussion' for purposes of

[26] *Ibid.*, p. 8.

achieving 'democracy' is not science . . . nonetheless I believe that in the modernization of Japan such values as 'democracy' and 'human rights' have played an 'important role' in providing the motive force in social and political development, and that these have provided important 'issues' for the various ideological camps. These are matters of *historical fact*, and as part of the science of experience they cannot be overlooked. Of course for some people or some states 'democracy' may not constitute a major problem in the process of modernization. But for a conference which took as its objective the discussion of 'modernization in Japan,' not to take under consideration such an important question was, in my opinion, unduly one-sided. This is not all. At a conference in which 'modernization' was conceived of as a process which would affect every society . . . each in its own time and at its own speed, a process which would embrace the social revolutions of Soviet Russia, Communist China and Asia and Africa, that [democracy] was not brought up for discussion at all left me most dissatisfied. If in analyzing the historical changes which affect Asia, Africa and Latin America today we ignore the value of 'democracy' or its *motive power* we will end in having no true analysis and, I believe, we will be mistaken in our assessment of the future of these societies. As for me, I would like to know whether the values of 'democracy' or the *social and political structure* which goes under the name of 'democracy' should be included within the syndrome or the 'working hypothesis' of the process of modernization conceived of in its world history sense."[27]

What answer are we to give Mr. Kawashima? One, which was never adequately expressed at Hakone, could have been a statement of faith somewhat along the lines of the recent Rockefeller Brothers report on the democratic idea. "The history of the last three centuries," it states, "is in large part the history of the democratic impulse. Democratic aspirations have moved with mounting force in the world, and any people that has felt their contagion has never been the same

[27] Kawashima Takeyoshi, "Kindai Nihon no shakaigakuteki kenkyū," in *Shisō*, 442 (1961.4), pp. 484-485.

afterward. Masquerades of democracy have sometimes been taken for the real thing. The power of democratic ideals is now so great that even the most militant opponents of democracy must speak the language of democracy to justify themselves to those they rule. A fundamental reason why our era is so unsettled and turbulent is simply that the attraction of democratic ideals has come to be felt everywhere in the world. It is the democratic dream that is keeping the world on edge."[28]

But a more skeptical atmosphere dominated the Hakone meeting and served to inhibit the Western participants from making such a simple affirmation. Mr. Schwartz's comment on this question was more characteristic. "Now, modernization as here defined has so far proven ambivalent or rather 'multivalent' in its relationship to many possibilities in the spheres of culture, politics, social structure, etc. It has also served many purposes, some of them contradictory. It is perhaps true that a general betterment of the economic lot of mankind is an end immanent as it were in the industrialization process, although even this may only be absolutely true in the long run. This does not mean that industrialization may not also serve quite different purposes such as the enhancement of state power for the struggle in the international sphere. It must not be forgotten that modernization proved quite compatible with the phenomenon of Nazi Germany and that the militaristic period in modern Japanese history probably advanced the industrial modernization of Japan.

"All of this is meant to suggest that among the hidden premises which we ought to avoid is an overly optimistic and overly pious bias in dealing with this term. Optimism is, of course, a relative concept. The American liberal may think that the whole process is moving by some beneficent fatality in a direction which favors his values. Some elements of the Japanese left who support 'Kindaika' may think that it is inevitably moving in the direction of something like the Chinese Commune. Whether modernization as such must

[28] *The Power of the Democratic Idea*, Sixth Report of the Rockefeller Brothers Fund Special Studies Project (New York, 1960), p. 1.

inevitably move in either direction is an entirely unproven assumption.

"I am not here suggesting that a pessimistic bias be substituted for the optimistic bias. There is, of course, a large literature which has been written to prove that modernization is leading us inevitably into a most unpromising wasteland. (Weber himself was by no means sanguine about the future.) What is required, I feel, is a sense of the ambivalence, the indeterminate relation of modernization to many possibilities. There may be certain inevitable social and cultural concomitants of the modernization process everywhere (urbanization?), but much has been asserted in this area which has by no means been demonstrated by historical fact."[29]

But there is another answer to Mr. Kawashima. Having agreed that the social concomitants of modernization lead to a greater rationality of social relationships, the question of democracy can be resolved into whether rationalization of the political and social aspects of society necessarily leads "in the long run" to the adoption of democratic values. This was a question which the Western scholars at Hakone found difficult to answer on empirical grounds alone. And it is one which is difficult to discuss without reference to political issues. The resolution between a ringing confidence in democracy and Mr. Schwartz's ambivalent attitude, if it is to come out in favor of democracy, would require a demonstration that neither the Fascist nor Communist forms of government represented stable (or inevitable) end products of the modernization proecss. There is, of course, considerable evidence that this is not at all unlikely. Certainly the Fascist societies of the period before World War II proved unstable in their attempt to create a national unity based on archaic racial symbols. The Communist insistence on an imposed unity by indoctrination must eventually create tensions which the system itself cannot resolve except by suppression or by loss of identity.[30] Modernization may indeed produce as its ideal

[29] Schwartz, Conference Paper, pp. 4-6.
[30] Robert Bellah, "Values and Social Change in Modern Japan," in *Asian Cultural Studies*, vol. 3 (1962.10), pp. 24-25.

society one based on democratic values, but the path to that ideal may lead through ambiguous territory.

Having investigated the terminological territory on either side of our descriptive definition of modernization we are prepared to take stock of where we now stand. Our discussion so far has served to isolate at least four levels at which the process of modernization might be described. We began with a "middle level" description from which we moved in two directions. In the first place we recognized that for each disciplinary interest a great deal of detailed criteria could be submitted which was admittedly partial in scope but specific to certain problems peculiar to the disciplines themselves. Our general descriptive definition, in effect, had drawn from these disciplinary insights a limited combination of basic symptoms of modernization which we then organized into a unified syndrome. We then went to the extreme of suggesting that the entire process of modernization could be summed up in the concept of rationality. Then returning half a step we found terms which described the effects of rationality as it took hold of certain major areas of society. Mechanization and industrialization of the economy, bureaucratization in government and social organization, the spread of ideas of progress and science in the intellectual sphere, and a widening range of diversity in the area of social relations and values, all appear to be symptoms of greater rationality of the human condition, whether for good or ill.

At Hakone we came to no new consensus on the meaning of modernization, but we gained new understanding of the conceptual structure of the problem we faced. We recognized that the process of modernization in all its complexity could hardly be confined to a single all-inclusive formulation. Rather we found ourselves seeking definitions at various levels of specificity or generality. Between these levels we have tried to maintain a thread of logical consistency. But the levels themselves are certainly not immutable. Our statements have fallen into certain modes of expression, not because these are necessarily inherent in the data, but because they conform to the levels of conceptual vocabulary to which we are accustomed. Yet behind these statements, and if we are not overly beguiled by our own vocabulary, we can claim some clearer insight into what cultural changes make up the modernization syndrome. We have, in other words, helped to clarify those areas of a modernizing society upon which we shall wish to focus our attention in our several annual seminars.

From descriptive definition we must turn to the consideration of process. For having isolated the elements of change which seem most significant to us we can inquire about cause. It seems always easier to describe the drama of change than to explain what brings it about. The few "grand systems" which attempt to account for historical change in the large have in the main been the work of speculative philosophers. But Hegel's view of the dialectic process or Toynbee's concept of the life cycle of cultures stretch the mind beyond our empirical experience. The more limited attempts at causal explanation have usually consisted of descriptions of certain outstanding events under the assumption that they constitute a first cause. Accordingly historical change is explained as the work of great men, of great ideas, or as the product of interaction in the social and economic spheres.

The problem of identifying cause is not unlike the task of descriptive definition in its intellectual requirements. We were confronted at Hakone with a number of stereotyped answers derived in the main from theories about social behavior which rested on the magnification of certain aspects of social change in preference to others. The Marxist emphasis on class tension as the moving force in social change, Max Weber's stress upon the role of changing values, the view that modernization was primarily the product of the spread of science, all had their advocates. We have no quarrel with these theories as such, if each is regarded hypothetically as an explanation within certain limited contexts. But we must be skeptical of them as dogmas or as unitary explanations of modernization.

But skepticism is chiefly a defensive virtue. Between complete intellectual neutralism and dogmatic commitment to some theoretical line there are a number of intermediate positions. The common ground between the advocates of an open approach to modernization contains fewer dramatic landmarks, but the terrain is more safely traveled. On this we could agree: that we are in the presence of a very general phenomenon whereby societies have tended over the course of time to become increasingly complex and specialized in their functions, that, except for certain isolated instances, they have tended to improve their technological equipment, increase the utilization of human and natural resources, and expand the volume of mass participation in the political, economic, and intellectual life of the whole. Can we not say, then, that the process of rationalization has tended to pick up momentum as human society has gained the means to purposefully achieve rational control of its physical and social environment? This apparently basic movement has worked upon the structure of each society, creating pressures and tensions within it until at a given time a concurrence of changes or incipient changes in many sectors has suddenly projected the society into a period of rapid or revolutionary transformation. There are obviously certain critical turning points in this process. Modernization has generally taken place under revolutionary conditions. But the combination of factors which set off revolution within one society is apt to be quite different from that which activated another. The comparative study of societies undergoing modernization can therefore be most useful in leading to a sharper sense of understanding of some of the basic changes and the kinds of transitional crises which appear to be common to a number of cases. But the acceptance of a formula of change derived from one society as normal for all others is certainly not justified.

If we are reluctant to say more about the causes of modernization at this point, it is because our discussions have urged caution upon us. It is possible of course to retrace our arguments on definition, changing the nouns and adjectives of our earlier statement into verbs and adverbs and assuming that each symptom of change which we have listed contains some elements of causal necessity. But the explanation of *why* societies push toward greater urbanization, bureaucratization, secularization, or whatever modern trend we have in mind still eludes us. A more productive subject of inquiry, therefore, has seemed to be the quest for pattern and sequence in the modernization process. The history of modernization in actual societies can yield to classification of sequential patterns and types of revolutionary crises according to broad categories. Historical data on modernizing societies can be cut in many different ways, of course, and according to many degrees of detail. The recent work of Cyril Black differentiates six styles of modernization.[31] At the Hakone meeting Messrs. Rosovsky and Levy suggested a fourfold division, first between indigenous and non-indigenous modernizers and then between old societies with fully developed traditional cultures (Japan would be one) and young societies emerging in relatively empty lands (such as the U.S. or the countries of Africa). But there is no need to seek agreement on such categories. The uncomplicated approach taken by Mr. Reischauer is as useful as any, particularly as a point of departure for the analysis of the Japanese case.

According to Mr. Reischauer "Modernization has taken place under three very different historical settings: 1, in nations in which the elements of modernization for the most part first appeared through a relatively slow evolutionary process; 2, in nations with highly developed, complex civilizations in which the major elements of modernization were first introduced from the outside; and 3, in nations or sub-national areas of relatively primitive culture in which elements of modernization have been recently injected. In the first category could be listed the countries of northwest Europe and their cultural extensions overseas; in the second the major countries of Asia, North Africa and Latin America, and in the third the rest of Africa and parts of Oceania. Naturally these categories are by no means clear-cut but provide rather a continuum. For example, parts of south and east Europe (and also Japan to some extent) might be regarded as transi-

[31] Cyril E. Black, "Political Modernization in Historical Perspective" (Princeton, 1960, mimeo.), pp. 12-22.

34

tional between types 1 and 2, and parts of Southeast Asia transitional between types 2 and 3.

"We should also bear in mind that the countries of the world undergoing modernization have very distinctive traditional cultures. There are first of all the large zones of Christian, Islamic, South Asian and East Asian civilizations and, within each of these, clear cultural distinctions between national units. The more primitive areas also have their cultural variations. There is every reason to believe that these inherited cultural differences will profoundly affect the whole process of modernization and the eventual outcome . . .

"From all this we can conclude that there are and will continue to be great variations in modernization and no one case can therefore be considered typical. In particular, we should guard against the assumption that the historical and causal sequence in which the characteristics of modernization first appeared in northwest Europe is somehow the norm. Actually the slow, evolutionary development of the features of modernization in this particular area not only makes it untypical for the world as a whole but also makes the analysis of modernization much more difficult there than in other areas where it has developed much more suddenly and as a much clearer break with previous traditions and technology . . . Since modernization is a world-wide phenomenon, its general nature can only be understood through a careful comparison of many local examples."[32]

We should add that Japan's modernization can best be understood when it too is put into the perspective of other local examples. As one of the late modernizing societies Japan naturally followed a pattern which has many points in common with other countries outside of western Europe. Yet a close comparison with such supposedly comparable countries as China and Turkey reveals the most startling differences. "Japan is a curiously mixed case," Mr. Reischauer's observation continued. "For anything involving cultural peculiarities, China and Korea would offer the best comparisons. According to historical type, Japan can be fruitfully compared with

[32] Reischauer, Conference Paper, pp. 2-4.

all the other highly developed nations of Asia, but in some ways the comparisons with Russia and east Europe might be even more interesting. According to stage, only the early phases of Japanese modernization can be better compared with south and east Europe and to some extent with northwest Europe and North America. On the other hand, comparisons with the early phases of modernization in northwestern Europe or with any phase of modernization in the more primitive areas of Africa would be hazardous."[33]

If the over-all pattern of Japan's modernization defies easy categorization (other than the very obvious one of being a late modernizer), internal events are no more easily dealt with. The study of the modernization of Japan is inevitably that of the interplay of external and indigenous events; it is compounded of culture change and of culture contact. While on the one hand we may feel we have the advantage of knowing the nature and strength of modernizing impulses which impinged upon Japan from outside, it is no simple task to identify the interaction between these impulses and the Japanese matrix upon which they played.

In recent years if we have gained in knowledge at all in our comprehension of the modernization of Japan it has been through appreciation of the subtleties and intricacies of both the internal and external facets of this process. Greater precision in our knowledge of who or what from abroad reached Japanese shores makes it less necessary for us to talk about some vague idea of "Western impact." The more we know about precisely who among the Japanese were in touch with Westerners or how exactly the Japanese at large came to acquire their ideas about the West, the less we need to rely on the stereotyped images of Japan's imitative and faddistic "response" to the West. The recent reassessment of the Tokugawa period has placed a new emphasis upon the quality of Japan's receptivity. To rephrase Sansom's analogy, we are discovering that the hand that opened the door was as important as the one that produced the knock from outside.

But above all, a skeptical approach should give us renewed

[33] *Ibid.*, p. 6.

respect for empirical observation and make us less susceptible to assumptions that the Japanese story should have proceeded in a particular way. The comparison (usually to Japan's detriment) with the West need not dominate our judgment. And we can thereby try to avoid one of the most common tendencies in the appraisal of Japan's modernization, that which stems from chagrin over Japan's "failure" to advance at sufficient pace. To quote Mr. Schwartz a final time, "Both Western liberals and Japanese Marxists have often tended to explain modern Japanese history in terms of the conceptions of distortion and lag. The path of modern Japanese history is 'distorted' (presumably the word is used not in an ethical sense but in a social scientific sense) because it has not conformed to some Western model. The distortion is then often explained in terms of the lag. For some reason, certain aspects of traditional culture have managed to maintain their tenacious hold on Japanese society and inhibit and confine the modernization of Japan. Many of the Japanese theoreticians of *Kindaika* (as well as Western liberals) never consider the possibility that many of the features of Meiji Japan which they find most obnoxious may actually be concomitant to the Japanese modernization process itself. Were the authoritarian attitudes of the Meiji elites simply a function of 'feudal' attitudes or may they have, at least in part, reflected the nature of their modernizing effort itself? Is it possible to maintain in the twentieth century that 'authoritarianism' and 'modernization' are antithetical terms? To the extent that traditional habits and institutions have survived in modern Japan have they always inhibited modernization? Actually some of these habits and institutions were actually harnessed to the modernizing process and used to push it forward. Even if the authoritarian tendencies of the Meiji oligarchy were rooted in a 'feudal mentality' it must be pointed out that this 'feudal mentality' greatly facilitated the creation of a Weberian type of modern bureaucracy. This does not mean that there have been no genuine traditionalists in modern Japan. It does mean that one cannot explain modern Japanese history simply

37

in terms of a struggle between traditions and the modernization process."[34]

To many at the Hakone meeting the kind of double vision
which Mr. Schwartz advocates, the sense of openness to
change not only in the subject matter of history but in the
concepts of analysis themselves, seemed a substitution of
chaos for order, of a "no-system" approach instead of one
based on accepted theoretical certainties. At the outset of
the meeting Mr. Tōyama had asked, "Most Japanese scholars,
especially historians use 'modernization' in the sense of the
process of transition to a capitalistic society. . . . I would like
to have it made clear why a totally new conception, completely
divorced from [the usual modes of thought], is considered
necessary."[35] To some extent Mr. Tōyama answered his own
question in his post-conference newspaper report. In referring
to the American scholars he later wrote, "They insisted that
it was difficult to apply successfully such concepts as feudalism, capitalism, and socialism to a study of the history of
multifarious peoples of the world. They questioned whether
by adopting such concepts one would not fall into the bias
of interpreting the individual peculiarities of the modernization process of the several societies against the standard of
western European society, the very process for which these
concepts had originally been conceived as explanations. . . .
Recently in the Japanese academic world there has been a
willingness to question whether Japanese have not placed too
much emphasis on measuring the peculiarities of Japanese
society against an ideal type drawn from the history of the
rise of capitalism in England and France. Moreover it has
been suggested that one can hardly grasp the significance of
phenomena recently taking place both in America and Soviet
Russia (for instance the spread of 'mass society') if too much
attention is paid to social structure alone. Thus we can fully
appreciate the validity of the American approach. At the same

[34] Schwartz, Conference Paper, pp. 8-10.
[35] Tōyama Shigeki, "Kindaika to yū gainen ni kansuru oboegaki"
(Hakone Conference Paper, mimeo.), p. 1.

time it is essential that they recognize that Japanese scholars stand on a different problem consciousness."[36]

In the final analysis, as we reflect on problems of definition and of cause and pattern, it is this matter of problem awareness which is the real point at issue. For it is this particular quality which directs the scholar in his search for significant problems and satisfying answers. Differing viewpoints toward modernization may be argued in theoretical terms, but it is the kind of inquiry which these viewpoints generate which is the real issue at stake. Conversely, definitions are as much shaped by the questions scholars want to ask as by any theoretically objective data. And so definition and problem awareness proceed together, each helping to shape the other.

The problems which emerge from Mr. Tōyama's approach are clear enough. As he put it in his conference statement: "The greatest concern of our scholars until quite recently has been with the problem of how to democratize the politics and thought of our country. To achieve this end we have found it necessary to solve a number of academic problems such as the following:

1. Why was it that in spite of the dominant role of capitalistic economy in commerce and industry, there remained strong pre-modern factors in agriculture and the life of farming people?

2. Why was it that in spite of the establishment of modern institutions such as the Diet and public law, militarism and the dictatorial sway of the military and bureaucrats continued?

3. Why was it that in spite of the spread of education and the wholesale introduction of Western thought, even intellectuals, in deciding their everyday conduct, were strongly swayed by patriarchal considerations or by considerations of social status?

Such attitudes provide the starting point in their pursuit of the problem of 'modernization' in modern Japan after the Meiji Restoration."[37]

[36] Tōyama Shigeki, "Genjutsu to dentō wa chigau mo gakusha no kyōryoku wa kanō," *Mainichi Shimbun* (September 9, 1960).
[37] Tōyama, "oboegaki," pp. 2-3.

What questions emerge from an open approach to modernization such as the one we have tried to formulate in this essay? The test lies in large part in the future deliberations of the Conference on Modern Japan in the five seminars, each of which will consider modern Japan from a different direction. It is significant that the first seminar, organized by Mr. Jansen, takes up the subject of attitudes, for these are the most illusive and ambivalent elements of the modernizing process. As the essays which follow will indicate, the questions we have asked and the answers we have received conform to no stereotype. They range over familiar and unfamiliar territory, looking not for the simple but the complex answer. Stories which were once told in bold phrases of Western impact and native reaction, of samurai counter-revolutionaries and agrarian innovators, of economic imbalance and failures at democracy have been retold. In the retelling, some of the contrasts have lost their dramatic distinctions, but the nuances of color are more subtly revealed. Some of the villains—the samurai, the zaibatsu, the Meiji constitution, Confucianism—have been found less pernicious; others—the lower class samurai, the parasitic landlord, the warmongering general —have lost their clear identity. However, the new players have been presented with greater creditability. Our attention to empirical data is more precise, and reliance on general theory less confining. We have lost perhaps the comfort of certainty (within the limits of some conceptual system), yet we have gained in depth of appreciation of the total process of modern change in Japan.

Illustrative of the kind of answer which an open approach to familiar questions can give is the treatment of the role of Confucianism in Japan's modernization which appears in this volume. Gone is the picture of a hopelessly traditional society suddenly enlightened by the West. On closer scrutiny, the ideas commonly associated with Confucianism are found to contain elements which proved congenial to the modern ethos —loyalty over self, national over personal goals, emphasis on self-improvement and achievement. But these elements of Confucianism, though capable of nurturing the attitudes of modern science, did not produce them. The Tokugawa *yin* required a foreign *yang* to appear. The resulting synthesis was permanently and significantly different from the two, but it was often expressed in the same terms as had been used previously. Thus we have found it necessary to constantly reexamine the contents of familiar terms in the light of their changing meanings and in terms of changing social and cultural settings.[38] To be able to appreciate these multiple facets of the "traditional" ethos is certainly the essence of the kind of open approach to the problem of modernization which we hope to maintain in our seminars.

[38] Summarized by Marius Jansen in "Notes on Discussion, First Seminar, Conference on Modern Japan" (mimeo. 1962), pp. 16-17.

CHAPTER II

Changing Japanese Attitudes Toward Modernization

MARIUS B. JANSEN

WEBSTER'S definition of attitudes reads in part, "a state of mental or, especially, emotional readiness for some form of activity," and in the most general sense as "feeling, set, bearing, air." As used in this paper and volume, we may amplify this to mean "commonly shared value assumptions" as they affected the great questions that faced modern Japan. Much recent scholarship has been concerned with the manner in which Japan was mentally and emotionally prepared for the modern transformation; that transformation in turn knew several phases, and it is the shared assumptions and attitudes of those phases that concern us here. We proceed from no fixed or uniform theory of the relationship between attitudes and decisions beyond the assumption that attitudes and ideas played a significant role in Japan's ability or inability to adjust to the modern world of international and industrial organizations, and that investigation of these attitudes can help us to see the setting and way in which the Japanese in the last century have viewed their world.

In proceeding as they do, the papers can hope to cast new light on the times in which men lived, the problems with which they dealt, and the decisions they made. But by no means can they claim to show why particular decisions were made at particular points in time. For the process of reflection, weighing, and selection of alternatives, however orderly and inevitable it may seem in retrospect, is in actuality never so. At all points the resolutions achieved came about as the result of clashes of attitudes and interests, and at any given point the climate of opinion was more a constellation of attitudes than a harmonious blending of outlooks. The attitudes

43

in their totality only provided the setting, the elements of opinion and outlook, within which forces and alternatives could contend.

In Japan, as elsewhere, there was no lack of alternatives and of contingencies, human, national, and international. If success was attainable by only one path, the exploration of alternate paths to failure was not therefore ruled out. Thus when Perry brought his letter, powerful and intelligent men advocated differing responses to it. It is perfectly conceivable that Japan could have decided to resort to war to ward off the West, and indeed Tokugawa Nariaki advocated such a policy in full knowledge that the war would probably be lost. It would be worth the effort, he felt, because even defeat would re-create a martial consciousness and a national sense of crisis and of purpose among a ruling class grown soft and indolent. Had war, and defeat, come in the 1850's, the course of the next decades could well have been very different. A program of modernization would no doubt have come, since much of it had been foreshadowed in previous decades, but the authorities in whose interests it was carried on might well have held to a very different timetable and a different interest. Again, in the 1860's it made a difference which of the contending powers proved victorious. Both leaders and opponents of the Tokugawa shogunate were conscious of the need for steps that would create a more unified, "modernized" state; the shogunate sought to destroy the great fiefs of the southwest as prelude to national unification, while leaders of those domains sought the destruction of the Tokugawa as prelude to unification under their own leadership. However similar the goals, the premises of the two groups were sufficiently different to have altered fundamentally the nature of the resulting system. Tokugawa hegemony would probably, for instance, have spared Japan the Emperor system. Thus throughout the recent century contingencies of time, place, and person provided an abundance of alternative paths the country might have followed.

But although the outcome was not inevitable, "attitudes" had a remarkable consistency of focus, and it can be maintained that Japanese attitudes have enough continuity and coherence to serve as fitting subjects with which to begin consideration of Japanese modernization. The continuity may be seen as the product of inherited cultural factors, and the coherence as growing from the dimension of the cataclysmic crises through which the country passed. Japan's insularity, its frequently narrow range of alternative intellectual positions, its failure to develop a framework of universal, supranational values, helped provide the setting. And the dimension of the crises presented by the West, as it broke into Japan's insularity, the critical importance and effectiveness of the imperial cult as a determinant of outlooks in Imperial Japan, followed by the crushing defeat and close contact with the West in the form of the Allied Occupation, have helped provide the coherence. It thus becomes possible to discern something of a general climate of opinion and attitudes, a "style," in which representative reactions can be investigated; it becomes reasonable to speak of a "Meiji," a "Taishō," and a "Shōwa" Japan. And because the stimuli were of such an order as to produce something approaching consensus (in concern, if not in solutions) in a society not deeply divided or specialized in religion or thought, there is good reason to discuss attitudes and images.

It may also be suggested that, however distinctive the Japanese setting and tradition, these studies of Japan can have considerable reference value for the study of modernization in other settings. The self-conscious antitheses of "tradition" and "modern" so tenaciously retained by many Japanese are also held in many other cultural settings, however different the agents and the alternatives may be. The papers on Chinese Confucianism by Hellmut Wilhelm and Indian modernization by Stephen Hay show both the limits and the advantages of such comparisons. One sees that a parallel intellectual tradition (Confucianism) can nevertheless produce "attitudes" very different from those in Japan, and that a more intimate association with the West in India finds "modernizers" for a time sharing Western, instead of leading Asian, responses to their problems.

Particular attitudes need to be considered in some detail, but also in their setting, in relation to other views which make up the over-all pattern in which they exist. In the case of Japan, this can most usefully be done by noting the changing image which Japanese have held of their own and of other countries. It must of course be remembered that information about such countries—and about the Japanese past—changed in quality and quantity. Furthermore the other countries—Japan's models of attraction or repulsion—were themselves in constant change. Thus there were objective as well as subjective bases for changing attitudes, even toward the Japanese tradition, which was more or less in process of creation by ideologists of nationalism. Ideas and attitudes do not exist in isolation, but in a network of interconnection in which each supports or complements the other; they cannot undergo change without corresponding extension or contraction of their fellows. In this sense Japanese attitudes toward China, toward the West, and toward the Japanese tradition, may be singled out as particularly rewarding areas for study.

Within these interdependent ideas and attitudes, one can study the whole through the study of any one. At the same time, at a given period certain attitudes can be determinants, and play the principal role in molding others. It makes a difference, as Joseph Levenson has pointed out, whether one places constitutionalism in his past because he ascribes value to it, or ascribes value to it because he thinks that he discerns it in that past.[1] In the case of nineteenth century Japan, the discussion about abolishing feudal subdivisions for being out of harmony with Japan's true past was only superficially concerned with that past. More important was the need to establish a state structure for which, in the language of the time, future generations would need to "feel no shame."[2] At some points the Japanese obsession with China, with the West, or

[1] *Liang Ch'i-ch'ao and the Mind of Modern China* (Cambridge, Harvard University Press, 1953), p. 43.

[2] For one of many instances of such wording in late Tokugawa days, see the Satsuma-Tosa agreement of 1867, in *Sakamoto Ryōma kankei monjo* (Tokyo, 1925), I, pp. 310-311.

with the native tradition, seems to overshadow, and to determine, all other concerns.

These qualifications made, it becomes appropriate to suggest some of the principal divisions and guidelines that may be used for the consideration of changing Japanese attitudes toward modernization, both to explain the setting in which these papers were put together and the discussion that accompanied their presentation. It is hardly necessary to point out that these notes can best serve as points of reference for the more detailed papers, which will treat individual persons, periods, and themes. There can, indeed, be no pretense of adequacy for a subject so broad, not least because research along many of these lines is as yet hardly underway in Japan itself. What, then, are the principal problems of periodization, characterization, and delimitation which can be put forth for the study of changing attitudes toward modernization in Japan?

Mid-Tokugawa: The Eighteenth Century

The century between Genroku and Bunka is one in which Tokugawa institutions and attitudes reached something of a plateau in coherence and consistency. The Japanese world had been at peace for most of a century, and the country closed beyond the memory of men still active. The abnormality of military rule and rank, developed under the pressures of sixteenth century warfare, had been codified into the normality of peacetime and stylized in the ritual of Tokugawa ceremonial.[3] From the center, where the authority of an emperor who was denied all power and freedom was invoked to legitimize the authority of the military despots, through the domains, which a warrior class administered as civil servants from their urban bases, to the countryside, whose produce supported a society and economy grown increasingly complex, contradictions were resolved to make possible the endurance in peace time of arrangements worked out for military emer-

[3] Maruyama Masao, "Kaikoku," in *Tenkanki rinri shisō*, vol. 11 of *Koza: gendai rinri* (Tokyo, 1959), pp. 82ff.

gency. The persistence into the 1860's of the institutions of the seventeenth century gives evidence of the success with which this resolution was accomplished. At the same time, however, the attitudes and values which had become prevalent in the eighteenth century helped clarify both the stability and the dynamics for change of Tokugawa Japan.

Of the three variables—attitudes toward China, toward the West, and toward the Japanese tradition—which invite consideration, those toward China and the Chinese tradition were undoubtedly at the forefront of the eighteenth century intellectuals' world outlook. Tokugawa writers sometimes began with the phrase, "although ours is a small island country" in unspoken reference to the colossus on the mainland. Their leaders' efforts to convert them in the Chinese written tradition, and their isolation from the West, made the China-view very nearly a determinant for many of them. More than ever before, large numbers of Japanese lived in the Chinese cultural sphere. Many of the Tokugawa Confucianists accepted, as Arthur Wright points out, the Chinese Confucianists' image of "China," and their occasional regret at being born outer barbarians brought them the wrath of their contemporaries and rivals.[4] It is possible to see in some of this exaggerated praise a Tokugawa variant of the Meiji deprecation and self-abasement before the West. No doubt, the abasement should more often than not be described as ritual and elegiac rather than deeply rooted. China had not impinged upon the *kangakusha* as a political force or strategic problem, and if

---

[4] "The Study of Chinese Civilization," in *Journal of the History of Ideas*, XXI, 2 (1960), pp. 233-255, particularly a quotation from Ise Sadatake (1717-1784) criticizing Japanese Confucianists who, "though they are born in this country . . . know nothing of its morality, its practices, its ancient ways, its customs. . . . Let them cease eating the rice produced in this land and starve to death, the sooner the better." A century later Fukuzawa expressed similar scorn for traditional, impractical scholarship and derided its practitioners as "rice consuming dictionaries" of no use to their country and a "hindrance to its economy." *Fukuzawa Yukichi senshū* (Tokyo, 1951), I, p. 96; also G. B. Sansom, *The Western World and Japan* (New York, 1950), p. 454.

they strove to master its wisdom they did not simultaneously have to fear its strength. Nonetheless their admiration and respect were great, and much of it survived well into the nineteenth century.

In the eighteenth century a rival strain of thought, that of the exponents of national learning, the *kokugakusha*, emerged to challenge the *kangakusha's* worship of China. Even so, the very virulence of the attacks these men leveled against the Chinese tradition, and the vituperation with which they attacked their China-oriented contemporaries, served to indicate how surely they measured the prestige and power of the Chinese tradition.[5]

Despite these divergencies of view, both camps shared a largely favorable view of their own society and of Tokugawa rule. They tended to praise it for the peace and order that had been brought out of the chaos of the fifteenth and sixteenth century wars through the wisdom of shogun and daimyo. These achievements meant that those in authority merited the respect and loyalty of their inferiors. Most writers felt they should begin with statements of gratitude to their betters. A classic summary is that of the Confucian scholar Muro Kyūsō (1658-1734), who was grateful for the benefits he had received from his parents, from his lord ("we can live without starving or freezing, and can bring up our families. How can we forget our lord's grace? . . . if we do not know how to serve our lord and our parents, how do we differ from the beasts?") and from the teachings of the Sages ("whereby we know the Way"). For Muro and the majority of his educated counterparts, these three graces were the "center of all goodness."[6] Others might arrange them differently, but even among scholars of Western learning at the end of the century the atmosphere was one of gratification that the times permitted indulgence of their wish to study.

---

[5] See Horst Hammitsch, "Kangaku und Kokugaku: Ein Beitrag zur Geistesgeschichte der Tokugawa Zeit," *Monumenta Nipponica*, II, I (1939), pp. 1-24, for some representative polemics.

[6] On Muro, George W. Knox, tr., "A Japanese Philosopher," *Transactions of the Asiatic Society of Japan* [*TASJ*], 20 (1892), I, pp. 1-133.

The kind of national cooperation in studies of Western armaments at the end of the Tokugawa period was unthinkable in a day when Sugita Gempaku (1733-1817) and his friends had to work out a trial and error translation despite the existence of men who could have helped them, but would not, out of fear of losing their monopoly. Gempaku's pseudonym was Kyūkō, and the nine blessings in which he rejoiced were a *rangakusha's* approximation of Kyūsō's: living in a time of peace, being raised in the capital, enjoying friendship with high and low, longevity, having a stipend, not being too poor, achieving fame, having progeny, and enjoying vigor in old age.[7] Gempaku had to count some of his blessings twice to make them nine, but his list serves as an interesting reminder of the non-military, non-hierarchic pleasures he found in his "feudal" world. If one takes Muro and Sugita as representative, or simply as important, intellectual types, it is apparent that it is still early to speak of attitudes toward modernization among the elite, and that the climate of the day was more nearly a relaxed approval of the times than a frenetic concern for changes to ward off disaster.

Nevertheless there was room for much diversity and conflict of opinion within the framework of agreement that things were better than they had been. The full range of Confucian thought of eighteenth century Japan is only now beginning to come into view as questions of its relevance to the subsequent process of modernization are beginning to be asked.[8] Some of those questions and answers form the burden of later sections in this volume. It is appropriate, however, to indicate their nature and significance here. Although the principal postulates of the Confucian schools in Manchu China and Tokugawa Japan were extremely close, and although it is possible to find a comparable emphasis for almost any position

[7] Eikoh Ma, "Japan's Encounter with Western Science," *Bulletin of the History of Medicine*, XXXIII, 4 (1959), p. 325.

[8] Thus in addition to Maruyama Masao (see Craig, below) writers like Takeyama Michio stress the role of Confucianism in secularization and rationalism.

present in one society in the other, the full thrust of the doctrines differed considerably.

The Confucian literati in China were ideologically *and* institutionally committed in a way that their Japanese counterparts were not. The Japanese Confucianists were aware of alternate forms of political organization, centralized (*gunken*) and "feudal" (*hōken*), and conscious, as R. P. Dore points out, that their country had followed a sequence between these which was the reverse of that chosen by China. The Japanese Confucianist learned of necessity to live with the fact that his country did not, in its formal political organization, incorporate the ideal Way of the Sages. If he was inclined to grant the shogun full authority, as was Ogyū Sorai, he sought to increase his command over his subordinates and over the court; if he held for the Imperial Court, as others did, his problems were even greater.

In the process some scholars developed a tendency to separate the Japanese experience from the Chinese ideal, or, rather, to separate the Confucian ideal from China. Ogyū Sorai worked out an operational definition of "Sages" whereby those worthies ceased to be specific individuals, encumbered with a given historical and political precedent, and became instead a classification type for wise political system builders. In this manner the full Confucian ideal could be said to have been unrealized in China, but within the grasp of Japan. Having universalized those values previously held by his contemporaries to be inextricably associated with China, Sorai could then particularize them and argue for their realization in a Japanese version.[9] Orthodoxy, in other words, was less specific and confining for the Japanese Confucianist. It was not closely associated with a functioning despotism, and it had less burden of present reality. There was a more selective, competitive, and flexible procedure into which the ideas and arguments of the Japanese Confucianist could be fitted. The Tokugawa Confucianist can at times be seen as forerun-

[9] J. R. McEwan, *The Political Writings of Ogyū Sorai* (Cambridge University Press, 1962), p. 30.

ner of administrative innovation and experimentation; his Ch'ing counterpart, restricted in what he could see without, was more likely to look within.

In the Chinese setting, changes described by Hellmut Wilhelm took the form of psychological interiorization, of increased concern with the principles or ideal forms, and less with the specific embodiment or practical applications. In Tokugawa Japan, on the other hand, where even the Wang Yang-ming tradition of interiorization became associated with political reformers,[10] the principal thrust seems to have been one of greater practicality, of application rather than of ethical introspection, and of separation and investigation of (in terms of the Neo-Confucian synthesis) material forms as well as ideal principles. For all of this the diversity of the Tokugawa scene, in which the Tokugawa regime did not represent an ideal principal of government as the Chinese did for Imperial Confucianism, was in part responsible.

And in addition to this the daimyo system of Tokugawa days, with its multiple opportunities for employment of the relatively modest number of eighteenth century scholars, made possible and even encouraged a variety of view and heterodoxy quite unlike the massive unity of Imperial China, where an examination system served as guarantor of orthodoxy and approved avenue to power. The full attempt on the part of bakufu legislators to encourage unity came only at the end of the eighteenth century, and even then many daimyo consciously tried to minimize the impact which this conformity might have for their specialist retainers. In part Japan may have benefited in that its Confucian system was, by Chinese standards, underdeveloped. As the need and prevalence of education rose in the eighteenth century, concern with its content also grew, and the Neo-Confucian synthesis was declared official only in the 1790's under Matsudaira Sadanobu. Even then, many daimyo did their best to minimize the impact of this proscription for their Confucian specialists.[11]

[10] Notably, Kumazawa Banzan (1619-1691) and numerous Restoration figures.

[11] In Fukuoka, for instance, the daimyo at first replaced the deviant

No emphasis on heterodoxy and variety may be permitted to obscure the fact that eighteenth century Japan was overwhelmingly Confucian in outlook and values. It is true, in Maruyama Masao's terms, that while doctrines could vary, the basic categories through which the Japanese of that day saw their world were Confucian. For most Confucian scholars the daimyo were thought of as contemporary embodiments of the Chou lords, and the *bushi* the *shih* of the classics. Whether or not it was like Chou China, however, this system of categories and allegiances, geared to a military society of regional divisions, provided a social order capable of transmitting messages of authority with great efficiency. Personal submission was combined with devotion to the group, and this pattern could, in time, be translated into regional, and national loyalties when once the units of competition and threat should have increased in size and strength.

Related to the content of Confucian teaching was the fact of change within Japanese society with which that teaching had to deal. All writers and administrators of the eighteenth century accepted as a fact and a problem the rapid change within their society. From 1700 on the shortage of currency, its adulteration and consequent devaluation, the change of status and prestige whereby merchants began to rival the urbanized samurai, and village headmen to replace them as effective leaders of local society, brought fears of social and moral disorganization. Ogyū Sorai wrote of the stages of regimes and speculated on a possible latter day for the Tokugawa, and he and others groped for measures whereby such trends might be reversed or slowed. Thus the very speed of social change in eighteenth century Japan served to rule out a static view of the Japanese world. The rising standards of education provide one instance. Demands of specialization and the struggle for achievement made the authorities' efforts

---

(Sorai) schoolmaster with his disciple, and closed the school only after it burned some years later. *Nihon kyōikushi shiryō* (Tokyo, 1890), 5, pp. 296-297. I am indebted to Albert Altman for this and the following reference.

to encourage learning essential. Ronald Dore shows that educational opportunities grew rapidly in the second half of the eighteenth century, and figures for domains bear this out.[12] Domain schools, which Sorai reported as exceptional in the early part of the century, were standard by its close, and the relation between educational opportunities and administrative expectation and performance could not fail to be direct.[13]

Eighteenth century Japan was thus responding to its internal needs of intellectual, social, and economic change and growth in many ways. But no cataclysmic crisis had yet appeared to challenge the bases of the society, and no sharply fundamental or revisionist proposals—beyond those conventional to the Confucian agrarianists—had yet been brought forward. Basic changes had not yet become critical or urgent, but change was everywhere a fact with which administrators and thinkers had to deal.

Late Tokugawa

The intellectual history of Japan in the first half of the nineteenth century is dominated by the consciousness of domestic weakness and foreign threat. The relatively optimistic tone of the eighteenth century writers who paused to itemize their good fortune changed to sharp warnings that there was little time left in which to work out solutions for the problems that faced Japan. The political history of the last decades of Tokugawa rule centers around reforms that were attempted both at the center and in the domains. As the awareness of danger grew, patterns of deference between daimyo and shogun and between retainer and daimyo began to change; as writings about the *gaikan*, or foreign threat, increased in volume, young enthusiasts were being conditioned by the talk of crisis and by the rush of preparedness measures to play their role in the violence and struggle that lay ahead. Peace

[12] Thus in all Japan only 28 of the 227 han schools ultimately established were in being in 1750. Ishikawa Ken, *Nihon gakkōshi no kenkyū* (Tokyo, 1960), p. 263.

[13] R. P. Dore, "Talent and the Social Order in Japan," *Past and Present* (1962).

and order, so much praised a few years before, now came to seem shameful because their product was weakness instead of strength. And because the root of the difficulty lay in the West, which had already humiliated China, it was the West which was the principal determinant of the attitudes with which the historian needs to deal.

In one sense the history of the period records the process whereby the Japanese learned to face a new kind of world. Traditional Japan, as Mushakoji Kinhide points out, had known a "they" and "we," with China furnishing the "they."[14] The temporary appearance of the Westerners in pre-Tokugawa days and Japan's continued contact with the Dutch in Nagasaki had not altered this dichotomy. Europe remained somewhere on the periphery, a remembered danger and a present convenience. But the new international society of the nineteenth century found a Japan suddenly squarely between East and West, and the reorientation of thought and attitude which this required is of interest. This confrontation had to some degree been prepared for by the *rangakusha,* whose studies had received active government support from at least the early decades of the century. Their books and warnings were furthermore able to find root because of two elements in the Tokugawa social and intellectual setting. Japan's feudal political order, in which autonomous domains maintained cautious and suspicious attitudes toward their neighbors, in some sense prefigured the role of the Powers in the new international society. Conceptually, the Confucian Way of Heaven, a Way to which both China and Japan had had to conform, forecast the late Tokugawa interest in international law as a superior, universally valid norm, and provided some rationalization for treating with the new arrivals from Western seas. It thus became possible to some extent to apply existing categories to the changed situation.[15] However inadequate those categories might be to Japan's long-range needs, their utility in the moment of crisis was undoubtedly great.

[14] "Nihonjin no kaigai ishiki," *Shisō* (June 1961), pp. 718-734.
[15] Maruyama, "Kaikoku," *op.cit.*

The quaint nature of the expressions of benevolence and impartiality with which the Confucianists explained why it was moral to treat with the Westerners should not be allowed to conceal the importance of the bridge to reality which they constructed with their arguments.

For many Japanese this learning process had the happy result of discovery that the problems which faced their society, however pressing, were not entirely unique or without precedent. Nakaoka Shintarō, on reading Fukuzawa's *Seiyō jijō*, found comfort in the fact that Washington too had had to raise an army to drive the barbarians out of his country.[16] The process of internationalization received its classical expression in Sakuma Shōzan's invocation of Confucius: "When I was twenty I realized that I play a part in my local state. After I was thirty I realized that I play a part in the affairs of the nation. After I was forty I realized that I play a part in the affairs of the entire world."[17] Domestic political order and classical tradition both helped prepare Japanese to relate their country and its problems to the new international society they had to enter.

Since China had played such a central role in the world view of the Japanese, word of its humiliation and defeat by the West was an important factor in the development of the nineteenth century attitudes. Many had access to the details of that defeat—government officials, official Confucianists, scholars of Western learning—and many more heard the story through them. Soon published documents spread the word to all who could read. No group was more affected by these reports than the Confucian scholars who had leaned toward

---

[16] "The oppression of the English king became more heavy every day, and the American people suffered. At that point a man named Washington complained of the people's hardships. . . . He carried out exclusion (*jōi*) and drove out the barbarians . . ." From a document reprinted in Hirao Michio, ed., *Ishin Kinnō ibun sensho: Sakamoto Ryōma, Nakaoka Shintarō* (Tokyo, 1943), pp. 325-333; partially translated in Jansen, *Sakamoto Ryōma and the Meiji Restoration* (Princeton University Press, 1961), p. 251.

[17] Tr. Charles S. Terry, "Sakuma Shōzan and his Seiken-roku" (Columbia University unpublished Master's Essay, 1951), p. 86.

China; their only possible conclusion was that the Ch'ing dynasty had fallen far short of its professed standards, and they warned that Japan should do better. But in the process they inevitably experienced a shift in their assessment of cultural excellence, and they were not likely to be reproached again with calling themselves, as some had done, "Eastern barbarians."

van Gulik has taken as representative the response of an important Confucian, Shionoya Tōin (1810-1867).[18] Tōin served as advisor to Mizuno Tadakuni, the chief architect of the bakufu's Tempō reforms between 1841 and 1843, and through his position he undoubtedly had access to some of the reports of the Hollanders at Nagasaki.[19] But soon better, because more credible, sources for the Chinese defeat came into Japan in the form of books from China. A collection of documents about China's war with England was soon reissued in a Japanese edition by a Kyushu school,[20] and in 1843 an Edo Sinologue also published an account of the Opium War. But it was above all Wei Yuan's *Hai-kuo t'u-chih*, whose 1847 edition Shionoya edited for a Japanese reprint, which informed his generation of Japanese.

Tōin's case provides evidence of an intellectual and psychological shock of major proportions. His essay *Kakkaron*, which appeared in print in 1859, is full of helpless rage against Western culture and morality; the very script of Western books fills him with loathing.[21] For men like him the Chinese

---

[18] "Kakkaron: A Japanese Echo of the Opium War," *Monumenta Serica* (1939), IV, pp. 478-545.

[19] For such intelligence, see a questionnaire addressed to the Dutch in 1842 which C. R. Boxer, *Jan Compagnie in Japan* (The Hague, 1950), App. V, pp. 185-187, provides. "QUESTION: Why have the Tartars lost, since they are said to be brave enough? ANS. Bravery alone is not sufficient, the art of war demands something more. No outlandish power can compete with a European one, as can be seen by the great realm of China which has been conquered by only four thousand men."

[20] Meirindō, in all probability the Takanabe-han (present Miyazaki) school founded in 1777 with two Chinese on its faculty; it continued to the end of Tokugawa. *Nihon Rekishi Daijiten* (Tokyo, 1959), 18, p. 78.

[21] Tōin described it as "confused and irregular, wriggling like

foundations of their value structure had proven, in van Gulik's words, "to be mere quicksand, . . . the *jusha*, having nothing to fall back upon, were left entirely helpless . . . the foreign problem affected them to the core of their being: they lost their self-esteem, and suffered from all the psychological throes which such a loss implies."[22] From men wounded so basically, no creative response was to be expected, and writers like Shionoya Tōin or Ōhashi Totsuan, another Confucianist who rejected the West completely,[23] provide in their negations emphatic concluding chords to the thought that had been dominant throughout most of the Tokugawa period.

Not all Confucianists, of course, were restricted to impotent fury. In some measure, as Albert Craig points out, Tokugawa intellectual life had prepared positions from which a more constructive response was possible. Sakuma Shōzan, for one, found in Wei Yuan's work confirmation of ideas already formed in his mind. He found it remarkable that "Wei and I were born in different places, and did not even know each other's name. Is it not singular that we both wrote lamenting the times during the same year, and that our views were in accord without having met? We really must be called comrades from separate lands."[24] Perhaps one can differentiate between intellectuals (like Tōin) committed to ideas and administrators concerned with them more instrumentally. Certainly responsible administrators from many parts of Japan (Yoshida Tōyō of Tosa, for instance) read and found in the *Hai-kuo t'u-chih* confirmation of their ideas that Japan might withstand the West by undertaking drastic reforms.

The same attitude was held by the scholars of Western

---

snakes or larvae of mosquitos. The straight ones are like dog's teeth, the round ones are like worms. The crooked ones are like the forelegs of a mantis, the stretched ones are like slime lines left by snails. They resemble dried bones or decaying skulls, rotten bellies of dead snakes or parched vipers." van Gulik, pp. 542-543.

[22] *loc.cit.*

[23] Carmen Blacker, "Ōhashi Totsuan: A Study in Anti-Western Thought," *TASJ* (Nov. 1959), Third Series, vol. 7, pp. 147-168.

[24] Terry, *op.cit.*, p. 73.

learning, the vast majority of whom pursued their specialty from a firm base in Confucian values.[25] For many of them, the cultural crisis that lay ahead was nearly as full of strain as it was for their more orthodox contemporaries. Despite the charges of obscurantists and zenophobes, they did not think better of the West than did their contemporaries, but they did think about it more. And since their specialization was suddenly shown to be of critical importance for the country at large and for their domain in particular, their sense of crisis differed considerably from that exhibited by Shionoya Tōin or Ōhashi Totsuan.

For all persuasions, however, the evaluation of China, both as civilization and as country, was inevitably and permanently altered. The deference and respect of the past would soon change to a kindness bordering on condescension. Katsu Rintarō and others would now think in terms of a regenerated and strengthened Japan leading its mainland neighbor. The path had been opened to the "Ōkuma Doctrine" of the end of the century, whereby Japan would repay its longstanding cultural debt by restoring China to a place of honor in an East Asia free of Western domination. Tokugawa Confucianists had sometimes posed as a moral problem the possibility of an invading army from China led by their revered Mencius; but the new formulation was more likely to be in terms of an army sent to rescue Mencius.

Meanwhile a desire to disaffiliate from those aspects of "China" and "Asia" that suggested weakness and submission soon became evident. In 1860 Ambassador Muragaki, Awaji no Kami, when his ship took on supplies in Angola on its return to Japan from Washington, noted in his diary that "we come to discover that the natives of India and Africa both belong to one and the same tribe of whom that Buddha must have been a chieftain. If so, methinks it absurd to worship Buddha or Amitabha at our altar; perhaps more absurd it is that our priests shave their heads in imitation of these

[25] Well shown by Numata Jirō, *Bakumatsu yōgaku shi* (Tokyo, 1952).

natives' frizzled hair, wear a surplice of bold brocade in the same fashion as these natives cover themselves with shawl-like cloths, and carry their bowl of offering in the same manner as these natives use coconut cups to eat food from."[26] Godai Tomoatsu, in London in 1862, wrote that the English considered Japanese more enterprising and forward-looking than Chinese, and speculated on the possibility of using Chinese and Indian laborers under Japanese direction to create an East Asian center of industrial economic power. He concluded that Japan should also restrict, if not jettison, its use of the Chinese writing system which had served for so long as symbol of culture and morality.[27] A similar conclusion was reached by Shimizu Usaburō, a member of the Tokugawa Akitake (Mimbu) party to France, in 1867.[28]

As "China" fell in the scale of values, "West" inevitably rose. Not, to be sure, in the same way; virtually all writers convinced themselves of the importance of preserving their cultural values while utilizing the practical aspects of Western civilization. Nevertheless it proved to be more complicated; Fukuzawa's remembered scorn for the old, traditional learning could hardly stop at its application, but had to go on to encompass social attitudes and ultimately social values. As Maruyama points out, slogans of selection were simply unworkable in times of crisis, for the process could not be planned or controlled.[29]

The process of appreciation and escalation of Western influence and example took many forms. Among the earliest were efforts to identify Confucian values of order in the West, thereby elevating the Westerners from their usual category of beasts to men.[30] The American "Republic," translated

[26] *Kōkai Nikki: The Diary of the First Japanese Embassy to the United States of America* (Tokyo, 1958), p. 144.

[27] Tomoatsu kai, ed., *Kindai no ijin: ko Godai Tomoatsu den* (Tokyo, 1921), p. 336.

[28] Osatake, Takeki, *Iteki no kuni e* (Tokyo, 1939), p. 369.

[29] "Kokutai," *op.cit.*

[30] For one of many traditional obscurantist verdicts, Carmen Blacker, "Ōhashi Totsuan," p. 156. "The Westerners are like beasts. They have a system of monogamy which forbids them to keep concubines, even

kyōwa (harmony), fortunately became associated for some time with the concord that term implied. Yokoi Shōnan, learning of Washington's refusal to serve a third term, noted that the virtues of Yao and Shun were not wanting in so distant a land as America.[31] And Ambassador Muragaki wrote of Washington, D.C. in 1860 that "The capital city should be quiet, like Washington. A simple, thrifty way of living will then be encouraged among its citizens."[32]

Increased knowledge of Western history served also to create fascination with figures of will and force in that history, men who had broken through the patterns of their society and time. The repute of Napoleon in late Tokugawa times serves as example. Information he gained at Nagasaki from a Dutch doctor who had accompanied the Grand Army to Russia furnished Rai Sanyō with the material for his "Song of the French King" (1818), in which Napoleon's Russian exploits and disasters served as example to alert his countrymen to foreign military prowess and, by implication, the need for national defense. Sanyō's numerous errors (among them the statement that Napoleon had fled to America) were avoided by his successor Takahashi Sakusaemon (the bakufu translator who was imprisoned for trading von Siebold a map of Japan for a biography of Napoleon). He issued the "Complete Account of the Emperor Napoleon Bonaparte" (*Bonaparutei Tei shimatsu*) in 1825. In this concern with the man of force we can recognize some of the background for the early Meiji delight in revolt and revolution, which saw fruit in stories of Washington, Danton, and Robespierre.[33]

---

though the wife may be childless and the family line in danger of dying out." (Aizawa Seishisai.)

[31] Kimura Tsuyoshi, *Bummei kaika* (Tokyo, 1954), p. 262.

[32] *Kōkai Nikki*, p. 120. At other times, however, as when the embassy was shown Smithsonian mummies displayed side by side with animals, Muragaki concluded that "these foreigners did not earn their nickname of 'barbarians' for nothing." *Ibid.*, p. 104.

[33] Gotō Sueo, "Meiji Ishin zengo ni okeru Naporeon no eikyō," in *Shimada Kenji Kyōju kanreki kinen rombun shū: Hikaku bungaku hikaku bunka* (Tokyo, 1961), pp. 329-348.

In time the same figures and stories could serve to convey other messages. Koseki San'ei's account of Napoleon of 1837, which was based upon yet another Dutch biography, had the incidental effect of introducing the word "liberty" in its nineteenth century, romantic use into Japan, by having Napoleon as a young man join in wild acclaim (*"Jiyū banzai!"*) at Lyons for Schiller's *William Tell*.[34] And by the 1860's Japanese visitors to France were ready to see more than military prowess; the bakufu emissary Kurimoto Joun was able to conclude that the *Code Napoléon* was the Emperor's greatest achievement, one which Japan should make every effort to adapt and introduce. This late Tokugawa conviction survived into early Meiji days, when the government experimented with a code drawn up by the French jurist Boissonade.

As "West" came gradually to occupy the center of the stage the image of "Japan" necessarily changed in importance and content. The remembered image of classical antiquity, in which the Emperor had governed a centralized realm, was seen as closer to the European model, and that model began to seem more appropriate, because more successful, than the supra-national state of China. The scholars of national learning were prepared with arguments as to why this should be so, and they occasionally found themselves so close to their *rangakusha* contemporaries that, as Itō Tasaburō has pointed out, Buddhists sometimes charged them with being secret Christians.[35] Their link with the Japanese past gave them an acceptable position from which to advocate reorganization of the political order. *Kokugakusha* began to serve as ghost-writers in the way that Confucianists had formerly; Iwakura Tomomi hired one, Tamamatsu Misao, to put his memoranda into acceptable form. And, as men of many positions began to think self-consciously about the structure of their political order (as when Nakaoko Shintarō asked himself whether

[34] Kimura, "Jiyū wa itsu hajimete Nihon ni haite kita ka," *op.cit.*, p. 96.

[35] "Kokugaku to yōgaku," *Rekishigaku kenkyū* (1937), 7, no. 3, pp. 2-34.

feudalism was a good thing for Japan), the alternative, a system of prefectures and provinces, could be shown to have roots and therefore legitimacy within the Japanese tradition.

Late Tokugawa years thus saw a radical revision of attitudes. There was, it must be repeated, an air of urgency and crisis about all of it, and this made kaleidoscopic changes possible and indeed inevitable for many. The attitudes were formed under the guns of Western warships, which, in Maruyama's words, seemed in their dignity and perseverance "the symbol of the modern sovereign state with its solid power for organization and calculation, as well as firm diplomacy."[36] Policies advocated could differ, but the crisis to which they were variant responses was a constant. In the long run the nature of the challenge and its point of origin dictated the broad lines of response. The changes required were so basic that they precipitated a ferment of thought and action by men of all ranks and types. Even the opinions of the long-powerless Emperor, as Hershel Webb points out, could assume significance in a period of divided counsel. Out of this welter of contesting groups and opinions came the Meiji Restoration.

Meiji

The years between the Tokugawa fall and the turn of the century furnish another natural unit for consideration. The first two decades, into the mid 1880's, were full of contradictions, false starts, and confusion. For although the concern with the West was constant and overwhelming, the policies advocated varied a great deal. The government experimented with suppression of Buddhism and elevation of Restoration Shintō, then sought to blend elements of both into a synthetic creed that was to serve the national purposes, and finally fell back upon an official ideology that was a mixed bag of Shintō and Confucian values. The ritual of Tokugawa status-structured society was abandoned, frequently to the distress of Japanese who were uncertain how to behave. From the

[36] "Kaikoku," *op.cit.*

peasant who refused to mount his horse in response to Fuku-zawa's reminder of new rulings of equality of classes[37] to daimyo anxious to know the correct procedure to follow in consorting with dancing girls, everyone hoped for clear state-ment of a new code of procedure. This was some time in coming, and the creation of a new nobility in 1884 may serve as one indication of the time required for the creation of a "modern," more egalitarian, hierarchy and ritual.[38]

It would therefore be possible to subdivide these years by distinguishing between the early period, when the govern-ment tried to arouse and activate the country and thereby released energies imperfectly controlled and channeled, and the later or constitutional era, when the government's efforts went to restrain rather than to stimulate popular energies and enthusiasms.

The periods overlap, but the shift of Itō Hirobumi's posi-tion on matters of educational policy in the debate between Mori Arinori and the conservatives[39] indicates somewhat the demarcations between them. It is often tempting to distinguish between government leaders and writers or thinkers. Few had the prolonged, intimate knowledge of the West of a Mori Arinori, and their framework of thought and action was very different from that of the Indian modernizers discussed below

[37] For Fukuzawa, *Autobiography*, tr. Kiyooka (Tokyo, 1938), p. 261.

[38] Maruyama, "Kaikoku," p. 98, quotes a daimyo inquiry whether men of his station should visit restaurants and licensed quarters with formal retinue or secretly, and whether they should call singing girls to their restaurant rooms, or quietly invite them to their own resi-dences instead. "At this time of innovation," it concludes, "we should like to know the correct way to conduct ourselves . . ." That it required some time to develop a new hierarchy of authority and in-fluence is also shown by the well-documented accounts of arguments within the leadership group between men whose formal responsibilities would have suggested different behavior. Thus Kido and Mori quar-reled violently in Washington in 1872, and in 1898, when the first "party" cabinet brought another group of "equals" to power, Foreign Minister and Premier Ōkuma faced insubordination from Minister to the United States Hoshi.

[39] Hayashi Takeji, "Kindai kyōiku kōsō to Mori Arinori," *Chūō kōron* (Sept. 1962), pp. 208-218.

by Stephen Hay. To some degree, as Katō Shūichi has put it, they received Westernization from books and not from direct contact with the West, and could change the book when useful. When they visited the West, they frequently returned more aware of their "Japaneseness" than when they first set out; more convinced of the need for united national effort to achieve equality. But it would be going too far to see them as opportunists among idealists; for their reactions were to a large extent those of their countrymen. Uchimura too found his homeland becoming beautiful to him in the face of his experience of American society and attitudes, and the transition from unjustified enthusiasm about the West to skepticism, from self-abasement to self-assertion in regard to things Japanese, was typical. It is also one of the distinguishing features of the Meiji period that a class of "intellectuals" had not as yet clearly emerged, and that most men of letters shared the goals and hopes of their contemporaries in government service. Those goals were to stimulate and organize a national response within the framework of existing institutions in order to overcome the humiliation of weakness and inequality.

For the first three decades of Meiji there was a reasonable, almost a remarkable coherence about Japanese attitudes toward modernization, toward the Japanese tradition, and toward Asia. If one looks at these decades as a unit, the most striking thing remains, as Sansom phrased it, "the alacrity with which the country as a whole seized upon the dogma of perfectibility and threw itself without misgivings into the task of self-improvement."[40] The notions that improvement of the nation was possible through determined effort, and that the times required this if Japan was to maintain its independence, were universal. The Western intruders themselves had given evidence of what could be done through determination and scientific application. The early attractions of Western figures of will like Napoleon was of a piece; the ubiquitous pages of Samuel Smiles' *Self Help* (first translated 1870) and the higher rationale found in the arguments

[40] *Western World*, p. 313.

of Herbert Spencer, brought home the same lesson of progress through effort and survival of the progressive.

The early advocates of enlightenment lived in a heady expectation of great advances. Tsuda Masamichi and Nishi Amane emphasized the cumulative nature of knowledge, technology, and advance. Fukuzawa Yukichi stressed similar themes throughout his career. Ueki Emori carried this view farther than most, and held for an unrestricted, illimitable, solitary individual perfectionism of the most complete sort.[41] Ueki could express his perspective of individual perfectionism only in the hyperbole of the religious traditions he knew: "I will be the Jesus of Jesus . . . the spiritual king of the world . . . Ueki Daimyōjin . . . Ueki Daibosatsu . . . Ueki the Lord, Ueki Amida Buddha."[42] But such sentiments were not common, and they were not really as disruptive of the social or cultural integration as they sound. Even for Ueki, Confucian ideas had not wholly disappeared; the conviction that a natural order (the *dōri* of the Confucianists) existed and lay beyond the individual, remained to reconcile his self-assertion with a higher order.[43]

This note of self-improvement and advancement characterizes almost everything in the Meiji period. It was not the fully integrated, scientific view of "progress" through an organic process of regular and predictable growth as Western disciples of Herbert Spencer worked it out, but rather a general conviction that change was possible, desirable, and manageable, and that it came to those who applied themselves regularly and tenaciously. A disciplined and largely humorless quest characterized the Meiji period. Its origins were not, of

---

[41] Ienaga Saburō, *Kakumei shisō no senkusha: Ueki Emori no hito to shisō* (Tokyo, 1955), pp. 179-188, discusses Ueki's failure to develop a logic of negation (on which see also R. Bellah, below).

[42] *Ibid.*, p. 182.

[43] John W. Ward makes the same point for the West by pointing out that Emerson's "grandly isolated man . . . is a chilling ideal, unless, that is, one can share the assumption . . . that there was an order which existed apart from society, a natural order which ultimately validated the rejections of the artificial order of society . . ." "Individualism Today," *Yale Review* (Spring 1960), p. 383.

course, entirely Western; there was as much in the Tokugawa self-help and self-discipline schools of Ninomiya Son-
toku and Ishida Baigan to support these efforts as there was
in the Victorian writers, but for some time argument from
Western authority and example was more effective.

Together with progress so defined, a note of devotion and
service to country dominated the language, and no doubt the
thought, of the Meiji period. Even if it was not quite so compelling an objective as men later remembered in their autobiographies, it remains the fact that contemporary writings,
diaries, and press kept the national good constantly before the
private and public mind. The priority given the national purpose also dictated the way in which the Victorian creed of self-
improvement was most commonly applied. For a generation
Smiles, Mills, and others who might have been expected to
become the apostles of individual betterment and freedom
found application as exponents of national betterment and
rights. Just as the traditional slogan *fukoku-kyōhei*, calling
for wealth and power, was moved from domain to national
level in application, so the advice which Smiles (whose chapters began as talks to factory boys anxious to get on in life)
advanced—hard work, thrift, concentration on the serious,
avoidance of romance and imagination—convinced his readers
that their country, a poor boy in the family of nations, could
become a land of property and power.[44] Mill's arguments for
representation in taxation were applied in arguments for
tariff autonomy. Everywhere in Meiji Japan one is struck
by the stress on dedication and responsibility to what is
described as the national interest. For Ueki, one did the
nation a disservice if he failed to advance himself in ability and
action; Fukuzawa thought it his life work to educate the
nation, and writers like Kitamura Tōkoku turned to letters
in order to create a modern literature for which the country
need feel no shame.[45]

[44] Note also Sansom's reminder that an early translation of *Robinson
Crusoe* provided a foreword pointing out the docetic value of the book
for those anxious to develop an island. *Western World*, p. 398.

[45] Tōyama Shigeki, "Nihon kindaika to Tōkoku no kokumin bungaku
ron," *Bungaku*, vol. 20 (1952), 5, pp. 1-8.

Implicit in the exhortation to avoid future shame was the reminder of the ignominy of Japan's present weakness and backwardness, and this note of self-abasement runs through the life histories of Meiji men of all strata. The government, as Sansom long ago pointed out, found shame and ridicule from the West its most useful argument in ordering the abandonment of customs of nudity, sanitation, and the like.[46] Meiji Christian leaders' struggle with the discovery and conviction of personal inadequacy and sin was couched in terms familiar to the West.[47] More striking was the desire of the government to devise institutions, laws, and even buildings that would win the favor of the West. Instances of such insecurity abound at many levels, but they are most marked at the higher levels of society where Japanese were most likely to be familiar with Western example and practice.[48]

No doubt much of this was inevitable in a setting in which the Western world loomed so large. The Charter Oath of 1868 indicated that learning would be sought throughout the world, and except for a relatively powerless few no one seriously questioned the importance of Westernization as a policy. It was understood that most of the secrets necessary for national survival and strength were to be found in the West, and no better evidence of this can be found than the dispatching of the greater part of the top leadership group to the Western world in 1872. This too was a continuation of late Tokugawa policy, as the Mimbu embassy of 1867 had scheduled special subjects to be investigated once the Paris Exposition was over. Nevertheless the Iwakura mission represented something new in scale and commitment. Its official

[46] *Western World*, p. 385.

[47] John F. Howes, "Japanese Christians and American Missionaries," below, discusses the ambivalences in the relationship between Japanese Christians and the West.

[48] Thus Ōkubo Toshimichi wrote of his new Western-style house in 1876 "even foreigners to whom I have shown the house have praised it, so I am quite pleased." Quoted by S. D. Brown, "Ōkubo Toshimichi: His Political and Economic Policies in Early Meiji Japan," *Journal of Asian Studies* [*JAS*; before 1956, *FEQ*] (February 1962), XXI, 2, p. 191.

journal, the five volume report compiled by Kume Kunitake, stands as a monument to the careful, unemotional, and materialistic interest of the ambassadors as they toured the Western world. It is the last and greatest of the documents filed by Japanese learning missions.[49]

Westernization was a device as well as a policy. It is obviously in this category that one must place the discussion in Fukuzawa's paper about the international advantages to be gained from a formal declaration for Christianity as the national religion,[50] and Foreign Minister Inoue Kaoru's statement that it would be necessary to make of Japan "a newly Westernized country among the nations of Asia," in order to achieve repeal of the unequal treaties that had been inherited from Tokugawa days.[51] The expression of this conviction, the international social club built in 1883 and christened the Rokumeikan, was described by Ōkura Kihachirō (who later built the Imperial Hotel) as being a part of tactics as carefully worked out as those of Ōishi Kuranosuke and his 47 *rōnin* in Genroku times.[52] Even the name selected for the club (Deer Cry Pavilion) is of interest, for it was taken from a banquet poem (#183) in the *Book of Songs* which Waley renders as:

> Yu, yu, cry the deer
> Nibbling the black southernwood in the field.
> I have a lucky guest.
> Let me play my zither, blow my reed-organ,
> Blow my reed-organ, trill their tongues,
> Take up the baskets of offerings

[49] *Tokumei zenken taishi Bei-O kairan jikki* (Tokyo, 1876), 5 vols. See also the excellent study of Kume by Haga Tōru, "Meiji shoki ichi chishikijin no seiyō taiken" in *Hikaku bungaku hikaku bunka*, above, pp. 349-386.

[50] "We do not propose that a majority of our people should become Christians, a small proportion would be enough. All that is necessary is to accept the name of a Christian country." Quoted by Sansom in *Western World*, pp. 475-476.

[51] Quoted by Watanabe Ikujirō, *Nihon kinsei gaikōshi* (Tokyo, 1938), p. 56.

[52] Quoted by Kimura, *Bummei kaika*, pp. 52-53.

> Here is a man that loves me,
> And will teach me the ways of Chou.

Whether as sincere admiration or crafty tactic, the Meiji policies of Westernization clearly reflected the overwhelming importance of the West in the latter half of the nineteenth century.

The very enthusiasm of the Westernization mood provoked misgivings about the degree to which it was necessary to learn "the ways of Chou" and provided the opening for a return of the Confucianists, who now appeared as defenders of the Japanese, and not the Chinese, tradition. Their spokesmen were numerous, but the common element was to be found in warnings that the native tradition ought not to be jettisoned so uncritically. The magazine *Nihon* and its writers, respected members of the Genrōin like Tani Kanjō, intellectuals like Nishimura Shigeki,[53] and professional Confucianists like Motoda Eifu, all lamented an excessive orientation toward the West, especially toward Germany and called for a renewal of interest in the traditional culture and values of Japan. The comeback of the Japanese tradition marked the full maturity of the Meiji system.

The West also played a full part in this process. Negatively, the failure of Western powers to grant Japan treaty revision and concessions in the 1880's accelerated dissatisfaction with rapid emulation of the West. Positively, the encouragement given to advocates of Japanese culture by connoisseurs like Ernest Fenollosa and others—and the Paris artists' response to the wood block prints they discovered—stimulated men like Okakura Tenshin to try to revive interest in the arts and philosophy of Japan. In these ways, as Hellmut Wilhelm has pointed out, a kind of "neo-traditionalism," in which the native "myth" is fostered in response to European expectations, resulted, and the final blend was in some measure the

[53] Donald H. Shively, "Nishimura Shigeki: A Confucian View of Modernization," below, and "Motoda Eifu, Confucian Tutor to the Meiji Emperor," in David S. Nivison, Arthur F. Wright, eds., *Confucianism in Action* (Stanford University Press, 1959).

product of a dialogue between East and West. In addition, the Japanese discovery that the West was not a monolithic cultural unit, and that science and religion were at war in the West, made Japanese aware of the possibility and even necessity of choice and selection.[54]

The center of the Japanese tradition so conceived was the Emperor system. This engrossing and endlessly complex problem is treated separately by H. Webb. All Japanese seem to have fallen under its spell. Iconoclasts like Ueki Emori, who noted in his diary dreams in which he violated the Empress, and the novelist Fukuzawa Shichirō, who aroused the nation with a fantasy of imperial executions as recently as 1960, testify to the centrality of the institution and cult quite as much as the official panegyrists and worshippers. But numerous gradations of respect for and utilization of the Emperor could exist within the pattern of the cult, and its ultimate content seems to have been the product of subtle but far-reaching changes. In the 1880's the Sun Goddess and Confucius returned to inspire the dream of the final Meiji constitutionalist attempt, to have a harmonious, united Diet striving to show forth the beauty of a total state structure, one conceivable only under the august sponsorship of a sovereign above politics and yet present in the very matrix of the political process.

The Japanese "tradition," as revised and revived in the 1880's, was itself a dynamic response to external and internal stimuli. For a time it was still possible, and indeed necessary, to debate its essence and nature, and it was only upon the full implementation of the education and political policies of the 1880's that it became possible to speak of a new "orthodoxy" which stood to thwart or impede the personal, individ-

[54] See Robert S. Schwantes, "Christianity *versus* Science: A Conflict of Ideas in Meiji Japan," *FEQ* (1953), XII, 2, pp. 123-132; for Fenollosa, L. W. Chisolm, *Fenollosa: The Far East and American Culture* (Yale University Press, 1963). H. Kishimoto, "Modernization *versus* Westernization in the East," *Journal of World History* VII, 4 (1963), pp. 871-874, emphasizes the distinctions that need to be drawn between "Western" and "modern."

ual appropriation of what had in the first round of modernization been claimed for the larger national unit.

During all of this the role of "China" and "Asia" served
largely to illustrate the importance of the "West" in Japanese
thought. In a setting in which success was measured by the
degree to which Japan could show itself able to adopt the
Western model, only political opponents of the leaders would
champion the cause of closer ties with Asia.

Korean and, in late Meiji times, Chinese refugees—revolu-
tionaries and reformers—found protectors and friends among
the Meiji "liberals" and among the "reactionaries," both of
whom thought their government was neglecting its proper
Asian responsibilities in its headlong drive for Westernization
and Western favor. It was particularly the out-of-power
liberals like Ōi Kentarō who fell in love with the notion of
a new Pan-Asianism, wherein Japan would provide leadership
for reform movements in neighboring lands. They saw in such
activities hopes for an increase in political freedom in Japan
itself. Since their field of political maneuver within Japan was
limited, they were drawn to Asian activities. The role and
ideal of the Restoration activists came easily to mind, and they
styled themselves "China rōnin." However interesting their
lives, it is important not to exaggerate the numbers or importance of these men. They had friends in rather high places
(Fukuzawa, Ōkuma, Itagaki, Inukai) and they were popular
and romantic figures, but their cause did not loom very large
in numbers or, one suspects, in popular interest. They were
important more as reminders of the image of Japan held by
Korean and Chinese reformers as a land of modernity and
progress, able to repulse the West—than for the influence
they had within their own society.

Even more difficult to measure is the influence of the fore-
runners of the later ultranationalists, zealots for the old virtues
and values, who cooperated with their government's opponents in Asian adventures and domestic insurrections. Individually colorful and collectively well-publicized in later
years, one suspects that their chief importance came at a later
date when military and industrial support was available for

particular projects, and that until then they were little more than reminders of the variety and severity of dislocations that resulted from strains of the modernization process in Meiji Japan.

Imperial Japan

The sweeping institutional and organizational changes of the Meiji period were for the most part managed by a narrow elite which was largely agreed on its goals, goals which were phrased in national and not in individual terms. The individual application and appropriation lay in the future. What counted was the national group; standing aside from that group, or leaving it, was not a permissible or even, for most, a practical alternative. Direct and intensive contact with the outside world was still possible for very few, and for most Japanese horizons were circumscribed by the outline of their four islands.

Inevitably, the period which followed was marked by growing divisions within the larger group. For the most part these divisions grew out of the successes of the Meiji reforms as professionalized specialists replaced the broadly experienced elite of the Meiji years. The common background of samurai and Confucian training and joint participation in the Restoration days was replaced by intensive education and training in one of the numerous bureaucracies that now arose, and generalized regional allegiance gave way to a narrower obligation to clique. At the same time, a clearer awareness of what modernization meant for Japan made it necessary to attempt to reconcile "tradition" and "modernity" and to derive a personal meaning out of goals that had long been taken for granted as natural and essential. This increased complexity and ambivalence, this questioning and looking back, may be taken as a sign of the emergence of Imperial Japan.

One important "new" element in the formation of attitudes was the rising consciousness of Japan's new modernity. Attitudes toward *Japanese* modernization, as fact and future, provide the historian with some of his most interesting materials. These attitudes began to be sharply differentiated, by group and affiliation, and twentieth century Japan, in Robert Scalapino's phrase (for the 1960's), began to emerge as an open society made up of closed components.[55]

Japan's victory over China in 1895 coincided with the publication of a new monthly which catered to the interests of the urban sector. *Taiyō* mirrored the growing maturity and independence of its readers; it began with adulatory pictorial essays devoted to the Meiji leaders, and shifted soon to searching discussions of Japan's new role and problems.

The first issues provided in symposium form discussions of the meaning of Japan's victory over China. These set forth the alternate positions held in future discussions of cultural policy, and since many of them were by highly important figures they deserve brief mention. The initial response to the war had been overwhelmingly joyous in Japan. Christians, journalists, and educators had rallied to the cause of a government they had alternately criticized and supported, seeing it now for the first time as fully their own. As the theretofore liberal journalist Tokutomi recalled, "When the war with China broke out I put aside all thought of *hambatsu* government, of Satsuma and Chōshū; I saw that the times demanded that we confront Manchu China with a united country, and I prepared to sacrifice whatever was mine."[56] Nevertheless victory reopened questions of direction and policy that had been temporarily put aside during the united war effort.

The modernizers called for greater effort to remake their society. Kume Kunitake, chronicler of the Iwakura mission, and recently forced to resign his chair in history at Tokyo University because of studies which treated the Shintō mythol-

---

[55] Robert S. Scalapino, Junnosuke Masumi, *Parties and Politics in Contemporary Japan* (Berkeley, 1962), p. 145.

[56] For Tokutomi, *Sohō jiden* (Tokyo, 1935), p. 293. The best survey of attitudes is to be found in Oka Yoshitake, "Ni-Shi sensō to tōji ni okeru tai-gai ishiki," *Kokka gakkai zasshi* (1954, 1955), 68, nos. 3, 4, pp. 101-129, and nos. 5, 6, pp. 223-254, a continuation of his earlier discussion of treaty-reform efforts and contemporary attitudes. "Jōyaku kaisei ron ni awawareta tōji no tai-gai ishiki," *ibid.* (1953), 67, nos. 1-2, pp. 1-24, 183-206.

ogy objectively, called for a great reform in the educational world. Japan's victory over China, he wrote, represented the defeat of a philosophical and social order centered in China to which Japan had belonged until Meiji. It was a world of class governments and social divisions. The old Confucian virtues, which elevated status and submission, were now as much defeated as were the Ch'ing armies. The new era would be one of specialization, of distinction between *bun* (letters) and *bu* (arms), and Japan's victory should be credited to her having begun this separation and specialization. Kume concluded that the laws of social evolution made Chinese political philosophy—and Mencius—seem primitive and underdeveloped; greater liberality and equality must come as logical antitheses to the old order whose end was now so evident.[57]

Fukuzawa Yukichi announced that Japan had fully lived down the shame of the past. It had done this through combining patriotism with the enlightenment of *bummei kaika*, and the only conceivable path that remained was one of further advance along the same road. With victory achieved, commerce should take precedence over guns, and Japan should become a nation of scholars striving for civilization and enlightenment.[58]

Tsubouchi Shōyō, for his part, was less prepared to elevate *bun* at the cost of *bu*. He announced the arrival of a new age of culture which would match that of Periclean Athens, but stressed that this had become possible through arms and war. He wrote that war made a nation out of a people, and cited European authors and examples to buttress his argument of the critical importance of war in a nation's history.

A second group of writers preferred to emphasize the importance of spirit and values for the Imperial Japan that had been born. Tani Kanjō, in a "sermon" preached on a Confucian text at the recently founded *Shibun Gakkai*, stressed the importance of spiritual orientation, and took his examples from areas as distant as Switzerland and Montenegro to

[57] *Taiyō*, 1, "Gakkai no daikakushin," pp. 3-8.
[58] *Taiyō*, 2, "Yukichi Ō no jiji iken," pp. 360-361; a lecture given before 30 members of the lower house of the Diet.

show that one could avoid the shame of defeat only through cultivating spirit. Fujisawa Nangaku, the son of a Takamatsu *jusha*, argued that post-war education would have to be based more than ever before on spiritual values (*seishin*). *Bun* and *bu*, he argued in traditional manner, could never be separated without peril to the nation; and a state structure and policy of properly aesthetic proportions must be created by combining them carefully.[59] And Inoue Tetsujirō, that pillar of future philosophical orthodoxy, compared Japan's victory over China to the Roman conquest of Greece. But while he excoriated Chinese (and Indian) weakness, he reminded his readers that Oriental, especially Chinese, learning and philosophy were of supreme nobility and remained part of the life stream of Japanese culture. It followed that they were superior to what could be found in the West, and that a Japan which was entering the main stream of international scholarship, as it was of international politics, should look to its own standards and traditions.[60]

These pieces foreshadowed the main varieties of argument that would be used in the half century ahead. The problem of reconciling traditional with modern, and of determining the proper balance of *bun* with *bu*, continued to occupy polemicists and scholars throughout the next half century. One can see prefigured the positions of men as different as Araki Sadao and Yoshino Sakuzō in these discussions of 1895. Unhappily, the tripartite intervention soon removed the best arguments of the modernizers by providing further shame and inequality. Japan had not yet achieved its minimum goals in international society, and spirit and arms had even greater roles to play in the next decade.

One could select many dates for the beginning of Imperial Japan; 1887, the date of the first great wave of national indignation aroused by the failure of the plans for treaty revi-

[59] *Ibid.*, 3, pp. 416-418. In this he echoes the wording, repeated in each version of the Tokugawa *Buke shohattō*, that "from of old, *bun* has been the left, *bu* the right, neither complete without the other." Cf., *Tokugawa Kinreikō* (Tokyo, 1897), 1, p. 91.

[60] *Taiyō*, 1, pp. 13-17, "Sensō go no gakugei."

sion,[61] or 1890, the implementation of Constitution and Rescript on Education, or 1895. Yet the decade between Shimonoseki and Portsmouth marks the center of the process, and 1900 serves as a convenient milestone. The date has in its favor Japan's full realization of European imperialist designs on China, and knowledge of Russian advances in Manchuria, the failure of two attempts at change in China, the second concluded by the Boxer intervention in which Japan emerged for the first time as full member in the "Western" community. There was also the investment of the Chinese indemnity in a steel and iron industry about to make Japan a major industrial power with heavy reliance upon raw materials from the mainland. The domestic situation showed equally significant changes. Itō Hirobumi, the greatest of the oligarchs, condescended to organize and lead a political party in order to command support in the lower house of the Diet. In that same house the extension of suffrage through lowering of the tax qualification had been made, and the first bill calling for universal manhood suffrage submitted. An Imperial ordinance institutionalized the power of the military high command through the provision calling for active service representatives in the cabinet, and a new police law replaced the *ad hoc* measures of earlier Meiji days with an integrated, minatory response to the nascent social movement.

The exhilaration of the war against China was not sustained by the events which followed. For the most part the romantic, intense affiliations of earlier Meiji gave way to more complex and considered outlooks. The world of Imperial Japan was a much less friendly place. No traveler would go abroad again expecting, as had Uchimura, to find that in America the rocks would ring with praises or the streets be peopled by the ranks of the elect.[62] The optimism that characterized the

[61] This is the preference of Kōsaka Masaaki, "Meiji no Nihon to sekai," in *Konoe Kazan Kō gojūnensatsu kinen ronshū. Ajiya: Kako to genzai* (Tokyo, 1955), p. 231, and of Delmer Brown, *Nationalism in Japan* (Berkeley, 1955), pp. 112ff.

[62] "How I Became a Christian," reprinted in *Uchimura Kanzō zenshū* (Tokyo, 1933), 15, pp. 80-81. It may be suggested, however, that early travelers to Communist China were equally optimistic.

rush toward perfectibility in Meiji was increasingly replaced by the misgivings about the process of industrialization and social change. The banalities of the political novelists of the 1880's had already given way to the introspective reveries of the modern writers. The exultant war songs of the Sino-Japanese War, when Progress was conquering a decadent past, would give way to the melancholy songs of the Russo-Japanese War with their nostalgia for the green of Japan after the red clay of Manchuria.[63] The war against Russia would, indeed, be immeasurably more costly and more sobering. Its symbols represented tragedy and sacrifice, whether of responsibility, like Nogi, or commitment, like Hirose Takeo.[64]

The first decade of the twentieth century was critical for the formation of attitudes in Imperial Japan. The bright dream of progress was fading. The ideal of full partnership with the West had been achieved at tremendous cost in lives and treasure, only to bring the immigration restrictions and warnings about a coming race war that showed amicable relations in international society were by no means assured.

The attitudes of pessimism and doubt that developed were by no means restricted to the intellectuals, although they held them in the most complex and interesting manner. The genrō themselves were full of doubt about the policies of the succes-

---

[63] Tamai Kensuke, "Gunka," *Bungaku* (1955), 23, no. 12, pp. 32-39.

[64] Hirose, a young naval officer who died a hero's death in early operations at Port Arthur, was deified as a god of war and became a fitting subject for elementary school textbook lessons on nationalism. But a recent discovery of his papers reveals that during his years (1898-1902) in Russia he became deeply drawn to Russian culture and Russians. To one, a naval officer in the Russian fleet, he wrote in Russian just before his final mission: "Our countries are now at war. I am more sorry than I can say that this is so. Still, this is a war between countries, and it does not in the least change the warm personal feelings I have always had for you. On the contrary, I seem to be more fond of you than ever, precisely because we are in such a situation. . . . At this very moment I am taking my ship on a mission to try to block your harbor. Farewell, dear friend, fare thee well!" Shimada Kenji, *Roshiya ni okeru Hirose Takeo* (Tokyo, 1961), pp. 313-314. This would seem at least as remarkable as Katayama's famous handshake with Plekhanov at Amsterdam.

sor statesmen they had selected for office. It seemed to Yamagata, Matsukata, and Inoue that the government was spending too much, that its foreign debt was too large, and that the future was anything but bright. Yamagata himself was persuaded of the probability of an East-West clash in the future. He and his colleagues were also disturbed to see the growing emphasis on personal and material benefits among the people; this they found an unworthy contrast to the national and (as they saw it in retrospect from their spacious villas) disinterested motives they had had themselves.[65]

Sectional responses to national crises were also shown in 1912 by the tilt between War Minister Uehara and Prime Minister Saionji over the issue of increasing the size of the army. Uehara's stubborn refusal to give way and his willingness to jettison the very pattern of Meiji constitutionalism to win his point if needed showed some of the possibilities inherent in the special interest groups that had now become entrenched within the state structure. Even within the army, as this and later crises were to show, the presumed desires of the founder, Yamagata, were no longer necessarily the key to the resolution of disputes. The business community, so long the beneficiary of special tax and subsidy benefits from the modernizing regime, also showed signs of restiveness and determination to have its interest considered.

But the strains of the period were most sharply etched in the malaise of the intellectuals. More than any other group they were aware of the contradictions forced upon them by the ideology of the family state, and they were more likely to ask themselves whether they were "modern" or "Japanese" than their contemporaries. The intellectuals also were becoming more numerous, and they were no longer as sure of employment as they had been; less of an elite, they were also more critical of their society. The curious incident of the anarchist plot which resulted in the execution of Kōtoku Shūsui furnishes an excellent symbol of this. For Tokutomi Roka, who electrified the students of the First Higher School

[65] Shinobu Seisaburō, *Taishō seiji shi* (Tokyo, 1953), I, pp. 211ff.

with a lecture discussing the event, the incident dramatically underscored the declining importance of political protest for the youth of late Meiji days. He appealed to his hearers (who included some of the most important intellectuals of post-World War II Japan) to remember the importance of caring enough to resist and revolt. It seemed to him more valuable to the national purpose than the blandly materialist, self-centered concerns he thought he saw dominating youth in the early decades of the twentieth century. Similar considerations were to soften condemnations of youthful resisters in the 1930's and 1960's. For writers the Kōtoku incident was more important for what it showed than for its content. A Nagai Kafū was suddenly and movingly reminded of the impracticality of an intellectual, individual revolt against the unfairness of his state. It had been possible for a Zola to defend Dreyfus, and yet it would be impossible for his Japanese counterpart in letters to do so. For a brief moment the lack of a tradition of opposition, the lack of opportunity to influence their countrymen (even from exile: the cost of insularity) seems to have struck a number of important intellectuals and to have confirmed them in what was anyway their initial inclination: withdrawal, retreat, or indifference to the political issues of their day.[66]

There was much more at work here than the efficiency of the modern police state, for that state was neither as efficient nor as awesome as later apologists for inaction would have their readers believe. The facts of the Kōtoku incident, for instance, were widely available despite the official censorship. In education (as when the "liberal" parties assailed Katsura's education budget and policies) and in civil rights the pressure came usually not from government, which preferred to favor the "modernists" (like Minobe in the 1930's) and acted only when its hand was forced, but from forces within Japanese society. Colleagues, neighbors, publicists, relatives—these were the people who hounded the Kumes, the reformers, and

[66] I have profited from an unpublished paper by Fred. Notehelfer, "The Significance of the 'High Treason Trial' of 1911 in the eyes of three Meiji Thinkers."

the liberals, with threats of ostracism and shame for having lowered Japan or Japanese values before the world.

For the few who were inclined to resist there was lacking a generally accepted framework of universal values on which they could base their arguments. In Maruyama's perceptive comment, the atrophy of the Confucian values after the middle of the Meiji period and the failure to develop alternative transcendental ideals which might replace them—an agreed-upon mandate of heaven or of history—made it difficult to restrain, and easy to promote, the ideologies of family state and divine nation. The poverty and limitations of political discourse to be found in even the Yoshinos and Minobes illustrate the handicaps which Meiji ideology posed for the modernization of political theory and action.

Imperial Japan with its multiple bureaucracies[67] therefore provided an unlikely home for advocates of individual conscience and solitary opposition. Hence the importance of Uchimura Kanzō for later generations.[68] His defiance of convention and ideology in refusing to bow to the Emperor's portrait and his refusal to enter the establishment of even Japanese Christianity provided one of the very few instances of what contemporary Japanese seek as "modern" conduct, an isolated case in which the values, as well as the matter, of "modernization" became individually appropriated.

Imperial Japan thus saw the emergence of the modern intellectual in a complex social and philosophical setting. For the historian it now becomes futile to try to single out and arrange in the order of importance Japanese attitudes toward China, toward the West, and toward the Japanese tradition.

---

[67] Note the weary, though extreme, conclusion of Peter Quennell on his colleagues after a period as lecturer at a university in the 1930's; "Modern Japan is a paradise of bureaucrats; every lecturer at a government school or university thinks of himself primarily as an official. . . . 'The Professor,' explained a friend who knew him well, 'is a sort of policeman; you must never forget that. He has read English literature and learned his subject, as a policeman learns the contents of his little book.'" *A Superficial Journey through Tokyo and Peking* (London, n.d.), p. 99.

[68] See John F. Howes, Chapter X, and Robert N. Bellah, Chapter XI, below.

That "tradition," however, was becoming part of the individual baggage of each school boy in a way it never had before. Imperial Japan sought to affect and fix attitudes at their beginning, by developing standardized public school textbooks which were first introduced in 1903. Thereafter generations of lower school students received the mythology as truth, and scholars were well advised to turn their critical approach to other areas of inquiry.[69] "Kokutai" gradually became a subject for serious and devout investigation, its ambiguities shrouded in language designed to ward off definition and exactness. Beginning as a trickle, the tide of books devoted to *kokutai* became a flood, until it stood as a catalogue classification for libraries.[70] The strains of maintaining so artificial and irrelevant a mythology were very great, and persistent and vigilant effort was required to defend the indefensible.[71] The 1920's, years during which a questioning attitude toward the national ideology became noticeably stronger, were also years of well-subsidized organizations devoted to the protection of the National "Essence" and "Foundation."

Despite this increased awareness of the Japanese tradition, the Japanese concern with the West may perhaps be described as somewhat less compulsive in the twentieth century's early decades. During these same years the West itself changed thoroughly. Neither unapproachable nor invincible, it proved to be less monolithic, less doctrinaire, less confident of its own blessings. Imperial Germany and Imperial Russia, two of the principal concerns of modern Japan's emulators and strategists, both disappeared, the latter replaced by a new source of

[69] Karazawa Tomitarō, *Kyōkasho no rekishi* (Tokyo, 1956), 2 vols., provides the fullest history of textbooks of modern Japan.

[70] John Paul Reed, *Kokutai* (Chicago, 1940), p. 211, provides figures for publication of books on Japanese ideology; beginning modestly (1 in 1908), they increase slowly (10 in 1911), decline during the 1920's (6 in 1923), then mount steadily in the 1930's (36 in 1930 and 98 in 1934).

[71] Thomas C. Smith, "Old Values and New Techniques in the Modernization of Japan," *FEQ* (1955), XIV, 3, pp. 355-363, lays major stress on the populous and conservative agricultural sector in suggesting reasons for the success of these efforts.

attraction for radicals and of fear for traditionalists; the United States became the new rival in Pacific affairs, and Japan an important competitor in Western markets. It therefore becomes meaningless to try to characterize attitudes toward the "West," and requires rather a detailed study of sectional responses and problems to individual problems and issues.

During the same years Asia was changing, and with it Japanese attitudes toward Asia. The crash of the traditional political order in China ended discussion about the kind of alliance with China that the Meiji leaders had once hoped for, and instead it became conventional to point out that there was no longer a Chinese government with which to cooperate. For a time this was very nearly true, and the chaos of the war lord era made individual and idealistic projects of aid ineffective unless they were backed up by organizational support from government or army. In the process idealism was certain to give way to opportunism; loans to war lords, aggression veiled and unveiled, and friendships made and broken, served to increase Chinese mistrust and Japanese frustration. The record of Japanese control in Korea, despite its impressive technological achievements, was also not of such a nature as to increase the confidence of Japan's other continental neighbors, and the Siberian intervention added to charges of Japanese aggressiveness which in turn helped produce hurt and angry responses. An additional important element in Japan's attitudes toward China was the fact that a new scholarly tradition, based upon historicism, was producing a literature which, despite important dissents, tended to conclude that Chinese culture was an immutable way of life in which republican institutions and modern nationalism had made only superficial impressions, and that a strong helping hand in defending the traditional culture would reap gratitude and cooperation. Scholars like Naitō Torajirō who popularized "unchanging China" also wrote persuasively of China's backwardness, stagnation, and corruption, and tended to create an image of a land in which any change, including a reversal to earlier, more traditional, conditions would be preferable. These views made important contributions to an unflattering image of China in the 1920's and to the efforts of the 1930's to "lead" China in the name of the "common culture" which Japan and her neighbor had known since antiquity.[72]

Another element in Japan's attitudes toward China was the fact that Japan's success in modernization and the victory over Russia, followed hard by the Western promises of self-determination held out during World War I, had helped accelerate trends of nationalism everywhere in Asia. Cultural admiration of Japan remained (though weakened by increasing opportunity for Chinese to seek Westernization at its source) but political admiration was something else again. The image of a young, imaginative Japan was being replaced by that of a mature and dogmatic neighbor, while the Japanese image of China had changed from that of a land of ineffectual but gentlemanly literati to an anarchic community led by youthful and impetuous republicans. Katō Kōmei, returning from China in 1913, commented that on a previous trip in 1899 he had found Chinese leaders older than those in Japan; now they were in their thirties, while Japan was ruled by old men.[73]

These changes represented more than the replacement of the idealism and adventure of the Meiji "China rōnin" by the dogmatism and insensitivity of their successors. They reflected instead the attainment of new stages of the modernization process in both China and Japan—stages less open to influence by individual activists, well-meaning or otherwise, because influence, in societies more activated and complex, re-

---

[72] Arthur F. Wright, op.cit., p. 248; Hisayuki Miyakawa, "An Outline of the Naitō Hypothesis and its Effects on Japanese Studies of China," *FEQ* (1955), XIV, 4, pp. 533-552. For works prepared by Inaba Iwakichi for the Imperial Army, John K. Fairbank and Masataka Banno, *Japanese Studies of Modern China* (Tokyo, 1955), pp. 230-232. But it should not be concluded that Naitō was in agreement with the China policy at all times; for his criticism of the Twenty-one Demands, *Taiyō*, 21, 9, pp. 55-61, "Ni-Shi kōshō ron."

[73] Ito Masanori, *Katō Kōmei den* (Tokyo, 1929), I, p. 737.

quired more organization and agreement, and was subject less to charisma and color than it was to corporate impact and response. In part, it may be suggested, the intellectual "style" in twentieth century Japan had changed from optimism and activism to pessimism and passivity because so many of the actors saw themselves removed from stage to balcony, becoming more and more part of a mass society in which there was less likelihood of "establishing one's name" because names were lost in the anonymity of the throng. In scholarly life a parallel process, whereby the restrictions of official ideology removed the great themes of responsible analysis from circulation, together with the breakdown of the comprehensive theories of nineteenth century progress with a resulting fragmentation and compartmentalization of knowledge, produced a diligent but pointless pursuit of highly specialized and rarefied topics and systems. It was a setting in which Marxism, with its comprehensive approach and apocalyptic vision, could make important, albeit covert headway; and future crises would find ground well prepared for its spread.

Although Imperial Japan ended only with the defeat of 1945, many of its attitudes changed qualitatively in the 1930's and some lived on thereafter. The ethos that pervaded Japan in the years after 1931, and the flight from reality that resulted, make an attempt to study attitudes at that point particularly important. Our scholarship on this period is still too new, and it is far from adequate to permit answers to some of the most basic questions we bring to it. Of the papers in this volume only two take up the period. We have had in the past much detail, but strikingly little explanation. There are shadowy and sinister groups, but almost no personalities apprehensible in their complexity. Much of what we do have is based upon too narrow a comparative framework, and emphasizes the unique nature of Japanese militarism and expansionism. Most pre-war Western writers and post-war Japanese commentators tended to stress, pejoratively, the consequences of Japan's experience as if it were in violation of some normal process of historical development. The future historian, conscious that modernizing societies in Egypt, Turkey, Burma, and Pakistan have seen their equivalent of Japan's military purists show discontent with parliamentary machinery, and recalling the role of the French forces in Algeria when discussing the efforts of the Kwantung army to force government decisions in Tokyo, may come with somewhat different questions and derive different conclusions. The distance and perspectives of the 1960's may permit a more reasoned and balanced approach to these problems.[74]

Many of the elements already discussed could be advanced in partial explanation of the shift in attitudes of the 1930's. The pace of domestic social change exacerbated divisions within society and increased the willingness of some to welcome the elevation of old-style national goals like patriotism. The nature of Japanese insularity and the consciousness of international disapproval and censure also made it possible to rally support for militarist actions, both as apologia and as explanations to head off further criticism which might only provoke further extremism. The sole "universal" values of the new order, those of the Emperor figure and cult, were national and particular rather than truly universal, and were combined with the historical failure to develop a tradition of individual opposition on grounds of conscience. With every pressure combining to encourage silence or assent, the mood and mode of expression swung steadily to the side of those who had the force and strength of convictions (somewhat in the way that forces could combine, in the 1950's, to encourage a drift toward "radical" opinions and attitudes).

It is also possible to find roots for different responses in the factors that have been discussed above. In some measure the schools of modernizers and of traditionalists remained juxtaposed as they had been. The same divisions were to be seen within each of the new bureaucracies that had arisen,

[74] Recent studies of army factionalism promise clarification and differentiation in the usual impression of insubordinate young officers. See James B. Crowley, "Japanese Army Factionalism in the 1930's," *JAS* (1962), XXI, 3, pp. 309-326.

including even the military. There, as elsewhere in modern Japan, issues of "spirit" and of "Western tools" became associated with other sources of dissatisfaction in Japanese society such as regionalism and cliquism.

Neither faction nor position was ever fully dominant, and no extremist faction ever succeeded to the extent that it changed the basic structure of government inherited from the Meiji period. From crisis to crisis decisions of this order were put off by men who, "moderates" and "militarists" alike, preferred to concentrate on the immediate strategic, diplomatic, or economic problem, hopeful that the morrow would bring an improved situation from which the solution would present itself.[75] Unhappily their expectations were not fulfilled, and this in part because they never met their problem head-on. This had, in fact, not been done since the Meiji period. One suspects it had been possible then only because there was at hand in the Restoration oligarchy a group, able to marshal all elements in the national power structure, which operated on the basis of mutual trust and esteem and was not afraid or hesitant to speak its mind. When the crisis occasioned by the 21 Demands subsided in June, 1915, the editor of *Taiyō*, Ukita Kazutami, foreshadowed the future by asking himself how the matter would have turned out if the *genrō* had not proved worthy of trust and capable of deliberation. Had it been left to the forces of "opinion" in a period of parties and factions which encourage extreme opinions, he asked, might not the country have been led to disaster? He concluded that the gods and *genrō* had saved a bad situation; a quarter century later the gods alone proved unequal to the task. Divided counsels, specialized bureaucracies, and a failure to develop, in absence of educated popular participation, a new united group at the center, led to national disaster.

[75] Thus Saionji, quoted by Harada: ". . . there is no use in saying, 'How distressing!' or 'I am at my wit's end!' This is probably one phenomenon of a transitional period. If one could only feel that this indeed is the time to put forth one's maximum effort, one might even find it a very interesting period . . ." Quoted by Takashi Oka, "Saionji and the Manchurian Crisis," *Papers on China* (Harvard, 1954), p. 58.

The frenzy of the 1930's has continued to torture the intellectuals of post-war Japan. Their ambivalent approach to the process and concept of "modernization," their deprecation of Japan's "achievements" and preference for familiar concepts like democracy and peace, constitute a logical and understandable exorcism of the irrationality of the recent past.

It may be appropriate to conclude these remarks with a few over-all considerations which bear on the continuities and discontinuities of the formation of attitudes in Japan's modern century.

The first relates to the grouping of responses. It has often been noted that the extremes of attraction to and rejection of outside tradition are related psychological phenomena, as are the extremes of self-abasement and cultural pride. It should prove rewarding to investigate the convergence of shifts in attitudes with movements of change in social and international relations. This has not as yet been seriously attempted for Japan. It may not be possible to establish a clear sequence of priority, but it should become possible to speak more positively than one can at present about such relationships, to see how relatively minor maladjustments so affect each other that correctible or adjustable vibrations become irreversible oscillations. What is needed is a more subtle and broadly-based understanding of the dynamics and interrelationships of change over a period of time.

A second and striking continuity is the importance of Japan's self-conscious and insular response. From Meiji through military to contemporary Japan, the prevalence of a discussion carried on in terms of self-awareness, self-identification, and self-realization is a conspicuous feature of the Japanese scene. The awareness of being different, of facing discontinuities of unique proportions, of suffering, and of "agony"—to use some of the terms one meets in the literature—seems to be constant in much of Japan's recent intellectual history. One may wish to question the uniqueness and the prevalence of such attitudes—Japan's discontinuities seem scarcely greater than those of many other parts of the non-Western world, and certainly no greater than China's—and the prevalence (since discussion in these terms brings one inevitably face to face with the most self-conscious group, the intellectuals) of such attitudes, but their existence in itself constitutes a verifiable fact of the greatest importance for anyone investigating the process of modernization in Japan.

Study of attitudes also confronts one with the phenomenon of the dedication of Japanese elites, frequently self-appointed, who have felt themselves born to set the world right. Their intensity and courage has been a constant dynamic and frequent boon. The *shishi* ideal with its endorsement of purity and action is an important heritage of modern Japan, and it has contributed much to the speed of the process of change. It has also been a source of danger and of violence, and much recent political history underscores Shaw's reminder that sincerity is fully compatible with stupidity.[76] It is important to seek the psychological mainsprings of such responses by studying the self and world image held by the activists.

Finally, in conducting such studies we need to be constantly aware of the fact that the change so characteristic of modern Japan has been as true *within* the concepts and slogans as in the society in which they were used. Phrases and slogans of "Japanism" as used by the Restoration *shishi*, Meiji traditionalists, twentieth century reactionaries, and military radicals changed profoundly in content and thrust. The 1930's did not represent a return to something old merely because old slogans were given new life any more than the Restoration represented an authentic return to antiquity. At each stage such slogans represented a changing, and not an unchanged, attitude toward modernization. Labels rather than attitudes, these slogans covered sets of values which were as different as were the persons and groups who seized upon them in their own psychological need and response.

[76] Noted by Howard S. Hibbett, "The Portrait of the Artist in Japanese Fiction," *FEQ* (1955), XIV, 3, p. 354.

PART TWO

The Tokugawa Setting

The modernization process in Japan is often dated from the Meiji Restoration of 1868 with its determination (announced in the Charter Oath of April of that year) to abandon absurd customs of the past and to seek knowledge throughout the world. Except for brief periods of extreme enthusiasm for all that was Western, however, the process of seeking knowledge was highly selective and pragmatic, with Japan's political and cultural leaders seldom losing sight of their basic goals, which were defined in terms of national wealth and power. The definition of those goals and the development of the pattern of interpretation within which they had meaning was a product of Tokugawa times, and the applicability of the measures that were selected was also determined by the social and institutional setting into which they were introduced. In Meiji, as earlier, Sir George Sansom's recent reminder holds: The Japanese "borrowed and discarded as seemed fit to them, performing eclectic feats which bear witness to the toughness of their native tradition."

By the end of the Tokugawa period that native tradition had known many transitions, and early nineteenth century Japanese society was one of great variety and complexity. In recent years historians have been increasingly concerned with efforts to characterize and identify elements of that setting that conditioned the modernization process. It would require a larger volume than this to do the subject justice, and the tremendous importance of the pre-Meiji setting will require study for many more years before an adequate balance sheet can be prepared.

For purposes of this collection two aspects of the Tokugawa scene are selected, both of which bear directly on the setting and speed of the nineteenth century program of reform. Both also figure importantly in the list of features essential to modern societies discussed by J. W. Hall. Among the cluster of characteristics there described, many relate to education. Quite aside from "widespread literacy," which receives separate listing, education is the prerequisite for realization of many of the other aspects of the modern polity. In the absence of twentieth century radio communications, the signboard, newspaper, and book were the only means available to a government trying to encourage, direct, and activate its people. It determined the degree of effective participation in social and economic processes, and involvement in and cooperation with the bureaucratic structure of government that was possible.

When R. P. Dore turns his attention to the educational scene in late-Tokugawa Japan his conclusions thus affect every aspect and level of understanding of the Meiji scene. Nowhere is the continuity between Tokugawa and Meiji more clearly seen. The pervasiveness of education, the growing network of schools for commoners as well as for the elite, the practicality and applicability that characterized Tokugawa education, and the values of concord, cooperation, and obligation inherent in its classics—values that kept paternalistic governments from fearing the effects of their diffusion—all show how extraordinarily the late feudal domain, in the interests of its regional and parochial wealth and power, prepared the way for a national regime which would carry over these same outlooks in the interests of the whole country to become one domain in a new and larger context.

The second aspect treated here relates to the content and thrust of the knowledge and values transmitted by Tokugawa education on its higher levels. The list of features of the modern state enumerated concludes with language describing a "rational and secular orientation of the individual to his environment based on the growth of scientific knowledge." A belief in progress and in man's ability to affect and in part control his environment was one of the principal elements stressed in the discussion of modernization which E. O. Reischauer prepared for the Hakone meeting; it is indeed one of the most striking contrasts between the modern and the medieval in the West, and it was one that struck many writers in Asia most forcefully when they first learned of it.[1]

In this respect, as in so many others, the Tokugawa scene was peculiarly conducive to the acceptance of what was to come from the West. As many writers have pointed out, the prevailing tone of intellectual life was secular. The Neo-Confucian philosophy that received official favor and which was the subject mat-

[1] Thus the eighteenth century Indian Muslim Abū Tāleb noted on his return from London, "The English have very peculiar opinions on the subject of *perfection*. They insist that it is merely an ideal quality, and depends entirely upon comparison; that mankind have risen, by degrees, from the state of savages to the exalted dignity of the great philosopher Newton . . ." quoted in Wm. T. de Bary, S. Hay, R. Weiler, and A. Yarrow, eds., *Sources of Indian Tradition* (New York, 1958), p. 565.

ter for virtually all higher schools was rationalist and avoided the concerns—emotional and metaphysical—of the Buddhist philosophies that had prevailed before the Tokugawa period opened. Although it gave way at times to other Confucian schools, and was on occasion combined in various ways with elements of veneration for the national (Shintō) tradition, in most respects the two moved in compartmentalized categories in which the gods rarely interfered with the impersonal and natural categories of the Confucianists. In the Japanese setting Confucian teachings served to reinforce values of duty, self-discipline, loyalty, and achievement—in honor to one's name and gratitude and respect to parents and superiors—and thus contributed to the dynamism and vitality of the social setting. Intellectually, those teachings led to many and varied pursuits. Many Confucian scholars compiled important works of classification and study in botany, and most of them concentrated on problems of political economy. Unlike their contemporaries in China, whose political speculations were necessarily bounded by the Confucian emperor who capped and closed their political universe, and who tended increasingly to interiorize their concerns of ethical and moral probity, the Japanese Confucianists produced a voluminous literature of political and economic analysis, much of it critical of the order they knew.

Albert Craig treats a representative of this tradition to investigate the degree to which it was prepared to deal with Western science. His discussion of this problem, when compared with the later contribution on Confucianism in China of the same period (VIII) illustrates the need to distinguish and differentiate with care; what is true of "Confucianism," here seen so differently in two disparate settings, could later be the case with "Western" and equally so with "nationalist," or "socialist," thought.

CHAPTER III

The Legacy of Tokugawa Education*

R. P. DORE

THOSE who look hopefully to Japan for "lessons" in how late-comers can industrialize and build effective national political institutions are apt to overlook one important respect in which mid-nineteenth century Japan differed from its Asian neighbors and from most of those societies which still count as underdeveloped today—Japan already had a developed system of formal school education. It was a system which was largely swept away in the modernizing enthusiasm of the 1870's, and it was a system which in many respects had to be swept away if Japan was to emerge as a modern industrial and military power. It was class-ridden, formalistic, backward-looking, out-of-date. But it was also intellectually sophisticated, disciplined, occasionally stimulating, and politically relevant. Whatever one's judgment of its value, the fact remains that this system shaped the generation which, in the last quarter of the nineteenth century, carried through the sweeping changes which laid the foundation of modern Japan. It is in this sense a legacy worth considering.

The first thing to be stressed is not simply the kind, but the sheer _amount of formal educa_tion that went on. If the Tokugawa period was a time of stagnation in some respects and of cyclical fluctuation in others, at least in the field of education there was a steady trend of growth. In Ieyasu's time a samurai who could express himself cogently on paper was a rarity, and illiteracy was normal. But gradually peace "civilized." Saikaku, at the end of the seventeenth century, already speaks of an illiterate samurai as sadly behind the times, and

* This paper covers substantially the same ground as the final chapter of the present writer's _Education in Tokugawa Japan_ (Routledge and University of California Press, 1964).

by the middle of the nineteenth century the situation was vastly different. Nearly every fief had its fief-endowed school and there were hundreds of private schools for samurai. By the time he was adult, the average samurai could not only read and write his own language, he was likely to have undergone a sufficiently prolonged and disciplined intellectual training to be able to read some Chinese as well.

If public provision for formal education was limited to the samurai class, the lower orders were already managing to provide very well for themselves. In the towns a good proportion of the population could read and write Japanese. Parents bought such education for their children, voluntarily and with hard cash, from teachers who derived their total income from fees. In country districts paternally disposed richer villagers did a great deal to supplement the operations of an otherwise private-enterprise system. At a very rough estimate it would seem that by the time of the Restoration forty to fifty percent of all Japanese boys, and perhaps fifteen percent of girls were getting some formal schooling outside their homes.[1]

[1] This estimate is derived from a combined use of the list of *terakoya* (with numbers of pupils) contained in volumes 8 and 9 of Mombushō, *Nihon kyoikushi-shiryō* (1890-1892) and the statistics for school attendance in 1874 and 1879 contained in the Mombushō's second and seventh *Nempō*. The *increase* in school attendance between 1868 and 1879 was calculated for three prefectures which seem to have been conscientiously reported on in the *terakoya* list. It was then assumed that the average rate of increase during this decade was the same in these prefectures as in the whole country and this factor was then used to project back the attendance rates in 1868 from the more certainly known rates in 1879. Supporting evidence from later Meiji surveys is fragmentary. In 1877 a survey, purportedly of all men and women over the age of six in Shiga prefecture, found 36 percent who could not write their own names. The corresponding proportion in a similar survey in Kagoshima in 1884 was as high as 81 percent, while in Okayama in 1890 the corresponding figure among all men and women *over thirty* was 48 percent. In Ishikawa in 1887 15 percent of conscripts (of about twenty years of age) were reported illiterate. Kagoshima is likely to have been fairly typical of the "frontier regions" of the south and north, Shiga of the central regions containing the bulk of the population. (Ministry of Education, *Fourteenth Annual Report of the Minister of State for the year 1886*, p. 48, and *Eighteenth* . . . *1890*, pp. 49-50.)

This suggests a spread of literacy greater than in most modern underdeveloped countries, and greater than in any European country at a comparable stage of economic development, with the possible exceptions of Prussia, Holland, and Scotland. It even compares favorably with some mid-nineteenth century European countries. As late as 1837 a British Select Committee found that in the major industrial towns only one child in four or five was ever getting to school,[2] and it may have been more than a desire to jolt his fellow-countrymen which prompted one Frenchman to write in 1877 that "primary education in Japan has achieved a level which should make us blush. . . . There is no village without its school, hardly a person who cannot read . . ."[3]

The Advantages of Literacy

What does widespread literacy do for a developing country? At the very least it ensures a positive attitude toward the process of deliberately acquiring new knowledge. The man who has in childhood submitted to some process of disciplined and conscious learning is more likely to respond to further training, be it in a conscript army, in a factory, or at lectures arranged by his village agricultural association. And such training can be more precise and efficient, and more nationally standardized if the written word can be used to supplement the spoken.

Secondly, the widespread nature of basic education, and education which was not forced on an unwilling populace, but supported by parents' voluntary choice and sacrifice, argues that Japanese society had already got over the first hurdle of a modernization process, the diffusion of a simple notion of the possibility of "improvement." In the ideal-

[2] Brian Simon, *Studies in the History of Education 1780-1870*, 1960, p. 170.

[3] Georges Bousquet, *Le Japon de Nos Jours*, 1877, vol. I, p. 337. The Dutch Chief Factor, Meijlan, had been equally impressed by the spread of education some years earlier, and claimed that everyone had at least minimal literacy. (Quoted in M. B. Jansen, Princeton University Press, *Sakamoto Ryōma and the Meiji Restoration*, 1961, p. 12.)

typical "traditional society," things are as they are, and the individual does not see himself as offered the choice of doing, or not doing, anything to alter his society or his position in it. Japan was not such a society. By taking thought one could add an inch to one's, or one's children's, stature, perhaps improve their opportunities in a material sense, certainly—in a society in which learning was generally valued—enhance their prestige and self-respect. This awareness, and desire for self-improvement, ensured that opportunities created by technological and political changes would be eagerly taken up. A competitive society could be more easily created because a large proportion of the population had been psychologically prepared to offer themselves as competitors. And where the notion of individual self-improvement was widely diffused the notion of national improvement could be more readily understood and accepted.

One must be careful not to overpaint the picture, of course. Still, by the Restoration, the majority of children, and perhaps even a majority of boys, were not going to school. In 1880 an official of the Ministry of Education could still urge that it was too soon to allow straight popular election of education committees because "there are districts where the people still do not appreciate the advantages of education; where they will be only too willing to spend a thousand pieces of gold on a dramatic troupe or a festival, but begrudge ten for a school, where they will lay out the red carpet for actors and wrestlers but show little respect for a teacher."[4] The picture was patchy; feudal separatism had produced wide regional differences in the spread of education and the prevailing enthusiasm for it. But the exceptional thing, compared with other societies at a comparable stage of economic development, is that the average level was so high. The ideological transition to an ambitious knowledge-seeking and qualification-seeking society had not only begun; it was well under way.

This growing desire for self-improvement is not, perhaps,

[4] *Kaisei kyōikurei seitei riyū*, 1880. in *Meiji bunka zenshū* (Tokyo, 1928), vol. 10, p. 401.

a question of the direct consequences of widespread education. Rather, the growth of education in the late Tokugawa period is in itself a symptom of growing mobility aspirations. It is important however that education was already established as a means to mobility. A good many commoners had got themselves a surname and two swords in some daimyo's service by virtue of their mastery of Chinese, or of Western learning. When the Restoration brought a more fluid society there was, as a consequence, a sufficient reservoir of people who sought to better themselves not simply by exploiting new opportunities of a traditional kind, but also by systematically acquiring new knowledge and skills.

Thirdly, the wide diffusion of a basic literacy meant that Japan had a better chance, when the modernization process started, of putting the nation's best intellectual resources to good use. Fewer potential Noguchis or Hoshi Tōrus remained mute and inglorious than would have been the case if a large proportion of the populace had not had the chance early in life to get over the first hurdle toward mental training and demonstrate to themselves—and to teachers who might provide access to helpful patronage—such talents as they might have.

Finally, there are the political implications of literacy. Already, in the Tokugawa period, the public notice board was an accepted means of communication between the rulers and the people. Administration by written directive could, in the Japan of 1870, reach down to the lowest level. It also may well be that the teachers of the existing popular schools helped to provide channels of communication. They were already there in the villages and country towns to act as the carriers of new ideas and of a new national consciousness to the people. Even granted the facilitating effects of the authoritarian traditions of feudal rule, the implementation of the new decrees, the new land registration system and the new civil registration system would have been much more difficult to accomplish if basic literacy had not been so widespread. The chances of rumor growing wildly out of fearful suspicion and leading to obstruction and revolt were much reduced when a majority, even of the peasants, could actually read the documents they were required to set their seals to. The early Meiji uprisings could have been much more serious than they were.

In sum, it was important that the Japanese populace was not just a sack of potatoes. The modernization of Japan was not simply a matter of top-level changes. It was also a cumulation of a mass of small initiatives by large numbers of people who could appreciate new possibilities, make new choices, or at the very least allow themselves to be persuaded to do for the first time something they had never done before. The new educational system which the Restoration government exerted itself to establish in the seventies was, of course, much more effective in all these ways than the mixture of mechanical repetition and gentle moralizing purveyed by the *terakoya* teachers, but this is not to underestimate the legacy of the *terakoya* system. It ensured that the generation which had passed childhood in 1870 did not have to be written off as lost. And without the traditions, the teachers, the buildings, and the established attitudes of the Tokugawa period, the development of the new system could never have been accomplished as fast as it was—and almost without government subsidy.[5]

The Samurai

The more interesting aspects of the legacy of Tokugawa education concern not so much the wide spread of basic literacy as the content of the education received by those

[5] After the first fine flourish of the 1872 program with its bold intentions of creating 53,760 new primary schools *de novo*, the central Government was forced finally to come to terms with the cloth from which its coat had to be cut. The revised ordinances of 1879 and 1880 permitted private schools (i.e., the existing *terakoya*) to function as substitutes for public schools if certified as efficient, and in the Ministry's explanation to the Senate of the 1880 order it is admitted that even in the public schools nine-tenths of the teachers had received no training from the new training colleges, and that most of them were "priests, monks (*shūgen*) or teachers of calligraphy"—i.e., former *terakoya* teachers. (*Kaisei kyōikurei seitei riyū*, pp. 299, 307.)

It is leaders who make the differences, the populace who make the stream.

who [assumed the positions of leadership and took the big decisions which launched Japan on the road to modernization.] How far can one trace the motives and the assumptions which guided their activities back to the education they had been given in the fief and private schools in which they had been trained?

Attitudes to Popular Education

One question concerning the attitudes bred in the samurai schools relates directly back to the topic of popular education. How was it that the new and still almost exclusively samurai government decided so early in the Meiji period to establish a system of universal elementary education? The apparent motives behind the policy varied; the utilitarian appeal in the preamble of the 1872 ordinance to self-interested individualism as the driving force of social progress, and the welfare argument of the drafters of the 1880 ordinance that state interference, otherwise undesirable, is justified in defence of helpless children against the thoughtlessness of parents, give place, in 1886 to the state-centered system of Mori Arinori, designed to produce a loyal as well as an enterprising citizenry. But the assumption that a single unified and compulsory system was necessary remained unchallenged. A literate populace, with some knowledge of geography and history as well as the three R's, was generally agreed to be an essential condition of the modern, civilized state.

Nowadays this is axiomatic, but in the 1870's it was not so. In Russia, an intellectual concerned with the conditions of economic progress could still say, in the 1890's, that "a good farm and a good factory constitute the best and the only possible school for the people."[6] Indeed, the utilitarian arguments for a universal education system which were borrowed from Fukuzawa by those who drafted the 1872 Ordinance had only in 1870 achieved victory in England after

[6] D. I. Pisarev, quoted by Alexander Gerschenkron, "The Problem of Economic Development in Russian Intellectual History of the Nineteenth Century" in E. J. Simmons, ed., *Continuity and Change in Russian and Soviet Thought* (Cambridge, Mass., 1955), p. 30.

a long struggle against the fears of "nearly the whole body of those who are rich (who) dread the consequences of teaching the people more than they dread the effects of their ignorance,"[7]—and then only after the growing organization of the working class had won it a partial right to the suffrage.

How was it that ideas which had only painfully fought their way to respectability in England in the teeth of class interest and class antagonism aroused no such opposition in Japan? The early plans of 1870-1871 for a divided school system with high schools for samurai and grade schools for the masses disappeared rapidly and without trace, at least in official policy. Surely the social cleavage between the samurai and the rest—a cleavage which still had legal backing—was no less than the gulf which divided the English working class from its betters. The cartoons of the time showing the humble commoner forehead-to-ground before arrogant samurai officials argue a social distance between the classes which not even England could match.

Part of the answer lies in the difference of class structure. Social distance between the classes is one thing; class antagonism is another. Japan may have been as much "two nations" as was England, but in England the two nations were at war. Peterloo, the trade unions, the Chartist movement, represented a growing threat to the traditional ruling class and to the new middle class. The samurai, in a pre-industrial Japan, faced no such threat; peasant revolts were the sporadic tantrums of irresponsible children, not symptoms of a growing, systematic disaffection. The lower orders in Japan still knew, and accepted, their place.[8] There was nothing in the situation

---

[7] Francis Place, writing in 1833. Quoted in Brian Simon, *op.cit.*, p. 169.

[8] And civil relationships across class barriers were easier to sustain as a result. Chamberlain puts the difference between Japan and England in the 1890's very nicely when he urges the English traveller in Japan to "be constantly polite and conciliatory in your demeanour towards the people. Whereas the lower classes at home are apt to resent suave manners and to imagine that he who addresses them politely wishes to deceive them or get something out of them, every

which prompted the Restoration leaders to think of a universal education system primarily in terms of its effect on the distribution of political power within the country.

The other part of the explanation lies in the attitudes toward education which prevailed in the Tokugawa period and which permeated the education the Restoration leaders had themselves received. The purpose of formal education was in the first place moral; to gain access—directly in the case of Chinese courses in the samurai schools, in watered-down versions in the *terakoya* copybooks—to the teachings of the Sages concerning the proper ordering of human relations. Secondly, it was a means to acquisition of certain useful or gracious skills; medicine, strategy, administration, Chinese prose-writing, or the generalized bookish erudition which made up Confucian scholarship. Thirdly, it was a means of acquiring that knowledge of men and affairs which would enable rulers to govern wisely.

None of these assumptions concerning the functions of education provided any reason for denying it to the lower classes. There was, indeed, every advantage in their getting moral instruction for the particularism of the ethic which the Confucian classics taught—or were interpreted as teaching—made it applicable equally to all segments of society. An appreciation of the proper nature of the five relationships was necessary both for masters and for servants, for elder and for younger brothers; in fact more important for servants and younger brother since their duties were more onerously prescribed. If commoners carried their studies further and acquired useful skills, this might have undesirable effects if it led them to neglect their proper duties, but on the other hand if they became really proficient these skills could be made use of. The specialists in Confucian learning, or medicine, or metallurgy, even when they belonged to the samurai class, had occupied only a lowly status within it. The unspecialized

Japanese, however humble, expects courtesy, being himself courteous."
B. H. Chamberlain and W. B. Mason, *A Handbook for Travellers in Japan*, 3rd ed. (London, 1891), p. 17.

governing samurai used them and patronized them; such deference as he gave them was mixed with condescension, and useful commoners could easily be incorporated in their ranks. The third element in a complete education—the knowledge of men and affairs necessary to the rulers of men—was the only one which would have been unbecoming the status of a commoner, but there was little chance that commoners would acquire such knowledge, and none that having acquired it they would be able to use it.

Consequently there is almost no unambiguous evidence of attempts by feudal authorities to prevent commoners from acquiring education in the Tokugawa period, and only occasional expressions of the view that they should be discouraged from going beyond basic literacy and moral instruction.[9] Such limited interference as there was with non-samurai schools consisted of measures to ensure that the texts used did contain a proper modicum of moral instruction, registration of teachers to ensure that undesirables did not settle in the fief, and the occasional awards of prizes and commendations to bright pupils which demonstrated the daimyo's benevolent concern. In a number of fiefs, commoners who had shown talent and promised to be useful were admitted to the fief schools. No fief administration went further and undertook a major investment of fief resources in educating its populace, but in the last decades of the period there were a number of writers who began urging that they should do so. They used the examples both of Chou China and of contemporary Holland as precedents, and they argued both from the need for moral instruction and—most explicitly in an 1863 memorial to the daimyo of Nambu by Oshima Takatō—from the need to mobilize all talents for the good of the fief.[10]

---

[9] See for instance Ogyū Sorai, *Taiheisaku* (*Nihon Bunko* Series, vol. 2), p. 30; Karashima Ken, *Gakusei wakumon* (*Nihon kyōikushi shiryō*, vol. 8), p. 11; Nishikawa Joken, *Hyakushō-bukuro* (*Nihon keizai sōsho*, vol. 5), p. 183; Yamana Bunsei, *Nōka-kun* (*Nihon keizai sōsho*, vol. 15), p. 580.

[10] See Horie Yasuzō, "Keizai seikatsu to ningen sonchō" in Kōsaka Masaaki, ed., *Ningen sonchō shisō no keifu*, 1961, p. 478. Other writers who urge a universal educational system are Shōji Kōgi (*Keizai*

Intellectual Equipment

The propagation by the schools of a general idea that education was a good thing was probably important in other ways for the attitudes with which the ex-samurai embarked on the course of modernizing their country. The value of basic literacy simply as training in being educated has already been mentioned. Such discipline the samurai had received in ample measure. The extraordinary thing is that curiosity and eagerness to learn also survived the education given in the schools of Chinese, for it would be difficult to think of a form of education better calculated to kill curiosity than the early stages of Chinese study—the endless repetition of barbaric pseudo-Japanese renderings of Chinese texts whose obscurities teachers never felt themselves called upon to explain. And yet—perhaps there was more stimulation in the later stages of study when meanings and not just readings became important—somehow curiosity did manage to survive. The indefatigable note-takers on foreign missions, the students who pumped the Clarks and the Janes dry of every piece of information they had to give, the thousands of government officials and technicians who embarked on the study of foreign languages or sought the instruction of foreign technicians are evidence enough.

Whatever might be said about its effect on curiosity (there still is not a non-pejorative word for "curiosity" in Japanese), the traditional education may have prepared its products for the acceptance of new knowledge in another way. The authoritarian teacher-pupil relation which was part and parcel of the schools' bookish pedagogic tradition required humility on the part of the pupil. Knowledge was imparted by the teacher to be accepted, not to be improved upon. And this attitude, given the initial decision to learn from the West, produced a humble attentiveness and an assiduous thoroughness. Every

---

mondō hiroku, 1841, in *Nihon keizai sōsho*, vol. 22, p. 77), Umetsuji Norikiyo (if he really is the author of *Yuniwa no ho*, 1843, *Nihon keizai sōsho*, vol. 21, pp. 488-492), and Satō Shinen (*Suitō hiroku*, 1857, *Nihon keizai taiten*, vol. 18, pp. 659-660).

detail went down into the notebook; every utterance of the foreign *sensei* was treated with solemn respect. Had the Tokugawa schools been mainly concerned to "teach people to think," had they encouraged the free play of ideas between teacher and pupil on a footing of near equality, many more steamships might have had their boilers ruined by men who thought they could run them by the light of pure reason before they got instructions in how to keep them filled with water.

There is another aspect of the efficacy of a Confucian education which is also more or less independent of the values or knowledge imparted. It "trained the mind." In the words of Tōbata Seiichi discussing how it was that the samurai were successful industrial pioneers, their education had given them a high "general intellectual level . . . not simply the ability to understand a single concrete body of knowledge, but an ability which could be applied to the understanding of other bodies of knowledge without falling to a lower level."[11] It is a difficult concept to express in these latter days when all cultures must be accounted "as good as" one another, and societies may be decently rated by per capita income or rate of economic growth but never, in the manner of our Victorian ancestors, by their "level of civilisation." Nevertheless, there are real differences of intellectual sophistication, one criterion of which might be the richness of the vocabulary available for the discriminating expression of abstract ideas. The new chemists of Meiji had to develop a whole set of new words to express new ways of classifying matter. However, the students of politics, law, or philosophy found that most of the conceptual distinctions found in their European models were already familiar and could be easily expressed in their own vocabulary. The need of the translators to coin a new word for "right" is well known. Perhaps the important thing is that so few such neologisms were needed and that the indigenous vocabulary which could be mobilized for the new translations was not the esoteric language of a small intellectual coterie, but the common property of a relatively large

[11] Arisawa Hiromi, Tōbata Seiichi, Nakayama Ichiro, *Keizai shutaisei kōza*, vol. 3, 1960, p. 17.

section of the nation.[12] The particular character of the Chinese script is also relevant. New words could be easily created in forms which left their etymological components clearly apparent and often made further explanation unnecessary. The reader of Mill in translation might conceivably read and take the sense of the word *"kenri"* without even realizing that this was a "new" word to translate the foreign concept of "right."[13]

The sophistication of the political vocabulary which samurai acquired in the Tokugawa schools was perhaps the most important of all. The development of Japan's commercial vocabulary in 1870 reflected simply the contemporary development of Japan's commercial institutions. But the political vocabulary which the educated samurai had at his disposal enabled him not merely to understand and describe the workings of his own society, but also to conceive of alternative forms of organization. Most samurai who got beyond the Four Books read some Chinese history; a good number read one or other of the Chinese legal codes. Many, thanks to Rai Sanyō, had some knowledge of Japan's own history.[14] They had had

[12] If one takes, as an example, a random page from an official memorandum justifying the imposition of compulsory education by arguments clearly derived from Western sources, a few of the new words stand out: "the *rights* of minors," "the government, i.e., the *collective force of society*," "in the *eye of the law*," but these are a small proportion of the indigenous abstract vocabulary; "to state a reason," "fixed interpretation," "impose a responsibility," "evasion," "essential criterion," "minimum period," etc. (*Kaisei kyōikurei seitei riyū*, pp. 402-403.)

[13] When Fukuzawa translated *Chambers Political Economy* in 1866 a Bakufu official objected strongly to its praise of *kyōsō*—Fukuzawa's translation of "competition." He had no difficulty in understanding the idea, only in accepting the notion that anything involving "conflict" could be considered praiseworthy. (Carmen Blacker, *Fukuzawa Yukichi*, Ph.D. thesis, University of London, 1957, p. 28.)

[14] According to Ishikawa Ken's count of texts recorded by the *Nihon kyoikushi shiryō* as used in fief schools at some time before they closed doors in early Meiji, two histories—the *Tso chuan* and the *Shih chi*—were used in more than 100 schools, and six others—the *Shih-pa-shih-lüeh*, the *Tzu-chih t'ung-chien*, the *Han shu*, the *Hou Han shu*, the *Kuo yü* and Rai Sanyō's *Nihon gaishi*—were used in more than fifty. (*Gakkō no hattatsu*, 1951, p. 248.)

some training in comparing and contrasting different principles of political organization. This may not have been a particularly refined or subtle knowledge, but, for instance, the mere fact that the contrast between a "feudal system" and a "system of centralized government"[15] was part of the stock in trade of the better-educated samurai mind in 1870 may explain a lot about the rapidity of political change in early Meiji.

The schools did more than teach a rudimentary form of political science; they also taught that such knowledge was an important qualification for successful government. From about 1780 onwards there was a growing tendency for fief edicts concerning the schools to define their function as the production of "men of talent" who can "serve the fief." Wisdom, strength of character, and intelligence were no longer the only qualities required for successful political leadership as they had been in Ieyasu's time; knowledge was thought to be necessary as well. Half a century of gradual permeation into the schools of the doctrines of Ogyū Sorai was beginning to have its effect. Though explicit adherence to "Sorai Confucianism" was to become generally tabooed at the end of the eighteenth century, what Maruyama Masao has seen as his central tenet[16]—that society was not a product of nature but an "artifice" created by the Sages and capable of being improved by a knowledge of their doctrines—had been incorporated among the general assumptions of Japanese intellectual life and there was hardly a Confucian teacher who was not prepared to memorialize his lord and tell him how, according to his knowledge and understanding of the Sages' doctrines, the institutions of his fief should be trans-

---

[15] The distinction is found even in a mediocre little compendium of Chinese grammar written in 1839, not for samurai but for commoners who wished to educate themselves. In a series of short general-knowledge sections at the end, the main point made under the heading of history is that there were two systems of government, *hōken-seido* and *gunken-seido*, and that China started with the first and went on to the second, while Japan reversed the process. (Yamamoto Shōitsu, *Dōjitsū*, reprinted in *Sentetsu icho kanseki kokujikai zenshū*, vol. 7.)

[16] *Nihon seijishisōshi kenkyū* (Tokyo, 1953), esp. pp. 208-222, 228.

formed. The permeation of this attitude can be ascribed not solely to Sorai's influence, but also to the development of schools, for the doctrine of the political importance of knowledge provided the schools with a valuable *raison d'être*. At a time when considerable persuasion was still needed to make daimyo endow schools, it was obviously as useful a doctrine for scholars to propagate as a healthy concern with the modernization of underdeveloped societies is for applicants to modern American foundations.

Whatever its origins, the doctrine had important consequences for the Meiji period. Without it, it is unlikely that one—and that the most specific—of the five articles of the Meiji Charter Oath would have spoken of seeking knowledge throughout the world as a means of strengthening the Imperial throne, or that, once allegiance had been transferred from Eastern to Western Sages, the Meiji leaders would have sought so assiduously for models of institutional reform in the societies of the West. It is also possible to argue that the innovations of the Meiji leaders were acceptable in part *because* they could claim to be the practical application of knowledge—of study of ancient Japanese tradition and of the modern West.[17]

Education and Political Attitudes

There was another side to this medal. If government required knowledge, then knowledge was for government. We have already defined the accepted Tokugawa version of the purposes of education as threefold—moral improvement, the acquisition of useful skills, and the broadening of wisdom and experience required for good government. The increasing

[17] An Englishman is perhaps more likely than most to be struck in modern Japan by the preference for the authority of theory and bookish knowledge as against the uncertainties of common sense and experience. It is something which reveals itself in such diverse things as the Marxism of the Socialist Party and the conservatives' faith in economic planning, the tyranny of the sex instruction manuals and the scientism of the composer who recently had the sounds of a temple bell electronically analyzed in order to resynthesize it in his music.

emphasis on the production of "men of talent" naturally en-
hanced the importance of the last two aims. The *jitsugaku*
of men like Satō Shinen was no other than an explicit elevation of these two aims into a philosophy of education. Of
the two it was the latter to which the Confucian teachers
could lay full claim to competence. They were slow in incorporating improved technical vocational training into their cur-
ricula. A little more mathematics and surveying, more formal-
ized medical training, more study of Chinese legal codes, a
few abortive attempts to teach the elements of contemporary
administrative practice was about all it amounted to. It was
Western learning which offered new and more attractive
skills, and its rapid growth in the nineteenth century—increasingly after 1850 in separate departments of the fief
schools—far outstripped the feeble efforts in this direction
by the Confucian teachers. Hence, "useful" education for men
of talent in the departments of Chinese learning was primarily
concerned with ends rather than with means, with the study
of history as a road to knowledge of guiding precedents for
government.

This overriding concern with politics was, perhaps, forti-
fied by the samurai's training in swordsmanship which
brought him face to face with the elemental power situation
in which the strong and skillful holds, but must exercise with
discretion, the power of life and death over the weak and
inept. It was certainly strengthened by the fact that, in a
still feudal Japan, power was decentralized, and in the bureaucracies of the fiefs very large numbers of men held, or
could reasonably seek to hold, positions which offered scope
for political initiative—a scope which was progressively
widened in the fluid Bakumatsu period, as traditional restraints gave way and routine administrative responses became inadequate to cope with new situations.

It has been suggested that in this sense the feudal system
provided an admirable training ground for political and administrative talent which stood the Meiji regime in good

stead.[18] The fief bureaucracies were, to pervert de Tocqueville's phrase, "the grade schools of oligarchy." This may well be true. One might add that they were the grade schools of opposition and revolt as well. The rebellions of the first decade, the Popular Rights Movement, the early development of party politics, the popular nationalism of the early twentieth century, the plots and assassinations in the terrorist *shishi* tradition right up to the present day, spring from much the same roots. Japan did not have to wait for the development of a middle class chafing under governmental restriction of its economic activities before a large section of the nation began to hold political opinions and seek to express them in action. The samurai, thanks in large part to the high political content of nineteenth century Confucian education, began the period of industrialization with their political consciousness well developed. Yamaji Aizan was not untypical when he declared "Politics is my mistress. I love politics, I adore politics, I live and breathe politics. My fate is bound up with the fate of the Japanese nation. The governance of the nation, the bringing of peace to the world (the phrase is from the *Ta hsüeh*) have been my study since youth."[19] The wonder of it is that any product of late Tokugawa Confucian training managed to devote himself to a career other than a political one, and indeed even some of their sons had difficulty in this regard. One, who decided eventually to become an engineer, reported the decision to his father in a letter full of fearful apology. His father had always brought him up to believe that "the purpose of *gakumon* was to cultivate oneself in order to rule the country," the study of letters as such being a secondary requirement, "so that, if

[18] Matsuda Michio, "Nihon no chishikijin" in *Kindai Nihon shisōshi kōza* (Tokyo, 1959), vol. 4, p. 13.

[19] Quoted (from *Aru hito ni kotooru sho*) in Uchida Yoshihiko, Shioda Shōhei, "Chishiki seinen no shoruikei" in *Kindai Nihon shisōshi kōza*, vol. 4, p. 249.

office does *not* come one's way, one can write something for the benefit of posterity."[20]

A slightly closer look at the nature of these political pre-occupations is necessary to explain why, among the opposition movements of post-Restoration Japan, one should see the Popular Rights movement, but not, say, the activities of the Seiyūkai, the young officers' *coups d'état* but not the suffrage movement, as especially rooted in this Tokugawa tradition. A passionate concern with national politics might partake (the division is a rough and ready one) in varying proportions of three elements: (a) a predilection for political activity as a vocation, the activity in itself and the exercise of power if that activity is successful providing its own satisfactions, (b) a desire to further the interests of sectional groups within the nation, and (c) a desire to promote policies which are conceived to be necessary for the welfare of the nation as a whole. Those historians who see the Meiji Restoration as primarily a bourgeois revolution, or who see in the petitions of the sake brewers and in the demands for a reduction in the land tax the core and essence of the Popular Rights movement, imply that the political concern of the Restoration activists and of the Meiji opposition was predominantly of type (b). This seems extremely doubtful. Let it be granted that such elements were far from absent in Meiji politics and that by the 1920's they played a dominant role, even overtly, in the national political scene. It still seems probable that in early Meiji Japan the first and third kind of motives were much more important ingredients of political activism than the second.

The first motive, to be sure, did not find explicit sanction in Confucian teachings. The exercise of political leadership

[20] Tanakadate Aikitsu, quoted from his biography by Nagai Michio, "Chishikijin no seisan-ruuto" in *ibid.*, vol. 4, p. 215. Nagai also quotes from the biography of Kitasato Shibasaburō who eventually became a doctor but only after much heart-searching for "ever since I breathed my first breath on this earth my ideals had been centered on the nation and the state" and he thought that anyone born with two arms and two legs should be ashamed to become a priest or a doctor.

was not, for the samurai, an acknowledged source of personal gratification, but a fulfillment of duty. So much for the explicit moral teachings; but the effect of studying history on youthful members of a military class could only too easily produce a different orientation. In large measure the history they read was the history of military adventure in which government and warfare, the responsibilities of power, and the glories of military victory were inextricably intertwined. Government might be a duty in the Tokugawa Confucian ethic, but military adventure, in the less codified samurai tradition, rein-forced by family legends of the exploits of sixteenth century ancestors and by Rai Sanyō's descriptions of the heroes of Japanese history, was sheer fun. Marius Jansen has recently recorded the zestful enjoyment with which Sakamoto Ryōma pursued his youthful career as a political activist,[21] and it was still in a spirit of military adventure that the heirs of the Bakumatsu *shishi* approached politics in the 1880's, and in 1936. Tokutomi Sohō complains in 1886 that too many of his friends in the Popular Rights movement "look on politics as a kind of sport, a form of amusement like letting off fire-works," and their bombastic rhetoric is always shooting off into flights of fantasy in which they picture themselves riding bravely along the banks of the Yalu, banners flying in the wind.[22] Better for Japanese youth, he says sadly, if they would choose as their heroes Adam Smith and John Watt instead of Napoleon and Bismarck, the idols of his day.[23] And if political activity was a substitute for military adventure there was always the danger that it would turn into the real thing; the sword was never far behind the pamphlet. A writer in 1883 deplores the fact that the political parties instead of competing with ideas concerning the proper form of the constitution which was to come, were concerned only to seize power when it came, and some of them, confusing *kempō* (constitution) with *kempō* (swordsmanship) were secretly

[21] *Sakamoto Ryōma and the Meiji Restoration,* see esp. pp. 153, 167, 171.

[22] *Shōrai no Nihon,* ed. of 1888, p. 204.

[23] *Ibid.,* p. 95.

polishing their military skills to this end.[24] It could well be argued that it is because a passionate concern with politics was originally allied in this way to the spirit of military adventure that the pattern of private enterprise violence has persisted in Japanese politics to a more advanced level of industrialization and modernization than in most other countries.

It was, of course, above all the third kind of passionate concern with politics, the desire to promote policies considered to be necessary for the nation as a whole, which was most specifically nurtured by the education the samurai received. In the Confucian tradition politics was not the art of the possible, the choice of lesser evils, the achievement of the best compromise between conflicting interests; a good policy was one which would benefit *everyone*. It was the political philosophy of an uncomplex society in which the chief potential conflict of interest lay between the producing ruled and the consuming rulers. Enlightened government consisted in the kind of benevolence which would enable the ruled to produce more in contentment to the benefit of all. When sectional conflict did rear its head among the ruled, as between peasant and merchant, it was resolved by a simple scale of priorities; the peasantry was of greatest importance to the welfare of the whole, hence its interest should be paramount. It is hardly surprising that men who received training in this kind of political philosophy—and received it at a time when the Japanese nation as a whole *did* have, in defense against foreign attack, one overriding common concern overshadowing all other political issues—should have developed a concern with politics of this nationally-oriented, rather than sectionally-oriented, sort. They were *yūkoku no shi*—men concerned with the fate of the *nation*.

There is another aspect of Confucian political training which is directly relevant to the opposition movements of post-Restoration Japan. It was, at least implicitly, a training in *principles*. As such it opened the possibility for every

---

[24] *Meiji jūrokunen kakuseitō seisuiki*, quoted in Hattori Shisō *Meiji no seijikatachi*, vol. 1 (Tokyo, 1950), p. 81.

man to become his own arbiter of the correct application of those principles to particular situations. True, one of the major principles inculcated was loyalty—to the head of one's household or to the head of one's fief—and it is true that, in a dominant version of this ethic, loyalty meant blind obedience. But Maruyama Masao has recently shown the persistence in the Tokugawa period of a different tradition which required the loyal servant to be his own judge of what was really in his lord's interest, even his own judge of what constituted benevolent rule—which he should support—and what constituted wickedness—against which he should remonstrate.[25] Such judgments required criteria above and beyond the simple principle of loyalty, and these history could provide. In Rai Sanyō's judgments of Japan's past rulers, for instance, there are implicit other principles of evaluation besides the overriding one of loyal devotion to the interests of the Emperor —the distinction between the "public" interest and "private" interest (pursuit of the one being, in the Chinese manner, in accord with the Way of Heaven, and the other morally reprehensible)[26] and the pragmatic principle of conformity with a vaguely defined "trend of the times."[27] Such principles provided criteria for the loyal servant to be his *own* judge of what constituted loyalty in a retainer, and what constituted good government (i.e., true devotion to the "public" interest of the people as a whole) in a ruler.

The last years of the Tokugawa period provided ample scope for this tradition to grow. Albert Craig has described how the loyalists of Chōshū could defy their lord on strictly moral grounds within the Confucian tradition. They claimed to be urging on him policies which were in the best interests of that lord's house as *they* interpreted them according to

[25] "Chūsei to hangyaku" in *Kindai Nihon shisōshi kōza*, vol. 6, 1960, pp. 393-397.

[26] Maruyama, *loc.cit.*

[27] Carmen Blacker, "Japanese Historical Writing in the Tokugawa Period" in W. G. Beasley and E. G. Pulleyblank, *Historians of China and Japan* (London, 1961), p. 262.

their principles.[28] The Restoration immeasurably widened the scope for this tradition to develop, if only so far as it weakened the force of the competing "loyalty-blind obedience" tradition. (In the new state, where the new object of loyalty was the Emperor and the nation, those not immediately in government employment owed no personal duty of submission to the Emperor's immediate servants in the way that the Tokugawa retainer owed a personal duty of submission to his lord.) It was, moreover, a time when by general agreement the State had to adopt innovating policies, and innovation, involving a choice between alternatives, requires principles of selection in a way in which the mere routine maintenance of a system of power (which was all that was required of administrators until 1853) may not. There was no lack in the Meiji period of vociferous ex-samurai voices offering to tell the government what those principles should be, and what were the just and proper policies which followed from them. The point to be made here—a point made by Maruyama in the article just quoted—is that (a) the hubris which permitted subordinates to offer advice to their superiors, (b) the notion that such advice could be offered by any independent thinker who knew the proper principles of judgment, and (c) some of the content of the principles assumed by government critics in the Meiji period—a notion of the public interest (variously interpreted to mean national glory or popular welfare) and of according with the "trend of the times" (the meaning of *jisei* becoming modified under the influence of Western doctrines of progress)[29] all had their roots in a Tokugawa tradition, a tradition of long standing

[28] *Chōshū in the Meiji Restoration* (Cambridge, 1961), pp. 160-161, 224, 352.

[29] See Carmen Blacker, *Fukuzawa Yukichi*, Ph.D. thesis, University of London, 1957, pp. 127-136, for a comparison of Fukuzawa's notion of *jisei* as a "general state of public opinion" limiting the actions of "great men," with that of Rai Sanyō. See also Tokutomi Sohō's *Shōrai no Nihon*, 1888, esp. pp. 193, 210, for a related, but more Spencerian concept of *hitsuzen no ikioi*, a kind of dynamic force compelling society along a road of inevitable progression from the military to the productive form of society.

but nurtured by study, particularly historical study, in the schools of the Tokugawa period. Fukuzawa's "spirit of independence" and Uchimura's conscience were not simply grown from foreign seeds.

Which consideration leads to a final aspect of the political emphases of late Tokugawa education—the element of continuity between the role of the Confucian scholar in Tokugawa Japan and that of the intellectual in the Meiji period. The Confucian teacher was the repository of wisdom concerning the principles of personal and political conduct, and as such he was honored—but not rewarded with income or with power. He knew, but he did not do. A Fujita Tōko, a *sensei* in a central position in his fief, was a rare exception. Even if he was concerned with principles rather than with skills, with the *gaku* which the educational philosophers spoke of as the root rather than with the *gei* which formed the mere branches, the teacher was still a specialist, and specialists, whether of swordsmanship or of letters, were traditionally ranked well below the all-round men who were expected to exercise leadership. (Only when they were actually giving a lecture would they be accorded the seat of honor.) Most scholars accepted their lowly position and took service in a daimyo's retinue; others more conscious of the ambiguity in the deference they were accorded, preserved their independence by setting themselves up in the big towns as private teachers.

A similar pattern persisted after the Restoration. Ōkubo is said to have spoken scornfully of Fukuzawa and the other *yōgakusha* as mere *geisha*—specialists in intellectual skills.[30] The philosopher-politician was as rare after the Meiji as before. But equally, the politically-minded philosopher was as common. Some, Katō Hiroyuki, Motoda Eifu, Nishimura Shigeki, were content to inherit the role of the hired scholar in government employ. Others, Fukuzawa, Tokutomi Sohō, Miyake Setsurei, Yamaji Aizan, Ueki Emori, the political journalists of Meiji, were in their roles, if not in their ideas, the heirs of Yoshida Shōin, Yasui Sokken, Sakuma Shōzan,

[30] Minamoto Ryōen, "Jitsugaku shikan no teishō," *Shisō no kagaku*, 35, Nov. 1961, p. 9.

the independent Confucian scholars who preserved a greater freedom to criticize.[31] They preached, they gave advice about politics, and their political concern was a national one, embracing the welfare of the nation as a whole in the traditional manner, rather than dealing with the politics of harmonizing conflicting sectional interests.

Merit

The nineteenth century stress on the function of the schools as breeding grounds for "men of talent" had another aspect. School organization became more competitive; merit was more explicitly rewarded. There is perhaps a natural tendency for teachers to reward superior performance, for only in their successful pupils can they take the measure of their own success, and the duller the subject matter the greater the need to add to intellectual curiosity the further stimulus of competition. This "natural" tendency toward the overt and invidious assessment of merit had been held in check in the early schools in deference to the status system. The possibility of status inferiors being ranked above their betters was one that had to be guarded against. From the beginning of the nineteenth century, however, two factors served to weaken this check. As schools became bigger and more rationally organized it became necessary to institutionalize some measurement of achievement in order to determine suitability for promotion from grade to grade. Secondly, the new emphasis on the need to produce "men of talent" required new incentives. Increasingly, prizes were given to those who excelled; seats of honor were awarded on the basis of merit rather than of rank; reductions of hereditary privileges were ordered for those whose performance was unsatisfactory. It was a slow and hesitant change, slower and more hesitant in the fief schools than in private schools such as that of Hirose Tansō, and carried through with the fullest rigor only in the private Dutch

[31] See Fukuzawa's argument for preferring (in terms of Katō Hiroyuki's rebuttal in the *Meiroku zasshi*, vol. 2) "prodding from outside" to "nourishing from within" in *Gakumon no susume* (*Fukuzawa Yukichi zenshū*, vol. 3, Tokyo, 1959), pp. 48-56.

academies such as that of Ogata Kōan. It was not always, moreover, that the logical consequences of this trend were followed beyond the school. The edicts which required the schools to produce men of talent only made sense if there was a real intention to give full scope in the fief bureaucracies for the talents which the schools produced. It is not hard to find explicit statements that this would be the policy, and doubtless it was this shift in overt ideals which made it possible in the last years of the regime for men of outstanding force of character to gain positions of leadership in some fiefs far above their hereditary entitlement. However, these were still exceptions in an emergency situation.

The entrenchment of rank distinctions in the bureaucracies of the Bakufu and the fiefs was too strong for the principle of appointment by merit to become fully institutionalized. It was one thing for emphasis on performance to develop in the schools where only approbation and symbolic prizes were at stake—and that among juniors. It was quite another thing for the same principles to be applied to alter the distribution of power between adult men. The schools were, as one fief edict put it, "outside the system." They did, nevertheless, familiarize the students who passed through them with the experience of competition and assessment by merit, and they did contribute to the development of the idea that ideally in the world of administration, too, the merit principle *ought* to operate. By the 1850's this had become a standard item in the program of every reformer who wrote a memorial to his daimyo, and it was no longer considered subversive but only a counsel of perfection. It was the widespread acceptance of this idea, to which the schools powerfully contributed, which made it possible, once the great shake-up had occurred, for men of modest hereditary rank to emerge not merely as the real, but also as the titular leaders of the nation.

Ambition

There is another aspect of the late Tokugawa stress on the production of "men of talent" which relates to one of the most interesting problems of the motives of Japan's nineteenth century modernizers. It led, as has been shown, on the one hand to a stress on political skills, on the other to the promotion of the merit principle. This was a dangerous combination since it could lead to the encouragement of personal ambition in competitive striving for the satisfactions of power. A conservative teacher upholding the traditional view of education as a means to the appreciation of moral duty knew what he was about when he argued against bringing explicit teaching of administrative skills into the schools. It would, he urged, encourage a concern with *kembo-kōri*—the "scheming manipulation of power for (personal) advantage."[32]

Power as such is neutral. Karashima's fear was that it would be used for self-aggrandizement. But it could also, and this was the justification of those who urged the development of *jitsugaku*, be used for altruistic ends. The edicts which speak of the need for "men of talent" qualify the phrase: "men of talent who can be useful to the fief." Competitive striving was permitted provided it was competition in service to the daimyo and to the fief. To seek office and power was legitimate if one's motive was not to achieve prestige and income but to utilize one's talents the more effectively (either, in the loyalty-obedience tradition, according to the definition of effectiveness imposed by superiors, or, more dangerously in the "protestant" tradition, according to one's own judgment of what constituted service). With the Meiji Restoration the definition of the collectivity to be served was altered. "Service to the nation" replaced "service to the fief"; "han nationalism" gave way to Japanese nationalism. But it was still essentially the same ideology of service which remained the overriding justification for all competitive striving, all individual initiatives which might, incidentally, bring the adventurous personal advancement.

It is easy enough to document the dominance of this ideology—in the utterances of the "community-centered entre-

[32] Karashima Ken, *Gakusei wakumon* (1816), *Nihon kyōikushi shiryō*, vol. 8, p. 5.

preneurs" like Shibusawa and Godai,[33] in the writings of the propagandists of the enlightenment who urge that everyone should get an education in order to be able the better to serve the state,[34] in the speeches of founders of universities who insist that their aim is to better the nation,[35] in the free use by every butcher, baker, and candlestick maker of the word *kokueki*—"benefit to the nation"—in the title of his business.[36]

But how far is this ideology a clue to the really operative motives? As Bellah has remarked about the Tokugawa period "the road to private aggrandisement was often the road of public service,"[37] and we have already remarked how the intrinsic satisfactions of power and political activity, as something not clearly distinguished from military adventure, provided an important motive for the activities of men like Sakamoto Ryōma who managed to "combine ambition with idealism," the readiness to sacrifice life and status in the Imperial cause with "the hope of fame and power which helped to make the risk worth while."[38] And Fukuzawa had no doubt about the importance of a coincidence of national and personal interest when he observed in 1877 that the people in the countryside who followed the new calendar and put out flags on the new national holidays were those who had done well for themselves under the new regime.[39]

Any assessment of the relative weight of personal ambition and devotion to the national interest in the motives of the men who led Japan in the Meiji period can only, at best, be

[33] See, e.g., Gustav Ranis, "The Community-Centered Entrepreneur in Japanese Development." *Explorations in Entrepreneurial History*, vol. 8, 2 Dec. 1955.

[34] Matsuzaki Minoru, *Bummei inaka mondō*, 1879, in *Meiji bunka zenshū*, vol. 20, 1930, p. 277.

[35] See, for example, speeches by Niijima (p. 222), Ono Azusa (p. 220), and the inscription by Fukuzawa for Mori's new commercial school (p. 207) quoted in Nagai Michio, "Chishikijin no seisan ruuto."

[36] Nakayama Taishō, ed., *Shimbun shūsei Meiji hennen-shi*, vol. 7 (Tokyo, 1940), p. 65.

[37] R. N. Bellah, *Tokugawa Religion* (Glencoe, Ill., 1957), p. 37.

[38] M. B. Jansen, *op.cit.*, p. 153.

[39] "Bunkenron" in *Fukuzawa Yukichi-zenshū*, vol. 4, 1959, p. 239.

approximate, and in any case must await the more competent hands of those who have made a close study of their recorded deeds and words. Here only a few general considerations will be attempted.

In the first place, for all the group-centered nature of the ideology, there seems (except in fiefs like Aizu and Satsuma which had a system of licensed children's gangs) to have been more in the early experiences of the young samurai to encourage an individual self-assertiveness than to develop a self-abnegating identification with the group. In the schools tuition was still individual; even where there was grading of classes by ability they were not usually taught as a class *en masse*, and in the group discussion sessions performances were individual, rather than cooperative. The history that was read was history of the heroic sort, the records of individual great men and villains. Military training was a matter of training in individual combat with the sword and the lance. True, for most of the period competitive jousts, which would have made one man the winner and one a loser, were banned between pupils of different teachers and even among pupils of the same teacher, but these prohibitions were almost universally lifted at the end of the period, and jousting became a popular sport. Attempts were made after the arrival of Perry to develop drill on Western lines, requiring each samurai to work as a member of a team. They seem not to have been very successful, however, and it was often only the lower-ranking foot-soldiers or specially recruited peasants who could be induced to train for such an inglorious type of warfare. Altogether teamwork was not a conspicuous feature of the young samurai's training. The playing fields of Eton, or at least those of Dr. Arnold's Rugby, would have been more suitably congruent with the Tokugawa collectivist ideology than the military sheds of the Meirinkan or the Kōdōkan.

It was a kind of training well calculated to develop strong egos, and yet there is good reason why Kamishima Jirō should have characterized the kind of individualism which it produced as *taigunshūteki*—individual self-assertion toward *the group*.[40] It was not a self-sufficient individualism but one which depended on the group's existence since it was primarily a desire to secure recognition and admiration from the group and power within it. The passion for public oratory of the early Meiji student[41] is a typical later expression of this kind of self-assertion; oratory requires an audience; fame can only be accorded by admirers, power can only be acknowledged by obedient followers.

As long as prestige and power were the chief objects of self-assertive ambition, it could be turned to group ends; the collectivist ethic could determine the *kind* of behavior which would earn approval, the kind of exercise of power which would be considered legitimate. The desire to enrich the nation and strengthen its defenses might not be "pure," but it was only in the service of such causes that the "impure" desire for power and glory could be satisfied.

There was a less obvious compatibility if personal ambition took the form of a desire for pecuniary gain. The businessman could easily ride two horses as long as what was good for Mitsubishi could be thought to be good for the country. But the man in public office could only enrich himself at the public expense, and it is clear that, at least in the opposition's version of the official ethic, a true devotion to the public interest required a certain personal asceticism in the public servant.[42] It seems, however, that such abstemiousness was not characteristic of Meiji government leaders. Official salary scales were generous[43] and so were expense accounts. The Meiji states-

[40] *Kindai Nihon no seishin kōzō* (Tokyo, 1961), p. 252.

[41] See, for instance, Tokutomi Roka's description of Friday nights at the "Kansai Gakuin." *Omoide no ki* (*Gendai Nihon bungaku zenshū*, vol. 12), p. 190.

[42] See the memorials of Tani Kanjō and Itagaki Taisuke, and the speech of Katsu Kaishū in *Meiji bunka zenshū*, vol. 3, 1929, pp. 463-464, 471, 482, 485.

[43] A Meiji minister could presumably live at least on the scale of a daimyo of the old regime. Ministerial salaries—personal salaries excluding perquisites such as ministerial mansions—were equal, in 1877, to about 1100 *koku* of rice; in 1890 to about 660 *koku*, the Prime Minister's salary being the equivalent respectively of 1750 and 1100

men enjoyed the good things of life, and some amassed sizable fortunes. They were not above corruption, not only from patriotic motives (buying the votes of despised politicians in the national interest) but also for personal ends. Tani Kanjō speaks, in his letter of resignation, of the various uses of patronage which soon became rife again within a year after the wholesale reforms of 1885 were supposed to have inaugurated a new era of official integrity :[44]

"Official appointments are used to reward those who have performed meritorious services, to help out old friends, to repay personal favours, to build up supporting cliques, to reward those who minister to personal pleasures, and even to blackmail into silence unofficial critics. Official appointments and official ranks are looked on as private property ; government revenue is treated as if it were private wealth."

It may be significant that he does not include in his indictment the actual sale of patronage for hard cash. Corruption seems mostly to have taken the form of misusing official position to give personal favors, and these were means of building up a coterie of followers who could offer, in their loyalty, a more direct and personal satisfaction of the desire for prestige. Wealth came as a by-product of this patronage, in the form of gifts from those friends and followers who were rich. Corruption, in other words, was rarely overtly contractual.

Wealth itself might be sought by the Meiji statesmen for a variety of reasons. It could be used to found a dynasty, to become, in the Matsukata manner, a *senzo* on a grand scale,[45] with the assurance of grateful descendants to honor one's memory. It could be spent, Itō-style, in the *geisha* houses where more intrinsic attractions were conjoined with the opportunity to strengthen the bonds of one's personal following

---

koku. (Calculated from figures given by Hattori Shisō, *Meiji no seijikatachi* [Tokyo, 1950], pp. 109-111.) Tani Kanjō claims that these salaries, in terms of the cost of living, were higher than anything found in the West (*op.cit.*, p. 464).

[44] *Meiji bunka zenshū*, vol. 3, p. 466, quoted by Hattori, p. 108.

[45] See Kamishima Jirō, *op.cit.*, p. 265, for the importance of "becoming a *senzo*" as a Meiji object of ambition.

in bibulous entertainment, and to acquire a reputation as a hard drinker and inexhaustible womanizer which was again a source of prestige in the samurai tradition. Alternatively it could be spent acquiring the large mansions of a Yamagata, at once a means of asserting one's prestigious status and of housing a large entourage of dependent followers.

In these ways the self-enrichment of the Meiji leaders may be seen as a by-product of the same vanity which was a partial inspiration of their public service. But it remains something of a puzzle nevertheless, for the ethic of devotion to the public good *was* a strong one, it *was* to some extent internalized, and the ascetic leader who drew a sharp line between public and private interest and lived an austerely frugal life *was* the ideal. Such an ideal has, of course, coexisted in many other societies with a large measure of official self-indulgence. It may be a rare society in which the thought that it will be charged to an expense account does not make it easier for the official to order an extra drink. But the *explicitness* of the patriotic ethic in Meiji Japan, and the sheer *frequency* of utterance of high-sounding sentiments about service to the nation would have led one to expect that Japan might be one of those rare societies. Because it was not, self-righteous hypocrisy was given a chance to grow.[46] They protested too much, and the divorce between oratory and practice relegated the pursuit of private interest to the realm of the furtive. An important by-product of this is that the secret pulling of strings, while presenting an outward appearance of righteous concern with the public welfare, has become the *normal* means

---

[46] This, in Fukuzawa's view, always was characteristic of samurai morality. Tokugawa samurai, he says in his *Gakumon no susume,* "were to all outward appearances model retainers, given to large talk of loyalty and service to the fief—'poverty is the rule of the samurai,' 'he who is nourished as a retainer should die in his master's service' —one would think they were about to seek their death in battle at any moment." And yet they were really nothing but "gilded pseudo-*chün-tzu.*" "Commissioners of Works would demand kickbacks from carpenters, Exchequer officials would take bribes from the merchants, and such behavior was almost standard practice in the households of the three hundred daimyo." (Quoted in Maruyama Masao, "Chūsei to hangyaku," p. 391.)

of promoting all kinds of "private" sectional interests. What was called in our earlier classification political concerns—the desire to further the interests of sectional groups within the nation—has shared in the furtiveness attaching to personal self-aggrandizement.[47] "Pressure group" may be a dirty word in other societies besides Japan, but it is not often that, as in Japan, the pressure group which is open and aboveboard in its activities, and blatantly unsecretive in its pursuit of private interest does not thereby mitigate its offence but merely compounds it.

For all that—to return to the Meiji leaders—the rhetorical ethic did have its restraining effect. Japan did not, as Tani Kanjō warned that it might,[48] follow the path of Egypt whose drive for national regeneration under Mahomet Ali foundered in its leaders' extravagant self-indulgence. Policy was always the result of a dialectic between the ideal and private interest, never solely guided by the latter. This again is something one might chalk up to the credit of Tokugawa education— not simply the content of the restraining ideal, but the fact that the Meiji leaders were trained in the calculation of all the consequences of political action, in the difficult art of subordinating immediate to long-term objectives, and in the habit of evaluating consequences and objectives in the light of abstract principles. These abilities are all part of that "rationality," the development of which some would see as the essence of the modernization process.

In Conclusion

In this discussion of the legacy of Tokugawa educational traditions it has been difficult to avoid ethical judgment of the value of that legacy, and the attempt to do so has doubtless at some points failed. However, the initial intention of this chapter was to elucidate some of the ways in which the Tokugawa traditions were favorable to the initiation of social

[47] See for the development of this point the remarks by Kyōgoku Junichi in Oka Yoshitake, ed., *Gendai Nihon no seiji katei* (Tokyo, 1958), p. 475.

[48] *op.cit.*, p. 469.

change and how far they account for the changes which did in fact take place. The attitudes to popular education, the sense of the contingency of social institutions on the human will, the training in abstract analysis, and the application of evaluating principles to policy, the development of a respect for merit rather than status, the stimulation of personal ambition, and the strengthening of a collectivist ideology have been singled out. At the same time one should not overlook those features which earned that tradition the denunciations of men like Fukuzawa—the dead formalism of its pedagogy, the veneration of the past, the emphasis on personal relations and on the passive absorption of knowledge rather than independent inquiry. It was a type of education which had to go in a modernizing country, but at least it had the honor of having carried the seeds of its own destruction.

CHAPTER IV

Science and Confucianism in Tokugawa Japan

ALBERT CRAIG

IN A modern society virtue is one thing and knowledge is something else. This has not always been so. The overtones of an earlier age in the West in which these two spheres had not yet been differentiated still linger on in a word such as wisdom.

This paper is an attempt to gauge the impact of Western thought, and more particularly, of Western scientific thought on the Chu Hsi Neo-Confucian tradition of Tokugawa Japan. I am not asking how scientific was science in the Tokugawa period; rather, I am inquiring into the effect that the introduction of Western science had on the structure of Chu Hsi Confucianism. My principal finding is that the acceptance of science created a tension, or more accurately, exacerbated a previously existing tension between virtue and knowledge in this school of Confucianism. This opened the way for a type of differentiation (one not fully achieved at the stage which I discuss) which finally led to the disintegration of the Chu Hsi position in Japan.

Western science did this not by simply confronting Confucianism as a new and better kind of knowledge; but subtly, even deviously, by infiltrating into the very heart of the Neo-Confucian metaphysical synthesis and working on it from within.[1] The leavening effect that this had on Tokugawa

[1] Why science had this effect in Japan, but not in China, is a very complex problem, one that is beyond the scope of this paper. Obviously, since the same system of Chu Hsi thought was present in China, the acceptance of science in Japan cannot be explained in terms of ideas alone. Equally obviously, this difference between the two countries does not rule out the particular structure of Chu Hsi Confucianism as one important element contributing to the acceptance of science in Tokugawa Japan. This paper is a fragment of a larger work in which

thought was such as to produce among some individuals in early nineteenth century Japan intellectual orientations singularly different from those of China in the same age. These were not without consequences in the early Meiji period.

Yamagata Bantō: Chōnin and Scholar

For this study I have chosen as my point of departure Yamagata Bantō (1748-1821). Born in a village in the cotton-growing area of Harima (in the present Hyōgo-ken), he was the second son in what was probably a relatively well-to-do peasant family. His older brother, in addition to farming, was a local merchant dealing in cotton thread.

Several generations earlier the brother of Bantō's grandfather had established a merchant house in Osaka. In the following generation two older brothers of Bantō's father had followed him to Osaka. At the age of 13 it was Bantō's destiny to succeed his uncle as the head of one of the branch houses of the Osaka establishment.

The head of the main house at this time was a man who approved of scholarship. Therefore, while working at the main house, Bantō was also sent to the Kaitokudō (Hall of Virtuous Cultivation), a semi-official school originally established by Osaka merchants to teach their sons the doctrines of the Chu Hsi school of Confucianism. In contrast to most schools in which samurai were given preferred positions, it was one in which "students would associate as equals without regard for differences in rank or wealth."[2]

From this school Bantō went on to study with Asada Gōryu, an Osaka astronomer, and his disciple, Takahashi Yoshitoki. Under their guidance he read the available translations of Western books, he at least handled the original Western works, and he viewed various scientific instruments

---

I am attempting to define the social and intellectual setting of science in Tokugawa Japan—making comparisions with China where possible.

[2] Hayashi Motoe (editor), *Nihon jimbutsushi taikei*, vol. 4 (Tokyo, 1959), p. 158.

imported from Europe through Nagasaki. Moreover, using his connections with Asada and others in Osaka, he was able in later years to enter the most prominent circles of Dutch studies in Edo, to meet and talk with Ōtsuki Gentaku and others of his school.

Bantō's life as an Osaka merchant is a Horatio Alger-like story of initial adversity overcome by frugality and hard work, and of subsequent success and honor. The merchant house which Bantō served had begun as a buyer and seller of rice, and expanded into money exchange and the risky business of loans to daimyo. In 1769 the head of the house died. The heir was only six. By 1771 the fortunes of the house had sunk to a mere sixty *kan* of silver—most of its capital being out on a loan to Sendai-han (which, plagued by ten years of poor harvests, could repay nothing). In 1772 Bantō took charge, but in spite of his efforts things improved very little for ten years. It was at this point that Bantō devised an ingenious scheme for marketing the rice of Sendai with greater profits both for that han and himself. By 1792 Sendai han had not only re-established its finances, but Bantō had more than recouped the fortunes of his house. At the time of his death, wildly prosperous, the house was a creditor to several tens of daimyo.[3]

Yamagata Bantō was at best a secondhand student of Dutch studies. In spite of this, his thought is of particular interest since, as an essayist and scholar by avocation, he more fully explored some of the implications of the union of Neo-Confucian metaphysics and Western science than did others who were more narrowly translators. The results of these philosophical inquiries were contained in his main work, *Daydreams (Yume no shiro)*. This was a mixture of philosophy, political economy, cultural geography, and astronomy, written as an intellectual guide for future generations of his family. It was written between 1802 and 1820 during his years of impending and almost total blindness.

In many ways Bantō was representative of the revival of Chu Hsi thought which occurred during the later years of

[3] *Ibid.*

the Tokugawa period. Even with government backing the revival was not able to return Confucian scholarship to the "purity" of the early Edo period; but for all the revival's eclectic tendencies, its vitality was impressive. Yamagata Bantō was a polymath, deeply read in the various schools of his day. Yet all of the heterogeneity of his thought was effectively encased within the framework of the Chu Hsi teachings. This was typical: virtually all of the non-medical scientific writings of the early nineteenth century appear to have been written within this framework.

The Rational, Moral Universe

"There is no hell, no heaven, no self—only man and the ten thousand things."

"In this world there are no gods, Buddhas, or ghosts, nor are there strange or miraculous things."[4]

Yamagata Bantō's thought in its basic structure contains very little that cannot be viewed within the categories of the Chu Hsi tradition. In the Chu Hsi metaphysics the ultimate principle, that which makes all things what they are, is designated as *ri*. Since *ri* may be known, it is at times translated as Reason or reason. Viewed as it is in itself, as an ultimate moral and ontological principle like Plato's Good, it is referred to as the Supreme Ultimate (*taikyoku*). The names given to aspects of *ri* should not suggest, however, that Reason or the Supreme Ultimate are entities with a separate existence. On the contrary, they exist only in the *ri*. And *ri* itself is to be discovered only in things as they are or in things as they may become.

The saltation from *ri* to the world of multiplicity—a problem for any philosophy that poses an ultimate and singular metaphysical principle—is explained by Chu Hsi in terms that are at best hazy. Though *ri* is primary in a logical and moral sense, it could not by itself produce the world. It is not a first cause or a Christian God. Only in conjunction with *ki*, a

[4] Yamagata Bantō, "Yume no shiro," in *Nihon keizai taiten*, vol. 37 (Tokyo, 1936), p. 644.

psycho-physical force or substance possessing varying degrees of fineness, is the world of the 10,000 things formed. The genesis of *ki* is never clearly stated. When asked, Chu Hsi always avoided the problem by saying that *ki*, like *ri*, was found only in things. There are some passages in his writings, however, which suggest that *ki* in itself is the primeval swirl, the chaos, organized by *ri* to form the universe. *Ki* is also identified with the *yin* and *yang* (in Japanese *in* and *yō*) and the five elements of earlier Chinese philosophy.

Bantō writes of man's position in the cosmos: "The man of wisdom seeks what is fundamental within *ri*, the ignorant man seeks it outside of *ri*, but though he may seek it there he will not find it. All things are born of heaven and earth by the unfathomable [interaction] of *yin* and *yang*. Among them man is the first. Therefore at the head of the 10,000 things, man uses the others. But, they are not created for him, he merely leads. Consequently, he must not covet them for selfish use. All things are the same. It is merely that one is in the highest position."[5]

This ontology forms the base of a philosophical position that, while grossly unscientific, is at the same time radically rationalistic; in it even those things that are inexplicable can be rationally viewed. Bantō writes: "No matter how one thinks of it, is it not wonderful that in the ten months following conception a body develops and a person is formed. And not humans alone; animals, birds, fish and insects: all are so. Food is eaten, it passes about within the body, and finally leaves as the two wastes. By this one lives: is this not strange and marvelous? But this is not done by grace of a god, nor by the command of men. It is solely the natural (*shizen no*) *ri* of heaven and earth."[6]

Bantō goes on to deduce from this *ri* a canon of economic rationality. Beyond the conventions do not waste time on vain superstitions. One's dead ancestors do not really exist in any meaningful sense. Pay attention to the job at hand: "Crows don't have sparrows, peonies don't bloom on plum

[5] *Ibid.*, pp. 589-590.
[6] *Ibid.*, p. 590.

trees, eggplants don't grow on melon vines. This is wondrous and yet in every case it is determined by *ri*. . . . Outside of this *dōri* can there be a god or a Buddha? Solely by the power (*toku*) of *yin* and *yang* the 10,000 things emerge. This appears most marvelous, yet it is not marvelous; it seems most strange, yet it is not strange. By the *dōri* of nature, life is achieved: the sages speak of this [process] and call it god (*shin*), but there is no god beyond this god. In connection with death they speak of spirits, but here too, after death there is no existence (*seikon*), nor mind nor will. Outside of this spirit there is no spirit. In every case there is but *ri*. What is there to seek beyond this. . . . So discriminate well. After knowing what the *ri* of god is, one will understand that the spirits of one's ancestors are none other than the *ri* in one's heart. . . . These should be worshipped as if they existed, but distinguish carefully. Be respectful when performing the rites, but at other times 'keep them at a distance' and work hard at your daily job. This is most important. May my descendants observe this scrupulously. This is the spirit I worship. Apart from it there are no gods or spirits to worship. Beware!'"[7]

Ri in man is called his nature (*sei*). Yet the *ri* in man is the same as that in all other things. This identity of the *ri* in man and the *ri* of the universe is crucial to Bantō's thought.

Man can know his *ri* or nature in two ways. One is by intuition, by directly grasping the *ri* within himself through meditation. Since man's essential nature is *ri*, man is basically good. He is normally, however, alienated from this inner goodness by bad or coarse *ki*. This he must refine by a combination of intellectual activity and ascetic discipline until his *ri*, as it were, shines forth. Thus intellectual advance and ethical cultivation are the same process. This is the locus of the identity of ethics and knowledge in Chu Hsi Confucianism.

In the original Chu Hsi synthesis, meditation (*seiza*) was very close, both in theory and practice, to Zen meditation. In Zen one looked into his own nature (*kenshō*) and, by so doing, realized the ultimate Buddha-nature. In the Chu Hsi form of

[7] *Ibid.*, pp. 590-591.

meditation, one "exhausted his nature" (*jinsei*) in order to penetrate the *ri*.[8] So close was the Chu Hsi position to that of Zen that many Ming and Ch'ing scholars criticized it as essentially Buddhist in character. In fact, however, there was one important difference. The *ri* within oneself that was to be penetrated in the Chu Hsi form of meditation was the same *ri* that pervaded all existing things: it was a positive concept. Contemplation of it was a form of this-worldly mysticism with rationalistic implications for action strikingly different from Zen mysticism with its framework of Buddhist philosophy.

To what extent did Bantō's thought mirror this contemplative side of Chu Hsi? One can best say that he accepted it as an integral part of the total structure of Chu Hsi thought. Bantō wrote, "the ancients while sitting arrived at the wonderful *ri*."[9] Therefore, "in all matters of human character and ethical action the sages must be taken as central."[10] But, there was very little talk of contemplation in Bantō's writings. In fact, he was much more concerned with active inquiry, the second way by which man may know the *ri*.

There were a number of phrases used by Chu Hsi to indicate the pursuit of *ri* in the universe. Bantō sedulously employed them all: *kakubutsu kyūri* (investigate things and penetrate the *ri*), *chichi kakubutsu* (gain knowledge and investigate things), and *sokubutsu kyūri* (look into things and penetrate the *ri*).

It is extremely difficult to say what such expressions originally meant. Were they intended to encourage an active observation of nature or did they merely refer to the passive contemplation of the essences of things? Certainly there was some of both, although in Chu Hsi the active elements were ultimately subordinate to the passive. One can at least say that a good measure of active observation was permitted, rationalized, and even encouraged by this conceptual framework. Chu Hsi wrote: "Drugs have no heat; heat is produced

[8] Maruyama Masao, *Nihon seiji shisōshi kenkyu* (Tokyo, 1952), p. 11.

[9] Yamagata, *op.cit.*, p. 106.

[10] *Ibid.*, p. 112.

after they are swallowed; this is their nature."[11] He also wrote that a ship can go only on water and a cart on land; these are their natures.[12] The nature of a thing lies beyond its form. The concern within this intellectual tradition for why a thing had to be what it was (*tōzen no ri*, or *shikaru yuen no ri*) led in China and Japan to inquiries into nature. In both countries Confucian scholars compiled catalogs of flora, fauna, and minerals. Kaibara Ekken writes in the introduction to his *Medicinal Herbs of Japan* (*Yamoto honzō*): "From the time of my childhood I was sickly and took pleasure in reading books on herbs and was interested in pursuing the study of the *ri* of things."[13] Matsuoka Joan (1669-1747) in a work on the same subject wrote: "This is not solely a basic text for doctors, it is truly a part of *kakubutsu kyūri*."[14]

The earliest work introducing Western science into Japan viewed science as primarily concerned with *ki*, the psycho-physical stuff, and not with the ethical *ri*. The *Kenkon bensetsu* (An Explanation of the Cosmos) (1658) which presented to Japan a round but geocentric world argued: "The scholars of barbarian learning do not know the *ri* of *yin* and *yang*; therefore, they do not know why heaven is heaven."[15] They say "that the four elements and not heaven are the source of all things. This is like knowing the mother and not the father. To know the mother and not the father is to be an animal."[16] That is to say, without understanding *ri* there is no knowledge of virtue and without virtue man is not human. This basic position was continued by Arai Ha-kuseki (1657-1725) who, distinguishing between Western science and Western religion, opened the way for Dutch studies in Japan. Hakuseki argued that Western science

[11] *Chu Tzu ch'üan-shu* 42 :7a.

[12] *Ibid.*, 42 :30a.

[13] Kaibara Ekken, "Yamato honzō," in *Ekken zenshū*, vol. 6 (Tokyo, 1911), p. 2.

[14] Bitō Masahide, "Edo jidai chūki ni okeru honzōgaku," in *Rekishi to bunka*, vol. 2 (Tokyo, 1957), p. 31.

[15] Mukai Kenshō, "Kenkon bensetsu," in *Bummei genryū sōsho*, vol. 2 (Tokyo, 1914), p. 54.

[16] *Ibid.*, p. 11.

was concerned with *ki* (i.e., it lacked a knowledge of the *ri* that was beyond the forms of *ki*), but was useful as practical knowledge.[17] In general, this view can be said to typify the first philosophic reaction to the importation of Western science.

However, by the period in which Hakuseki wrote, some were already viewing Western science as one branch of the study of *ri*. This marks the second stage of philosophic reaction to Western science; it represents the view that was most prevalent during the period of the greatest "scientific" activity in Tokugawa Japan. This view gradually gained in adherents throughout the eighteenth century. By 1791-1792 Motoki Ryōei could speak of Kepler and Galileo as "great scholars (*daiju*)" who had established the bases of the "study of *kyūri*";[18] and in the early nineteenth century in the preface of a work by Udagawa Yōan, it was stated: "The East has herbology (*honzō*) and that's all. In the West there is botany which truly is the study of *kyūri*."[19] Botany, he writes, is the discovery of "Linnaeus, a sage who has recently appeared in the world."[20]

Yamagata Bantō was in many respects representative of this rising tide of opinion that saw Western science as the study of *ri*.

Dark Worlds and Light: The Contemplation of Copernican Ri

"The most important area for the advance of knowledge and the investigation of things is astronomy. . . . We say it is the most important since only after heaven is there earth, only after earth man, and only after man the nine virtues. All of the things necessary for the way of government are derivative from heaven."[21]

---

[17] Arai Hakuseki, "Seiyō kibun," in *Arai Hakuseki zenshū*, vol. 4 (Tokyo, 1906), pp. 748-749.

[18] Inoue Tadashi, "Kyūri no hatten," *Rekishigaku kenkyū*, vol. 10, no. 7 (Tokyo, 1940), p. 14.

[19] *Bummei genryū sōsho*, vol. 2, p. 284.

[20] Bitō Masahide, *op.cit.*, p. 54.   [21] Yamagata, *op.cit.*, pp. 114-116.

For a knowledge of astronomy Bantō recommends the West: "There is no parallel, past or present in any country, for the knowledge that Europe has of astronomy. . . . [in the fields of] astronomy, geography, and medicine, those who emphasize and select what is old are stupid."[22] Bantō's view of the universe, which he also refers to as the "Supreme Ultimate," is of a plurality of heliocentric worlds continuous in space: "Fixed stars are all like suns. Between stars the areas where the light reaches are light worlds. In each light world there are things like the seven planets. Depending on the size of the sun, the planets will vary in number. The light world of our sun is one of these. Between light worlds there are dark worlds. . . . According to the theory of attraction all planets in a light world take the sun as their heart."[23]

Bantō admits that this postulates an astronomical order that is difficult to grasp: "If the earth is flying around, the mountains, rivers, vegetation, and houses all ought to fall off . . . and why do the waters of the sea remain as they are?"[24] His answer is gravity, but he points out that: "Even in Europe many disagreed when this was first propounded; and though they finally came around, it took a long time."[25]

One difficulty that arises with this theory is how it can be made to accord with *yin* and *yang*. According to the ancients, "heaven is *yang*, and earth is *yin*. Movement is a characteristic of *yang* and quietude of *yin*."[26] Consequently, if the earth is viewed as moving and the sun as unmoving, logical difficulties occur. This did not lead Bantō to jettison entirely the old theories nor to impugn the sages. It led instead to a theory of the relativity of motion: "Viewed from a cliff the boat moves, but if one is riding in a boat the cliff appears to draw away. Riding on a horse the wind blows in ones face, yet from the point of view of the wind, the face comes into it. . . . Seen from the sun the earth revolves, yet viewed from the earth the sun can be said to move. . . . From Kyoto Ōmi is to

[22] *Ibid.*, p. 112. [23] *Ibid.*, p. 117. [24] *Ibid.*, p. 96.
[25] *Ibid.*, p. 96. [26] *Ibid.*, p. 105.

the east and Osaka to the west . . . but from Edo all are to the west, and from Nagasaki all to the east."[27]

Central to this chapter, however, are the ethical overtones which Bantō ascribes to these astronomical findings. The *ri* uncovered by Western science are *"giri"* (virtuous *ri*) and *"dōri"* (ethical *ri*).[28] There is absolutely no distinction made between the *ri* of nature and that of ethics. There are certain ultimate questions regarding the limits of space and time (similar to Kant's antinomies) that Western science does not handle, but these only qualify its value. The moral overtones of Western science are revealed by Bantō in a most amazing passage (cribbed from the 1798 *Rekishō shinsho* by Shitsuki Tadao)[29] in which the heart of man is joined to the heart of the sun in contemplation of the universal *ri*: "Where does the universe begin and when will it end? Who made the universe, the original *ki*, or heaven and earth? When the immeasurable is joined to the immeasurable it becomes even more immeasurable. And yet, though there is no place in man that lacks this mysterious, unfathomable nature, it centers on his heart [or mind]. Heaven's strange, unfathomable nature is also everywhere, yet it centers on the sun. Thus, just as the functions of man all came from his heart, as the duties of the family proceed from the father, the affairs of a country from its offices, and the government of the empire from the court, so the strange process of the creation of heaven and earth all come from the sun. Thus, in carefully cultivating the self, in obeying the father, in serving the lord, and in standing in awe before the mysterious, unfathomable mandate of heaven, one joins in contemplation one's heart with that of the sun."[30]

This is an interesting quotation in several respects. Like the earlier quotation concerning the importance of astronomy, this clearly reflects a philosophical belief in a natural social order. The *ri* of the universe are at the same time the *ri*

[27] *Ibid.*, pp. 107-108.   [28] *Ibid.*, pp. 181, 590.
[29] Shitsuki Tadao, "Rekishō shinsho," in *Bummei genryū sōsho*, vol. 2 (Tokyo, 1914), p. 131.
[30] Yamagata, *op.cit.*, pp. 113-114.

governing all aspects of human conduct. This also contains an ethic of immanence: one's obligation to the universal *ri* can only be fulfilled by performing the particular familial and social duties of one's station. Both of these characteristics tend to inhibit social change. In the natural social order of the Tokugawa Chu Hsi school, unlike the view of the eighteenth century *philosophes* in Europe, society was seen as the embodiment, and not as a distortion, of the "natural order." And, the possibilities for action in terms of universal values were few: the contents of the abstract values of Confucianism were largely defined in the particular context of the Tokugawa social order.

At the same time, one must not overly discount the "rationality" of Chu Hsi Confucianism. Faced with a pluralism of light worlds, Bantō immediately assumes that the others are in general like our own. Conditions on other planets "vary only according to their size and their proximity to the sun." "All have soil and moisture—they are not like footballs or paper curtains."[31]

Under these conditions, by the process of continuous creation described earlier, "grass and trees will appear, insects will develop; if there are insects, fish, shellfish, animals and birds will not be absent, and finally there will be people too."[32] In Bantō's mind, this theory of continuous and progressive evolution is quite different from the creation myths and metaphysical fantasies of other schools. He points out that this theory is "an extrapolation from what we have on earth . . . and is quite unlike the slapdash arguments of the Buddhists and Shintoists."[33] He further qualifies his view of evolution with the naturalistic supposition that there are no people on Mercury or Venus "since these two planets are near to the sun and too hot." He does not, however, have a closed mind on this subject: "In Beppu in Bungo there are fish [living in the waters] of a hot spring. If these fish are put into [ordinary] water they will die in a day. Since this is so there may be people even in the heat."[34]

[31] *Ibid.*, p. 123.
[33] *Ibid.*, p. 134.
[32] *Ibid.*, pp. 123-124.
[34] *Ibid.*, p. 123.

When one considers the tremendous impact that Darwin had even on post-Newtonian Europe, it is ironic that Neo-Confucian rationalism—which could never have produced a Darwin—could accept, and even anticipate, the philosophical implications of his basic position without a tremor.

Holland as a Confucian Utopia

Yamagata Bantō's view of culture was Confucian and basically similar to that mentioned earlier in the *Kenkon bensetsu*: "Americans [i.e., Indians] are extremely stupid. They must be classed together with the ignorant Ainu of the present day. In general they do not study nor have they etiquette. They are but a step removed from the birds and beasts. Only by studying, finding the way, and knowing the proper forms of social behavior does man become man."[35]

There existed a long tradition in both China and Japan of viewing the West as barbarian. Bantō was not wholly immune to this heritage. At one point he writes: "All Europeans put profits first and [their] evil religion second."[36] He felt, moreover, that Europe was Christian and to Bantō Christianity was essentially like Buddhism: "Though one says that there is no limit to the evil of Buddhism, when one compares it with Christianity, [one can say that] it wins the minds of men but does not go as far as seizing their countries . . . [nevertheless] using Buddhism to fight Christianity is like using fire to put out a fire."[37] Such a criticism reminds one of Nishi Amane's comment that "Christianity is Buddhism with hair on it."[38]

Even admitting a certain ambivalence, Bantō's basic position was that the superiority of the West in its knowledge of the *ri* of science implied its possession of a superior level of moral practice. In truth, Bantō knew as little of the West as the Western philosophers of enlightened despotism knew of China. His account is therefore a description of what the West ought to be, given the excellence of its science: "The Western Europeans circle the globe. They advance in astronomy and

[35] *Ibid.*, p. 188.   [36] *Ibid.*, p. 188.
[37] *Ibid.*, p. 475.   [38] Inoue, *op.cit.*, p. 37.

make geographical observations; they understand the world as a whole. That they are loyal, filial, humane and virtuous goes without saying; they are addicted solely to advancing knowledge and investigating things, and do not waste their days on useless arts and skills. As for writing they have but 26 letters [in the three styles of], angular, cursive, and grass writing, abbreviations, punctuation marks and numbers, 100 letters in all. Therefore by the age of ten the national alphabet is completely mastered and they can set themselves to the investigation of things. Thus it is only natural that their wisdom and skills are extensive. Consequently when travelling through the various lands or crossing the 10,000 league seas they are not surprised no matter what natural phenomenon they encounter; when they first arrived and conversed with the Japanese their faces did not change color—they were at ease, even as if in their own country."[39]

Bantō attributes this happy state of affairs to a system of feudal rewards within the Western countries and to mercantilism in their relations with other countries: "[Our knowledge of] astronomy and geography increases year by year; therefore we ought not to remain bogged down in old theories. Westerners are adept at the various arts (*gei*); the Japanese and Chinese cannot compare with them. When one invents a new instrument or discovers a new skill he appeals to the authorities and his house is given a stipend and his expenses met without limit. If one is sick, he gives way to his son or disciple who will receive it in his place. Thus even if three or five generations pass there will be none who will not get it. For the development of astronomy and geography, ships and expenses are furnished for travel to all countries, there is no place that they do not reach. . . . In the country of the Dutch (*kōmō*) the king is the commander-in-chief of commerce. The origins of their world travels and of astronomy and geography are in commerce."[40]

Another implication of the partial superiority of the Western *ri* is a view of knowledge as progressive. In Bantō's

[39] Yamagata, *op.cit.*, p. 181.   [40] *Ibid.*, p. 67.

thought certain fundamental areas were settled by the classics and Sung philosophy, but many others were not: "Today the errors of the past are demonstrated and known. Since this is so, in the future as well, unknown areas will gradually be opened to research and in turn the errors of the present will be known. And those who follow after that will in turn know their errors. Therefore, is it not beneficial to [critically] discuss the past? Can we call those, who blindly believe books without weighing the relative merits of past and present, gentlemen (*kunshi*)?"[41] Considering that this was written more than twenty years before the Opium War it displays a surprisingly radical willingness to criticize the past as the ultimate source of truth.

Japan as a Non-Utopia

Bantō's view of Japan was complex since he was well read in its history and deeply versed in the functioning of its economy. It will suffice to say that he believed that Japan had originally been feudal (*hōken*), that it borrowed the bureaucratic system from China thereafter only to realize its shortcomings and return to feudalism. Bantō was satisfied with this, writing: "Ah! There is nothing outside of the feudal system."[42] This was after all the system of the sages of ancient China.

Within the feudal system each class had its appointed role. Bantō's views regarding the relative virtues of different social classes reveal that the intellectual consequences of his merchant status were almost nil. They also illustrate a more general point of interest: the most powerful members of the Osaka merchant community, because of financial ties to the han, tended to identify almost wholly with han interests and to think in the same categories as samurai bureaucrats. "The peasant is the base of the country. . . . Peasants are necessary, but the country could get along without artisans or merchants. Always act to benefit the peasants and accord them the superior position. But act to harm (*son wo tsukete*) the artisans and merchants and relegate them to an inferior position. In

---

[41] *Ibid.*, p. 112.　　　　　　　[42] *Ibid.*, p. 277.

disputes between peasants and merchants, give the decision to the peasant most of the time. Artisans and merchants urge the people to extravagance. Luxury goods must be prohibited. Among the merchants, place those in legitimate businesses above, those who amuse the people below, and those who pander to the people even below that. Plan to increase the peasants, if only by one person; desire to diminish the artisans and merchants, if only by one person. Forbid the peasants to engage in crafts or trade. These are the rules for enriching the country."[43]

His generally low appreciation of the function of merchants in society was coupled with a specific concern for Japan's national image. He speaks of "the rapacity and greed of the merchants and lower officials" at Nagasaki, and of Japan's ignorance of foreign trade. These will lead "the countries of the world to laugh at Japan" and so "damage the national polity (*kokutai*)."[44] For Bantō, the physiocratic perfection of Japan's feudal system and the value he placed on its national polity did not mean that all was well. Contrasting the Japanese with the Dutch, he wrote: "If our samurai went to such a distant foreign land, how afraid they would be. From this one can discern [by contrast] the intellectual strength of the Westerners. How true it is! The Japanese and Chinese, although they begin their study of [Chinese] characters as children, cannot master them in a lifetime. In addition, they fritter away their days on Buddhism, poetry, tea ceremonies, Nō songs, classical dancing, and other useless arts. In order to make a living they perform various arts and actions and are unable to truly study loyalty, filial piety, humanity and righteousness, or to cultivate the self, much less to become conversant in astronomy, geography and other sciences (*giri*), or to advance their knowledge and investigate things. Consequently, though they are depraved and unrighteous, they feel no shame. . . . They only feel that the present customs of our country are right."[45]

Bantō explains these shortcomings in terms of economic

[43] *Ibid.*, p. 303.   [44] *Ibid.*, p. 297.   [45] *Ibid.*, p. 181.

necessity: "Since our people are busy making a living, even though they act unrighteously, they feel that it is enough merely to care for their wives and children, and they know no shame. Ignorant and untalented, they are duped by those who believe in demons, gods and Buddhas and incur needless expenses. They commit wrongs and pursue profit alone, becoming more and more illiterate. How sad this is!"[46]

Science and Metaphysics in Late Tokugawa Chu Hsi Thought

In the West the rise of science had great repercussions in the area of social and political theory. It would not be too much to say that, if one may separate science from technology, before 1750 science contributed more to social theory than it did to industry. This was certainly one source of the social and political dynamism of the modern West. In Japan science seems to have had no comparable consequences. How can this be explained?

The most important reason is that during the Tokugawa period science was never really grasped as science. It was much more the rational classification of the results of translators. Japan advanced, as it were, in three rapid hops, from a geocentric to a heliocentric and then to a Newtonian picture of the universe. All three pictures were virtually non-mathematical. Moreover, they were usually pictures gleaned from the popularizers, not the creators, of the sciences. Until very late, progress in science was progress in language, without the necessary union of empiricism and theory. Bantō, for all of his appreciation of Western science, could write that Japan was lucky in that it "could reap the benefits [of science] without working for them."[47] By the late Tokugawa period when a somewhat truer picture of science began to emerge, the political situation had become so complex that it is difficult to say which changes were due to science and which to other factors.

A second reason why science had only a limited influence

[46] *Ibid.*, p. 182.　　　　　　　[47] *Ibid.*, p. 116.

on the Tokugawa world-view was the sponge-like character of the rationalism of Neo-Confucianism. This was, to be sure, one intellectual factor making possible the acceptance of Western science in Japan—though this alone cannot explain its acceptance. Yet, at the same time, it also permitted Japan to absorb a considerable amount of the results of Western science without major alterations in the structure of Confucianism. The whole question of what is rational is not simple. The structure of medieval Christian thought, at least in its syntax, was largely Greek. In a sense this was more rational than any philosophy of China or Japan. Yet, within it large areas were posted as off-limits to reason. In the Western system the balance between Greek rationality and the requirements of a revealed religion was extremely delicate. Any increased input into the former could force a shift all along the line. Therefore the results of the science that developed within this system of thought were often resisted. In Japanese Chu Hsi thought the sharpness and tightness of Greek logic was totally lacking. In its place was a sort of harmonic organicism in which everything ultimately derived from the *ri*, which as we have noted was a relatively undifferentiated concept. However, while admitting its amorphous nature, one should also note that in this world-view nothing was beyond the limits of reason. And there was no source of resistance to the results of science: its organic character permitted the substitution of Western theories for Chinese theories, or the harmonic juxtaposition of the two, without basic shifts in the concept of organism itself.

A third reason often given for the small influence of science on other areas of thought is that science was viewed as essentially instrumental in character and peripheral to the main emphases in Tokugawa thought. This contention, however, can be questioned. It is true that Arai Hakuseki sanctioned science only as a morally inferior area of learning, as a practical tool. And this view seems to continue until the end of the Tokugawa period: Sakuma Shōzan's dictum "Eastern virtues and Western skills" immediately comes to mind, and similar passages can also be found in Bantō. These views would seem to suggest that the Western learning was compartmentalized and sealed off from the sensitive inner workings of Tokugawa thought. But this was not so. As we have seen, such an interpretation wholly glosses over the admission of Western science into the holy of holies of Neo-Confucianism, the category of *ri*. Its acceptance there had consequences in a wide range of areas producing: a progressive view of knowledge; the acceptance of a foreign [barbarian] country as a Confucian moral model, one not wholly lacking in institutional implications, and a fairly astringent critique of Japan. Of course, in the early nineteenth century very few people held such views. Yet it does mirror a pattern of reaction to the West that was completely lacking in China and one that in some ways prefigures *bummei kaika*, the "enlightenment" thought of the early Meiji period.

The acceptance of Western science as *ri* was also the beginning of a process by which basic concepts of the Tokugawa world-view were reinterpreted and in turn subverted, by having read into them a Western content. But it was only after the Restoration, in the writings of the Meirokusha (The Meiji Six Society), that this process was completed.

At the stage represented by Yamagata Bantō, the tension between the foreign elements and the total Confucian conceptual scheme was minimal—largely because he knew so little of either science or the West. Little by little, however, things became more complex. Consider the view given in the preface to the 1851 *Kikai kanran kōgi*, a work on physics, by Kawamoto Kōmin: "Physics is that study that investigates the *ri* of heaven and earth, of the 10,000 things. . . . For several centuries our country has been at peace; the arts flourish, men of wisdom appear in great number. . . . Western studies rise rapidly; numerous translations are made; yet the vast majority deal merely with drugs and therapies, few go into essentials. Therefore I will attempt to explain one or two here: The human body functions in relation to an external environment. It can't be understood without bringing in things external to it. The field that teaches the *ri* of the body's functions is called physiology; it is one branch of physics. Those who study medicine should first investigate the *ri* of the 10,000 things in physics, next master physiology, and only last turn to pathology. These fields are fundamental. Therapy is derivative."[48]

Here we begin to see the idea of a hierarchy of sciences integrated in theory. And with this new sophistication came an increased emphasis among specialists in Western studies on the "laws" of nature and on experimental procedures. Japanese science moved from Benjamin Franklin's experiment with the kite—duplicated early in the nineteenth century —to slightly more elaborate devices. As the Western contexts of the earlier accepted sciences such as medicine and astronomy were explored, other fields such as physics and physiology were encountered. More knowledge of these led to a greater appreciation of their potentials. And, in spite of occasional persecutions, the growing awareness of foreign activities in the seas surrounding Japan led to an increased concern with means for coping with the West. But at the same time, expansion within the sciences created more tensions within the philosophical synthesis of science and Confucianism.

For one thing *kakubutsu kyūri* (investigate things and penetrate the *ri*) that had previously been only a handmaiden to contemplative moral concerns now became central. As this occurred, it was used to sanction action within a wide range of disciplines outside of the few mentioned in the classics (such as herbology). It is significant to note that the mainstream of the development of science in the Tokugawa period did not require the negation of *ri* as a universal and partly intuitable natural reason. Rather, the concept of *ri* was reinterpreted, and a new stress was given to those ideas within the Chu Hsi philosophy which could be viewed as encouraging an experimental science.

As this occurred, the contemplative implications of *ri* subsided into latency. Since contemplation had earlier been a dominant emphasis within the Chu Hsi position, the keystone

[48] Kawamoto Kōmin, *Kikai kanran kōgi*, in *Nihon kagaku koten zenshū*, vol. 6 (Tokyo, 1942), pp. 13-14.

of a moral hierarchy extending from man to the political order, the shift described above produced considerable structural torque within the philosophy as a whole. Perhaps the point of greatest tension was the question of the moral character of *ri*. More and more it became obvious that the analytical concerns of the sciences had little direct concern with ethics. This implicitly raised the question: was the *ri* of the natural world the same as the *ri* of ethics? This question could not be posed, however, for within this tradition the necessary categories were lacking. The concern with this problem can be seen in Sakuma Shōzan.

Shōzan's intellectual affiliations are clear: "I have received chiefly the teachings of the Ch'eng-Chu [Hsi] school and with this I [seek to] penetrate the *ri* of the 10,000 things and of heaven and earth."[49] He is equally clear in his identification of this *ri* with the content of Western science: "In the present age, visiting the five continents and penetrating all of their studies and sciences (*butsuri*) is of course the true meaning of the Chu Hsi [teachings]."[50] Other statements to the same effect occur frequently in his writings. He sets forth as one of the five pleasures of the gentleman: "to have been born after the Westerners discovered their theories and to know a *ri* that the sages never knew."[51] But, he adds that "with Western studies alone there is no consideration of virtue (*dōtoku giri*)."[52] Here is an implict recognition of two different types of *ri*. Shōzan knew far more about Western society than Yamagata Bantō. He knew too much to perpetuate the fallacy that the Western nations were semi-ideal Confucian states. Shōzan also knew far more of Western science. In terms of his Chu Hsi philosophy this posed a contradiction which Shōzan could not resolve: how could the West have so great a knowledge of the *ri* of science and so little knowledge of the *ri* of ethics when these were

---

[49] Kaneko Takanosuke, *Sakuma Shōzan no hito to shisō* (Tokyo, 1943), p. 20.
[50] *Dai Nihon shisō zenshū*, vol. 17 (Tokyo, 1931), p. 308.
[51] *Ibid.*, p. 249.
[52] Kaneko, *op.cit.*, p. 31.

really the same *ri*? This problem never became explicit in his writings, yet, insofar as I have been able to discover, Shōzan scrupulously distinguished in his usage of terms between the *ri* of things (*butsuri*) and the *ri* of virtue (*dōri*). This illustrates a sensitivity in this area of a sort that Yamagata Bantō never felt to be necessary.

It is not accidental that Ōhashi Totsuan should appear at this stage of awareness of Western science and criticize it as logic-chopping. This is not the true study of *ri*, he writes, rather it is "a means of destroying the *ri*."[53] By this time it was obvious to friend and foe alike that the *ri* of the West was somehow different from that of the Sung philosophers. It was not until after the Restoration, however, that this distinction was made explicit, destroying the fundamental premise of the Chu Hsi synthesis.

Nishi Amane, a Bakufu scholar and one of the first Japanese sent abroad during the bakumatsu period, wrote from Holland in 1862 that Western "philosophy is better at explaining the *ri* of man's nature than the Ch'eng-Chu [Hsi] teachings."[54] Eight years later Nishi was able to describe the problem that had never become explicit in Shōzan's writings: "It is not a question of Westerners not knowing the *ri*." Within the *ri* they "make various distinctions and are even more precise than we are."[55]

With Nishi Amane and others who study abroad, Western learning expands into the humanities and social sciences. Where tension had earlier been created by injecting Western content into the world of the 10,000 things, the same process of subversion by reinterpretation now began in the area of morality. The Chu Hsi system had been able to tolerate the degree of reinterpretation of *ri* that had been forced upon it by the acceptance of the infantile science of the Tokugawa period. But, it could not absorb Western philosophical categories with the same ease. That Nishi's purpose was syncretic rather than destructive can be discerned from the title of his work published in 1874: "A New Theory of the Unity of All

[53] Inoue, *op.cit.*, p. 32.   [54] *Ibid.*, p. 37.
[55] *Ibid.*, p. 37.

Ethical Systems" (*Hyakuichi shinron*). But, the consequence of this work was the final destruction of the Chu Hsi concept of *ri*. Nishi makes a clear distinction between the *ri* of things and that of ethics. The former (*butsuri*) is *a priori* (*senten teki*); man cannot transgress against it; and in it man is one object among others. The latter (*shinri*), in contrast, is *a posteriori*; man ought not to transgress against it; and in it man is a subject and alone.[56] This resolves the contradiction present in Sakuma Shōzan. It also marks the formal severance of the nexus between knowledge of the natural world and ethics.

Conclusion: Science and Chu Hsi Philosophy in the Context of Tokugawa Thought

All who write on Tokugawa thought must at some point ask themselves how their work relates to Maruyama Masao's brilliant elucidation of the development of the school of Ancient Learning in his *Nihon seiji shisōshi kenkyū*. This is a particularly important question in the case of this paper since Professor Maruyama finds a split between ethics and nature in the thought of Itō Jinsai and Ogyū Sorai that in some respects seem to prefigure the differentiation that occurs only much later in the Tokugawa Chu Hsi tradition. Was this later differentiation, which appears first in the writings of Nishi Amane, not related to the earlier developments in the school of Ancient Learning?

I feel that they were not at all related in respect to the distinction between ethics and nature as areas of knowledge. They were related in other ways. The problem can best be put into historical perspective by distinguishing between four major periods in Tokugawa Confucian thought.[57]

The first was the period of the establishment of the Chu Hsi orthodoxy by Hayashi Razan and Fujiwara Seika. This involved the separation of Confucianism from Buddhism, and

[56] *Meiji bunka zenshū*, vol. 15 (Tokyo, 1929), pp. 264-268.

[57] For some of the material in this gross sketch of Tokugawa intellectual development I am indebted to Sagara Tōru, *Kinsei Nihon jukyō undō no keifu* (Tokyo, 1955).

the propagation of a relatively pure form of Chu Hsi Confucianism as an official philosophy to legitimate Tokugawa rule and to prepare warriors for the task of civil administration.

A second period, which saw its full development only in the latter half of the seventeenth century, was marked by the emergence of a number of individual philosophers such as Nakae Tōju and Kumazawa Banzan in the Wang Yang-ming tradition, and Yamaga Sokō, Itō Jinsai and Ogyū Sorai, who are conventionally grouped together as representative of the school of Ancient Learning. It would distort their thought to say that these men challenged the Tokugawa political order : they did not. They did, however, alter the structure of Chu Hsi Confucian thought metaphysically and socially, creating potentials that had not existed in the earlier period. Professor Maruyama, for example, sees in the philosophy of Chu Hsi a medieval world-view : a philosophy in which a particular social order is taken as a natural order. The attack by the school of Ancient Learning on this assumption of a natural social order he finds comparable, in many respects, to the attack on Thomistic philosophy by the nominalists of late medieval Europe.

A third period of great complexity was characterized by a number of overlapping developments. Academies arose, usually based on one or another of the systems of thought formed during the second period. Contention and competition grew between the followers of these different schools of thought. Contention itself was viewed as an evil, as a force inimical to social harmony, and men tried variously to reconcile the differences between the separate schools. Maruyama's analysis of the way in which Motoori Norinaga incorporated into his National Learning a large portion of the structure of Ogyū Sorai's Confucianism illustrates the way in which different systems of thought were joined at this time.[58] "Eclectic syncretism" may best describe the intellectual temper of the eighteenth century in Japan. Of special importance to this

[58] Maruyama Masao, *op.cit.*, p. 140.

paper was the revival of Chu Hsi Confucianism which occurred during this third period. In part this drew energies from a larger intellectual reaction to the lack of emphasis on individual cultivation in the teachings of Ogyū Sorai. Prominent among the leaders of this revival was Nakai Chikuzan (1730-1804), a teacher of Yamagata Bantō.

The fourth period began in 1790 following the bakufu's prohibition of heterodox teachings. Like the third, this was a complex period and difficult to describe since the philosophical diversity of the preceding period was compounded by the early nineteenth century reaction to the "barbarian" menace. I feel that it can best be viewed as a time during which the eclectic syncretistic tendencies of the third period were re-encased within the framework of the Chu Hsi orthodoxy.

The strength of this revival can only be understood by considering a few of the conditioning factors. At the outset, some scholars protested bitterly against the bakufu order. But, such protests faded very rapidly. In general there was a high level of individual anxiety to comply with the official position. Kameda Bōsai, for example, one of the "five great teachers" in Edo at this time, was said to have had one thousand *hatamoto* disciples. They soon disappeared, however, and he was forced to close his school.[59] The effects of this prohibition became nation-wide in 1795 when the *rōjū* Matsudaira Nobuaki, rising to power within the bakufu, sent an even more immoderate order to the han prohibiting the appointment as officials of men schooled in heterodox teachings.

It is also significant that this revival occurred just as the general level of education was advancing rapidly. (See the article by Ronald Dore in this volume or John Hall's article on the Tokugawa *jusha* in *Confucianism in Action*.) Numerically, the effect of the Chu Hsi revival at this time was far greater than had been the case with earlier intellectual trends. As a consequence, in the bakumatsu period, both pro-bakufu and pro-imperial forces (but especially the latter) saw Japanese society largely from the assumptions of a Chu Hsi natural social order.

[59] Sagara, *op.cit.*, p. 188.

In many ways Yamagata Bantō was a characteristic thinker of this fourth period. Fundamentally he rejected the teachings of the school of Ancient Learning. He wrote, for example, that "in the teachings of Sorai there is much that is poisonous."[60] And, as we have noted, he made no distinction between the *ri* of ethics and that of nature. But, at a less fundamental level, he accepted portions of Sorai's argument. He wrote, for example, that the universe cannot be known and cannot be measured. This is an idea that undoubtedly can be traced back to the school of Ancient Learning. Yet, for Bantō, incomprehensibility as a category was ultimately subordinated to intelligibility. Through *ri* even that which appears unknowable can be grasped. Sorai's ideas give to Bantō's writing on this subject a veneer of sophistication. But Bantō's structure is that of Chu Hsi.

The ultimacy of *ri* as a natural law of sorts also conditioned the characteristic late Tokugawa attitude to the authority of the sages. They were men who had sought the truth and found a portion of it. Therefore, they could be taken as guides to action. The truth, however, was above the sages and open to all men. Others had also discovered portions of the truth and could be taken as models along with the sages. The system was not closed.

Finally, when we examine the differentiation between ethics and the natural world that eventually developed within the Chu Hsi tradition in late Tokugawa Japan, we find that both in context and content it was completely different from the earlier distinction made in the writings of Itō Jinsai and Ogyū Sorai. As Professor Maruyama has pointed out, both of these men reject *ri* as a basic category relevant to human action. Both do this in order to give greater emphasis to practical, human concerns (Jinsai to ethics and Sorai to politics). By rejecting the relevance of *ri* they were rejecting its contemplative implications. Jinsai did this by denying outright the ultimacy of *ri*. For Jinsai, *ri* exists only in *ki* (the psycho-physical stuff); *ki* is basic. Sorai did not deny *ri* as

[60] Yamagata, *op.cit.*, p. 422.

such. He felt, as did the Chu Hsi school, that things are what they are because of their *ri*. But, only the sages could know this *ri* and they received their knowledge from Heaven, not by study. The knowledge of the sages was therefore absolute, and beyond the reach of ordinary men in a later age. Learning therefore is identified with the study of the classics. And even the classics do not present information concerning the *ri*. They only contain the practical applications of such knowledge made by the sages. This practical basis for action defines the limits of human knowledge. Beyond this fundamentalist and a-theoretical guide, there is nothing.

In order to formulate a philosophical basis for more practical human concerns both men distinguish between ethics and nature. This rescues ethics from the stillness of a timeless nature. Jinsai contrasts the way of man (*jindō*) with the way of Heaven (*tendō*); Sorai contrasts the *ri* of order (*jōri*) with the *ri* of ethics (*dōri*). Yet, what is fundamental here, in contrast to the acceptance of scientific thought within the Chu Hsi framework, is that the differentiation is wholly directed toward the ethical side of things. Nature is made autonomous only to become a dead category. Beyond this it is ignored, or worse, subjected to an empty respect. Sorai writes: "Is it not extremely disrespectful to speak of knowing Heaven." And, "to measure the *ri* of Heaven against one's own [small] wisdom is disrespectful to Heaven and makes light of the sages."[61] In the same work Sorai also writes: "That which is Heaven can not be known; the sages were in awe of heaven."[62]

In the case of Nishi Amane, the differentiation between *shinri* and *butsuri* was just the opposite: it was as concerned with freeing science from ethics as with freeing ethics from nature. Nishi wrote in a tradition that took the universe as an object of knowledge as well as respect. Nishi's distinction between *shinri* and *butsuri* was borrowed from Western philosophy; it did not come from within the Chu Hsi tradition. Nishi wrote of it as "something regarding which no

[61] Maruyama Masao, *op. cit.*, p. 81.
[62] *Ibid.*, p. 81.

distinction has been made in either China or Japan since ancient times."[63] Yet, he used this distinction to make explicit a difference that had been felt within the Tokugawa Chu Hsi tradition since the time of Sakuma Shōzan: a difference arising from the value placed on science, rather than ethics.

[63] *Meiji bunka zenshū*, vol. 15, p. 263. In contrast to this distinction between ethics and science Nishi acknowledges that the distinction between ethics and law had been made previously, although with insufficient clarity, by others both in China and Japan—including Ogyū Sorai. See *ibid.*, p. 262.

PART THREE

The Symbol and the Substance of Power

However numerous the advantages which Tokugawa Japan bequeathed to the Meiji modernizers, the Restoration of 1868 remains a decisive break. Only after the abolition of the shogunate was there a genuine effort to centralize and activate loyalties and efforts previously expended in competitive maneuvering and wasteful duplication. Since the Restoration took place in a setting of international competition and peril and under circumstances of national humiliation, a symbol of the national tradition around which all factions could unite was urgently needed. The school of national learning which had grown up during the Tokugawa peace provided one in the person of a semi-divine emperor, embodiment of the native wisdom. The imperial institution, lauded in this manner, had also the support of the Confucian tradition, for its application of Chinese political values had served to arm as many attacks on shogunal usurpation of political prerogatives as had the Shintō enthusiasm.

The way to appropriation of this advantage was greatly eased in that the emperor, the best possible symbol of legitimacy and continuity, was associated with the existing Tokugawa political institutions in only the most shadowy manner; restoration could be explained as a resolution of contradictions, and did not have to be phrased in terms of revolutionary overturn. Legitimacy was not challenged so much as it was affirmed.

Herschel Webb's study of attitudes toward the imperial institution describes the radical changes in the esteem in which the emperor was held in Tokugawa and Meiji times and opens the whole subject of the nature and significance of the imperial institution. Steeped as it is in the psychology and values of the Japanese tradition, this is an area of inquiry peculiarly resistant to characterization and definition. Nowhere can one see more sharply the unyielding elements of the cultural core of Japan; for despite the restoration of power in the name of antiquity and the near deification of the emperor's person, despite a constitution which reserved essential powers for his personal prerogative, the actual role, power, and influence of the modern emperor remained in many ways as obscure and indefinite as that of his ancestors. And since, despite a constitution that might have made him a functioning autocrat, he served rather as symbol, this modern use of tradition and confusion of symbol with substance, in an age before image manipulation by political planners with modern media, deserves to be described as creative, and not traditional, much less derivative, statecraft.

Donald H. Shively moves a step closer to the decision process with his study of Nishimura Shigeki, a man who functioned as educator, participant, and critic in the modernization process. A case study like this shows as nothing else could do the impossibility of making neat, sharp distinctions between categories of "modernizer-Westernizer" and "Confucian-traditionalist," and reminds us that the consensus on what was to be done about nation-building in the face of the foreign threat transcended intramural differentiations of emphasis. Nishimura was above all a Confucian scholar, but this in no wise prevented his avid study of Western learning and joining in the association formed by advocates of enlightenment in 1873. Conscious that his country was "but one corner of the whole globe," he urged his countrymen to "gain the greatness of America and the strength of England and France." And yet he deplored alike the excessive imitation of the 1880's and the "bigoted and obstinate and stupid scholarship" of Shintō enthusiasts. His moral basis remained that of the Confucian classics he had so long expounded, and in the success of his efforts to secure recognition for this code as foundation of the modern education system his influence far outlived his life. In this process of developing a moral and ethical basis for a modern state, to the end that a populace activated through education should nevertheless find its moral guidelines in the wisdom of the Japanese past—without falling into Shintō fanaticism—Nishimura may stand as epitome of much of his age and generation. Generalizations about "conservative" and "progressives" like those of "traditionalist" and "Westernizer" acquire the proper shadings—to the extent that they survive at all—only in the light of such careers.

With consideration of Yamagata Aritomo, the subject of the essay by Roger F. Hackett, we come to the center of the Meiji leadership group. In contrast to the men of ideas and words taken up hitherto, Yamagata was pre-eminently a man of action. Others might talk about ideology, but he implemented, and thereby gave meaning and reality to their ideas. His many-sided career, varied even for the Meiji oligarchs, embraced roles affecting the military, bureaucracy, local government, political leadership, and finally, from semi-retirement, elder statesmen. Throughout he was a man of few words, even among a group known for the most part for its reticence, and his developing attitudes and concerns can be traced most effectively by close scrutiny of his actions.

Yamagata and his peers, like Nishimura, fit no neat category, and instead show in their pattern of activity how responsibility and practicality required the refraction of many rays into a single stream of some consistency. He was heir of all that has been discussed: the education of the Tokugawa era, which affected him when his rank and status were still modest and which made him see education of the masses as a form of mobilization and conscription as a form of education; the Confucian scale of values, combining paternalism with low regard for the independent capacity of the populace; devotion to the imperial cause, and willingness to assume that he and his fellows spoke for it; and an unemotional, practical bent which made him able to distinguish between means and ends, and willing to change the former if thereby he could be more confident of the ability to salvage the latter. Meiji Japan was fortunate in having as its leaders a group of men who had grown up in circumstances of adversity and national insecurity, and who, having known the luxury of rashness and intemperate action in their early years before the stakes were high, were thereafter content to hold their country's risks to the minimum until its resources were prepared, meanwhile conscious that institutional innovation and activation of their countrymen furnished a challenge worthy of their best efforts.

CHAPTER V

The Development of an Orthodox Attitude Toward the Imperial Institution in the Nineteenth Century

HERSCHEL WEBB

S URELY there is no more amazing instance in world history of the use of traditionalist means to radical ends than when the leaders of early Meiji masked the political changes which they had made with the label of an "imperial restoration." The effect was not only to give unprecedented policies the color of great antiquity, but also to make it appear that what was in fact an administration by relatively lowly placed new men proceeded instead from the most highly pedigreed and unquestionably legitimate of all possible sources.

That phrase, "imperial restoration," brings to mind an entire system of thought regarding the modern Japanese state and the historical process through which it came into being. In its essentials this theory holds that the Restoration was first of all a return of political power by the shogunate, which had long usurped it, to the imperial dynasty, to whom it rightfully belonged. The Meiji government, then, was government by the emperor, or at least was carried out by the emperor's chosen ministers and in accordance with imperial will. This theory further holds that in the period before the Meiji Restoration, and extending back at least to the late seventeenth century, there was an influential tradition of thought (which I shall here call "loyalist") which offered as a political ideal much the same kind of political settlement for the emperor and the government as the Restoration achieved.

Such, in brief, is the view which one might call the orthodox Japanese interpretation of Restoration history and the post-Restoration state. It is associated with the governing oligarchy of the Meiji period, and its purely legal aspects are to be seen most clearly in the Constitution of 1889, certain other statutes, and the official commentaries upon them. In its broader implications, particularly those relating to historical developments, the interpretation may be found in the histories approved for use in the public school system of prewar Japan and in general in the works of Japanese historians of a conservative or traditionalist cast.[1]

It is not necessary to dwell here on the many criticisms that both the political scientist and the historian can make against this theory. It has long been apparent to most Japanese and Western students of the subject that the actual status of the emperor in modern Japan has been more than somewhat at variance with the lofty position asserted for him in the Meiji Constitution. If the emperors of late nineteenth and early twentieth century Japan were not merely figureheads, neither were they the actual rulers of the country. Furthermore, the historical process leading to the Restoration was far too complex to permit description in terms of a single loyalist or restorationist movement in Tokugawa times.

Nevertheless, the orthodox theory of the Restoration is a fruitful object of study. It offers a glimpse of the ideal relationship envisaged by Meiji leaders between the emperor and the government, and therefore shows something of their system of ethical values and their motives for political action. Their professed beliefs may, furthermore, be studied most profitably in the light of that loyalist tradition which they claimed as their intellectual inheritance. Loyalist thought was not, to be sure, the only influence on the ideas or the achievement of the architects of the new Japan, but by their own acknowledgment it was one of the most important. Moreover, those very elements of mid-Meiji theory that cannot be

---

[1] For a general discussion of modern Japanese treatments of the history of the Meiji Restoration, see Tōyama Shigeki, *Meiji ishin* (Tokyo, 1952), pp. 1-11. A conspicuous example of the orthodox interpretation is *Ishin shi* (6 vols., Tokyo, 1939-1941), compiled under the auspices of the Ministry of Education. One of the few authentic and articulate presentations in English is Robert King Hall (ed.), *Kokutai no hongi. Cardinal Principles of the National Entity of Japan* (Cambridge, Harvard University Press, 1949).

accounted for by means of the loyalist tradition will show most clearly the oligarchs' imaginative use of national tradition and the way in which they fitted themselves for the solution of unprecedented national problems.

It is easiest to define this loyalist tradition if one takes as one's base point the body of official thought regarding the emperor in the latter part of the nineteenth century, and then works backward, tracing as far back as possible its ideological ancestry. The men who formulated the orthodox theory of the Meiji state are generally agreed to have been the senior governing bureaucrats of the period in which the Constitution was drafted. Most of the members of this group had participated actively in the Restoration of 1868. Of course, the group which I call "restorationist" also included men who did not remain in the government long enough to take part in the drafting of the Constitution. Some of these, such as Saigō, Itagaki, Ōkuma, and Gotō, became dissociated from the governing oligarchy on account of policy splits of the 1870's. Others, notably Sakamoto Ryōma, Yokoi Shōnan, Ōkubo and Kido, were removed by death.

The restorationists in turn had emerged from a group largely composed of dissident samurai, *gōshi*, and *rōnin* who between 1858 and 1865 imparted to the continuing loyalist catchword *"sonnō"* ("revere the emperor") a radically anti-shogunal meaning. The *sonnō* faction of that time had studied under, or been influenced by the doctrines of, mid-nineteenth century Confucian teachers of a nationalistic bent such as Yoshida Shōin, Fujita Tōko, and Aizawa Seishisai. Several traditions contributed to their thought on the imperial institution, but that which shaped it most concretely can be traced to Fujita Yūkoku and other Confucians of the Mito School of about 1800 and still further back to Confucians of the late seventeenth and early eighteenth century such as Yamazaki Ansai, Yamaga Sokō, and the early Mito School. Those men too had intellectual forebears, who would have to be considered in a complete account of loyalist thought, but whom I shall ignore here, as their influence on nineteenth century attitudes was remote.

Most members of this long tradition were in one way or another avid students of history, and their formulations of the ideal role of the emperor were usually conditioned by their appraisal of the condition of the throne in their own time, and a comparison with what it had been in past ages. Therefore, I shall frame the discussion of loyalist ideas in the context of the actual relationship that existed at different stages between the throne and the Japanese state.[2]

I shall begin before the Tokugawa unification in that period of turmoil known as *sengoku jidai*, "the period of the warring states." From that time until the early twentieth century, I discern four main phases in the condition of Japanese emperors, and these correspond roughly to the periods which historians know as *sengoku*, Tokugawa, Bakumatsu, and Meiji.

In the first of these periods, extending from the late fifteenth to the early seventeenth century, the treatment accorded the sovereign was proverbially wretched. The imperial capital and palace were in ruins at the end of the Ōnin War (1477), and no one had the money or inclination to restore them to their former condition. Poverty hampered even the ritual activities of the emperors, which had been all that was left to them when centuries of "deputies" had usurped their effective powers of state. The enthronement ceremony of the

[2] The words "nation," "state," "government," "rule," and "sovereignty" will be used below in a non-technical sense, but it is hoped that certain contrasts which I mean to imply by means of them will be clear. The Japanese "nation," as used here, includes all of the implications and associations which we normally assign to the word "Japan," including the land, the people, and their society. "State" has a narrower meaning, referring to the political organization of the same community. The "government" is a body of men who wield effective political powers. The government "rules." But "sovereignty" is the ultimate authority in the state, which Japanese loyalists considered to belong to the emperor. I use the words "emperor," "sovereign," and "monarch" more or less interchangeably, and I refer to that man's office as the "imperial institution" or "the throne." On the other hand, "the court," in a Tokugawa period context, denotes the entire body of men who resided within the palace compound in Kyoto as advisers, administrators, or servants for the emperor.

Emperor Go-Kashiwabara (r. 1500-1526) was delayed twenty years for lack of funds, and even then was shorn of its customary splendor. Go-Nara Tennō (r. 1526-1557), the poorest of the lot, is said to have sold his autographs for cash and went unburied for a time after his death. Little majesty surrounded so impoverished an institution. Military upstarts consorted with emperors as though they had been casual acquaintances or servants.

Yet, for all that this implies, there was on the purely human side something less unfavorable about the treatment which *sengoku* emperors received from their subjects. They had, relatively speaking, a considerable degree of personal freedom, freedom to go about the city or the countryside and to come into contact with people of different classes and factions. They also had another kind of freedom more relevant to my discussion. That was the opportunity, qualified but real, to participate in politics. In however debased a state, their office had the power of its ancient magical or ritual associations. It symbolized legitimate authority even when none existed. The holder of the office ought not to be treated roughly and rarely was. On the contrary, his support added to a cause, given freely as a human being, was potentially a thing of great value. Hence he enjoyed, as most past emperors had not, an important freedom of ethical choice, namely to back one or another side in the factional struggles that distinguished the age. In 1469, for example, the Emperor Go-Tsuchimikado gave his support to Ashikaga Yoshimasa in the struggle with his brother Yoshimi. Sixteenth century barons of the Uesugi, Hōjō, and other families coveted imperial favor, which could not be won by threats of physical violence, and hence had to be courted by appeals to the personal choice of the sovereign. The relationship between the Emperor Ōgimachi and Oda Nobunaga was one of mutual respect with a realization that each had much to gain from the support of the other. In 1580 the emperor's intervention made a settlement possible between Nobunaga and the Hongan-ji. On another occasion an imperial remonstrance against Nobunaga was effective in causing the latter to postpone his planned attack on the Kōya-san monastery.

Such examples show that the emperors in those years were influential political figures. Of course, they were not rulers. Ōgimachi Tennō had nothing like the personal power of Nobunaga. None of the *sengoku* emperors was even in a position to contend for actual political strength of that degree, for that would have required control of fighting men and weapons, which they lacked. Moreover, there is no denying that even the small degree of personal freedom and influence which they did achieve was at the price of a large measure of the traditional dignity and awe of the imperial office.

With the restoration of peace and order in the first few years of the seventeenth century, the condition of the imperial institution changed profoundly. For us today, the most striking change was the imposition by the Tokugawa shogunate of unprecedented restrictions on the personal freedom of the emperor and the court. Inevitably this meant a total suppression of the influence of the Kyoto court in political matters. Some of the new restrictions were written into law with the *Kuge sho-hatto*, "Laws regarding the imperial court," of 1615.[3] In these, the shogunate assumed the power to veto appointments and resignations of all the most important officials of the court; to bestow titles of nobility, previously considered to be the prerogative solely of the emperor, on members of the military aristocracy; and to govern certain Buddhist monasteries which had previously been under the control of the imperial family or the Kyoto court. Some other restrictions date from the same period, but seem to have been informal rules of procedure rather than laws imposed by the shogunate. One of the most important of these was the curtailment of the physical freedom of the emperor (and even of other members of the imperial family) to travel. From 1626 to 1863 no emperor left the compound of his palace, except when fires or other emergencies required that the

---

[3] For a text see *Tokugawa kinrei-kō* (Tokyo, 1931), I, pp. 1-4. The laws are discussed in Tsuji Zennosuke, *Nihon bunka-shi* (Tokyo, 1952), v, pp. 142-151.

palace itself be moved.[4] Abdicated sovereigns seem not to have been hampered to the same extent as sovereigns actually on the throne, though there is evidence that even with those individuals the shogunate kept travel to a minimum. The Shugaku-in villa, which had been furnished early in the seventeenth century as an imperial pleasure resort, lies scarcely outside the city of Kyoto, but was in disuse entirely from 1732 to 1823. When the retired Emperor Kōkaku visited it for the first time in the latter year, it seemed to many in the shogunal government to be a dangerous breach of precedent.[5] The obvious result of this policy was to protect the emperor and his family from every contact with people not authorized to associate with him by his own ministers or those of the shogunate.

Another restriction on imperial freedom was that even though the Kyoto court was self-governing in everyday matters, the emperor himself was usually a less influential figure within the court than certain of his ministers of high-ranking *kuge* families. For instance, it was these ministers who approved Kōkaku's request to be allowed to go to the Shugaku-in before they referred the matter to shogunal officials. In another famous case, a group of *kuge* officials actually deposed the Emperor Go-Sai in 1663, on grounds that certain national misfortunes of the time must be due to a lack of imperial virtue.[6]

Despite the utter impotence of the Kyoto court in the state and the near impotence of the emperor in the court, there are several respects in which the Tokugawa shoguns' treatment of the throne represented a distinct improvement over that which *sengoku* society had accorded it. Ceremonial respect for the institution was the universal attitude shown by the military aristocracy, and this was no doubt merely the outward manifestation of sincere reverence and awe. The material circumstances of the court were much improved. Its members were no longer ill-housed or shabbily clothed. There

---

[4] Hosokawa Junjirō et al. (comp.), *Koji ruien* (Tokyo, 1931-1936), XII, pp. 587, 68off.

[5] *Ibid.*, pp. 747-748. [6] *Ibid.*, pp. 564-565.

was plenty of money for them to maintain dignity in their rituals and ceremonies. Historians frequently speak of the impoverishment of the court in the Tokugawa period. It was impoverished by comparison with Versailles or even with Edo, but by earlier Japanese standards it was not.

I have stressed the great contrast in the throne's external condition between the *sengoku* and Tokugawa periods because that contrast had such an important part in shaping the attitude toward the institution which prevailed (among those who were concerned with it at all) until well into the nineteenth century. We should not forget that whatever criticisms imperial loyalists may from time to time have leveled against the shogunate for its treatment of the emperor, a recurrent theme in their writings is the idea that the first Tokugawa shogun, by setting the country in order and improving the material circumstances of the court, had exemplified the proper attitude of a subject toward the throne.

I should like to cite two interesting documents of the early eighteenth century which illustrate this point of view. The author was Asaka Tampaku (1656-1737), a retainer of the Mito han who is most famous as one of the compilers of the *Dai Nihon shi*. Tampaku is credited with having been one of the three or four most influential scholars in formulating the imperial loyalist ideas with which the work of the early Mito School is imbued. Many of these ideas are expressed in their most articulate form in Tampaku's book *Dai Nihon shi ronsan*, a group of essays on Japanese history which were originally intended to be appended to the various chapters of the *Dai Nihon shi*. He seems to me to have been almost the perfect exemplar in his time of the tradition that came in the next century to be known as *sonnō*. His work was known to officials of the Kyoto court, with whom he corresponded. In a letter to one of them, he described his high regard for the achievements of the Tokugawa family. Prior to Ieyasu's time, he said, the family had been confined to the province of Mikawa. "Surrounded by enemies, they nevertheless managed to maintain their position. There was nothing secretive or occult about the way in which they finally established the empire.

Their sincerity brought unity to the people, and their considerate treatment brought peace. They transmitted their virtues to later generations, and thus firmly united the hearts of the people. . . . The line passed to Ieyasu, whose valor was bestowed on him by Heaven, and the people submitted to his benevolent rule. . . . He joined the fragments of the country together, and treated the feudal lords according to the rites. . . ."[7]

In another writing of Tampaku, an essay entitled "Resso seiseki no jo" ("On the achievements of our ancestors"), he was explicit in attributing Ieyasu's success to his exemplary treatment of the throne. In it he says: "Nobunaga and Hideyoshi were aware in a rough way of the reverence due to the emperor, but they were not sincere about it in their hearts. . . . When Ieyasu put the country in order, he caused the feudal lords to submit to the emperor's rule. He rebuilt the imperial palace and restored its defenses. He presented rich lands to the throne so that plentiful sacrifices could be offered to the gods. . . . Great was the reverence which he showed to the emperor. . . . Respect for the emperor laid the basis for profound peace."[8]

Tampaku's attitude toward the imperial institution, as stated here, is disappointingly vague in many ways, but no more so than the other expressions of loyalist sentiment written before the middle of the nineteenth century. There is no hint that the throne might play an active role in the state, nor is it made clear what attitude one should accord to the personal views of any particular emperor. Yet here we may at least deduce an essential element in the loyalist ideal: it demanded consideration for the material well-being of the emperor and the court, with the aim that the purely ritual functions of the imperial office could be carried out in proper style. The contrast drawn here between Nobunaga and the Tokugawa shoguns had nothing to do with the fact that the former befriended an emperor and occasionally listened to what he had to

[7] "Tō Shissei ni itasu no sho," in Takasu Yoshijirō (ed.), *Mito gaku taikei* (Tokyo, 1942-1943), VI, pp. 413-414.
[8] "Resso seiseki no jo," in *Mito gaku taikei*, VI, p. 367.

say, while the latter silenced emperors and imprisoned them. Rather it lay in the attitudes shown in the two periods toward the throne's ceremonial or symbolic role. Tampaku's comparison can perhaps be paraphrased as follows: Nobunaga's behavior implied that the throne had power to command men's loyalty and hence might be useful in obtaining power for him; the Tokugawa shoguns, on the other hand, by restoring the throne to its ancient sacrosanct dignity and material splendor recognized that the ultimate end which the imperial institution might achieve was not the political power of a man or a family, but something of far greater worth, national unity and order. "Respect for the emperor laid the basis for profound peace."

Of course, this formulation of ideas cannot stand as a description of the actual views which *sengoku* and Tokugawa rulers took of the imperial institution. What Tampaku's words illustrate is his own ideas of the proper condition of the throne and the proper behavior of subjects in regard to it. This attitude belongs to Tampaku's age—the turn of the eighteenth century—and could probably not have existed much earlier. That is, it was surely conditioned by historical retrospect, the knowledge that the Tokugawa family had restored order after centuries of chaos and that their peaceful rule had endured for a century. The idea that *sengoku* Japan was badly governed and that the Tokugawa shoguns ruled well is a commonplace in writings of the Tokugawa period. Imperial loyalists from the late seventeenth to the early nineteenth century did not depart in any respect from that commonly accepted point of view. Their contribution to historical thought lay solely in the view that the Tokugawa achievement would not have been possible without reverence for the throne and the attention to its material well-being that was the outward manifestation of that reverence.

Loyalist thought often postulated a clear relationship between the throne and the government, but the throne's part in the relationship was always passive. The government was to assume the duties of protecting the emperor, respecting him, and giving heed in their policies to the ethical values which he symbolized, but of the emperor nothing was expected except that he continue to be there. There is a famous passage from an early nineteenth century work, the *Seimei-ron* ("On the rectification of names") by Fujita Yūkoku (1774-1826), which illustrates the one-sided nature of this relationship. Yūkoku, like Asaka Tampaku, was a Confucian scholar and retainer of the Mito han. His son Fujita Tōko (1806-1855) was one of the most illustrious retainers of the loyalist daimyo Tokugawa Nariaki in the Bakumatsu period. Both the father and the son are considered to have typified the positions taken by loyalists in their respective ages. Yūkoku said: "If the shogunate reveres the imperial house, all the feudal lords will respect the shogunate. If the feudal lords respect the shogunate, the ministers and officials will honor the feudal lords. In this way high and low will give support to each other, and the entire country will be in accord. What qualities enable the shogunate to unite the country? Above, its reverent attitude toward the emperor, and below, its protective treatment of the feudal lords. Its rule, however, is nothing more than the exercise of the emperor's sovereignty. . . ."[9]

There is little need to underline the implications of this interesting statement. The gist of it, expanded further on in the same essay, is that the shogun's rule is legitimate only if he recognizes his own subordination to the emperor. Yūkoku finds a classic summation of his attitude in the phrase: "As Heaven has not two suns, earth has not two masters." Confucian doctrine of the rectification of names asserts that in any social relationship the parties must recognize the inequalities of station that exist between them. Subjects, for example, must admit that they are subjects, and not aspire to the treatment that should be accorded only to sovereigns. "Earth's master," the sovereign, the recipient of Heaven's mandate, was the emperor, not the shogun. The first requirement for good government was that the shogun realize this. Yet, there is not a hint here that the *government* of Japan was or ought to be anything but the government of the Tokugawa shoguns.

Thus, what strikes one most of all in this—and indeed in

[9] Kikuchi Kenjirō (ed.), *Yūkoku zenshū* (Tokyo, 1935), p. 229.

the whole body of Confucian loyalist writings before the Bakumatsu period—is its essential conservatism in regard to existing political institutions. However, there is nothing surprising about their general satisfaction with the state of things as they were. Until the nineteenth century there lived in their minds a historical contrast between the orderly and stable regime under which they lived and the deplorable chaos that had existed in the *sengoku* period.

The condition of the monarchy changed again in the Bakumatsu period. A series of historical events between 1846 and 1858 profoundly modified the circumstances of the court and the relationship that had existed between the emperor and the shogunal government. In brief, the change amounted to a reemergence of the throne into the field of national politics. The emperor and his court regained something of the freedom and influence which they had lost with the Tokugawa unification, but simultaneously there was a loss of some of the reverential awe from subjects which loyalist thought considered to be the one supreme mark of a harmonious society. The loyalists' espousal of this ideal did not change, but they were forced by circumstances to think out new ways of applying the ideal in the realm of political policy.

Two nodal events of the period will illustrate the changed relationship between the throne and the government. Both of them occurred as the direct result of threats from abroad that could not be dealt with by the shogunate's traditional means. The first event, in 1846, was the despatch to Edo, in the name of the youthful Emperor Kōmei, of a gently critical letter requesting that coastal defenses be strengthened and "the Imperial mind be set at ease."[10] The second event was the emperor's refusal to ratify the 1858 treaty with the United States after it had been submitted to him for his approval by the shogunal government. The throne's letter of 1846 in its modest way marked the appearance of a new factor for the

[10] For a text of the letter see Ishin Shiryō Hensan Jimukyoku (comp.), *Ishin shi* (Tokyo, 1941), II, p. 27. A translation appears in Edwin Borden Lee, *The political career of Ii Naosuke* (Unpublished Ph.D. dissertation, Columbia University, 1960), pp. 25-26.

government and the loyalists to reckon with, namely imperial will, actively expressed by the court itself. The refusal to approve the 1858 treaty conclusively demonstrated that the imperial will might extend to matters of specific state policy and that it might be contrary to the wishes of the shogunate.

In this situation it was natural that the opinions of emperors should again have become an object for contention between opposing political factions, much as the freely expressed support of emperors had been a thing of great value sought in the struggles of the *sengoku* period. Furthermore, the possibility that an emperor might express a preference for some other faction than one's own naturally created in the groups that lacked the emperor's favor much the same inclination to flout the imperial will that had seemed to loyalists to disfigure the attitude which *sengoku* society displayed toward the throne.

It must be admitted that the personal freedom and influence of the Bakumatsu Emperor, Kōmei, is a vexatious historical problem. It is not easy to know when the emperor himself made decisions, and when other agencies in and around the court made them and then sanctified them by attributing them to the emperor. It is clear that the *kuge* ministers' power to influence or restrain the sovereign continued even after the shogunate's system of controls over the court had begun to break down. We should therefore understand the newly emerging imperial will more in an institutional than a personal sense.

This should be taken as a caution lest we pursue the analogy between the *sengoku* throne and the Bakumatsu throne further than the facts allow, but it holds good at least in the following respects. Both ages witnessed fierce struggles for power between factions each of which could plausibly argue that its policies were broadly in accordance with what the emperor represented. The emperors in the two periods shared the opportunity of signifying by personal choice which factions were truly their own. They therefore enjoyed a significant degree of influence in helping to decide in what way and by whom harmony was to be restored. On the other hand, by allying with particular factions the throne in both ages was exposed to contemptuous treatment from its subjects that seriously compromised its traditional dignity.

Let us now compare the loyalist view in the Bakumatsu period with what it had been before. As has been indicated, loyalism had long been a force for institutional conservatism and had furthermore postulated for the throne no more than a passive role in its relations with the government. In the Bakumatsu period, the loyalists were usually political dissidents, and many of them (including those at the forefront of the movement in the 1860's) even offered quite radical programs of political action. Moreover, since the very emergence of the imperial institution as an active agent in politics enabled this radical group to claim for themselves the label of loyalist, their ideas as to the proper role of the throne in the state tended increasingly to center around the ideal of government *by* the emperor, rather than government merely in his name. Despite all this, I believe that the thought of the loyalists continued throughout this period to be profoundly conservative, and that so far as the political role of the emperor as a human being was concerned there remained at the base of loyalist opinion a deep-seated idea that imperial government, at best, need not imply the active intervention of the emperor in politics. This is a paradox, but I think that it will be explained by reference to the specific content of loyalist political motives in the 1860's.

During the time of Ii Naosuke's autocratic rule as *tairō* (1858-1860), the main stream of loyalist sentiment was of course anti-shogunate, but that is not to say that it was the same as the policy later known as *tōbaku*, "to overthrow the shogunate." The attack was more narrowly directed at specific shogunal policies, among which the two most important were accedence to foreign demands and the domination of the shogunal government by a certain clique of *fudai* elements (Ii's faction) at the expense of other able daimyos. The movement to preserve Japanese exclusion was in every sense conservative to the core, and the movement to broaden the base of power within the shogunate was defended on the grounds that shogunal councils more broadly representative of the interests of the whole country would be more effective in the fight against the foreigners. The Emperor Kōmei (as he spoke through his court) was known to be deeply conservative about almost everything, but his conservatism had been most clearly manifested in regard to the issue of national seclusion.

It was not just a lucky accident that the emperor's views here happened to coincide with those of the faction which we know as loyalist. Most of Japan was conservative on this point. The minority who were not—those, for example, who believed that foreign trade was the answer to Japan's economic problems—came to their position through experiences that neither the loyalists nor the Kyoto court had been exposed to. Furthermore, virtually everyone was unhappy at being compelled to end seclusion on terms set by the Western powers. Ii Naosuke and his faction were as disturbed as anyone else at that painful necessity, but responsibility required them to succumb to the necessity as a less unbearable alternative to national extinction. The opposition loyalists, who by their very nature as dissidents lacked the responsibility of conceiving practical plans of action, failed to perceive the alternatives in the same way, and they could claim with perfect honesty that the emperor didn't either. It is thus easy enough to explain how the conservatism of the loyalists in regard to seclusion, or to the protection of the country from foreign domination, was translated into radicalism in regard to the institution of the shogunate. Faced with a choice between preserving fundamental values and preserving existing institutions, they could not but sacrifice the institutions. In Marius Jansen's excellent study of Sakamoto Ryōma there is described the very ingenious way in which Nakaoka Shintarō justified the *kaikoku* ("open the country") position which he had reached by 1866 as another and more practical form of *jōi* ("expel the barbarians"). The justification was, I think, sincere. It was also another instance of the same principle that when the *value* of national independence was at stake, it might be necessary to sacrifice the *institution* of the seclusion system.

The loyalists' abandonment of the "passive-emperor-principle" in favor of the principle that the emperor ought to hold real political power appears to be a more fundamental change in their program during the Bakumatsu period. Here too, however, the new development may be explained as an application of the old—and continuing—belief to a new situation. Once the imperial will had been expressed on a political issue—as in 1858—it was natural that loyalists should have demanded that it be obeyed. None of them, of course, implied that by expressing his will in this fashion the emperor had overstepped the proper bounds of his political role. In fact, throughout the period many loyalists (for example, those of Tokugawa Nariaki's faction before 1860, the activist *rōnin* and *kuge* in Kyoto in the early 1860's, and spokesmen for the Satsuma and Chōshū han after the 1866 Chōshū expedition) openly courted imperial favor in their search for ideological ammunition for their side. This is positive evidence that loyalists recognized the new active role of the throne in politics, but it scarcely proves that they envisioned the perpetuation of that role as a permanent ingredient of an ideal state. I should like to offer certain evidences that they did not so believe, but I fully admit that they are indirect and not conclusive.

First, all loyalists believed that the objective situation which necessitated the direct expression of imperial will was deplorable. The occasion for the emperor's reemergence was associated in their minds with national disunity and governmental weakness, and as loyalists they described those conditions as a lack of harmony between the throne and the government. They did not say specifically that if harmony were restored, the emperor ought to revert to his traditional passive role, but that is at least a plausible extension of their argument.

Second, when one examines the specific content of the political program of the loyalists as it developed in the 1860's, one is struck by the fact that those portions of it that dealt with administration—foreign policy, the powers of the han and the shogunate, deliberative councils, etc.—became more and more explicit, but that the references to the emperor remained thoroughly vague and ambiguous. The loyalists, who from the time of the Chōshū expedition could be called restorationists, customarily began their manifestoes of political action with the demand that "political power be returned to the emperor." Yet when one reads further in them, one finds that the *exercise* of power, as opposed to its theoretical location, was to be entrusted to other agencies. There is a clear implication that these effective agencies of government ought to be loyal to the emperor, but there is little indication that this implied the emperor's active help in showing his ministers what the concrete manifestations of loyalty might be.

Third, there is the evidence that some of the loyalists on occasion ignored the expressed wishes of the emperor when those conflicted with their own. The most conspicuous occasion of this kind was the abortive invasion of Kyoto by Chōshū loyalists in August 1864. In the previous year, the Emperor Kōmei had protested to the daimyos of Aizu and Satsuma that the loyalist leaders in Kyoto had got out of hand. In a coup of September 1863, troops of the two han expelled from Kyoto the Chōshū loyalists as well as Sanjō Sanetomi and other loyalist *kuge*. The attempted invasion by Chōshū elements in the next summer was as direct an affront to the imperial will as any shown by the shogunal forces in the Bakumatsu period. Such behavior seems hypocritical in the extreme. While it was not necessarily typical of the actions of all of the loyalists in this period, it nevertheless involved people, particularly Sanjō, who remained at the center of the restorationist movement. Whether or not it was hypocritical, it bespeaks for the restorationists a system of political values in which general ethical precepts and particular objectives of policy took priority over the expressed opinions of the emperor. The ethical precepts to which I refer included the familiar ideal of reverence to the throne, as well as the insistence on several other traditional values. Yet, when one examines the concrete program which loyalists thought of as means of translating their ethical values into action, one is forced to the conclusion that imperial loyalty in their minds was directed more to what the imperial office symbolized than to the man who held it.

In short, loyalist thought in the Bakumatsu period seems to me to have been a direct outgrowth of the earlier tradition and to have shared many of the same essential characteristics. It was first of all a vehicle for deep conservatism toward national values. It was even conservative in respect to existing institutions except for those (such as the shogunate and the seclusion system) whose maintenance was thought to place the national values in jeopardy. The loyalist ideal continued to stress a relationship between the throne and the government which was distinguished more by the attitudes and treatment it required from the government upward to the throne than by any reciprocal activities of a political kind demanded of the emperor. These ingredients of past loyalist tradition continued, but political crisis and the new role of the imperial institution in politics caused them to be modified or reapplied. Loyalists listened to the emperor's voice, and though they were sometimes embarrassed by what it said to them, they were forced to come to terms with it. The message which it conveyed to them was that there was grave disharmony between the throne and the government. They described the settlement which they achieved in 1867 and 1868 as a wresting away from the shogunate of ultimate political power (*taiken*) and restoring it to the throne. With it harmony was also restored. The imperial voice no longer spoke to dissidents.

Whether it spoke to anybody in instruction or protest, even to the restorationists in the government, is of course another question. The facts of the emperor's condition after the Restoration—the fourth phase in my over-all historical view—are such as to leave the matter in substantial doubt, but they are still instructive in illustrating the development of attitudes toward the throne in the nineteenth century. There are echoes, though faint, in the settlement of Meiji of the settlement achieved by the first Tokugawa shogun. The state improved the material condition of the court and invested it with new glamour and awe. Criticism of the throne was silenced, and a system went into effect which made it difficult, if not impossible, for there to be open disagreements between the imperial court and the government. Whereas the means which the Tokugawa shoguns had used to this end had been elaborate and cumbersome, the Meiji restorationists employed a device which was simplicity itself. They obliterated the 300 miles of geographic distance between the emperor and the government and ensconced him in the inmost councils of state. If he spoke at all to his subjects, he spoke through them.

Then, as 250 years earlier, the new exaltation of the imperial office went hand in hand with a new restriction of the emperor's personal freedom. The power to register a protest with society at large against the way things are going is a very real manifestation of political freedom, whether or not it is accompanied by the power to effect changes in the trend.

In comparing the two emperors, Kōmei and Meiji, a distinction must be made between the influence each enjoyed on account of his personal qualities or the receptivity to his wishes of those around him, and the power each held due to the institutional position of the throne in the state. It is the latter, not the former, which is at issue in this discussion. There is no doubt that both men had ample opportunity to give advice to their intimate associates, and those of the Meiji Emperor possessed effective political power to a degree that those of his father had not. Furthermore, the Meiji Emperor clearly had the opportunity of gaining the experience with matters of state that would have made his opinions valuable to his subordinates. One may even go much further, and conclude that he had yet another advantage of an intangible nature that gave him far greater personal authority than either his proximity to the effective government or his political experience can explain. This intangible factor was none other than that very spirit of loyalty to the throne that Meiji governors and governed alike spoke of as the chief integrating force in the state. If, as I believe, that force was directed more to the emperor as a symbol than to the emperor as a person, nevertheless it had usually been considered by the restorationists and by their successors to preclude the outright flouting of the emperor's personal will.

However, what was really noteworthy about the throne in Meiji times was its effective isolation from the rest of society outside the established governmental authorities. Its isolation prevented dissidents from influencing the emperor, and restricted his freedom to speak directly to them. In this respect the position of the imperial institution then was similar to what it had been through most of the Tokugawa period, but very dissimilar from its condition between the 1840's and the 1860's.

Both Kōmei and Meiji were figures of political importance in ways in which their immediate predecessors had not been, but the particular strengths which the two enjoyed were opposite in kind and mutually incompatible. New powers were acquired at the sacrifice of old, and the Restoration, far from being merely a return to power of the imperial dynasty, was rather a neutralization of imperial power, a regularization in which a new harmony between the throne and the government necessarily entailed a loss of the emperor's freedom to influence historical change by choosing his own faction. The monarch had enjoyed this freedom briefly in the closing years of the shogunate, but the Meiji Emperor did not.

Post-restoration loyalist sentiment responded to the changed condition of the throne in two main ways. First, it stressed the happy contrast between the shabby state to which the throne had fallen by late Tokugawa times and the exalted condition to which it had later been restored. This contrast once again tended to emphasize the passive character of the throne in its relationship with the state. Second, the restorationists began to describe the policies of the government, regardless of who actually decided them, as emanating from the emperor, or representing the imperial will. "Imperial will," used in this sense, is a far different kind of thing from, say, the wishes expressed by the Emperor Kōmei in 1863 when he requested that the lawlessness of the Chōshū loyalists be controlled. It is much more similar to that vague imperial sanction which, according to loyalists of the early nineteenth century, legitimized the rule of the Tokugawa shoguns. Though the Meiji oligarchs' use of the emperor's name resembled an old Japanese pattern of political behavior, it led, I think, to an important new concept of the throne and the state, to which I shall return in the last portion of this paper.

It remains first to restate the aspects of the loyalist tradition that did not change—or that changed only in their application to passing situations—and to indicate the implications which they held for historical developments in the Meiji period.

From first to last the ethical principles upheld by loyalists applied to how the emperor should be treated rather than what he should do. Some of these principles demanded respect from subjects and the maintenance of a high standard of material well-being for the court. These had little to do with policy. Other principles, however, were indirectly concerned with policy, since they demanded that the government act in accordance with the values which the emperor symbolized. Most of the specific content of loyalist writings is a delineation of what those values were. All of them belonged to the traditional Japanese ethical system. In particular the most frequently emphasized were national independence, national historic continuity, national unity, harmony within the government, and harmony between rulers and ruled. Secondarily, from time to time loyalists took the imperial institution to stand for institutional conservatism, using the imperial name in arguments for the support of seclusion, or the power of the shogunate or the han.

The Meiji oligarchs were custodians of this tradition of thought about the emperor, and consciously or unconsciously they made use of it in pursuing their radically modernizing policies. Some parts of the tradition were positive aids to them and to modernization: (1) The passive and symbolic character of the throne assisted them, as it had assisted most of the Tokugawa shoguns, by veiling such imperial discontent as may have existed and making it difficult for dissidents to add the imperial voice to their complaints; (2) The emperor symbolized national unity, a precondition for successful policies of modernization or of any other kind; (3) He symbolized national continuity, and his presence had helped to make the transition from shogunal rule relatively orderly and bloodless; (4) He symbolized national independence, hence freedom from foreign restraints and the national strength necessary to maintain that freedom; even quite radical institutional changes could be made palatable if they contributed to that conservative ideal.

In short, the overwhelmingly conservative associations of the imperial institution might be said to have been useful to the modernizers to the degree that they gave them freedom of action and placed a conservative face even on quite radical policies. But there was clearly something about the loyalist tradition that was not conducive to modernization and that might even endanger the success of policies if they were too destructive of native traditions. Saigō Takamori, the most famous conservative dissident of the early Meiji period, protested to the government that its policies went much too far, and he appealed to the name of the emperor in defense of his own conservatism. The protest was ultimately unsuccessful. The oligarchs weathered the shock which it produced and emerged stronger than before, but the danger that there might be other similar crises remained. It would have been highly valuable to the oligarchs if they had been able to find some new formulation of the emperor's role which would neutralize its conservative associations, when those would have hindered their purposes, but which would still allow them to make use of those associations when conservatism was needed. It is my belief that they did find such a formulation, or to be more exact that at some time in the middle years of the Meiji period there came into being a new attitude toward the throne significantly different from earlier tradition which served the purposes of the oligarchy in precisely that way. I have indicated above that this new attitude was a changed interpretation of the concept, "the imperial will."

This part of my paper is hardest of all to document, but I would offer tentatively the thesis that in the late nineteenth century, while the power of the throne remained more symbolic than actual, the substance behind the symbol subtly changed. From being a symbol of Japan itself, its people, or their history, the emperor came in addition to stand for the power of the state. The imperial will then ceased to mean merely the ethical axioms of traditional Japanese society, but took on the new meaning of the expressed decisions of the emperor's government.

There is a large part of this thesis that few would deny. Obviously the imperial institution in the Meiji period entered into a more intimate relationship with the agencies of government than it had had since the early Heian period. It is equally obvious that the dissociation of the throne from politics in the intervening centuries had tended to create a body of thought in which the throne stood for ethical values—the ideal basis for the exercise of power—rather than for power itself. Equally, the Meiji system lent itself to a reidentification of the throne with political power. The results of this reidentification are to be seen most clearly in the references to the emperor in the Meiji Constitution, and earlier than that in the draft proposal for a constitution which Iwakura Tomomi submitted to other members of the government in July, 1881.[11] There can be no doubt that in those documents the throne represents state power, limited only as the undescribed agencies for the exercise of the emperor's power should determine.

But I return to my other main point, which is less universally recognized, namely that the attitude toward the throne implied in the oligarchs' use of it was new with them. There is nothing in the long line of imperial loyalist thought which tended to so close an identification of the throne with state power. In fact the tradition demanded that the government be ethically responsible to the throne for its acts, and hence that the two terms in the relationship be recognized as distinct. If, as I believe, the architects of the Meiji Restoration had themselves initially postulated their program on that traditional view, then the specifically political character of the emperor in the later Meiji state must be seen as a new development.

I can only speculate on where the new attitude came from.

[11] For relevant passages and a discussion of them see Ishii Ryōsuke, *Tennō* (Tokyo, 1951), pp. 196-206.

Perhaps it was an indigenous development naturally enough explained by the new opportunity which the oligarchs enjoyed of identifying the monarch with their own power. Or perhaps its origins are to be sought in those Western traditions of authoritarian monarchy that Meiji governors studied so assiduously before turning to the drafting of their new constitution. If the new ingredient in Japanese state theory was alien in origin, it was rapidly absorbed, and came to color much of the modern Japanese thought on the nature of the monarchy.

I submit in conclusion that in the Meiji period, when the emperor entered a new relationship with the actual structure of governmental power, official theory also developed to justify his position in the state. There has been a tendency to describe the new orthodoxy that resulted primarily as an idea that the emperor should exercise authority, rather than being simply a symbol of authority. I believe that this is an inaccurate description, that the framers of the orthodox theory were content in fact that the powers of the throne should remain in normal circumstances more symbolic than real. The new ingredient of the theory is rather a new referent of the symbol: the power of the state as something above and detached from the rest of Japanese society.

Does the emperor symbolize the nation itself, with all of the values of order and morality which the Japanese have conceived for it, or does he stand for the authority of the state? Both equations have been present in the thought of modern Japanese on the significance of the throne. The one has roots in ancient tradition; the other was newly grafted on to it after the Restoration. Whatever its referent, the symbol connoted power. In the one case it was the power of the ingrained beliefs of a whole people about social and political norms. In the other it was the power of the leaders of society to make policies which would effect change, within limits which they themselves should determine. So long as the traditional values of society remained unchallenged, the older view served adequately the purposes of solidly established government and even aided in the orderly transfer of power from an old and moribund government to one which was new and vigorous. But for the purposes of a government intent on refashioning to the very foundations many of traditional society's most cherished institutions the newer view was clearly superior.

CHAPTER VI

Nishimura Shigeki: A Confucian View of Modernization

DONALD H. SHIVELY

IN THE middle of the nineteenth century the Japanese were shocked into the realization that they could no longer keep the barbarians at bay by the traditional means. They discovered that in order to cope with the mounting pressure for trade concessions, which, in the experience of other Asian countries, had resulted in encroachments upon their sovereignty, some drastic innovations were required in organization and methods. The most important of these was the modernization of those segments of the culture necessary to make Japan into a military power which need no longer be fearful of foreign aggression. The ambition for military strength not only

Bibliographical Note: Nishimura Shigeki (pen name Hakuō) wrote over 130 books and 200 articles. Most of the articles and several of the more important books are contained in the *Hakuō sōsho* (hereafter *Sōsho*) (2 vols., 1909, 1912). The official biography, compiled by his Society, the Nihon Kōdōkai, is *Hakuō Nishimura Shigeki den* (hereafter *Den*) (2 vols., 1933). The principal published autobiographical records are *Ōjiroku* (*Hakuō zensho*, vol. 2, 1905) and *Kiokuroku* (1961). All of the preceding were published in Tokyo by the Nihon Kōdōkai. Other important biographies are Kaigo Tokiomi, *Nishimura Shigeki*, Sugiura Jūgō (Nihon kyōikuka bunko, vol. 44) (Tokyo, Hokkai shuppansha, 1937) and Yoshida Kumaji, *Nishimura Shigeki* (Nihon kyōiku sentetsu sōsho, vol. 20) (Tokyo, Bunkyō shoin, 1942). Two articles which proved particularly valuable were Ienaga Saburō, "Nishimura Shigeki ron," in his *Nihon kindai shisōshi kenkyū* (1954), pp. 133-168, and Motoyama Yukihiko "(Meiji zenhanki ni okeru) Nishimura Shigeki no kyōiku shisō," in *Sōritsu nijūgo shūnen kinen rombunshū* (Kyoto Daigaku jimbunkagaku kenkyūjo, 1954), pp. 432-451. The author wishes to express his debt to Sadako Nakamura Ogata for assistance in preparing some of the materials used in this study, and his gratitude to Motoyama Yukihiko, Ronald Dore, and to many other friends who made suggestions concerning this paper.

launched the process; it continued to determine the priorities and emphasis during a century of modernization.

From the outset there was controversy over which elements were essential for modernization. This discussion became nationwide when, upon the arrival of Commodore Perry, the Tokugawa government took the unprecedented step of asking the daimyo for advice, and they in turn instructed their domain administrators and scholars to draft proposals. There was general agreement on the necessity of learning the use and manufacture of the latest Western military equipment, cannons, warships, and fortification; many believed it necessary to develop a modern industrial and commercial base for military strength. The question was also raised whether it might not be necessary to introduce some elements of Western political organization and philosophy; in other words, whether these were essential to provide the conditions under which a high level of commercial and military power could be developed. Although the Tokugawa government took the lead in this investigation in the attempt to modernize and strengthen itself, it was hampered by the lack of agreement among its supporters and the hostility of factions at the Imperial Court and among the daimyo. The internal forces set in motion by the impact of the West finally brought the old structure down, and it was replaced by a new regime which had the flexibility and imagination to institute a modernization program of revolutionary proportions.

The Restoration brought to power a dozen or two young reformers who, as quickly as their power mounted, swept away much of the feudal structure, not only political, but also social and economic. Upon seizing power, the new regime committed itself on the one hand to restoring the ancient imperial political institutions, and simultaneously on the other hand, to a considerable degree of modernization.

The apparent contradictions in these programs are brought out in the popular slogans which were used in these days to dramatize the programs for building national strength, restoring imperial rule, and modernizing the country. Like most Chinese and Japanese slogans, they were made up of two-character compounds, usually paired, to which the ideographic nature of the script and the clipped Sino-Japanese readings gave a terse and authoritative ring. These were particularly effective for a people raised from the first school reader on moral injunctions of similar form which commanded strong emotional adherence. The lack of precision of the short, ex-hortative phrases made it possible to rally wide popular support behind the government's program. The extraordinary effec-tiveness of such catch-phrases in rallying public opinion to causes of any political coloration has been a characteristic of modern Japanese politics to the present day. The fluctuations in popularity of the early Meiji slogans seem to trace the trends of the day.

The changing fashion of these slogans was taken as an indication of the fickleness of the Japanese people and gov-ernment by Nishimura Shigeki (1828-1902). He was an of-ficial of both the old and new regimes, a Confucian-oriented pioneer in modernization, and one of the most vocal moral critics of his times. He was also irritated by the misuse and misinterpretation of the slogans, and as a moralist, attempted to rectify the meaning of these terms in the public mind. It will be useful, therefore, in introducing this paper on Nishi-mura's ideas about the kind of modernization that Japan needed and his criticisms of the government's program, to view the developments of his day in terms of some of the slogans.

The battle cry of the Imperial Restoration campaign was *sonnō jōi* ("Revere the Emperor, Repel the Barbarians"), appealing both to anti-Bakufu and anti-foreign sentiment. However, as the new leaders had already decided to drop this avowed policy to close the ports, the "Repel the Barbarians" part of the slogan was hushed before the civil war had ended.

Revering the Emperor seemed to become absorbed into the broader program under the slogan *fukko* ("Restore An-tiquity"), by which was meant the resurrection of the political institutions and titles of the imperial bureaucracy at its height in the eighth century, even to the revival of the Jingi-kan "Council of Deities," ranked above the Council of State.

But like the Jingi-kan, which was reduced in status in 1871 and then abolished in 1872, the ancient imperial institutions, having served their temporary purpose, were gradually de-emphasized and reorganized or replaced by more European-type offices. Similarly, the use of Shintō to propagandize and bolster the new regime waned in the trend toward a secular state. As the movement by the court nobility to revive the *ancien régime* lost impetus, even the process of sanctifying the emperor was given scant attention for the next decade or more. The revival of antiquity was deemphasized as soon as the oligarchs felt strong enough to institute a full-scale program of modernization. They recognized that the commercial and military strength of Western nations was a product of their entire heritage, and that Japan, if she were to gain the strength of modern nations, must have a similar system of government and education.

The program to carry out this modernization of Japan was popularized by the slogan *bummei kaika* ("Civilization and Enlightenment"), which overshadowed all others throughout the 1870's and 1880's. It grew out of the emperor's Charter Oath of 1868, which forecast deliberative assemblies, participation of all classes in government, freedom of occupation, the search for knowledge throughout the world. It also decreed that "evil customs of the past shall be broken off and everything based upon the just laws of Nature." As this last statement suggests, the modernizers considered that many of the usages and practices connected with the feudal system were barbaric and shameful and that they must be replaced by the civilized practices of the West. The slogan "Civilization and Enlightenment" seems to have caught on particularly from about 1873 with the return of the Iwakura Mission from the United States and Europe. From 1871 to 1873 the government had instituted the prefectural system, postal system, modern coinage, Gregorian calendar, railways, national banks, and Western education systems. To some of the populace, these accomplishments were what the slogan meant, and they carried it onto the personal level with the imitation of Western dress, haircuts, food, and architecture. There was nowhere more talk of "Civilization and Enlightenment" than in the Meirokusha, "Meiji Six Society," named for the year of its formation in 1873 by the leading students of the West and the most progressive thinkers of the day to discuss the problems involved in the modernization of Japan. To some of the members of this Society, including Nishimura Shigeki who was one of the founders, the slogan meant first of all the movement for the advancement of the individual's knowledge and the development of his character and conduct.[1]

The slogan was general enough in usage so that no one was put in the awkward position of having to confess that he was opposed to civilization or enlightenment. On the point of specifically which segments of Japanese life should be modernized, however, there was wide range of opinion. There were those like Motoda Eifu (1818-1891) who favored as few changes as possible, who conceded the necessity to modernize the military forces, industry, and trade, but to whom the modern innovations being introduced into government were inferior to the idyllic political and moral conditions which he fancied had existed over a millennium before, during the golden age of Confucianism in Japan.[2] On the other extreme there were those who would remake the Japanese in the image of the European, inside and out, even though it would take conversion to Christianity or miscegenation or both to do it.

The adherents of such extreme views were few, however, for most of the political and intellectual leaders thought more in terms of how much and how rapidly Japan could be modernized without weakening the unity of the people. An essential consideration in maintaining unity and discipline was to preserve certain essential characteristics of Japanese culture

---

[1] Nishimura defined *bummei kaika* saying that it is a translation of the English word "civilization," but that "the Chinese translate 'civilization' as 'to advance in propriety and manners,' and if translated into colloquial Japanese it would be 'personal character becoming good.'" "Seigo kai" (April 1875), *Sōsho*, 2.12-13.

[2] See Shively, "Motoda Eifu: Confucian Lecturer to the Meiji Emperor," pp. 313-317 in *Confucianism in Action*, ed. D. S. Nivison and A. F. Wright (Stanford, 1959).

which were considered to have spiritual or moral value, among which the emperor system and the family system were two of the greatest sources of stability. The program of development through the first decades, therefore, cannot be defined exclusively in terms of "Civilization and Enlightenment" or Westernization, for the process of modernization in Japan relied also on the utilization of traditional elements suggested by the earlier slogan.

Nishimura pointed out in a talk before the Meirokusha in 1875 that the two slogans are contradictory: " 'Revere the Emperor, Repel the Barbarians' means to admire antiquity and despise the present, to respect superiors and to disdain inferiors, to hold one's own country in high esteem and to detest other countries. 'Civilization and Enlightenment' means to discard the old and take the new, to deprive those above and to benefit those below, to cast off the attitude of esteeming one's country and to be active in friendly relations with other countries."[3]

There was another slogan, however, which came closer than these slogans to the true character of Meiji Japan: *fukoku kyōhei* ("Enrich the Nation, Strengthen its Arms"). Although this had been a catchword from about the time of Perry's arrival, it had later become subsumed under "Civilization and Enlightenment." If the latter meant modernization in a broad sense, "Enrich the Nation, Strengthen its Arms" meant modernization in the selective way in which it was actually carried out in the Meiji period, that is, changing only those elements in the culture which inhibited the creation of a highly centralized state equipped with strong military forces supported by industrial power. Because such was the Meiji program, unencumbered by value judgments about the worth of modernization or Westernization, any suitable institutions and ideas could be incorporated, regardless of whether they came from the liberal West or the authoritarian West, whether they were native traditions or myths newly created.

The traditional elements which played an important part

[3] "Tekkan setsu" (1875), *Sōsho*, 2.38.

in Meiji Japan could not be reconciled with "Civilization and Enlightenment," but they served the purposes of "Enrich the Nation, Strengthen its Arms." Some were resurrected from the distant past, such as those concerned with the emperor system or with State Shintō. Most of these were *forcing* tradition. For example, the rehabilitation of ancient political institutions was almost as arbitrary as the introduction of Central European political institutions, but the two in fact often blended rather effectively, as in the hybrid peerage system of 1884. Other types of traditional elements which were alive in the culture were more legitimate. For example, some of the attitudes of the samurai class in Tokugawa society, which had seemed to be inundated for a time by the tide of "Civilization and Enlightenment," gradually rose again to play an important role in the family system, bushido, and the moral education of the Meiji period. These traditional elements were all present when the victory of "Enrich the Nation, Strengthen its Arms" became clear, and the slogan "Civilization and Enlightenment" died with the promulgation of the Constitution of 1889 (which was supposed to be a symbol of enlightenment) and the Imperial Rescript on Education of the next year.

It was this cause that Nishimura Shigeki had foremost in mind during his fifty years of public service, although his activities changed from feudal administrator to Meiji enlightener to moralist. He sharply disagreed, however, with the methods and priorities employed by the Meiji government in this program. He considered that the government had consistently shown its superficiality and lack of purpose by frequent changes of policy and by its travesty of the meaning of "civilization." This, in his opinion, was because it did not have established principles of morality to guide it, and refused to recognize that this was the fundamental requirement for strengthening the country. The great unifying and educating force of the Tokugawa period had been Neo-Confucian teachings which established the moral basis for personal conduct, social order, and national purpose. However, because Confucianism had served as the rationalization of the old

regime, it was rejected both by the advocates of enlightenment and by those bent on sanctifying the emperor. As Nishimura said, "The Way of Confucius and Mencius has fallen,
but the moral science of the Western countries has not yet
come in. This condition is like the time when the sun has set
but the moon has not yet risen."[4] And this was at a time of
Japan's great crisis, when government and people needed
special qualities for the urgent job of nation building—virtues
such as courage, dedication to duty, fortitude, frugality, and
patriotism, which would help them in making the sacrifices.
Nishimura said also that the Japanese should be selective,
willing to forgo many of the luxuries of Western civilization
until they had sufficient wealth and strength. Nishimura devoted the last decades of his life to the attempt to develop and
propagate a moral system to meet the needs of Japan in the
process of modernization, a system which would be the core
of the educational curriculum as Neo-Confucianism had been
before the Restoration, and which would guide the conduct of
all the people and serve as a moral basis for the government.

This was, especially in the terms in which Nishimura stated
it, a Confucian view of how to go about modernizing. Not
only this concept, but many of the elements which went into
it and the basic attitudes which he had toward society, were
carried over from his Confucian background. However, there
were many principles of Confucianism which he abandoned
or modified, and whatever his misconceptions about his own
knowledge of the West, it would only be misleading to speak
of him as a Confucianist except in the loosest Meiji usage.

When Nishimura first urged the necessity of a system of
morality for the nation, the oligarchs, failing to recognize in
the West any such system, did not seem to regard it to be an
essential condition for strength in modern states. By the late
1880's, however, as the age of constitutional government approached, when the sentiment of the people could no longer
be entirely ignored, some of the oligarchs began to sense the
utility of such a system. It would help to strengthen national

[4] "Shūshin chikoku nito ni arazaru ron" (1875), Sōsho, 2.6.

unity in the face of foreign religious and political doctrines
and to provide a common set of values such as they themselves
had received through their own Neo-Confucian school books.
To a considerable extent their attitudes of mind, and some of
the basic premises of their thinking, were molded by their
early education. It is not surprising, therefore, that there was
a growing awareness of the value of a national moral system,
based largely on traditional values, to unify the people undergoing the stress of rapid change. This led to the reemergence
of Confucian virtues as the basis of education in the Imperial
Rescript of 1890, a movement in which Nishimura had a
considerable role.

Although Nishimura had been one of the pioneers in the
enlightenment movement of 1873, we find him increasingly
associated with conservative and even reactionary movements,
not only in moral education, but also in his opposition to the
Westernization policy and treaty revision plans of the government in the late 1880's. Nishimura's dual role, apparently
contradictory, as enlightener and reactionary, suggests either
that he underwent a major change in his thought, or else that
he was inconsistent. Neither seems to have been the case.
Rather, his outlook differed from the prevailing ones on
points of priority and selectivity in the process of modernization. While his views might seem inconsistent or even anach-
ronistic in the late 1880's, they can be better appreciated if
we recognize that he had brought with him to the problems
of Meiji modernization an inordinate number of the basic
attitudes of a Tokugawa period Confucian-educated scholar.

From Tokugawa Official to Meiji Modernizer

Nishimura Shigeki was born in 1828, the eldest son of a
samurai in the service of the Hotta family, lord of Sakura.
This modest domain, assessed at 110,000 *koku*, was one of the
closest to Edo, and the Hotta were long prominent in the
councils of the Tokugawa Bakufu. The Hotta was one of
only four families from which the position of *Tairō*, the
Shogun's highest official, was usually filled. Nishimura's
father, Yoshiiku, like his grandfather before him, was assigned

the post of chief administrator of the subfief of Sano (14,000 *koku*). Yoshiiku, serving Hotta Masayoshi (1810-1864), who was one of the most progressive daimyo of the day and a member of the Senior Council (*rōjū*) from 1841 to 1843, made proposals to him on the reform of the bakufu. He also played an important part in developing education in the fief, including Dutch studies; he experimented in Western military methods, and cast and test-fired cannon.

Although Shigeki was only 22 when his father died in 1850, he was already well trained to succeed him. After preparation in the Confucian classics, he had studied the *Dainihonshi* and the *Nihon gaishi*. He received particular encouragement in his studies from the famous Confucian scholar, Yasui Sokken, who had been engaged for the domain school by his father. When he was twenty (*sai*) he read the *Shinron* of Aizawa Seishisai (1782-1863) of the nearby Mito domain, which set forth a bold program for reviving the spirit of the samurai and reforming the administration of the domains in preparation for dealing with the incursions of the foreign powers. Shigeki was deeply impressed with the proposals and agreed with them all except for Aizawa's vilification of the barbarians. Educated in an atmosphere of a double crisis, with the foreign menace exposing the weakness of the feudal system, his studies turned to Hayashi Shihei's work on coastal defense and translations of Dutch books on military tactics and gunnery.[5]

In 1851 he entered the school of Sakuma Shōzan (1811-1864) in Edo in order to improve his knowledge of Western gunnery. Shigeki reports in his autobiography the advice he received from Sakuma, who said: "Gunnery is the branch; Western studies is the root. You should engage in Western studies now. I studied Dutch books for the first time when I was thirty (*sai*). You are still young compared with when I began. You should set your aim and work hard at Western studies."[6] Shigeki writes that at that time he did not agree with this advice. His only objective was Western gunnery as

[5] *Den*, 1.1-34; Kaigo, pp. 8-18; *Ōjiroku*, pp. 1-28.
[6] *Ōjiroku*, pp. 35-36.

a means to repel the barbarians, and he was confident that Eastern learning was superior to Western in morality and government. But after thinking it over, he saw the reasonableness of his teacher's argument, and began the study of Dutch the next year.

During the following years he wrote a number of essays on Dutch books which he was studying—books on geography, products, navigation, and commerce—and discoursed on the importance of these subjects for Japan. As he put it in one of the essays: "If those in authority will learn about the products of the entire world, and learn the methods of manufacturing and commerce from this book, and thereafter, . . . if the plans are established for making the nation wealthy and strong, then we may succeed in surpassing England and France and overtaking Russia and America. . . ."[7] It appears that at 24 Shigeki was following in his father's steps as a progressive feudal administrator with a concern for national affairs. He had picked up the more radical proposals of the day, which, in the terms of the late Tokugawa period, were the beginnings of a plan for the modernization of Japan.

The necessity for a reexamination of Japan's situation was dramatized the next year by the arrival of Commodore Perry with an ultimatum demanding the opening of the country to trade. Nishimura was instructed by Lord Hotta to prepare a series of proposals on steps to be taken to deal with the foreign menace and the need for internal reforms, proposals which were forwarded to Abe Masahiro (1819-1857), head of the *rōjū*. A more original plan put forward by Nishimura at the same time was his proposal that, despite the rigid seclusion policy, the bakufu should permit him to go to Holland for three years of study in ordnance and fortification, to be concluded by a visit to "the various Western countries in order to investigate the climate, topography, and the nature of the people." Although this proposal came to naught because a senior official of the fief refused to forward it, it is an indication of Nishimura's pioneering spirit, coming as it did several

---

[7] Preface to *Sugen tsūron* (1862), *Den*, 1.209.

months before Yoshida Shōin made his ill-fated attempt to go abroad.[8]

During the next five years Nishimura prepared a large number of proposals on national issues for Hotta, who succeeded Abe as head of the *rōjū*. These proposals dealt with a large variety of problems, from the foreign challenge to reconstituting the spirit of the samurai class. Many of these suggestions can also be found in proposals made by other scholars during these years, such as curtailing the *sankin kōtai*, resettling samurai on the land, eliminating wasteful ceremonial and formal observances, abandoning obsolete traditions, and "opening up channels of expression." His proposal that officials be selected on the basis of intelligence and talent rather than lineage carried the suggestion that the conditions should be removed which favored officials who were conformists or unimaginative time-servers. He also proposed the clear differentiation of function between samurai who were civil and those who were military officials, with each official given authority within a defined area to make his decision alone and have sole responsibility for it. He proposed also that in order to carry on trade with foreigners, large ships should be built and trading stations be established abroad.[9]

Nishimura's direct involvement in foreign policy came in 1856, shortly before Townsend Harris reached Shimoda to negotiate a commercial treaty. At that time Hotta brought him into his office to deal with the documents pertaining to foreign affairs. Presumably he had a part in the development of the progressive policy of opening the country for trade, and, at the beginning of 1858, he accompanied Hotta as his secretary to Kyoto in the vain attempt to secure imperial sanction for the treaty to which the Tokugawa government was already committed.

Later in the year, when Hotta was eased out of the Bakufu councils by Ii Naosuke, Nishimura returned to his duties as a fief administrative official, which he performed for the next

[8] *Sōsho*, 1.329-331; *Den*, 1.119-124; Motoyama, p. 436.
[9] *Den*, 1.56-193, especially pp. 72-78, 100-101, 140-147, 172-177, 187-188.

twelve years until after the Meiji Restoration. He continued his study of Dutch, and in 1861 began to learn English under Tezuka Ritsuzō (1823-1878), the first teacher of English in Edo. This was a painstaking task, for although Tezuka, in collaboration with Nishi Amane, had written the first English grammar, there was no English-Japanese dictionary available; English books were translated via Dutch into Japanese. Another difficulty, according to Nishimura's autobiography, was that his study had to be conducted in great secrecy because of constant danger of assault by anti-foreign zealots.[10]

As a consequence of his studies and the English books he translated during these years, in 1868, when the Imperial government was restored, Nishimura was one of the nation's best informed Western experts. He was concerned that the Imperial Court, intent only on destroying the power of the Tokugawa adherents, might not be adequately informed about the danger of foreign intervention. He drafted, therefore, an analysis of the weaknesses of Japan and the steps that the government should take to overcome them, and sent it in the form of a memorial to Iwakura Tomomi in the fourth month of 1868. He stated that the weakness of Japan in comparison with Western nations was due primarily to differences of race, but that there were secondary causes of learning and tradition which could, at least, be remedied. He described the faults of Asian learning as follows: "So far, Asian learning has been concerned mainly with how to govern one country, and has not known how to apply itself broadly to the whole world. Therefore theories are narrow and tend to be bigoted. The distinction between lord and subject has been too severe, the difference between high and low too extreme. Trivialities and details are given careful attention, but world-shaking achievements are unknown. Within this small country, the people criticize each other's faults and expose each other's secrets. Therefore the intelligence of the people daily becomes more limited, their knowledge daily becomes narrower. They become impractical or go to extremes, and what they can see in

[10] *Ōjiroku*, p. 65; *Den*, 1.248.

their entire lives is confined to the walls of their school. These are the evils of Asian learning."

As he continues this discussion he appears to criticize the spirit of the Restoration: "Furthermore, the temperament of Asians is to prefer the old and abhor the new. When they reform the government they call it 'restoring antiquity' (*fukko*), and when they discuss morality they call it 'revering antiquity.' In manufacturing weapons they imitate the old system, and when they set up institutions they base them on ancient laws. In general, since opportunities in the world open up year by year, it cannot be that the ancient is superior to the present. . . . Also the temperament of Asians is to venerate empty words and not to discuss practical use. They consider long robes and wide sashes to be superior to short clothes and narrow sleeves, and they think of empty positions and hollow titles as superior to actual wealth and real flourishing. Therefore men's talents mostly tend to lack bearing and are not suitable for practical use. These are the peculiarities in taste of Asians."

The potentiality of the Japanese is also being restricted, he continued, by the Asian characteristics of petty quarrels and smallness of aims and ambition. "If we wish to extend the prestige of the nation abroad, we must get away from bigoted and narrow knowledge and views. Instead we must know the greatness of the five continents and learn that our country is but one corner of the whole globe. We must dissolve the hatred and discord within the country and establish great aspirations. We should consider the achievements of Empress Jingu, Toyotomi Hideyoshi, the Chin Emperor, and Han Wu-ti as too small to be our models, and take as our teachers Alexander, Caesar, Peter, and Napoleon. Then we can expect to gain the greatness of Russia and America and the strength of England and France." If such are to be Japan's ambitions, the first step is to set up a suitable form of government, then to proceed to enrich the nation and strengthen its arms. "The foundation for enriching the nation is to develop industry and trade; the foundation for strengthening its arms is to unite the people's minds through education."[11] To the second part of this program he was to devote the last decades of his life.

In the next decade, however, he was concerned less with unifying the minds of the people than with pioneer efforts to inform the public as well as the officials about the rest of the world. He made a reputation as an enlightener, first through the publication of his translations, and later through participation in the Meirokusha. Among his first publications were: *An Outline History of the World* (*Bankoku shiryaku*) (1869, revised and expanded in 1872), *Mirror of the History of the West* (*Taisei shikan*) (1869), *Chronology of Western History* (*Seishi nempyō*) (1870), *Household Economics* (*Kachū keizai*) (1873), *Essentials of Economics* (*Keizai yōshi*) (1874), and *A History of Education* (*Kyōiku shi*) (1875). He also wrote the eleventh and twelfth volumes of Uchida Masao's world geography, *Yochi shiryaku*, completing the work which had been left unfinished at the author's death.[12] In 1874 he also translated Laurens Hickok's *Moral Science*, published under the title of *Kyūshokisei kōgi*. Although these works are usually referred to as translations, Nishimura usually drew on material from a number of books in English and adapted the material for the Japanese reader.[13]

Nishimura's prefaces to his translations urged the Japanese to widen the horizons of their knowledge, stating, as in *An Outline History of the World*: "We take the sages and heroes of our own country and respect them and regard them as models to which nothing need be added. But we might not know that among the sages and heroes of the world are those who are superior to those that we praise of our own country. . . . Unless we are proficient in five different languages, we

[11] *Sōsho*, 1.368-370.

[12] He ranked this work as one of the three most important contributions to the enlightenment of the people made during the early years after the Restoration, together with Fukuzawa Yukichi's *Seiyō jijō* (*Conditions in the West*) and Nakamura Keiu's *Saikoku risshihen*, a translation of Samuel Smiles' *Self-Help*. *Den*, 1.319-335, 382-392.

[13] Laurens P. Hickok, *A System of Moral Science* (Schenectady, 1853). *Den*, 1.457-464.

cannot speak of breadth, and unless we read the books of all countries, we cannot speak of learning." Confucian scholars, because of their ignorance of the West, he continued, are one-sided and bigoted.[14]

Nishimura also stated that the systems of government of England and America, with their division of three powers, were the best in the world, while the weakness of Asian countries was in considerable part due to the organization of government. In Asia the rulers and bureaucrats attempted to hold the three powers concurrently because they were fearful of losing power. However, in time, as the peoples became better educated, they would clamor for popular rights, would rise, and take by force what was not being given to them. Rulers should look with caution at the rise of Cromwell.[15]

In his prefaces, Nishimura also developed the idea that it is the responsibility of the government not only to govern well, but also to provide the conditions under which people might prosper and the nation become wealthy. The government should therefore practice the virtues of justice, impartiality, and generosity.[16] Western nations were wealthy because the governments were just and fair in the protection of individual property and because the people were frugal and diligent.[17]

The proposal to establish the Meirokusha, the Society which assumed the leadership in the movement for enlightenment and intellectual advance, seems to have been originated by Mori Arinori upon his return from Washington in 1873, where he had been the Japanese *Chargé*. He pointed to the existence of learned societies in Western countries, and urged that Japanese scholars should abandon the tradition of remaining aloof from society, that they should hold public discussions and give lectures in order "to advance learning and to attempt to establish models of morality." Mori turned for help to Nishimura and he in turn enlisted the participation of Fukuzawa Yukichi, Nakamura Masanao, Katō Hiroyuki,

[14] Preface to *Bankoku shiryaku, Den*, 1.323-324.
[15] Preface to *Kōsei bankoku shiryaku, Den*, 1.328-330.
[16] Preface to *Seishi nempyō, Den*, 1.321.
[17] Preface to *Kachū keizai, Den*, 1.382-383.

Tsuda Masamichi, Nishi Amane, and Mitsukuri Rinshō—in short, the private scholars and officials best informed about the West.[18] Their monthly discussion meetings and lectures, open to the public and attended by many government officials, were for several years perhaps the most important channel for the introduction of information and ideas from the West; and the activities of the group became even more important with the launching of their journal, *Meiroku zasshi*, in 1874.

Nishimura not only played a leading role in the Meirokusha, but took the initiative in organizing in 1875 the Yōyōsha, a similar society for academic discussion. He contributed lectures and articles to these two societies on subjects ranging from political freedom, the rights and duties of citizens, the harmonizing of the government's program with the interests of the people, to trade protectionism, the tax system, language reform, and public morals. He advocated government assistance to vital industries, and the patriotic investment of the stipends of the former daimyo as capital for these industries. He argued for the necessity of checking the growth of Japan's population, suggesting to this end the encouragement of late marriage (as in the West) and a prohibition against keeping mistresses (which would also serve a moral purpose).[19]

Whatever the efficacy might have been of such proposals, we find him time and again making critical and original comments on the conditions and developments of the day. He observed in 1875 that the current practice of calling enemies of the Court *"zoku"* showed as much ignorance and bigotry as the habit, before the Age of Enlightenment, of calling the foreigners "barbarians." *"Zoku* is a word which means a person who steals or kills or threatens others, and it is not a word which means those who oppose the emperor. . . . That is a vile usage which is the practice in despotic monarchies, being caused by excessive respect for the sovereign. We ridicule the Chinese for excessive pride and self-esteem. However, strangely enough, in the use of this word *zoku* we have appropriated the distorted view of the Chinese without

[18] This account of the founding appears in *Ōjiroku*, pp. 164-166.
[19] *Den*, 1.401-422, 465-478.

any modification."[20] Nishimura's admonition was to no avail, for in the 1930's the "feudal custom" still prevailed of calling one's political opponents "*kokuzoku*," "traitors to the country."[21]

A matter of more consequence was the petition submitted by Itagaki, Soejima, Gotō, Etō, and others to the government in January, 1874, proposing the establishment of an elected house. The petition was summarily rejected, and several members of the Meirokusha, among them Mori, Nishi, and Katō, also wrote articles attacking the proposal. However, Nishimura submitted a petition in which he said that he did not know the petitioners himself, nor did he mean to argue the merits of their particular proposal. He would protest, however, that their proposal had not received careful study, and that it was being dismissed as without merit because it was written in passionate or excited language. Passion, said Nishimura, was not necessarily bad. There is good passion like the rebellion of Washington and Franklin, and bad passion like that of Robespierre and Danton. Nor was it inappropriate to consider seriously the establishment of a popularly elected body at this time. From the rational or theoretical point of view, such a government institution was just and fair. Furthermore, its practicality was demonstrated by the wealth and power of European countries and the United States. Nor was it too early to introduce such a body, for the English parliament began in 1265, and clever as the English people are, surely they were not more clever six hundred years ago than the Japanese are today. In recent years Japan had made rapid advances in building railways, steamships, and introducing electricity. However, these are the branches; but the root, the political system, had not yet been established. This is the most important question of the day, and the greatest priority should be given to the establishment of an elected body.[22]

Although such a statement might sound "liberal" in the context of 1874, Nishimura had rather little interest in West-

[20] "Zoku setsu" (1875), *Sōsho*, 2.10. [21] Ienaga, p. 150.
[22] *Den*, 1.396-398; text in *Sōsho*, 1.375-377.

ern political liberalism, nor did he have any political program for Japan. He stood, rather, for impartiality by the government, justice, and fairness. He was also for innovations which would make for national unity and strength.

Nishimura's service in the Meiji government began in 1873 when he was appointed Chief of the Compilation Section of the Ministry of Education, a post he served for thirteen years. Under his direction, the Section compiled not only textbooks, but the first large-scale dictionary and encyclopedia of modern times, and also edited the books prepared by the Translation Section.

Nishimura's activity as an enlightener led to his appointment in 1875 as Lecturer (*jikō*) on Western Books to the Meiji Emperor, replacing Katō Hiroyuki who had resigned. At this time Fukuba Bisei (1831-1907) lectured to the emperor on Japanese books, and Motoda Eifu (1818-1891) was the Lecturer on Chinese Books.[23] The next year he succeeded in being released from this duty of lecturing six times a week because of his work at the Ministry of Education, but it appears that in actuality he continued on a less formal appointment to lecture very frequently before the emperor for ten years and that he continued to give New Year lectures until 1894. He also served as a lecturer to four princes of the blood from 1877 to 1880, and in 1886 he left the Ministry of Education for a full-time appointment at the court.[24]

Nishimura the Conservative

During the first decade of the Meiji period, Nishimura appears, as we have seen, in the forefront of Japan's intellectual leaders, one of the very few who introduced Western history and ethics. He was a pioneer in the modernization of Japan in this period, but this cannot be said for the remainder of his career. It became increasingly evident that he was not in the main current of the times, in particular after 1876 when much of his activity shifted to insisting on moral reform as the first step in modernization. When Japanese officials and

[23] Shively, pp. 309-310.
[24] *Den*, 1.423-426.

students began to return from the United States and Europe by the dozens, Nishimura, who had never been abroad, could no longer speak with as much authority about the civilization of the West. He was distressed by the uncritical enthusiasm with which these younger men would transplant everything they found abroad without consideration of its appropriateness in Japan. He felt that the government was leading the people too rapidly to adopt Western ways, from political institutions to dress, and that unnecessary as well as precipitous changes were being made at the expense of important parts of the Japanese heritage.

For example, in lamenting the inadequacies of the new educational system, he wrote, in 1890: "If we had not lost the spirit of the education of the domain samurai when the domains were abolished, but had carried them over into the national education, we should not have lost the virtues of loyalty, filial piety, honor, and duty which had been cultivated for several centuries, nor would educated men today need to deplore that morality has fallen to the ground. . . . If today we want to develop moral education on national principles, we should take the former education as our model."[25] In the same year he also said that the Four Books of the Confucian classics were, to his knowledge, without rival in the world as texts for moral education, and should be used in the schools.[26] He also remembered nostalgically the institutions and observances which had supported the feudal code. He said that "there are not a few ways in which the ills of the day can be cured by selecting and using [Tokugawa] law, morality, economics, education, and customs (but not the entirety of these)."[27] Writing in 1894, he said: "The four things which helped to cultivate the martial spirit of the Japanese were the feudal system, harakiri, vendetta, and the wearing of swords. However, now these are all abolished. This

[25] "Nihon kyōiku ron" (April 1890), *Sōsho*, 2.451.

[26] "Shūshin kyōkasho no setsu" (August 1890), *Sōsho*, 2.539-540. Also, p. 238, below. A number of the examples in this and the following section of the chapter were suggested by Ienaga's article.

[27] *Sōsho*, 2.529.

is most regrettable. . . . The law forbidding the wearing of swords was issued in 1876 . . . and must be called a major blunder in governing. This excess should quickly be remedied today and the law of 1876 rescinded. . . ."[28]

Westernization in its worst sense for Nishimura came in the mid-1880's. This was Itō's sweeping reorganization of governmental offices and the opening of the Rokumeikan, the club which brought to Japan all of the trappings of the diplomatic social life of a European capital. Concerning the developments of these years, Nishimura's view was: ". . . the new administration of the Itō Cabinet imitated Europe and America in every detail in the legal system, customs, and ceremonial, and decked itself completely with foreign civilization. It gave special hospitality to foreigners, presenting such foreign amusements as balls, masquerades, tableaux vivants, assiduously sought to win their favor, and seemed to disregard and abandon the spirit of loyalty, filial piety, honor, duty, valor, and shame which had been the traditional foundation of our country since ancient times. The officials who were appointed were largely men of cleverness and flattery, and those who were simple and sturdy were always rejected. . . . After carrying on for one year, the customs and manners of the people became increasingly rash and flippant and frivolous."[29]

The display of Western institutions, and particularly of customs, was calculated in considerable part to impress the Western powers with the degree of Westernization that had taken place in Japan. In this way it was hoped that more favorable terms could be gained in revising the unequal treaties and in curtailing extraterritoriality. However, some of the concessions which the government was planning to make to the foreigners became known in July of 1889 to the officials of the Imperial Household Ministry. A group of them, comprised of Miura Gorō, Tani Kanjō, Soejima Taneomi, Motoda Eifu, and Nishimura Shigeki, began to hold meetings

[28] "Kokka dōtoku ron" (1894), *Sōsho*, 1.107-108; *Kiokuroku*, pp. 46-47.
[29] *Ōjiroku*, pp. 193-194. See also p. 69-70, above.

to plan their opposition, and they made visitations upon the cabinet ministers to express their objections.

Nishimura drafted a memorial in September in which he opposed the concession of unrestricted residence to foreigners on the grounds that this would result in the wealth and land of the country passing into their hands, and then the country would be taken from within. "What is the use of feeding the robbers in the room now, and vainly strengthening the gate and wall," he declared.[30] He also objected to the employment of foreign judges in mixed cases before the high court, as they would always be prejudiced in favor of foreigners. He argued that the foreign judges, in combination with the new Western-style law code, far from curtailing extraterritoriality, amounted to extending it throughout the country.[31] He protested further that the government was conducting the negotiations in secret in order to confront the people with a *fait accompli* before the first session of the Diet, "driving the ignorant people on to collision with these sly and greedy foreigners." If by any chance there were any mistakes made in these treaties, "and any part of the nation's prestige were damaged, even though the entire people would beg forgiveness for their crime before the spirits of the Imperial Ancestors, it would be too late." The existing treaties, with all their defects, at least kept the foreigners at a distance, and were less harmful than the new treaties being negotiated.[32] The protests of Nishimura and his colleagues contributed to the opposition which brought about the collapse of that series of negotiations.

The fear of foreign powers was very real to Nishimura even at this late date, thirty-six years after Perry's expedition. He said that "Western people did not attain naturally their rich nations and strong armaments. They reached today's wealth and strength by seizing the land and accumulating the wealth of other countries over several centuries."[33] And the

---

[30] "Jōyaku kaisei ni tsuki kengen," *Sōsho*, 1.397-411, p. 404.
[31] *Sōsho*, 1.405.   [32] *Sōsho*, 1.407-409.
[33] "Kōdōkai taii no enzetsu" (May 1890), *Sōsho*, 2.502.

process was continuing: "In recent years all the Western countries have the intention of extending their power in the Orient. Everybody has seen that France has taken Annam, England has overthrown Burma and seized the Komun Islands of Korea, Germany has seized the South Sea Islands, and Russia has been trying to expand her territory southward. Japan stands high out of the Eastern Sea, and since her geographical features are favorable and her products abundant, it is obvious that the Western powers have for some time been drooling over our country. It is not easy to maintain our independence being situated in such an imperiled place. . . . Therefore, in today's situation it is our urgent duty to unite the power of the entire people in order to preserve the independence of the country. . . ."[34]

He complained that most people were interested only in personal matters and not in the interests of the country. Merchants thought only of making profit by unethical means, party politicians wanted only to beat the opposition parties, and lawyers wanted to make profits on the misfortunes of others. "None turn their eyes abroad and wish to work together as a nation in order to vie with the white people for supremacy."[35]

From about 1886 on, Nishimura had even greater praise for traditional morality, saying that ". . . the beauty of our customs and manners, and the loftiness of our morality for over 2500 years since the beginning of our country, can be said to be unsurpassed in the world . . . ," and that "in Japan, there exists perfect moral teaching which is thousands and thousands of times superior to religions."[36] The spirit of the people should be given direction by fostering their devotion to the sacred imperial family, for it is a destiny unparalleled in the world that the nation had been ruled for 2,500 years by a single family of emperors of unmixed lineage.[37]

[34] "Nihon dōtoku ron" (Feb. 1887), *Sōsho*, 1.8.
[35] "Kōdōkai taii no enzetsu," *Sōsho*, 2.505-506.
[36] *Den*, 1.660, 663.
[37] "Nihon dōtoku ron," *Sōsho*, 1.91-92.

Nishimura the Progressive

On the basis of such statements, it is understandable that Nishimura had a reputation after 1876 of having turned conservative, or even reactionary, and that he had become an aggressive nationalist. Nishimura's general attitude, however, was not reactionary in the sense of wishing to restore or preserve the past. Rather, he believed that the proper way to progress was not to cut oneself off from the past. Sound progress would be made by remodeling existing institutions, modernizing them, instead of discarding them for new ones whose appropriateness to Japanese conditions was unpredictable. Although he believed Confucian texts to be the most suitable for school books, he pointed out the inadequacies of Confucianism as a doctrine for Japan's needs in the modern world. "There are five reasons why we should not follow the Confucian Way exclusively. First is that recently some Western studies, especially physiology and psychology, have become extremely refined in their investigation. However, Confucian theories do not coincide with these studies, and it is inevitable that they would obstruct each other. Second, Confucianism has many words of prohibition but few words of encouragement. Thus people become contented in being conservative and lack progressiveness. In the situation today, unless a progressive spirit is cultivated, it will be impossible to extend the prestige of the nation. Third, Confucianism is advantageous for ascendants and disadvantageous for descendants. The ascendants seem to have rights but no obligations and the descendants seem to have obligations but no rights. Although such an arrangement is necessary in putting a country in order, the abuse seems to be a little too excessive. Fourth, Confucianism has too many instances of respecting men and looking down on women and is not fair in discussing their relationship. Men are not blamed even if they keep several wives and mistresses, but it teaches that women should not remarry when their husbands die. There is much that seems extremely incompatible with present and future conditions. Fifth, Confucianism regards antiquity as good and the present as wrong, and demands on every occasion that we imitate the peaceful reigns of Yao and Shun and the Three Dynasties. . . . Under the present conditions of Japan, of course, it is not possible to imitate Yao, Shun, and the Three Dynasties, and moreover, we should not try."[38]

On another occasion he wrote: "Loyalty and filial piety, needless to say, are beautiful virtues. However, when Confucian scholars and scholars of Japanese studies expound them, they exaggerate them excessively and some miss the proper order of root and branches, importance and unimportance. The *Classic on Filial Piety* says that governing the nation, governing a province, governing oneself and the family, all can be done by means of filial piety. When we just hear this it sounds extremely reasonable, but the reality is definitely not accomplished in this way. In order to govern the nation there is a way and a technique. . . . If, by serving our father and mother well the nation would be well governed, it would be very easy, but this is definitely not the principle for governing a nation."[39] He also said: "Filial piety and brotherly love, which are limited to the family, are teachings which are extremely simple, whereas such principles as faithfulness and justice, since they are concerned with the whole of society, are important to study for many reasons and are extremely vital for their effect on the nation."[40]

On the traditional extended family, he said: "For the entire family to live in the same house was considered very noble in the Chinese morality of the later period, but in practice it does not serve any useful purpose. It is harmful in binding the promising and talented younger members of the family, and does not benefit society in the slightest."[41]

Although Nishimura said that moral education should be directed by the imperial household, he made no mention of

[38] *Ibid.*, pp. 23-24. Related to the shortcomings of Confucianism were his remarks on the inferiority of Eastern science, particularly: (1) its excessive reliance on books, (2) its exclusive use of the deductive method, (3) its lack of the comparative method. *Den*, 1.696.

[39] "Hakuō shigen," Ser. 2 (1881-1887), *Sōsho*, 1.534-535.

[40] "Jishikiroku" (1900), *Sōsho*, 1.661.

[41] "Nihon dōtoku ron," *Sōsho*, 1.51.

the descent of virtue from the divine imperial ancestors, and showed only hostility for mythology and Shintō. He said that the attempt to encourage Shintō through the Jingi-kan had failed because "its teachings could not keep pace with the rate of development of the people's intelligence at that time."[42] And also, ". . . if scholarship were limited to Japan, it would be similar to certain scholars of Japanese studies expounding the *Kojiki*, and it would become bigoted and obstinate and stupid scholarship."[43]

Nishimura gave extremely high priority to the development of strong military forces and to fostering the growth of patriotic spirit. However, his objective seems to have been only for the defense of the country. He did not follow his countrymen when they went on to chauvinism and aggression. He argued that a country was only secure when it had armaments appropriately scaled to its wealth, and that neither a rich country with weak armaments nor a poor country with strong armaments could long remain secure. In 1895, at the conclusion of the Sino-Japanese War, Nishimura wrote to Premier Itō saying that while Japan could follow the common practice of demanding an indemnity and territory, Japan should make only small claims. The Chinese terms should be accepted if at all possible in order to put an end to the war.[44] Two years later he wrote: "Aggression should not be

[42] *Ibid.*, p. 7.

[43] Speech at the Kaiseikō (1877), *Sōsho*, 2.52-53. Also, "Shintō, which was preached by Motoori, Hirata, and other elders, is superficial and inadequate to be made an academic subject at the University." "Daigaku no naka ni seigaku no ikka o mōkubeki setsu" (1879), *Sōsho*, 2.63. "Those who today profess to be scholars of Japanese studies (*kokugaku*) must leave the matter of reverence and faith entirely to Shintō teachers (regarding it as religion), and solely with the spirit of seeking truth and knowledge, engage in scholarship. However, when I observe the theories of the present scholars of Japanese studies, I see that many discuss facts with minds to a certain degree of reverence and faith. For example, when they discuss our country, there are many cases in which they say that what is not superior to other countries is superior, what is not so is so, what is new is old, and what is not certain is certain." "Shinjitsu kongō no kahi" (1889), *Sōsho*, 2.311.

[44] "Itō naikaku sōridaijin e kengan," *Sōsho*, 1.438; Ienaga, pp. 159-

made national policy. To invade another country is the act of a robber. Military preparations, the army and navy, should be put to use only in the defense of our own country. Relations with other countries should place all the emphasis on peace. Today many of the countries of the world avow peace on the outside, but in their hearts the greed to devour others is very strong. We must not learn this in the least. We should associate with each other in genuine peace, benefit each other by trade and other means, and we must not interfere in the internal affairs of other countries. (Our policy toward Korea up to now has indeed been a mistake.) Also we should not be eager to make alliances with other strong nations."[45]

Nishimura was also outspoken about other trends of the day which he considered dangerous. In 1894 he had the greatest distaste for those who had accumulated large fortunes, building up their businesses through governmental assistance.[46] He said that the rich became richer and the poor became poorer, while the laws of the country worked increasingly to the advantage of the rich. It was reasons such as these, he warned, which led in Western countries to the rise of socialist and communist parties.[47] He was opposed to Fukuzawa Yukichi's view that there was an urgent necessity to raise and protect a capitalist class, and that the gap between rich and poor was inevitable. Nishimura argued that the government should not take such a callous attitude toward poverty, which he said

---

160. Itō did not reply to the petition, and proceeded to make extensive territorial demands upon the Chinese, inviting the Triple Intervention. Nishimura wrote two years later: "If from the start he had listened to the warning of certain people, and not taken the Liaotung territory but had increased the indemnity somewhat, we would not have incurred this humiliation. However, in thinking it over deeply, I do not know but that this one blow, on the other hand, was good medicine for our country. If, on top of the fully successful war, we had completed fully successful negotiations, the arrogance of the officials and the people might be many times what it is today. . . ." "Zoku kokka dōtoku ron" (1897), *Sōsho*, 1.229.

[45] "Zoku kokka dōtoku ron" (1895), *Sōsho*, 1.232.

[46] "Kokka dōtoku ron," *Sōsho*, 1.215.

[47] "Jishikiroku," *Sōsho*, 1.678-679.

was caused less by laziness, as Fukuzawa claimed, than by unhappy circumstances.[48]

Nishimura did agree entirely with Fukuzawa, however, on the necessity of favoring the development of industry at the expense of agriculture as being the only way for Japan, with its increasing population, to reach the economic level of the West.[49] He also sounded like Fukuzawa when he said that Japanese merchants were uneducated and shortsighted, and that in order to be able to compete on the international market it would be necessary to train them in special commercial schools.[50] In these respects, at least, Nishimura had left far behind the physiocratic ideas of a Tokugawa official.

Nishimura insisted that the key to Japan's advance must be the development of independence of mind by the people. This was perhaps the most modern idea in Meiji Japan. It had received considerable discussion among the members of the Meirokusha, but Nishimura was one of the few who kept at the theme. He said that the main fault of the Japanese people was their "tendency to follow blindly, the weakness of the spirit of independence."[51] "In recent years among those who discuss government there are those called the conservatives. They wish to enrich the nation and strengthen its arms like Western countries but without losing the style of government that Japan has had up to the present. However, the wealth and strength of Western countries was attained by the extension of the people's rights; it was not attained by people dependent upon their governments. Therefore if we preserve the style of government that we have had up to the present, and unless the people completely lose their deferential and subservient character, we cannot attain the wealth and strength of Western countries."[52] On this same theme, he said that the people themselves must find out what is needed to make the Japanese people the best in the world and how

[48] "Kokka dōtoku ron," *Sōsho*, 1.222.
[49] "Jishikiroku," *Sōsho*, 1.699.
[50] "Kokka dōtoku ron," *Sōsho*, 1.206-207.
[51] "Nihon dōtoku ron," *Sōsho*, 1.11.
[52] "Hakuō shigen," Ser. 2, *Sōsho*, 1.538-539.

to achieve this. If they lack the independence to do this and wait for government encouragement, they will never succeed.[53] How fatal it is for the people to rely on the government is put squarely in his remarkable denouncement of the Constitution granted in the name of the Emperor in 1889: "There are things that are beautiful in name and beautiful in fact, and there are things that are beautiful in name but not beautiful in fact. The Meiji constitutional government is extremely beautiful in name. However, in fact it is not very different from the absolutist government of the old days. Why is this? The constitutions of Western countries were made by the strength of the people. Therefore they contain many benefits for the people. Our constitution was made entirely by administrative officials, and particularly by the hand of the domain clique (*hambatsu*). Therefore it is beneficial to the administrative officials, that is, the government. The people do not realize this. They try to struggle with the government for political power on the basis of this constitution. That is foolish."[54]

The World-View of a Progressive Tokugawa Administrator

Rather than having "gone conservative" to any significant degree, we find that on some subjects Nishimura was perhaps too progressive or modern for the Meiji oligarchs, while on others his conservatism was obstructing their program. However, his views seem internally consistent if we acknowledge that, because of differences in his background and temperament, the elements of progressiveness and tradition in his thought were differently arranged. Nishimura was for nineteen years a domain official, giving Lord Hotta advice— justified in Confucian moral terms—on every program of the day ranging from national and international affairs to those of the finances and administration of the domain, and even on how to educate his heir. However, Nishimura's ap-

---

[53] "Mikawa no kuni kakuchi enzetsu" (1895), *Sōsho*, 2.992-993.
[54] "Hakuō shigen," Ser. 3 (1887-1894), *Sōsho*, 1.606.

proach to Japan's problems after the Restoration when he became an early Meiji enlightener and then a moralist seems to have been based to a considerable degree on the same attitudes—those of a progressive administrator of the late Tokugawa period. While Nishimura might cite Western writings as well as Confucian works in support of his arguments, the mode of thought remained that of a domain administrator. Among the more characteristic of these attitudes were the following:

1. *Morality is the root*, the foundation for everything from one's personal life to the order of society and government. Therefore, moral training is the root of education, and all other fields of study are branches. Nishimura criticized the Meiji government for basing itself on legalism rather than on morality. He argued that morality is the root, and law is a branch which developed later. "Law is an instrument to prevent man from entering into evil, but it is not an instrument to lead him to good. . . . Law does not have educating power or the power to elevate morals and customs . . . it is only the power of morality that can make people's minds just, make morals and customs beautiful, elevate the conditions of society, and enhance the honor of the country everywhere."[55]

A corollary to this premise is that a nation must be united in agreement on a moral system which would be a guide for government as well as for conduct. Western countries have unity of government and teaching in Christianity, but Japan's present condition is desperate since it has lost the unity of moral spirit. It should be the primary objective of the government to teach morality.

That the moral condition of a nation was related to its rise and fall has always been a favorite theme of Confucianists in discussing Chinese and Japanese history. Nishimura found it equally true in the West, and liked to describe how Greece and Rome had risen to power when the people were industrious and strong-willed, but when they turned to indul-

[55] "Wakumon jūgojō" (1882), *Sōsho*, 1.991-992. Cf. "Nihon dōtoku ron," *Sōsho*, 1.16-17.

gence and the arts, the empires fell. The Japanese also, he said, had until recently possessed the spirit of simplicity and resoluteness, but "today [1873] their bad customs greatly resemble those of Greece and Rome. . . . What maintains a country well is solely the spirit and conduct of the people. . . ."[56]

2. *The officials and people must practice morality*, or the country will fall into disorder. The individual must cultivate morality first in himself, and then practice it in his family; and it will extend throughout his village and then through the country and beyond. The behavior of the people will determine the quality of the whole country. It is particularly important that the ruler and the ministers conduct themselves as models for the people. Morality would also give them the ability to judge what policies are most beneficial for the people and what are not. Nishimura frequently stated this theme, as in a speech before the Meirokusha in 1875 entitled "Moral Training and Governing the Country Are Not Two Roads." He first quoted Confucius and Mencius, but then said that since they are considered to be stupid by "those who pursue utility," he would also quote from the writings of Bentham and other Western sages to show the importance of moral conduct. He continued: "In recent years among high officials and the nobility there are those who do not regulate their private conduct and expose themselves to ridicule by intelligent people." These officials have shown their "loathing for barbarism and love for civilization" by issuing laws prohibiting such ugly and barbarous behavior as exposure of legs and urinating in public. However, the personal conduct of the officials and nobles is far uglier than urinating in public. As long as officials behave in such a way, even if the

[56] "Chingen issoku" (1873), *Sōsho*, 2.1-2. Thirteen years later Nishimura was still citing the cases of moral decay of Greece and Rome in the same terms, and had added the partition of Poland and the defeat of France: "A German scholar has stated that the outcome of the Franco-Prussian War of some years ago was the outcome of morality. He said that it was because the German soldiers had a strong spirit of loyalty, courage, and patriotism. . . ." "Nihon dōtoku ron," *Sōsho*, 1.8, 9, 13.

nation were enriched and its armaments were to become strong, it could not be called a civilized country. "We earnestly ask you, high officials and nobles, know deeply that moral training is the root of governing the country. From this moment reform your conduct at once, make your words a pattern for the realm, make your conduct a standard for the realm. The people will look up to the high officials, respecting them and loving them, and consequently manners and customs will be reformed and etiquette will be rectified . . . the whole nation will benefit greatly from this."[57]

3. *Morality must be based on reason*—on a rational and practical philosophy—and not on religion. Religions, such as Buddhism, Christianity, and Shintō, are based on superstition and faith, and are the product of a primitive age. Their supporters are to be found among people of the lower class, but as the people's "knowledge expands more and more, belief in miracles will fade away daily and belief in reason will grow daily," until the religions will have to become more rational or die out. Nishimura often quoted Auguste Comte in support of this Confucian view. The suitable morality for a people is one based on reason, such as Chinese Confucianism or European philosophy, and the needs of Japan would best be met by borrowing elements primarily from these two systems.[58]

4. *Follow the mean in making progress*. Nishimura wrote that "it is the law of Heaven that everything progresses without ceasing, and it is against the law of Heaven to cling to old customs and never change; but there is a natural order for the development of all things." He said, however, that "it is also against the law of Heaven to go against the natural order, to rush ahead and progress rapidly. Therefore the nation's government should of course emphasize progress but it should avoid rashness and it should follow the natural

[57] "Shūshin chikoku nito ni arazaru ron" (1875), *Sōsho*, 2.5-9.
[58] "Nihon dōtoku ron," *Sōsho*, 1.20, 21, 28; "Shūkyō no zento" (1886), *Sōsho*, 2.129-132. Nishimura used Comte's three stages of intellectual and social development: theological, metaphysical, and scientific.

order. In short, it should go the middle way between obstinacy and rashness."[59]

In an article written in 1887 entitled "Discussion of the Mean," Nishimura criticized the weakness of the Japanese for rushing to extreme positions, which he found illustrated by the slogans popular since the Restoration: Repel the Barbarians (*jōi*), Reject Buddhism (*haibutsu*), Civilization and Enlightenment (*bummei kaika*), Popular Rights (*minken*), Reject Confucianism (*haiju*), Women's Rights (*joken*). Such extreme opinions are as harmful as unjust opinions. Further, he said that "such virtues as loyalty, filial piety, benevolence, civility, and fidelity are all great virtues throughout the world. However, if the middle way is lost, these virtues lose much of their merit."[60]

This attitude of the middle road is also illustrated by the fact that in the early 1880's when Nishimura was being called a Confucian bigot by the Westernized reformers in the Ministry of Education, he was also warning against the undesirability of appointing as teachers "doctrinaire Confucianists who will drag forth their bigoted theories."[61]

5. *Practical statecraft* was emphasized by Nishimura in the proposals he wrote for his daimyo, under the influence, probably, of Practical Studies (*jitsugaku*) of the Mito School.

[59] "Kokka dōtoku ron," *Sōsho*, 1.102-103. Nishimura's statement suggests that he thought of progress in traditional terms, that is, the change which flows inevitably from natural causes rather than a more Western concept of progress as being achieved by more active human intervention or change.

[60] "Chū ron" (1887), *Sōsho*, 2.168-172.

[61] *Den*, 1.515, 549; "Wakumon jugojō" (1882-1883), *Sōsho*, 1.1019. The moderation and constancy of Nishimura's views were a point of pride to him. Writing about 1881, he said: "My views today have not changed greatly from those of thirty years ago. That is, a country should develop in a natural order, which means that it should not imitate indiscriminately the externals of other countries. Those who used to be barbarian repellers and were formerly inclined toward obstinacy are today inclined toward frivolity. At both times they lacked clarity of foresight. If my foresight of thirty years ago turned out today to be right, some of my foresights today of thirty years from now will also probably be right." "Hakuō shigen," *Sōsho*, 1.489.

In order to achieve the Confucian ideal of benevolent government, he was prepared to abandon what seemed to him no longer functional or efficient in the traditional practices. The essential techniques that the lord should use in performing his administrative responsibilities were *mei* and *dan*. *Mei* ("clarification") meant the examination of all of the relevant facts both in detail and in their whole context and the evaluation of the probable results of the alternate courses of action. *Dan* ("decisiveness") meant making the right decision at the opportune moment and executing it quickly and resolutely, regardless of popular opinion and resistance.[62] The essence of benevolent government was neither dogged adherence to tradition nor reckless, hasty reform; it was the proper use of *mei* and *dan* to effect timely reform in government and society. It was characteristic of Nishimura's advice both before and after the Restoration that he did not linger in abstract argument like many Confucianists, but based his reasoning on observed fact and proof, sometimes citing statistics to support his points. He wrote in 1886: "If we want to know the truth about things, we must search for the facts. Everything that fits the facts is true, and everything that does not fit the facts is not true. Fact is the measure which tests truth."[63]

6. *The proper use of Western learning* was to study only those fields which had practical utility in meeting the crises of the late Tokugawa period, and to eschew foreign ideas which might disrupt the existing order. However, on the eve of the Restoration, Nishimura entered those areas which had been considered dangerous, and before long he was criticizing those who did not study the history, political systems, and thought of Western nations.[64] Since morality was considered the root of a culture, was it not necessary to study the moral systems and the lessons of history of the foreigners in order

---

[62] *Den*, 1.70-71, 170-172. I am indebted to Professor Motoyama who, in his article and in personal discussions, suggested the importance in Nishimura's thought of "practical statecraft" as well as the role of a domain administrator.

[63] "Nihon dōtoku ron," *Sōsho*, 1.29.

[64] Preface to *Bankoku shiryaku* (1869), *Den*, 1.324-325.

to understand the basis of their institutions? However, the manner in which Nishimura in his writings drew moral illustrations from Western history was that of a Confucian scholar drawing on Chinese and Japanese history. His Western philosophers were moralists, Hickok and Winslow,[65] in whose works he found attitudes relatively untainted by Christianity, which could be used to give weight and acceptability to essentially Confucian values. In short, he drew selectively from Western materials for examples, precedents, and illustrations to support his basic premises about what he considered the proper moral principles for Japan. His selective attitude is illustrated by his advocacy of Western ethics as a field of study, because it "discards the outer skin of Western studies but takes its spirit."[66]

Far from minimizing the importance of learning from the West, however, Nishimura said that such study was essential for knowledge and morality as well, but that it must be done in the right way. The difficulty with the Meiji Westernizers, Nishimura said, was copying everything they knew of the West. Instead, they should increase their knowledge of the West tenfold, and then select only those things which are suitable for Japan. To do this selection and adaptation, however, they must also know Japan, but such people did not know their own country either.[67]

The specific needs of Japan should be considered, because what is good in the Western country may not be good in Japan due to differences of tradition, history, and racial characteristics. Students of the West say that "Chinese explanations are wide of the mark and useless while European and American theories are detailed and precise. . . . However, when we attempt to apply them to our country, I am not yet able to decide whether that which is wide of the mark and

[65] Nishimura published in 1882 a translation of part of Hubbard Winslow's *Moral Philosophy; Analytical, Synthetical, and Practical* (New York, 1858, 1866), under the title *Inshi dōtoku gaku.*

[66] "Daigaku no naka ni seigaku no ikka o mōkubeki setsu" (1879), *Sōsho,* 2.64.

[67] Speech at Kaiseikō (1877), *Sōsho,* 2.52.

useless is disadvantageous or whether that which is detailed and precise is advantageous. . . ." He took the example of medicine to argue that a mediocre physician using Oriental herbal medicine can do the patient no harm, while a physician using the powerful foreign drugs can easily kill the patient. "I wish that those who govern the country would first diagnose the disease and employ medicine afterwards."[68]

7. *Fear of Western expansion,* which all Japanese felt in 1853, was harbored by Nishimura to the end of his days, and was compounded by concern about foreign economic infiltration and the penetration of Christianity which would undermine the national polity. Nishimura also feared that the Japanese were in danger of losing many elements of their tradition, in manners, mores, and clothing, through the reckless acceptance of Western ways. In short, there was throughout his thinking the suspicion that any importation from the West which was not essential for the strengthening of Japan was to be avoided and might indeed be harmful.

8. *Arts and literature are ornaments,* and should be tolerated only when they do no harm to society. As he wrote in 1901: "It is to be lamented that people . . . do not realize that the manners and customs of the nation are destroyed by the fine arts. . . . So far as they do not harm manners and customs, it is all right for fine arts to exist as embellishments, but there is no reason to gamble with the destruction of manners and customs by allowing the fine arts to exist. Recently some painters in the foreign style have painted pictures of nude women and presented them for public exhibition. Their ugliness and obscenity make people vomit. The motives of the painters are transparent. There is no doubt that the authorities responsible for maintaining public morals should ban them."[69] When he discusses the theater he scolds like a Tokugawa period Confucianist: "Theater is not the school of morality but the school of evil, the bed of sin, the agent of defilement and defeat."[70]

[68] "Riron no rigai" (1878), *Sōsho,* 2.59-61.
[69] "Zoku jishikiroku" (1902), *Sōsho,* 1.777.
[70] "Wakumon jūgojō" (ca. 1882), *Sōsho,* 1.1002. In discussing the literature of the puppet plays, Nishimura said: "In our country, in

9. *Inequality of classes and sexes.* Although Nishimura did not take an orthodox Tokugawa position concerning family relationships, most of his social attitudes remained traditional. Seven years after the Restoration, he insisted that members of the former samurai class should receive favored treatment from the government because of their long service in supporting and maintaining the nation: "To lower them to the level of rights of the common people is like using silk clothes and cotton clothes in the same way. . . . If we mix two million members of the samurai class with thirty-three million common people, the spirit of loyalty, courage, honor, and duty will gradually disappear."[71] A decade later he wrote: "Divide the people of the whole nation into two classes: the families which know manners and those which do not. The families which know manners are the nobility, the samurai (the upper-class part) and the important farmer, artisan, and merchant families; and the families which do not know manners are the common people below them."[72]

Although he was interested in the education of women, he considered that they should not be given too much, and that it was a mistake to encourage them to be too active. In a speech given in 1889 while Principal of the Peeresses' School, he said: "Frivolous people are inclined to say that the old Eastern education of women is extremely subservient and bigoted and should be abolished quickly. This opinion is

---

about the Genroku period, there were Chikamatsu Monzaemon and Takeda Izumo, and others. The *jōruri* which they wrote were truly the extreme in lewdness and obscenity, and they depicted human emotions so evil as to be worse than in the books of Li-weng (Li Yu, 1611-ca. 1680). In the feudal age, among samurai, their books were extremely despised, and a samurai of good conduct would no more pick up such a book than he would pick up rubbish. In recent years, there are some among scholars who read them and admire the cleverness of their styles. The extreme is adding critical remarks and publishing them for the public. The most extreme is to praise the compositions as models of Japanese style, and to take excerpts and publish them." "Hakuō shigen," Ser. 1, *Sōsho*, 1.456.

[71] "Tento no setsu" (1875), *Sōsho*, 2.43.
[72] "Danjo aierabu no setsu" (1886), *Sōsho*, 2.157.

greatly mistaken. As is well known, the Eastern education of women emphasizes submissiveness and faithfulness. . . . In recent years, many foreigners who have stayed in this country a long time have admired the submissiveness and virtuousness of Japanese women."[73]

These habits of mind persisted in Nishimura in part because, by the time the domains were abolished, he was already forty-three, having had nineteen years of experience as a responsible administrative official of a domain. That such habits were less strong in the thinking of the oligarchs was probably due largely to differences in background and experience. Of the samurai oligarchs, only Saigō Takamori was as old as Nishimura. They all came from fiefs which had long been hostile toward the Tokugawa. Only a few of the samurai were old enough to have had administrative posts in their fiefs until the eve of the Restoration, at which time they rose to influence as radicals in their domain and led the drive against the Tokugawa.

Nishimura never lost his loyalty to his old domain, nor his admiration for some elements of the Tokugawa system. It is not surprising that he felt ill at ease with the new regime and considered his public career at an end, especially when he was sent to Kyoto as soon as the Restoration was proclaimed to plead the case of the Sano domain before the new government. In 1871 he declined an appointment to the Ministry of Military Affairs, but shortly afterwards accepted a position in the prefectural government of Imba, the territory of his old fief. He resigned within three months, however, protesting that he did not wish to carry out orders of which he disapproved, issued by petty officials who were making rash changes and who treated the people of that area as a conquered people. He moved to Tokyo at once and opened a private school at the Hotta residence for the children of leading families of the domain. Two years later, however, he accepted an appointment in the Ministry of Education, but he did not forget his lord; in 1887, over twenty years after

[73] "Joshi kyōiku ron" (1889), *Sōsho*, 2.358-359.

his death, he wrote a series of treatises defending Lord Hotta's service to the Bakufu.

Against this background of experiences, it becomes difficult to evaluate Nishimura's criticisms of the policies and personal character of the oligarchs from the Satsuma and Chōshū domains. While the criticisms are always couched in moral terms, we cannot be sure to what extent they were based on other, unstated prejudices, such as the premises of a Tokugawa period administrator, his loyalties to the old domain, or personal disappointment.

The extent of Nishimura's hostility to the reforms of the Meiji government is shown in a general assessment he made of the new system compared with the Tokugawa system. Compared with the Tokugawa system, he found that there were some advantages but also some disadvantages in the new economic system, coinage, military system, and architecture. However, he rated as worse than before the tax system, education, calendar, government organization, social system, the courts, customs, manners and dress; and the law, he said, was much worse. He concluded that it was nonsense to praise the accomplishments of the period of "civilization."[74]

Morality for Modern Japan

The changes made after the Restoration were ill-conceived and chaotic, in Nishimura's view, because the nation had lost its moral foundations, and government and people were chasing helter-skelter after Western notions. Time and resources were being wasted. He became increasingly concerned that Japan lacked the material and spiritual strength to carry on a "Civilization and Enlightenment" movement at the same time as that to "Enrich the Nation and Strengthen its Arms." Both the government and the people failed to recognize the proper priority, and were failing to distinguish between root and branch. Most people thought of the two movements as the same kind of thing which could be attained

[74] Although it has not been possible to date this essay precisely, it appears to have been written shortly before 1882. "Hakuō shigen," Ser. 1, *Sōsho*, 1.502.

by the same means. Nishimura said in 1877 that he had thought so himself, until reading in Western history and philosophy brought the realization that the sequence and methods are different in the historical process. Western countries achieved their present strength by first increasing their wealth and then building strong military forces during the sixteenth and seventeenth centuries. Only after this was done did they proceed to the development of "civilization" in the eighteenth and nineteenth centuries.

The program for "Enriching the Country, Strengthening its Arms" was to: (1) make laws stringent, (2) esteem ranks and titles, (3) cultivate simplicity and sturdiness, (4) prohibit frivolity and indolence, (5) value integrity and a sense of shame, (6) develop the spirit of patriotism, (7) admire bravery and constancy, and (8) prohibit extravagance and sumptuousness. However, the program for "Civilization and Enlightenment" would (1) make literature flourish, (2) make technology thrive, (3) make laws detailed, (4) refine theories, (5) make apparatus intricate, (6) broaden international friendship, (7) promote the fine arts, and (8) make clothing, food, and houses beautiful. Since Japan could not achieve both programs at once, the effort should be divided eighty percent on the former and twenty percent on the latter, with the understanding that anything may be sacrificed from the latter which might impede the former.[75] Nishimura, still proposing the same scheme thirteen years later, in 1889, said that although actually the effort should be one hundred percent on the former, there would be too much popular sentiment against this; a concession of twenty percent to the latter would be practical.[76] To achieve this end, the proper virtues must be cultivated in the people, in the case of adults, through the establishment of societies devoted to the propagation of morality. For children and the future generations, the entire

[75] "Fukoku kyōhei setsu" (1877), *Sōsho*, 2.55-59.

[76] Nishimura added some further items to the two programs in 1889. "Bummei kaika no ben" (Nov. 1889), *Sōsho*, 2.403-406; "Bummei kaika no junjo" (Nov. 1889), *Sōsho*, 2.409, 415-426.

basis of the educational system must be centered on these virtues.[77]

Unable to make any headway among his colleagues in the Ministry of Education, Nishimura formed a small society in 1876 which he called the Tōkyō Shūshingakusha (Tokyo Society for Moral Training).[78] Four years later, when the membership had reached 32, he began the publication of a journal, the *Shūshingakusha sōsetsu*. In the opening article, proclaiming the purpose of the Society, he stated: "Since the Restoration of the Imperial Government, there has been advance in all of the hundred matters and daily we are progressing toward enlightenment. Only in the one matter of morality we seem, in comparison to the feudal period, to be losing ground."[79] He argued again that all other knowledge and study will be in vain if moral character is neglected, a judgment which he supported by quotations from Pestalozzi. The objectives of the society would be to help the members to develop their own moral character in order that they may help others conduct themselves properly in their respective roles in society.

In 1884 Nishimura reorganized the Society as the Nihon Kōdōkai (Japanese Society for the Investigation of the Way), now with 328 members, and broadened its scope to the dual function of inquiry into moral principles and their propagation.[80] In 1887 Nishimura reorganized the Society again, this time altering in the title the character *kō* ("investigation") to a homonym meaning "expansion," and it thus became "Society

[77] Motoyama, p. 443.

[78] The term *shūshingaku* is what in English is called "moral philosophy," Nishimura explained, in the Preface to his translation of Hickok. *Den*, 1.458.

[79] *Den*, 1.440.

[80] *Den*, 1.553-556. As part of the program of investigating moral principles, Nishimura made assignments among the Society members for the writing of a history of Japanese morality, the translation of Comte, *Course of Positive Philosophy*; Walter Bagehot, *Physics and Politics*; and Kuei Chen-ch'uan (Yu-kang, 1506-1571), *Chu-tzu hui-hsien*, none of which seems to have been completed.

for the Expansion of the Way."[81] Thanks to the conservative reaction against rapid Westernization during these years, and the new interest in traditional values and culture, the Society mushroomed until in 1902, the year of Nishimura's death, it had 130 local chapters and 10,000 members—an extraordinary membership for a private society at this time.[82]

During 1886 Nishimura became increasingly alarmed by the reforms of the Itō Cabinet, which aped the externals of Western civilization and abandoned Japanese morality. Unable to hold his peace, Nishimura delivered public lectures at Tokyo University on three successive days and published them under the title of *Nihon dōtoku ron* (Discourse on Japanese Morality).[83] He said that all of the systems of moral philosophy which Japan had ever had had been adopted from other countries. It was now necessary to seek again for truth all over the world, selecting the elements best suited, and combine them into a perfect system for Japan.[84] Confucianism itself would not suffice because of the inadequacies already enumerated. Buddhism, Christianity, and Shintō were unsuitable because they were religions, and, in addition, each of them had particular shortcomings and dangers which he detailed. The fifth system, Western philosophy, had many

[81] *Den*, 1.762-765. The journal of the Society was the *Kōdōkai zasshi*, but its publication was suspended by the government in 1889 because of an article opposing the granting of land possession rights to foreigners. It resumed publication the same year under the title *Nihon kōdōkai sōki*.

[82] Kaigo, pp. 6-7.

[83] Nishimura sent copies of the *Nihon dōtoku ron* to Cabinet ministers and other prominent officials. According to Nishimura's autobiography, Mori was extremely pleased with the work, gave it the approval of the Ministry of Education, and planned to have it used as a textbook in high schools. Prime Minister Itō was very displeased with the book, saying that "it slanders the new government and obstructs the progress of the administration." *Ōjiroku*, p. 194. Itō's annoyance was aggravated by his belief that the lectures were related to a document attacking his reforms which was written by his own Minister of Agriculture and Commerce, Tani Kanjō. *Den*, 1.595. Mori reviewed Nishimura's book, suggested verbal changes, and managed to mollify Itō somewhat.

[84] *Den*, 1.649, 655, 534-535.

fine points, but in addition to the difficulty of understanding it and the paucity of Japanese who had studied it, there were four ways in which it too seemed unsatisfactory, not in its substance, but in its suitability as a foundation for Japanese morality: (1) While it places great stress on the discussion of knowledge, it gives little emphasis to personal conduct. (2) It does not have a method of cultivating peace of mind or heart—composure of mind that will not be agitated or fearful on encountering suffering and danger. (3) Philosophers are too eager to excel over philosophers of the past; they therefore dissent, exaggerating minor points of difference. This is in contrast to Confucian scholars who adhere to the words of the sages. Both miss the middle way. (4) There are many schools, all disagreeing with one another, and therefore there is no unanimity to serve as a basis for a moral system.[85] These "inadequacies," significantly, are ones which would be keenly felt by a Japanese Confucianist.

Nishimura said that although none of the systems in itself was satisfactory, by drawing on all of them, and mostly on Confucianism and Western philosophy, Japan was in a unique position to combine Eastern and Western philosophy into a new system.[86] He gave the impression of impartiality, appearing to place Confucianism and Western philosophy on an equal footing. In practice, however, Nishimura's procedure was to build from a set of Confucian attitudes, eliminating only those which he considered no longer suitable, and drawing on the West for elements which would supplement and support, but not be in conflict with, his basically Confucian scheme. It was possible to add Western elements without apparent contradiction because of his superficial understanding of what he was borrowing. He did not realize, it seems, that by superimposing these on the Confucian rationalism he was changing the implications of the Western principles. What he borrowed from the West, moreover, was not "philosophy," but rather practical moral maxims which were not too difficult to naturalize. He said that "the reason why [Confucianism] looks

[85] "Nihon dōtoku ron," *Sōsho*, 1.7, 23-27.
[86] "Tōyō tetsugaku no zento" (Sept. 1889), *Den*, 2.1-3.

bigoted and inapplicable today is merely because it lacks the scholarship techniques of civilization." These he also borrowed from the West as embellishments to modernize Confucianism.[87]

These activities took place immediately after Nishimura was appointed a Court Councilor and resigned from the Ministry of Education.[88] Shortly before, he had been assigned the task, on the request of the Empress it is said, of compiling an ethics textbook on the meritorious deeds of women in Eastern and Western history. The book was to be a companion volume to Motoda Eifu's text, *Yōgaku kōyō*, which had ostensibly been written by Imperial Command, and which was distributed to every school in Japan in 1881. Nishimura's book, the *Fujokagami* (Mirror for Women), was published in 1887 and similarly disseminated.[89] In 1885 he was given the responsibility of planning and supervising the education of the Crown Prince, in which task he was assisted by Motoda.

During the years at Court he was probably in frequent association with Motoda, who had also joined in the opposition to the revision of the treaties. Motoda's view of moral education was that the Emperor should be the model of virtue for the entire people as the recipient of the ancestral precepts which were transmitted from the Sun Goddess through the unbroken line of the Imperial Family. These precepts happened to coincide with the Confucian teachings introduced into Japan during the reign of Emperor Ōjin (ca. 400). Motoda had written a number of memoranda to Cabinet Ministers, which claimed to be "expressions of the Imperial

---

[87] "Nihon dōtoku ron," *Sōsho*, 1.21.

[88] *Den*, 1.560-562.

[89] *Den*, 1.565-566. In February 1886, Mori asked Nishimura informally if he would accept the presidency of Tokyo University in order to undertake a major reorganization of the University. Nishimura declined, saying that he had his own ideas of how it should be reformed, but as he felt that his whole plan would not be approved and acceptance of only part of it would be meaningless, he would not wish to be appointed. *Ōjiroku*, pp. 192-193. In 1888, he was appointed Principal of the Peeresses's School, but was instructed to resign from this position five years later, at the instigation, he says, of Itō. *Ōjiroku*, pp 238-240.

Will," urging that these precepts be the basis of the morals courses in the schools, and that these courses should be the heart of the curriculum. Under this prodding, the Ministry of Education issued the statement in 1881 that thereafter the guiding principles of education would be loyalty, filial piety, and patriotism.[90] Because of changes in the Ministry and consequent reversals of policy, however, little was done to implement this program. Motoda's most serious setback was the appointment of Mori as Minister of Education in 1885.[91]

Nishimura, during his more than ten years in the Ministry, had similarly been frustrated in his efforts to have greater emphasis placed on the moral training courses. Perhaps his association with Motoda helped him to develop the proposal. in 1887 that the Imperial Household should take over the direction of moral education and issue textbooks for this purpose, following, he said, the precedents of the Ch'ing Emperors, K'ang-hsi and Yung-cheng.[92] He won the support of Court Councilors Soejima Taneomi, Sasaki Takayuki, and Sano Tsunetami, and in turn the Lord Keeper of the Privy Seal, Sanjō Sanetomi, and the Minister of the Imperial Household, Hijikata Hisamoto. The latter presented the plan to Mori, who became enraged at what he considered a criticism of his program. The plan was therefore put aside.[93]

In February of 1889 Mori was assassinated, and the same month Nishimura presented a plan to Hijikata, calling for the establishment in the Imperial Household Ministry of an office with the Confucian-sounding name of Meirin'in (Clarifying Ethics Institute). To it would be appointed scholars outstanding for their learning and virtue to supervise and inspect moral education in all schools from primary to university, to approve morals textbooks, and to compile new ones. He also proposed that an imperial rescript be issued at once to establish the basis of the people's moral education wholly

[90] Shively, p. 328. [91] Shively, pp. 328-329.
[92] The *Sheng-yu kuang-hsun*, issued by K'ang-hsi and elaborated by Yung-cheng. See F. W. Baller, *The Sacred Edict* (Shanghai: American Presbyterian Mission Press, 2nd ed., 1907). *Ōjiroku*, p. 197.
[93] *Den*, 1.705.

in the Imperial Household.[94] Although the office was not established, Nishimura's seems to have been the first suggestion that an imperial rescript be issued to establish the basis of moral education, an action actually taken in October of 1890.

Nishimura wrote a large number of speeches and articles on moral education during 1889 and 1890. His advocacy of Confucian books as the foundation for a national morality, much more openly stated than ever before, was more acceptable in the conservative reaction of the late 1880's. One of the clearest statements of his views at this time was a Memorial submitted to the Minister of Education in April of 1889 when, after a detailed criticism of the entire educational system, he discussed moral teaching: ". . . it should not be difficult to establish the foundation of moral education in our country today. For almost two thousand years since the *Analects* came to the Court of Ōjin in our country, the essential part of the history of education lies in nothing else but the Confucian Way. . . . If traditional education had not been destroyed at the beginning of Meiji, the educators today would not have lost direction in moral education. Thus the Confucian Way which has formed the morality of the Japanese people since the times of our ancestors, cannot be discarded even if we were to try to discard it. Especially the Four Books—the *Analects, Mencius, Great Learning*, and the *Mean* —in my opinion, can be said to be so far the best teachings in the world. Therefore, it is most proper to establish the foundation of moral education on Confucian books today. . . . When the Confucian Way is used, its spirit alone should be taken, and I hope that the name Confucianism will not be used. The name Confucianism has for some time been disliked by the people, so that there are many who would not believe in the substance because of the name." He added that as there were things in the Four Books which did not suit the times, only those parts which were appropriate should be used. Moreover, "although you use Confucianism, you should not use traditional pedantic Confucianists as teachers, but persons

[94] *Den,* 1.705-708.

who are versed in at least Japanese history and Chinese Confucianism, and also Western philosophy (especially moral philosophy), whose conduct is trusted by the public, and who have undertaken the study of cultivating peace of mind."[95]

Although Nishimura may have first suggested it, there is no evidence that he had anything to do with the composing of the Imperial Rescript of Education. It was drafted by Inoue Kowashi, but much of the content was provided by Motoda Eifu, with suggestions by a number of others who helped to make the Confucian elements less overt. Actually the content of the Rescript seems not to have been very far from Nishimura's position. It differed mainly in placing more emphasis than he would have on hierarchal and family relationships, and it contained mystical statements about the sanctity of the emperor and his ancestors. Although there is a suggestion of some of the universal values of the West, it did not include the cultivation by the individual of a spirit of independence and self-reliance. Nishimura's position, in short, was somewhat more progressive and more universal. The Rescript, however, came closer to serving Nishimura's program for the needs of Japan than any other act of the oligarchs.

It is apparent that Nishimura's program as well as his moral system, while derived in part from Confucian attitudes, were much more of an individual development than any traditional system of Confucianism. In attempting to understand how they were derived, we have taken into account his background and experiences, from the inertia morality of his early education to his bitter experiences as a supporter of the Tokugawa regime. Perhaps of greater importance, but more difficult to assess, were the factors of his temperament and individual needs, which caused him to develop a system which would rationalize his personal predilections. However, the theme that we find consistent through all of his actions and his development of a moral system is his dedication to his country.

[95] *Sōsho*, 1.422-423.

He selected moral principles which he considered would serve her most urgent requirements.

The reestablishment of a prescribed doctrine of moral education for the nation illustrates that Japan in the process of modernization was a curious blending of tradition with Westernization. Nishimura's was perhaps an extreme case in point, for in his activities as a student of the West, he kept feudal values as his guides and never lost the essentially Confucian world-view. During the years when Western ways were being copied most feverishly, he felt at odds with the trends of the day and advocated adherence to a nationwide, unified moral system—an idea from Japanese tradition which was much out of fashion at that time. Nishimura considered it a contribution to Japan's modernization, in fact its very foundation, to develop such a code for modern needs. For this purpose he would synthesize Eastern and Western philosophy, not in the search of truth as he claimed, but to develop a practical moral system for Japan's specific requirements. He also proposed to propagate his system in modern ways—through a national, standardized educational system and through a mass-membership society, complete with a women's auxiliary.

Such activities may not sound as though they would have very much to do with the process of modernization. However, Japan had lost the security of the comprehensive common moral tradition to which it was accustomed, and many leaders in government and education began to feel the need of such a system to unify the nation and give stability to its social and political structure during times when rapid change was essential in many sectors. While we might not consider it to be a necessary condition of modernization in other societies, there was no question about its short-run benefits in speeding modernization in the case of Japan. The system shows again how the impressive, Westernized exterior of modern Japan has been braced by the judicious use of tradition.

Other modernizers, more Western than Nishimura, placed their emphasis on ideals of natural rights, popular sovereignty, equality of classes and sexes, and language reform, but their ideas outran their times. Similarly, Nishimura's more progressive suggestions attracted little attention, but when he applied tradition to current problems, some of his ideas were eventually picked up and utilized. They better fitted the essentially conservative nature of Meiji society which was on the middle road between Westernization and nativistic reaction, the quickest way to national strength. While Nishimura's thought remained fundamentally unchanged, government and people veered far toward Westernization for a decade or more, and then, when the general stream swung back, part of it at least swerved across his course. His activities served to strengthen Japan, it is true, but ironically they contributed to the ideology of the authoritarian state and chauvinism—both of which he deplored. As a moralist who preferred the more abstract elements in Confucianism such as truth, justice, fairness, and humanitarianism, he was unsympathetic to such selfish interests. As an idealist, his ultimate objective for Japan, once it had achieved strength, was to be a moral force in the cause of justice and humanity among the nations of the world. Did any Meiji oligarchs conceive of this as the ultimate objective of the modernization of Japan?

CHAPTER VII

The Meiji Leaders and Modernization: The Case of Yamagata Aritomo

ROGER F. HACKETT

ONE approach to the understanding of the modernization of Japan is to examine the motives and attitudes of those who planned the changes. Developments after the Restoration were, of course, the product of countless changes which occurred at every level of society, from the peasants who were persuaded that things could be different to the intellectuals who formulated and communicated general ideas on why things should be different. At the center of this process of change were those who had come to power in the Restoration movement and who controlled the newly formed political regime. It was a small group which held the power of decision—perhaps fifteen or twenty. Their resourcefulness in responding to the external crisis facing Japan in the nineteenth century has frequently been cited as a major explanation of Japan's successful transition to the modern world.

To account for this celebrated accomplishment both the objectives sought and the measures adopted by the Meiji leaders need to be examined. What views did they hold of the goals toward which the nation should move? What did they conceive to be the desirable steps for reaching those goals? My purpose is to explore some of the attitudes and actions, as they relate to the modernization of Japan, of a major figure, Yamagata Aritomo (1839-1922). It is not assumed that the Meiji rulers shared all the same views toward modern change, though on many issues there was striking unanimity. But through an examination of Yamagata's thoughts and deeds perhaps some light will be shed on the nature and role of the leadership in the modernization of Japan.

243

National Goals

The decisions which launched Japan on the road to modernization were fundamentally related to the world-wide expansion of the Western nations. Perry had demonstrated that Japan could no longer live in isolation as a self-contained world, but this was only the most convincing of a series of impulses Japan had received in the nineteenth century which multiplied the evidence of the advantages enjoyed by the West. In the "Great Tokugawa Debate" over the opening of Japan to trade, neither party denied the seriousness of the foreign threat nor the superiority of Western arms: Tokugawa writers familiar with China's plight wrote frequently of the deficiencies of Japan's defenses and the dangers courted by that condition. Yamagata and his circle of Chōshū samurai listened to Yoshida Shōin warn them that "If a nation in this struggling world should be surrounded by nations of an aggressive inclination and should remain inactive, it would certainly be destined to decline and become obscure."[1] Foreign military actions in 1863 and 1864 against Satsuma and Chōshū demonstrated the superior force backing the trade and diplomacy of the Western powers. Thus the seriousness of the external threat was recognized long before 1868, but an effective, centrally coordinated response to the challenge had to await the Restoration.

The primary goal of the Meiji leaders was to develop the capacity to preserve the nation's independence, to gain enough power to prevent external encroachment. The aim was "to establish the independence of our country and to increase the nation's strength in facing the Western powers,"[2] as Yamagata once put it, and "to preserve the nation's rights and advantages among the powers,"[3] as he expressed it on another occasion. Linked with this aim was the objective of securing unity within Japan. The last shogun had given as his reason

[1] Henry van Straelen, *Yoshida Shōin* (1952), p. 79.
[2] Tokutomi Iichirō, *Kōshaku Yamagata Aritomo den* (1933), III, p. 108. (Hereafter, *Yamagata den*.)
[3] *Yamagata den*, III, p. 108.

for resigning the need for the government to be "directed from one central authority"[4] in order that the nation might maintain itself in the face of foreign pressure. The need for unity was reiterated in the proposal of the five western daimyo in surrendering their land registers: "There must be one central body of government, and one universal authority which must be preserved intact."[5] Again, in the Imperial Rescript abolishing the han in 1871 the question was asked, unless the han were abolished "How is it possible for Us . . . to give protection and tranquility to the people, and to maintain equality with foreign nations?"[6]

If the first aim of the Meiji rulers was to achieve national strength and independence, the second was to gain acceptance into the comity of Western nations. There was more than the desire for Japan to hold its own in the modern rivalry and struggle between nations; there was the ambition to be accepted as a civilized nation, with the standing of a Great Power. Addressing the city fathers in Sacramento, California in 1872 as a member of the Iwakura mission, Itō Hirobumi put it in these words: "We come to study your strength, that, by adopting widely your better ways, we may hereafter be stronger ourselves. . . . We shall labor to place Japan on an equal basis, in the future, with those countries whose modern civilization is now our guide."[7] At the end of the century, Itō, in a similar statement, said that the country had aimed "to secure . . . prosperity, strength, and culture, and the consequent recognized status of membership upon an equal footing in the family of the most powerful and civilized nations of the world."[8]

Independence, unity, and equality with the civilized powers were the justifications for military reorganization, educational

[4] Walter W. McLaren (ed.), *Japanese Government Documents* (1914), p. 2.

[5] McLaren, *Documents*, p. 29.

[6] *Ibid.*, p. 33.

[7] Quoted in Charles Lanman (ed.), *Leaders of the Meiji Restoration in America* (1931), p. 19.

[8] Okuma Shigenobu (ed.), *Fifty Years of New Japan* (1910), pp. 125-126.

reforms, political changes, and other radical changes initiated by the Meiji government. But neither the frequent reiteration of these goals nor their widespread acceptance as the reasons for change diminish their importance. It might be argued that self-preservation left no genuine alternative and so that the articulation of goals had little to do with Japan's capacity to change. Yet weight ought to be given to the influence exerted by the formulation of clear cut goals on the means for achieving them. In the first place, warning of threats to Japan's independence communicated a sense of urgency which helped to produce an environment less hostile to innovation. The claim that strength must be gathered in order to survive doubtless inspired greater efforts and broader support than otherwise would have been the case. In the second place, the open admission of inferiority and the need to learn from more advanced nations aided both the acceptance of radical measures and the alacrity with which foreign knowledge was pursued. One is tempted to feel that the confession of deficiencies affected both the capacity and the confidence of the Japanese to learn.

In any case, reforms were guided in directions which would not only advance the national interests but, at the same time, earn the respect of foreign powers and, hopefully, equality with them. An unusual example of this comes from the pen of Yamagata in an account of his efforts to strengthen the nation by developing a local government system in the 1880's. As in the case of most Meiji reforms, foreign advice had been sought and Western models carefully studied. "If you ask why I had a European, Mr. Mosse, draft the law," wrote Yamagata, "even though there was to be found the spirit of self-government in the *goningumi*, *shōya*, *nanushi*, and *toshiyori*, it was in order to be in step with the institutions extant among the great powers of Europe and America . . . and the German system was adopted as the model because it was the most suitable."[9]

[9] Yamagata Aritomo, "Chōhei seido oyobi jichi seido kakuritsu no enkaku" in *Meiji kensei keizai shiron* (1919), p. 401.

While the policies of the early Meiji period were carried out within the framework of the national goals outlined above, the framework itself was altered by the remarkable success of those policies. By the 1880's unity within Japan was no longer threatened by the revolts of the discontented, and the attention of the government moved to a concern for the moral and spiritual unity of the nation. The divisive effect of disgruntled ex-samurai lashing out at a government which had undermined their economic and social position was replaced by the activities of political groups challenging the rulers to share their power. As a consequence, the attitude toward unity on the part of the leaders changed from the organization of power to overcome physical resistance to the construction of political institutions and the promulgation of laws which would restrain and confine competing centers of political strength which, they believed, contributed to the nation's political and moral disunity. Similarly, the attitude toward the adoption of Western ways designed to convince foreign powers that Japan was a civilized nation—an effort which reached giddy heights in the late 1880's—swerved in a different direction. Interest was redirected to elements of Japan's traditional society which were pointed to as being every bit as civilized as what the Western powers displayed. Furthermore, as the nation grew in international stature and confidence replaced fear, some Japanese spoke of transmitting to China and Korea those aspects of Western civilization which she had adopted. Writing fifty years after the treaty with Perry, Ōkuma Shigenobu declared with smug satisfaction, "We desire, by the cooperation of our Anglo-Saxon friends, to engage in a glorious humanitarian work of civilizing and developing two Oriental nations now deeply sunk in misery, so that they, too, may someday be able to write semi-centennial stories of progress as we are now doing."[10]

The most important shift in the attitude of the Meiji leaders occurred in their views toward Japan's international goals. Not unnaturally, foreign relations were conceived of

[10] Okuma, *Fifty Years of New Japan*, p. 53.

in somewhat limited terms as the Meiji nation emerged. National security first meant defense of the home islands; the aim of independence did not require a thrust abroad. However, as Japan's strength increased it enabled her to play a more active part in international affairs. One angle from which to view the changing attitude of the leadership toward Japan's foreign goals is through the evolution of Yamagata's thinking concerning the requirements of Japan's national security. In his inaugural speech as Prime Minister before the first Diet in 1890, Yamagata outlined the broad objectives the nation should pursue. He declared that the continual goal of the nation must be "to preserve our independence and enhance our national position." In the words that followed he defined the nation's security in the following terms: "The independence and security of the nation depend first upon the protection of the line of sovereignty (*shukensen*) and then the line of advantage (*riekiesen*) . . . if we wish to maintain the nation's independence among the powers of the world at the present time, it is not enough to guard only the line of sovereignty; we must also defend the line of advantage . . . and within the limits of the nation's resources gradually strive for that position. For this reason, it is necessary to make comparatively large appropriations for our army and navy."[11] The precise extent of these "lines" was not made clear in the speech, although they clearly referred to the territorial boundary of the nation and to an area beyond which Japan should seek dominant influence. However, documents which have come to light more recently reveal that Yamagata thought of Tsushima island as the national boundary to the west and Korea as the "line of advantage" setting off a buffer zone of protection which, if in unfriendly hands, would threaten the nation's security.[12] He predicted Korea would become the center of conflict when the Russian trans-Siberian railway was completed. Because Korea's independence would then be

[11] *Yamagata den*, III, pp. 4-5.

[12] This document is printed in *Nihon gaikōshi kenkyū: Meiji jidai* (Studies in the History of Japan's Foreign Relations: Meiji Period), Tokyo (1957), pp. 192-195.

threatened and, if lost, would push back "the line of advantage" to Tsushima island, he argued for an agreement between China, England, Germany, and Japan to guarantee Korea's independence.

Japan's victory over China in 1895 called for a change in attitude toward the goal of the nation's security. In a memorandum calling for the expansion of the army and the navy submitted at about the time that the Treaty of Shimonoseki was being signed, Yamagata outlined the reasons for that need. He expressed fear at the growing strength of Russia, evidenced by the construction of the trans-Siberian railway, as well as the growing strength of other Western powers. He argued that "our military preparedness up to this time has been used chiefly to maintain the line of sovereignty. However, if we are to make the result of the recent war something more than a hollow victory and move on to become the leader of the East Asia, it will be absolutely necessary to extend the line of advantage. Our present military strength is inadequate for maintaining our new line of sovereignty; it follows that it is inadequate for extending the line of advantage and gaining dominance in East Asia."[13]

For Yamagata, victory had changed the nation's international goals. Japan should now strive to be a leading power in the Far East and build up the military forces to sustain that task. His strategic thinking and military planning were the products of careful study and a keen appreciation of the elements of international power rivalry. His changing "line of advantage" required the constant military expansion that provided a major stimulus to the growth of Japan's economy. It also required, in his view, the development of strong patriotism and unity through discipline and education. In order to protect the "line of advantage," he once declared, "the essential requirements are, first, military preparedness and, second, education."[14] The continuing justification for military preparedness, however, was the real or potential threat posed

[13] *Yamagata den,* iii, pp. 241-242.
[14] *Nihon gaikōshi kenkyū: Meiji jidai,* p. 195.

by foreign powers: first by the Western nations generally, then by Russia, and finally, after 1914, by his vision of a world-wide racial struggle between the white and colored races.

Some Measures for Achieving National Goals

It is commonly remarked that the Meiji oligarchs had no blueprint, no grand design, for transforming the country into a modern nation; rather that they were hardheaded, practical statesmen concerned more with pragmatic solutions to concrete problems as they arose. Without wholly denying this, the declared policy "to select from the various institutions prevailing among enlightened nations such as are best suited to our present condition, and adapt them, in general reforms,"[15] gave some form to the process. The principle of selection and the priority of reforms were determined by pragmatic tests, but the decision to emulate Western achievements affected the whole procedure. Furthermore, from the outset the Meiji leaders were sensitive to the interrelatedness of military requirements, political reforms, economic development, and other aspects of modernization. One illustration of this is Yamagata's memorandum objecting to the decision to send troops to Formosa in 1874. In it he warned against the premature use of the newly formed army and declared that the nation's strength depended as much upon economic development and raising the level of the people's welfare and intelligence as it did upon military undertakings.[16] The recognition, early in the Meiji period, of the interdependence of political unity and the development of a centralized army further illustrates this awareness.

Since military inferiority was the most convincing measure of the threat of the West, the need for a national military system utilizing modern weapons and techniques was widely accepted from the outset of the Meiji era. The adoption of

[15] From the letter of the Meiji Emperor delivered to President Grant by Iwakura in 1872. Quoted in Lanman, *Leaders of the Meiji Restoration in America*, p. 29.

[16] *Yamagata den*, II, pp. 346-352.

Western arms had been under way for some years before the Restoration; Chōshū and Satsuma had achieved a critical advantage in their struggle with the Bakufu by the rapidity and success with which they armed and trained some of their troops with Western weapons. Having played a decisive influence in the pre-Restoration fighting, it was natural that the military modernization would be expected to play a crucial part in unifying the nation.

The initial stages of this process were hindered more by political obstacles than technological difficulties. In the memorial submitted by the Tosa han inviting the shogun to abrogate his political powers in 1867, it was pointed out that "military preparations being one of the primary requirements, we need surplus guards for the Imperial Court and a military headquarters established somewhere in the Kyoto-Osaka area."[17] This recognition of the need for both an Imperial military force and a central headquarters was intimately related to the question of centralized political authority. After returning to Japan in September 1870, following a twelve month tour of Europe, Yamagata was asked to become Assistant Vice-Minister of Military Affairs. His experience and performance in Chōshū before the Restoration and his feats during the Restoration fighting, as well as his newly acquired knowledge of foreign military systems, made him a logical choice for such a post. He was eager to apply his knowledge and experience in organizing a national army, but he was persuaded that a unified political framework would first have to replace feudal autonomy. In this he followed the lead of Omura Masujirō, who served as Vice-Minister of Military Affairs until his assassination in 1869, and who had outlined the military reforms which were later put into effect. Omura had been convinced that military modernization required the abolition of the fiefs, the end of the samurai's privileges, and the introduction of universal military conscription. Omura's convictions became Yamagata's. "Upon my return to Japan," he recalled, "I felt that the fiefs must be abolished, but at that time the new government lacked the power to enforce such

[17] Osatake Takeshi, *Meiji bunka sōsetsu* (1934), p. 172.

a measure. Feeling that there was no choice but to await the proper time, I dedicated my efforts to the unification of military strength which I felt to be the most important task."[18]

For Yamagata, the first step toward unification was to persuade Satsuma to place its troops under the direct authority of the Tokyo government. In March of 1868 a guard unit composed of contingents from several han and totaling some four hundred men had been organized under a court bureau.[19] Friction had developed between Saigō Takamori and others and, as a consequence, Satsuma troops, the strongest contingent in the nation, had returned to Kagoshima. So when in February 1871 the decision was made to organize an Imperial Bodyguard with troops from Chōshū, Tosa, and Satsuma, it was first necessary to persuade Saigō to cooperate. The approach was to appeal to him on grounds of patriotism and the need to shift traditional allegiances from the han to the nation. Yamagata claims to have put it to Saigō in these terms: "When soldiers from three fiefs are organized in an Imperial Bodyguard they would naturally lose their status as han vassals. Satsuma men must be willing even to turn against the Satsuma lord if the occasion demands it. Similarly Tosa and Chōshū soldiers must be prepared to disobey their lords. In other words, we must organize an Imperial Bodyguard in reality as well as in name."[20] Saigō agreed.

The point to be noted here is that the decision to establish a Western type military organization to back up the new government required a preliminary political arrangement. Moreover, it was not until the fiefs were abolished in 1871 that the major step in the unification of military power—the inauguration of a military conscription system—could be taken. In turn, it was not possible to do away with the fiefs until sufficient military strength had been created to assure the success of that major political reform. By April 1871, an Imperial Bodyguard constituting the first important military unit under the direct command of the Emperor was organized.

[18] Yamagata, in *Meiji kensei keizai shiron*, p. 377.
[19] Matsushita Yoshio, *Wadai no kaigun rikugun shi* (1937), p. 31.
[20] Yamagata, *Meiji kensei keizai shiron*, p. 379.

The unit was no larger than 10,000 men but it did represent the cooperation of three major fiefs and the willingness to back up the government. With this nucleus of military power it was possible for the first time to undertake drastic political reforms with some confidence. "In order to realize the aim of the Restoration of the Emperor," Yamagata reasoned, "all orders must come from one source. If all orders are to emanate from one source we must first abolish the fiefs. . . . In abolishing the fiefs and establishing the prefectures it will be difficult to prevent the opposition of certain ex-daimyo and vassals. In some cases it will probably require suppression by military force."[21] He labeled the death of the fiefs the "second restoration," and claimed that "it made possible for the first time the actual realization of the Imperial Restoration."[22]

Military Conscription

Following the abolition of the feudal political order in 1871, the establishment of a conscription system became one of the government's main efforts. It is with this undertaking and the building of the new army that Yamagata was so intimately connected. These labors have been widely lauded. Even Yoshino Sakuzō, an otherwise bitter critic of the oligarchs, complimented them in the 1920's by conceding that "If Yamagata were to receive the thanks of the Japanese people a hundred years from now it would be for this one thing alone."[23] This would be a less acceptable judgment today, but that the adoption of conscription had profound consequence is generally appreciated. Despite this there is very little literature on the subject of the modernizing effect of the development of a Western-style army in Japan, or, for that matter, in any country.

Despite the far-reaching implications of such a decision, universal military conscription was launched early and with apparent ease. Perhaps part of the explanation of the quick

[21] *Ibid.*, p. 385.
[22] *Ibid.*, p. 386.
[23] Yoshino Sakuzō, "Rekishigan ni aizuru Yamagata kō," *Chūo kōron*, March 1922, p. 71.

adoption of this change was the widespread recognition that a dependable method was needed for organizing a national military force loyal to the Emperor and ready to enforce domestic order while the control of the central government was being solidified. In a memorial to the government six months after the abolition of the fiefs, Yamagata declared that "The immediate concern of the Military Department is with domestic affairs while external matters are of future significance."[24] So the need for internal security was a prime factor in the decision to adopt a new military system, and Sansom's judgment that "it was the most effective single measure that the government was able to take in its campaign to consolidate authority,"[25] seems valid. At the same time, however, Yamagata's memorial went on to argue that, "If adequate preparations are made against the outside world, there will be no cause for anxiety over internal matters. At present our military strength, aside from the Imperial Bodyguard established merely to protect the Palace and Emperor, includes only the troops of the four garrisons numbering twenty battalions. These are assigned to maintain internal security not external defense. . . . But with the significant changes resulting from the dissolution of the han armies and the collection of weapons, circumstances are appropriate for determining a policy for external defense." Thus the long-range objective of providing the nation military security in an unfriendly world was a second factor in the development of a national basis for military mobilization.

But why universal military conscription? Why not an elite army composed of ex-samurai? As a matter of fact, there was some opposition to military service regardless of class. General Tani Kanjō, for example, proposed that all the sons of *shizoku* should serve as soldiers first, with punishments to those who refused, while the common people should be selected for service only after the *shizoku* were trained.[26] Some of Saigō's subordinates opposed universal conscription

---

[24] Memorial in *Yamagata den*, II, pp. 200-205.
[25] Sir George Sansom, *The Western World and Japan* (1950), p. 326.
[26] Matsushita Yoshio, *Chōheirei seitei shi* (1943), p. 119.

on grounds that peasants could never become the high quality soldiers the nation required. Torio Koyata, a Chōshū general, opposed the plan claiming that the spirit of the samurai would be weakened, and Maebara Issei, another Chōshū clansman, who followed Omura as the Vice-Minister of Military Affairs and preceded Yamagata's promotion to that office, went along with plans to build a standing army exclusively of *shizoku*.

Success turned on several considerations. One important factor was that almost all European nations built their armies on the foundation of a universal conscription system. "Although standing armies vary with each country," read the 1872 memorial of Yamagata and his colleagues, "even such small countries as Belgium and Holland have at least forty-five thousand regulars and . . . all European countries have reserves."[27] Adopting Western practices formed a basis for many of the major Meiji reforms, but it was peculiarly important for military reforms. A modern army is by its very nature a comparative institution; its ultimate objective is to protect the nation from foreign threats and unless it can compare favorably with foreign military power it does not fulfill its purpose. To rate favorably, therefore, military forces must compare well by international standards.

A second reason aiding the adoption of conscription was the success that various fiefs had had in organizing military units made up of members of more than one class. Yamagata's experiences as a leader in the *Kiheitai* in Chōshū, and his knowledge of the rudimentary conscription systems adopted in Tosa and Wakayama prior to the Restoration, satisfied him that the non-samurai classes were capable of learning methods of modern warfare. Thirdly, a key factor in the adoption of conscription was the role played by Saigō. As the most powerful military figure in the nation, Saigō never openly expressed himself in opposition to the plan; indeed he maintained a stern silence while the arguments for and against conscription were being exchanged. Privately, however, he encouraged the idea of conscription through the sup-

[27] *Yamagata den*, II, p. 201.

port of his younger brother, Saigō Tsugumichi, the Assistant Vice-Minister in the Military Department, and at the same time he worked to weaken the most violent opposition of his own clansmen. Fourthly, Yamagata argued that universal conscription should be adopted because it could be regarded as an integral part of the national educational process which would strengthen the nation. He contended that, "If boys enter grammar school at six, high school at thirteen and graduate at nineteen, after which, from their twentieth year, they spend a few years as soldiers, in the end all will become soldiers and no one will be without education. In due course the nation will become a great civil and military university."[28] This was a position calculated to appeal to broad support.

Finally, the inclusion of liberal exemption provisions in the Conscription Act of January 10, 1873, suggests that compromises were felt necessary both to win its acceptance and to insure its enforcement in the face of opposition. The law provided for seven years of military service after the age of twenty, three years in the regular army and four years in the reserves, but it included seven types of exemptions. Some of these categories, such as household heads and their heirs, those in certain stipulated professions, government officials, clearly favored the *shizoku* class. The exemption for household heads and heirs, designed to give stability to families, did not in itself favor the *shizoku*, but the fact that the *shizoku* class monopolized the professions and officialdom meant a large group of this class received preferential treatment.[29] In the long run, all opposition to conscription was not overcome by these concessions, but the enactment of the law was clearly aided by these accommodations. When opposition no longer threatened the regime many of these concessions were withdrawn.

Once the decision was made to strengthen the nation by conscripting all males for military service in imitation of European, especially French, models, forces were set in

---

[28] Matsushita, *Chōheirei seitei shi*, p. 121.
[29] See text of conscription law in *ibid.*, pp. 137-966.

motion which contributed to the process of modernization. For example, it represented a radically new experience for most of the youth who entered the forces. Since the population was predominantly rural it required recruits to move into the towns where garrisons were located. This meant not only an abrupt introduction of the rural peasant into a new urban environment, it also meant, at least temporarily, the breaking of family and village ties of civilian life for the more impersonal world of the armed forces. The hierarchic organization and the stern discipline present in the army probably allowed the young recruit more psychological security and an easier introduction into a changing world than was the case of his village friend who gave up his land for the attractions of the city and was caught up in the process of being urbanized. Nevertheless, through conscription the village peasant came in touch for the first time with many new ideas and practices. He was introduced, for example, to Western style clothes for, despite the motley array of semi-Westernized clothes which may be seen in any photograph of the earliest modernized military forces of Japan, in due course regulations required all soldiers to adopt Western style uniforms. A regular allowance as payment for service was probably the first monthly salary most peasant conscripts had ever received. Living habits were undoubtedly altered as the recruits were housed in barracks equipped with beds, stoves, and electric lights. It is alleged that the custom of smoking cigarettes spread throughout the country largely because the recruits picked up the habit in the army. More important, many peasants received their earliest introduction to reading and writing and technical skills.[30]

One thing led to another. Cloth for military uniforms and knitted socks for the soldiers, originally imported at great cost, were soon being made by Japanese manufacturers. Requirements for supplying food to a growing army gave birth to a canning industry. Literacy had the consequence of broadening their outlook, books and magazines exposed soldiers

[30] Shibusawa Keizo (ed.), *Japanese Life and Culture in the Meiji Era* (1958), p. 306.

to some of the new thoughts of the age. Wholly aside from the high-level decisions to establish and develop industries to support the foundations of defense, the ramifications of the decision to adopt universal military conscription were endless.

Yet it was hardly Yamagata's intention to initiate conscription in order to introduce country boys to city ways. It was adopted in order to increase the unity and strength of the nation. Although the incorporation of Western technology and organizational methods were the first steps to that end, it was soon discovered that an efficient military force also required morale and discipline. Moreover, in the face of uncertainties in the infancy of the new order, it was essential to instill unquestioned loyalty to the nation. Army authorities were, therefore, concerned that radical thoughts being publicized in the 1870's would harm discipline. The concern seemed amply justified when some of the ringleaders of the army mutiny of 1878 were found to have supported agitation against the methods of the oligarchy.[31] Stern action was called for in the face of this "spiritual weakness."

In the development of the Meiji military ideology, the ambivalent character of Japan's encounter with the West is well illustrated. On the one hand, loyal, drilled, and disciplined military services were developed with the new Western techniques, but on the other, the spirit of loyalty and discipline were inculcated by resuscitating traditional ideals. Unity and loyalty were buttressed by external and internal elements reinforcing each other. From one point of view the sense of national unity was forced upon Japan by the necessity to cope with external pressures, it was induced by the belief that without unity national independence could not be sustained. From another point of view the feeling of loyalty toward the nation was a product of the belief in Japan's own unique historical development; it was thus encouraged by a sense

[31] Fifty-three soldiers were executed before a firing squad and 218 were punished for their part in this mutiny. A complete account of the Takebashi Mutiny is found in Matsushita, *Wadai no kaigun rikugun shi* (1937).

of national continuity and integrity. When these reinforcing elements were applied to military reforms it meant that coping with the West required both the adoption of Western military techniques and weapons to meet international standards of power, and the invoking of values of the past to promote standards of conduct essential for a unified army. New methods and old ideals were effectively joined or, in other words, a native ethic was combined with a borrowed technique.

A sequence of measures adopted in the 1870's and the early 1880's may be identified as the basis for developing discipline and obedience and unswerving allegiance to the imperial government. These measures contained both positive and negative elements. In the regulations handbooks issued to soldiers after 1872, loyalty to the Emperor was emphasized as the guiding principle. In the "Admonition to Soldiers" (*Gunjin kunkai*) circulated to all the military units in 1878, an appeal was made to all military personnel to adopt loyalty, bravery, and obedience as guiding ideals. These unifying ideals were amplified and elevated in the Imperial Rescript to Soldiers and Sailors issued in 1881 (*Gunjin chokuyū*). It was made clear that belief in these guiding virtues were part of Japan's historical development, and that the respected values of the past should be revived to strengthen the institutions of the present.[32]

There was, of course, a strong rational element in the building of the modern army along Western lines. At the same time, there was a ritualistic element which developed as the heart of the spirit of the military forces. The secular duty of defending the nation through obligatory military service was combined with the sacred duty of loyal service to the imperial government. The tendency of restoring more traditional values to give cohesion to a borrowed institution was not uncommon in Meiji Japan—the educational system comes

[32] I have attempted to show how the major author of these regulations relied upon samurai virtues to encourage army discipline in my article, "Nishi Amane—A Tokugawa-Meiji Bureaucrat," *Journal of Asian Studies* (1959), XVIII, p. 2.

readily to mind. But it was discernible earlier in the armed forces and for two different reasons: first, the obvious truth that no military establishment could long survive without loyal obedience; secondly, because the military institution could more quickly become modernized than other social institutions and then could be advanced by appealing to more ritualistic types of behavior.

The negative elements included in the measures to strengthen the armed forces were directed at keeping the army independent of political influences and prohibiting soldiers from participating in political activities. The "Admonition to Soldiers" warned military personnel that "such behavior as questioning imperial policies, or expressing private opinions on important laws, or criticizing the published regulations of the government, runs counter to the duty of a soldier."[33] The Regulations for Public Meetings and Associations issued by the government in 1880 was specifically designed to combat anti-government activities and warned that, "No military and naval men now on active service or in the first or second reserves may attend any meeting where politics form the subject of address or deliberation. Neither may they become members of any political association."[34] In part, at least, the Military Police were organized early in 1881 because, as the Order of the Council of State read, "The movement for popular government is spreading throughout the country and clashes are occurring between the citizens and the authorities as well as between soldiers and police."[35] Finally, in the "Rescript for Soldiers and Sailors" the first article proclaimed that loyalty was the essential duty of the soldier and sailor and warned him "neither to be led astray by current opinions nor meddle in politics, but with single heart to fulfill your essential duty of loyalty."[36] The extension of this principle of isolating the military from politics is found in the regulation Yamagata originated in May 1900

[33] *Yamagata den*, II, p. 774.
[34] *Ibid.*, II, p. 775.
[35] Matsushita Yoshio, *Meiji gunsei shiron* (1938), II, p. 215.
[36] Text in Hillis Lory, *Japan's Military Masters*, appendix.

which required the service ministers in the cabinet to be regular officers of the highest rank.

These regulations and laws sponsored by Yamagata make clear his conviction that military modernization required more than a quick adoption of the superior military technology of the West. No Meiji leader disagreed with Yamagata's statement that "The first requirement of the new government was to establish its authority by assembling actual military power."[37] The establishment of internal unity and the meeting of the external challenge were related objectives, both served by a modern military service based on universal military conscription. But the authority and discipline required demanded duty, loyalty, and rejection of political influences. In Yamagata's view, military modernization required, aside from the assimilation of new techniques and weapons, a national discipline of a sort that was best stimulated by recourse to values and virtues sanctioned by tradition.

Yamagata tended to take a similar view toward the problems of internal political development. When he assisted in the creation of political institutions he carried with him the conviction that the disciplined loyalty of the people and the limitation of popular political activities were necessary for the attainment of national goals. Indeed, Yamagata's apparent test of the acceptability of Western-style political institutions was their contribution to national unity. In the growing conflict between the demands for greater political freedom and the government's domination of Meiji politics, he came down heavily on the latter side. He promoted controls to limit political dissidence and encouraged legislation designed to increase support for the national interest. This can best be seen in his part in the development of a new local government system, and in his views of constitutional government and political parties.

Local Government

In the years following the formation of prefectures in 1871, successive steps were taken to reduce local autonomy

[37] Yamagata, *Meiji kensei keizai shiron*, p. 377.

by creating local bodies more susceptible to centralized control. In 1872, the number of prefectures was reduced and each in turn subdivided into smaller administrative units; in 1874, the prefectures were placed under the supervision and control of the Home Ministry. Growing demands for greater participation in local government led to the formation of prefectural assemblies in 1878. A measure of local self-government existed, but the frequent reference to an "autonomous system" (*jichi seido*) is somewhat misleading because all local units were subject, within the area of authority delegated to them, to centralized supervision. Furthermore, in 1880 there was no standardization and no legal framework specifying the rights and obligations of local units.

When plans were being drawn up for a new political framework in the 1880's, Yamagata expressed an interest in the arrangement of the local government system. He wrote Itō in Europe that information on this aspect of government should be sought from acknowledged authorities. It was his conviction that a local government system should be worked out prior to the promulgation of the constitution, and although he met some resistance on this point he won his way. As Home Minister he sat at the head of a committee for drafting a local government system which wrote the laws which were finally put into effect in 1888 and 1890.

In developing these laws Yamagata relied heavily on foreign experience. Albert Mosse, a leading pupil of the distinguished Prussian legal authority, Rudolph Gneist, is best known for his assistance in the preparation of the Meiji Constitution, but during his four years in Japan, from 1886 to 1890, he played a far more significant part in the drafting of local government laws.[38] As we have seen, Yamagata felt that the German local government system should be adopted as the model both because it was more suitable and because it was the system in a Great Power with which Japan wished to feel equal. In addition to Mosse's first-hand guidance and assistance, a second-hand source of acknowledged value was

[38] Osatake Takeshi, *Nihon kenseishi taikō* (1938), II, p. 681.

a biography of Stein, the Prussian statesman, by J. R. Seeley, Regius Professor of Modern History at Cambridge. Itō had come across Seeley's three volume work in his travels in Europe and immediately sent them to Yamagata who had them translated. He was so impressed by what he read about Stein that he wrote a laudatory preface to the completed translation and ordered that it be circulated to all officials concerned with the administration of local government.

It is not difficult to imagine the pleasure with which Yamagata must have read Seeley's analysis of Stein's Municipal Reform. One reference in particular must have found a sympathetic response: Seeley wrote, "There is, indeed, something in the law which reminds us of the great principle of the military reorganization on which Scharnhorst was meditating at the very same time. As the military reform ended in the state taking possession of three whole years in the life of every citizen, and partial possession of four more, so does this law enact that a citizen may be called upon to serve his own town gratuitously for three years, and, as a general rule, that he may be expected to serve for six."[39] This relationship between local government and military service was reflected in Yamagata's view that conscription and local self-government were twin pillars supporting the state, representing complementary services binding the people to the central government and strengthening the unity of the nation. He must have gained encouragement in that the theories and practices of a civilized European power sanctioned this attitude.

Stein's broader purposes likewise suited Yamagata's beliefs. Before the adoption of his municipal law, Stein argued that participation in local affairs "is a most beneficial manifestation of patriotic national feeling; if all cooperation is refused the result is discontent and opposition, which will break out in manifold forms or must be suppressed by violent measures which are destructive of the spirit."[40] Yamagata, guilty him-

[39] J. R. Seeley, *Life and Times of Stein* (1879), II, pp. 244-245.
[40] Quoted by Guy S. Ford, *Stein and the Era of Reform in Prussia* (1922), p. 226.

self of high handed measures to control the opposition, echoed these words in his own account of the preparation of the local government laws: "To my mind the influence of local autonomy contributed to the workings of constitutional government because it tended to develop public spirit and political knowledge and experience ... moreover, to the extent it contributed to a civic spirit it naturally lessened dissatisfaction with the government and its leaders."[41] As the activities of the political parties were causing Home Minister Yamagata grave difficulties at the time that legislation was being drafted, it was not unnatural that one of his hopes in the development of a local government system at the local level was to dissuade able men from participating in the popular political party and lure them into the local government administration.

The laws of 1888 and 1890 defining the organization of town, village, district, and prefectural governments increased the area of jurisdiction of local officials and allowed the local citizenry to select some of their representatives. Local responsibility was increased, however, not with a view to the development of democratic habits of mind at the grass roots but as the most effective way of preserving order and stability in the countryside. National unity, the raising of the standards of political administration which would earn the respect of foreign powers, and the organization of local government to strengthen the central government were the major objectives. Subjection of each administrative level of the supervision and control of the next gave the central government a higher degree of control than before. The broad powers reserved for the Home Minister at the apex of the triangle left little room for real decisions or initiative at the local level. Decentralization was limited, duties were delegated, and policies were executed from above and were not the expression of the will of the people from below. These characteristics of the local government laws were stressed in Yamagata's oral instructions to local officials in 1890. He told the assembled officials that, "Before everything, what you have to consider

[41] Yamagata, *Meiji kensei keizai shiron*, p. 406.

is that the people may be directed into the route most conducive to their interests, and that you yourselves may follow
the path of duty without error, favor, or affection. The executive power is of the imperial prerogative, and those delegated
to wield it should stand aloof from political parties and be
guided solely by consideration of the general good in the
discharge of their duties."[42]

In effect, what was accomplished was the bureaucratization
of the ablest local citizens. And in the increasing bureaucratic
organization of local government through these new laws one
observes a basic tendency of the process of modernization.
The laws codified the rights and responsibilities of levels of
government, differentiating levels of the political structure.
In this achievement Western models were explicitly followed.
But what was important to Yamagata was the expectation that
orderly government would be served and that in return for
a modicum of local responsibility loyal support of the government's goals would be given.

Transcendental Politics

In common with his colleagues, Yamagata accepted certain
Western political institutions, such as the constitution and
political parties, as a part of the modern development of Japan
and as a way to erase the stigma of the unequal treaties. "If
we wish to be sure of the future," he wrote a friend in 1880,
"it will be necessary to enact a constitution, open a national
assembly and establish foundations for a nation based upon
laws."[43] But he favored a cautious, gradual approach. He
had taken the position that a constitutional assembly should
first be convened by selecting the ablest men of the prefectural
assemblies and that after some years it should be allowed to
evolve into a national assembly. He felt that a constitution
should be designed to safeguard the powers of the emperor
and to define the limits of the people's rights. He also hoped
that it would strengthen the nation by encouraging support

[42] McLaren, *Documents*, p. 420.
[43] *Yamagata den*, III, p. 309.

of the government. "It is not unique," he had remarked "for a statesman to direct popular sentiment to lie with the government."

Yamagata was pleased enough with the Meiji Constitution to judge its enactment the "third restoration."[44] But he was troubled about parliamentary politics, especially with the possibilities of the diminution of the central government's authority. Unlike many Japanese travelers to Europe he had not been dazzled by constitutional practices abroad. During his first trip to Europe in 1869 he reported to Kido with misgivings that "even in England the King had lost much of his former power"[45] and added that it would be most undesirable if the Emperor's authority should be similarly reduced. On his second trip his earlier doubts about parliamentary government were strengthened. He registered his skepticism by reporting that, "In observing the various assemblies and election methods during my travels in Europe, I find that calm, mature discussion generally arouses little response while the reputation and influence of those advocating the empty theories of extremism gradually increases, the phenomenon varying in proportion to the development of the culture. . . . Administrative power is centralized, but in practice executive authority shifts to the legislature, with both groups advancing selfish policies thereby doing untold damage to the state."[46]

Nothing stands out more clearly in the political career of Yamagata than his dogged insistence that it was the government's responsibility to rule at the pleasure of the Emperor, and that a clear distinction should always be made between the government ruling on behalf of the Emperor and the parties owing loyalty to their own objectives. He was most insistent that the civil and military bureaucracies remain clear of partisan politics and that no party be permitted to control the cabinet and wield the decisive executive power. Initially there was general agreement among the Meiji leaders

[44] *Yamagata den,* II, p. 1060.
[45] *Ibid.,* II, p. 29.
[46] *Ibid.,* II, p. 1051.

that political parties should be excluded from power and that cabinet members should be responsible solely to the Emperor whom they served as advisers. They argued that it would be a violation of the constitution if ministers were to be responsible to the Diet or to a party. "I do not consider that cabinets organized on a party basis are consistent with the spirit of a Constitution enacted by the Emperor,"[47] was a sentiment Yamagata never tired of expressing.

This stand was sharply challenged by Itō's proposal to form a party in 1898. The vigor of the opposition of his fellow oligarchs to this suggestion delayed his plans, but Itō was not prevented from ushering in the Ōkuma-Itagaki party cabinet, a development which led Yamagata to talk gloomily of the "downfall of the Meiji government." Even before the formation of this short-lived party cabinet, Yamagata had been forced to the belief that party governments might appear. As he put it to Matsukata, "Speculating on the future, on the basis of the present situation, the formation of a party cabinet may some day be unavoidable; but, of course, this cannot be approved of in the light of the history of the Meiji government and the spirit of the constitution."[48]

Yamagata's attitude toward political parties was characteristic of most of the Meiji oligarchs. He recognized the validity of political parties in a constitutional system and the right of parties and interest groups to express sentiments in opposition to the government. The presence of two parties opposed to the government's policies, however, caused him concern and led him to encourage political groups friendly to the cabinet. It was his hope that a third party might exist which would counter-balance or at least frustrate any joint effort of the major parties to thwart the policy of the government.

Nevertheless, to his dying day Yamagata believed that the power of any popular party should be limited and never be allowed to gain control of the government. When Itō formed the *Seiyūkai*, Yamagata reported to the Emperor, "My

[47] *Japan Weekly Mail*, November 19, 1898.
[48] *Yamagata den*, III, pp. 309-310.

interpretation of the constitution differs from that of Itō and Ōkuma. I am absolutely opposed to a party cabinet. My only hope is that Imperial authority will be extended and Imperial prestige will not decline."[49] Hara Kei was persuaded in 1906 that it was futile "to hope for the fulfillment of constitutional government during Yamagata's lifetime."[50] Even after he was serving as prime minister of a party cabinet, and only three months before his assassination, Hara wrote in his diary, "Yamagata even now hasn't given up the thought of checking political parties."[51]

The consistency with which Yamagata held this view runs like a tough thread through the whole fabric of Meiji political history. The thinking of some of the other Meiji leaders with respect to the proper role of political parties underwent some change. It might be argued that Yamagata's adjustment to political realities, such as his understanding with the *Kenseitō* during his second ministry, or his acceptance of Hara as Prime Minister in 1918, reflected a tempering of his views, but it is doubtful. He clung to the position that a competitive political system multiplied divisions within society and detracted from national unity to which all should be sacrificed. He preferred a paternal government standing impartially over the people, working to compose their differences, protecting them from dangerous political ideas, and inspiring them to loyal support. It was his hope that constitutional government might provide a means of channeling political dissidence into paths least harmful to the accomplishment of the national goals. He had, of course, hoped that the military service and local government system would contribute to that same end.

Final Observations

I have chosen to examine a few of the activities in which Yamagata was engaged during a long, active, and influential career. He was not a man of ideas, he contributed little to the ideological shifts; rather, he was an institutional innovator

[49] Watanabe Ikujirō, *Meiji Tennō to hohitsu no hitobito*, pp. 278-279.
[50] *Hara Kei nikki*, III, p. 212. Entry of July 16, 1906.
[51] *Hara Kei nikki*, IX, p. 391. Entry of August 3, 1921.

and a manipulator of men. Yet through his development of military conscription, his involvement in organizing a local government system, and his constitutional politics, we can get a notion of his attitude toward the modernization of Japan. He conceived the establishment of each of these institutions as an important step in developing an up-to-date nation, and each innovation contributed significantly to stability, to the maintenance of independence and unity, and to winning foreign acceptance of Japan's modern, civilized state. All three institutions were based on foreign models, yet he did not regard modernization as an exotic venture. He viewed it as the realistic common sense acceptance of foreign practices suited to Japan's condition and valuable in the achievement of Japan's goals.

Although among the educated population of Meiji Japan there was a broad spectrum of attitudes toward the changes following the Restoration, the range of opinion among those holding power was more limited. The goals which they defined for the nation and toward which they attempted to guide developments evolved naturally and received widespread support. There were differences, however, concerning the priority of reforms and disagreement over the tempo of modernization. Yamagata was first concerned with the quick adoption of universal military conscription as a basis for developing the power of the state. He proved himself an efficient innovator; at the same time, as I have suggested, he incorporated traditional features in the reforms he helped to bring about.

There were, in fact, elements of both change and continuity in many of the Meiji reforms. Innovations were carried out within a mental and moral framework of the traditional past. Itō's claim that Japan didn't lack "mental and moral fiber" but only the "scientific, technical, and materialistic side of modern civilization,"[52] was a judgment shared by the Meiji leaders. They did not feel alienated from older values, they were never conscious of breaking with the past. For them the past was not bankrupt so that modernization was seen more

[52] Okuma (ed.), *Fifty Years of New Japan*, p. 124.

as the addition of Western ways. There were imaginative minds in search of a new society in Meiji Japan, but those controlling the government were seeking to up-date their society without upsetting the old base. Contrast, for example, Fukuzawa's conviction that "the independence of a nation springs from the independent spirit of its citizens," and his belief that Japan could not survive "if the old slavish spirit"[53] persisted with Yamagata's belief that Japan could not hold its own unless the past were strengthened. Both sentiments were entertained in Meiji Japan, but those in power did not see the pattern of Japan's future in the West.

In the modernization of Japan the relation between the principles of change and continuity took different forms. At one moment they conflicted, at another they existed side by side. What was most striking, however, was the way in which features of the traditional past contributed to the successful process of change. This was true of some of the innovations with which Yamagata was associated: traditional ideology was harnessed to strengthen the modernized army; concepts of a citizenry restricted in its rights and obedient to official-dom were hitched to a more modern local government system. Yamagata's conservative outlook, his preoccupation with the evolution of controls to encourage support of the government were combined with his acceptance of some Western institutions and the resolution to carry out modern reforms.

In examining the personal motivation of Yamagata we are confronted with difficulties. Clearly personal ambition and private drives moved him but he justified his deeds in the name of the national interest and the greater glory of the imperial power. Perhaps it is only a trait of the military approach to problems, but his preoccupation with preserving, protecting, and defending seemed to have formed the basis of much of his thinking. Fear of the foreign menace conditioned the hasty drive to construct the components of national power. Since, in the last analysis, the military establishment is maintained for the defense of the nation, it was perhaps natural

[53] Kiyooka Eiichi (tr.), *Autobiography of Fukuzawa Yukichi* (1934), p. 337.

for Yamagata to have been concerned with the nation's potential enemies and the extent of the threat they posed. His constant demands for greater military preparedness were based upon such estimates. Fear of Russia dominated his thinking for much of the Meiji period and was the basis of his advocacy of an alliance with Britain. His fear of a worldwide racial war between the white and colored peoples encouraged him to press the government for a closer association with the Chinese. His part in engineering an agreement with Russia in 1916 was designed to frustrate an "all-white" alliance which might fatally weaken Japan's position in a future racial struggle.

When we turn to Yamagata's attitude toward domestic developments, one might propose a similar basis for his attitudes. He was always concerned to protect the throne from what he regarded as threats and to defend the government against the encroachments of the popular political parties. In a word, he was inclined to conceive of political life in the framework of military operations, estimating his enemies and preparing to defend in ways he considered appropriate what he considered of central importance. One can imagine how he might have viewed the problems of political leadership: the "line of sovereignty" to be protected at all costs was the Imperial institution and the oligarchs were members of a supreme headquarters responsible for the strategy for defending the inner citadel. The civil and military bureaucracies, with top military personnel and the highest ranking civil servants comprising an elite corps, constituted the major defensive forces to be maneuvered. The Privy Council, the House of Peers, certain groups within the House of Representatives, and other units, might represent the "line of advantage," with permanent alliances formed with factions within each of those bodies sympathetic to his concept of government to bolster this protective zone. In this scheme, of course, the enemy was represented by the popular political parties and groups within the civil population questioning the legitimacy of the existing order and demanding greater political freedoms. Compromise with the opposition forces concen trated in the House of Representatives was an acceptable and sometimes necessary tactical move to gain limited objectives.

This outlook reflected Yamagata's low regard for the political activities of the populace. He had high regard for the ability of the people to serve the nation when properly led and educated, but a low opinion of their ability to act responsibly. He found the ideology and program of the movement for popular rights radical and unacceptable. To counteract what he believed to be the debilitating influence of popular movements he advocated suppressive measures, such as the Peace Preservation Law of 1887. In 1879 he complained of the arrogance, suspicion of the government, crude competition for wealth and position, the reckless acts in the name of foreign words like "freedom" of a large segment of the population. To counter this decay of moral standards he supported legislation, such as the Educational Rescript, to revive "good morals and manners." He believed his fears that radical thoughts were gnawing at the foundations of the state were shockingly confirmed by the alleged plot on the life of the emperor in 1908. "To think I have lived to witness the day when the destruction of the imperial order was advocated," was Yamagata's sad and bitter reaction. At the end of his life he repeatedly warned that radical ideas were spreading and irresponsible outbursts were menacing the nation.

In his attitude toward external affairs, politics, and the people he showed himself to be an arch-conservative. Yet Yamagata's attitude toward modernization was ambivalent. On the one hand, as a major architect of the Meiji state he fostered innovations that incorporated the achievements of Western science and technology; on the other hand, he advocated controls to suppress the political and social consequences of sweeping changes. He shared the dilemma of the conservative leaders: how to control forces released by the technological and political changes necessary to preserve unity and independence. The resolution he attempted was to use the central value of loyalty to the Imperial order both to justify and legitimize changes contributing to those ends as well as to sanction controls over consequences which weakened the ability to reach those goals. Yamagata's lasting fear was that a modernized future would bury the past which he felt necessary for building the present.

The Meiji leaders were autocrats who displayed resourceful statecraft. They were successful adapters of the components of modernity; their performance was remarkable but their prescription required the continuation of traditional authoritarianism in new form. They believed that the steps they took would lead the nation into the modern world. Their strong leadership provided the stable guidance which facilitated rapid and successful modernization.

PART FOUR

Cultural Contrasts: China and India

From the time the Conference on Modern Japan was organized, it was agreed that cross-cultural comparisons would be utilized where appropriate in order to see the Japanese case in different perspective. In considering changing attitudes toward modernization, the two aspects that came to mind most immediately were the bearing of a comparable (Confucian) tradition of thought in the different social and political setting of China, and the response to Western thought of early modernizers in India. The case of China provides a look at "pure" Confucianism on its home grounds, the second case, a view of the Western impact in a setting of total domination from abroad. The one turns inward, the other outward; Japan had known something of the first and was determined to know nothing of the second. However different the cases might prove to be, they might nevertheless provide occasion for reexamination of concepts and generalizations long applied to Japan.

Hellmut Wilhelm discusses the state of Chinese Confucianism on the eve of the nineteenth century Western impact. The period of Manchu domination, like that of the Tokugawa shogunate, represented the final stage of political and intellectual integration under the old order. During the centuries of peace and order many of the same schools and positions developed among Confucian scholars on both sides of the China Sea. Neither community of intellectuals was in close touch with the other; although imports of books from China provided one of the important sources of access to the non-Japanese world, Japanese Confucianists owed more to Chinese scholars who sought refuge in Japan after the fall of the Ming than they did to their contemporaries under Manchu rule. Nor was there much reason to expect curiosity about Confucian scholarship in Japan on the part of Chinese literati; although there were a few signs of prior development of some positions in Japan, all the signs point to parallel, rather than derivative, developments among the two philosophical and educational communities.[1]

Despite the existence of parallel schools of interpretation and specialization in China and Japan, however, the total thrust of the Confucian persuasion in China was extremely different. As suggested above,[2] the philosophy was tied to a functioning order of government in China; its ideals were supposedly embodied in the imperial autocrat who functioned also as ideological arbiter, and whose preferences, determined by official scholars and diffused by preparation for the examination system through which officialdom was recruited, limited the variety and degree of political speculation that was possible. Confucian values of legitimacy and loyalty, which pointed to a powerless emperor in Japan, led to a functioning political order in Peking. The resultant dynamics and tensions and the force of the philosophical tradition were consequently very different. Hellmut Wilhelm's examination of the psychological interiorization and increased

[1] A convenient summary of the Chinese influence in Tokugawa Japan can be found in Yoshikawa Kōjirō, *Nihon no shinjō* (Tokyo, 1960), of which pp. 1-133 are subtitled "Uke-ireru no rekishi: Nihon kangaku shoshi" (A History of Acceptance: A Short History of the Study of China in Japan).

[2] Pp. 51-52.

concern with ideal forms of the Ch'ing masters thus reminds us of the dangers of loose generalization about "tradition" and "Confucian." Despite the similarity of language and the identical texts in which guidance was sought, one seems to be dealing with an entirely different tradition.

Once the West knocked at the door, these differences became more striking still. The Manchus sought to manipulate the Confucian tradition to prevent political change which would unseat them, and reached a compromise with Western imperialists, ruling out the nationalism which might have turned against them. Had the Tokugawa regime carried on with European-French assistance, a comparable situation might have arisen. Instead the Meiji leadership was able to utilize nationalism in the interests of an imperial tradition under Confucian slogans and values—deferring for over a generation the possibility that popular nationalism might be turned against them.[3]

Stephen Hay's essay on Rammohun Roy, one of the first and most important advocates of modernization in India, shows that differentiation within categories of "Western" and "modern" is as necessary as in discussions of tradition. The "West" in the Indian experience of course represented a contact far more special and intense than in its East Asian context; the cultural setting was at the outset in any case less national than were those of China and Japan,

[3] For further development of this point, see Masao Maruyama, "Nationalism in Japan: Its Theoretical Background and Prospects," in *Thought and Behaviour in Modern Japanese Politics* (ed. Ivan Morris, Oxford University Press: London, 1963), pp. 135-156.

and the addition of a British to earlier levels of Persian-Islamic influence, and of Company to Mughal rule in Bengal, may on that account have provided less cultural shock than would otherwise have been the case. Whatever the case, one is struck in the quotations at hand by the almost total lack of the resentment with which contemporary Chinese and Japanese saw the Westerners invade their precincts, and by the speculation that the foreign yoke "would lead most speedily and surely to the amelioration of the native inhabitants." (Although it might be suggested that much of the Meiji scorn for "Chinese learning" and Nishimura's misgivings about "bigoted, obstinate, and stupid" Shintoists were comparable to Roy's deprecation of Sanskrit learning.)

The depth of Roy's participation in Western intellectual life (and his earlier exposure to related strands of thought in the Islamic tradition) is equally worthy of note. He followed the values of Christian Britain to their Greek and Hebrew roots, and was able to debate the very core of the Western intellectual tradition from the inside. And yet he did not surrender to that tradition completely or permanently; instead he brought to bear on it and on his own the power of reason in the interests of "enlightenment" and "progress."

Against this background the author suggests refinement of some terms, in the interests of recognition of the interplay between the traditional and the new. It has already been recognized that in the Japanese context this dialogue between the two was much in evidence, and that useful precedents lay at hand from the earlier adaptation of the Chinese examples. In this it is probable that the Japanese experience is fundamentally no different from that of other distinctive civilizations, although the alternation between periods of insular isolation and external orientation have made it more easily remarked.

CHAPTER VIII

Chinese Confucianism on the Eve of the Great Encounter[*]

HELLMUT WILHELM

IN THE context of this paper the term "Confucianism" will be used with two different intentions.[1] It is used to connote a system (or the systems) of thought derived from the mainstream of the Chinese intellectual tradition which is usually, and with good reason, traced back to Confucius and his school. In this sense, Confucianism should be understood as a school of philosophy, investigating, at it does, the facts and principles of reality and of human nature and conduct. Thus we have to deal here with a group (or groups) of philosophers who maintained and developed the intellectual heritage of the past. More particularly, we have to deal with those philosophers of the Confucian school who represent the stage of development of this school at the time when China was about to meet what Margaret Mead once called "the juggernaut of modern civilization."

On the other hand the term "Confucianism" is used to connote the Court ideology of the same period. In this sense the term should be understood as a discipline of political science. Its contents here will deal with the assertions and aims of the politico-social program of late Imperial China,

[*] This paper is based on data gathered during research for a monograph to be entitled "Trends of Thought in 19th Century China." Further documentation for some of the points made here will be forthcoming in this monograph. The topic of the monograph was suggested by, and much of the research for it was conducted under the auspices of, the Modern Chinese History Project, University of Washington. Research time was also provided by the courtesy of the Council of the Humanities, Princeton University.

[1] See Arthur Wright's preface and David Nivison's introduction to the volume *Confucianism in Action* (Stanford, 1959), for a plea to differentiate the content of this term whenever applied.

Confucianist ideology being one of her supreme tools of governance.

Once established, this differentiation is, however, difficult to maintain with any degree of neatness when applied to our period. No disciplinary barriers existed to delimitate these two aspects of Confucianism. On the one hand, the philosophers were, with rare exceptions, simultaneously acting as Court functionaries in a more or less exalted station. Thus their philosophizing was, at least as a rule, tainted for professional reasons by the propagandizing and indoctrinating functions of Court ideology. Since Confucianism had from the outset proclaimed public service as the most appropriate form of conduct for the educated, sustenance of his social position tended to be a determinant of the philosopher's theorizing. It is gratifying to note to what extent this pragmatic trap was avoided or circumvented by a number of philosophers whose intellectual integrity rendered them the responsible servants, and not unfrequently the victims, of the cause of the human mind. The Imperial ideologists, that is to say the Emperors and the Court politicians, on the other hand, assumed for authority the philosophers' garb. This do-it-yourself philosophizing proceeded as a rule with supreme disregard of the philosophers' world and of the current stage of intellectual development, and it was frequently carried on with an amazing degree of hypocrisy and callousness. Generally speaking, however, the functions of the philosopher and the functions of the politician were not clearly separated, and it is frequently difficult if not impossible to put a certain phenomenon or a certain individual squarely into one or the other camp.

Imperial Confucianism

During Ch'ing times, the fate of Confucianism in any sense was also heavily determined by the fact that China was ruled by a foreign dynasty. To be sure, among the articles of statecraft which the Manchus had taken over from preceding periods,[2] ideology as an instrument of control loomed large. Already in 1656 the Shun-chih Emperor said: "Controlling the universe, my first concern is to correct people's minds. To correct people's minds, my first concern is to exorcize heterodox skills."

This role of ideology was maintained by all subsequent Manchu Emperors, even though the terminology used reflected the personality of the Emperor and the progress of time. In an early K'ang-hsi edict of 1670 it is stated: "In my endeavor to bring about supreme control in the world, laws and regulations are not my only concern, but I put transformation through indoctrination first."

The most consistently used term for ideological practices was "to correct people's minds" (*cheng jen hsin*).[3] In Yung-cheng (1723-1735) edicts, however, the term "mind-washing" (*hsi hsin*) or "mind-washing and thought-cleansing" (*hsi hsin ti lü*) is preferred. The educational process and scholarship in general are squarely put to this task. As again the Yung-cheng Emperor once put it in 1735: "The supreme usefulness of reading books consists solely in fostering the way of cultivating one's personality and controlling people."

Or in another edict: "The state does not support scholars merely to stimulate literary talent . . . but in order to inspire due respect in the people toward their rulers and ancestors."[4]

The contents of government ideology were also settled quite early. In the Shun-chih edict, mentioned above, the emperor still states: "The three systems of teaching: Confucianism, Buddhism, and Taoism prevail simultaneously and they all make people do good and discard evil."

However, already under his rule these contents were narrowed down to Confucianism of the Chu Hsi brand, or, more precisely—to be fair to Chu Hsi—to certain tenets and slogans

[2] See Franz Michael, *The Origin of Manchu Rule in China* (Baltimore, 1942), Introduction.

[3] For Tao-kuang examples see *Tung-hua hsü-lu*, Tao-kuang 10, 1 r and 40, 4 r.

[4] Quoted by Nivison, *op.cit.* p. 223.

culled from Chu Hsi's comprehensive writings. By government order of 1652, textbooks in schools were limited to those of the Ch'eng-Chu school;[5] and the aging K'ang-hsi Emperor once opined: "Since the years of my minority, I have been genuinely fond of studying. Of all books there was not one which I would not peruse and recite. Each time I found in the writings of authors of all dynasties that a word or a phrase would be slightly out of harmony with the 'principle' and 'correct judgment,'[6] this was pointed out without fail by later critics. Only the Sung Confucianist, Master Chu, in all the books he wrote or compiled which comment on the multitude of Classics and expound the Way and the Principle, is always clear and distinct. . . . Throughout the last five hundred years, scholars have not dared to criticize him.[7] In my opinion, of those who advanced culture after K'ung and Meng, the merits of Master Chu are most extensive. . . ." And in consequence the place of Chu Hsi in official worship was raised from the status of a "Former Worthy" to that of a "Man of Genius."[8]

The institutional expressions of this Imperial decision are well known and do not have to be gone into here. To control the gentry ideologically, the examination system served;[9] its integrity was jealously guarded even at a time when honesty was not any more the prevailing attitude in other branches of the administration.[10] To control the commoners, the K'ang-

[5] *Ch'ing hsü t'ung-k'ao* 98.

[6] Li and i, the terms by which Chu Hsi Neo-Confucianism was usually referred to.

[7] Disregarding Imperial ignorance of actually existing criticism of this kind, the Emperor fails to take into account that the prevailing hesitance to criticize Chu Hsi was due to Imperial fiat rather than to the inherent unassailability of Chu's system.

[8] *Shih-lu*, Sheng-tsu 249, 7 v-8 r. Edict dated March 12, 1712.

[9] See Chung-li Chang, *The Chinese Gentry* (Seattle, 1955), esp. Part III.

[10] See for instance the famous "examination case" of 1859 (Hummel, *Eminent Chinese of the Ch'ing Period* [*ECCP*] 667 and numerous entries in the *Shih-lu*) which led to the execution of at least four high officials, including a Mongol bannerman, in addition to those who died in prison during the period of investigation.

hsi Emperor emulated the first Ming Emperor in selecting a number of slogans from the Chu Hsi system; these were elaborated upon by the Yung-cheng Emperor and—known as the Sacred Edict—were made the basis of continuous ideological indoctrination.[11] James Legge has aptly applied the term "Imperial Confucianism" to this system.[12]

Also in official worship a status distinction was then made between the three doctrines (or religions). When it was brought to the Tao-kuang (1821-1850) Emperor's attention that in several districts of Shansi province there existed temples of the Three Religions, he decreed that it was inappropriate "that the Exalted Saint and Foremost Teacher be revered and sacrificed to in the same temple as Buddha and Laotzu." Governors-General and Governors were made responsible in all provinces to correct this situation "for the glorification of the orthodox doctrine."[13]

Up to this point the attitude of the Manchu Emperors does not differ essentially from those of non-conquest dynasties. The Manchus may have been more elaborate, more rigid, and to a certain extent more skillful than their predecessors in earlier periods in applying the ideological device. The quality of their ideological policy was, however, determined by political principles developed earlier. Nevertheless, in one point the situation differed fundamentally; none of the Manchu Emperors showed any personal commitment to the ideological system that they thus employed. To be sure, Emperors of earlier dynasties had also found ways to make political contingency prevail over doctrinal directives; with few exceptions, however, they would not have found it sagacious to do so bluntly and without a proper dogmatic garb. Furthermore, the Manchu Emperors, with the possible exception of the first two, did not feel committed to anything beyond the

[11] See Chapt. 6 of K. C. Hsiao, *Rural China* (Seattle, 1960).

[12] James Legge, "Imperial Confucianism. Four lectures, delivered during the Easter and Michaelmas Terms of 1877, in the Taylor Institution, Oxford, on Imperial Confucianism, or the Sixteen Maxims of the K'ang-hsi Period." *The China Review* 6 (1877-1878), pp. 147-158; 223-235; 299-310; 363-374.

[13] *Tung-hua hsü lu*, Tao-kuang 34, 1 r.

maintenance and extension of their personal power and prestige. And in the case of the first two, where a sincere personal
absorption in spiritual and intellectual values cannot be denied,
the attraction of Buddhism seems to have been on the whole
stronger. Later Manchu Emperors did not share this addic-
tion, and, beginning with the Chia-ch'ing (1796-1820) Emperor, utterly lacked any understanding in the fields of philosophy and literature and said so openly. For the Tao-kuang
Emperor the "clever manipulation of literature," that is to
say creative writing, was as abhorrent as unreliability and
cliquishness among officials.[14] He once demoted the Governor
of Hunan for not having restrained one of his subordinates
from distributing his poetry commercially, a way of behaving
which he considered utterly unethical.[15]

Nor is this all. The same freedom from any commitment
to an ideological system was claimed not only for the Emperor personally but also for his Manchu bannermen. In 1836
the Tao-kuang Emperor discharged and fined to the amount
of two years' salary an Imperial Prince, a Beitzu, a Manchu
Banner General, and a Manchu Lieutenant General because
a Manchu bannerman under their charge had taken part in
a *chin-shih* examination without having been previously examined in horsemanship and archery as stipulated by the Hui-
tien. The special joke in this case was that the bannerman in
question was crippled.[16] In a number of other cases it is made
clear that this was not an individual occurrence which happened to irk the Emperor, but that a distinct policy was here
at play. In 1822 the Emperor denied financial assistance to an
academy for the education of bannermen in Hsi-an, stating
that in the education of bannermen only the Manchurian
language, horseback-riding, and archery should be emphasized. "Whoever has a mind to read books and study to
enhance his promotion should be privately responsible for
supplying instruction and the necessary money."[17] In another

[14] *Ibid.* Tao-kuang 33, 1 v-2 r.
[15] *Ibid.* 1 r-v.
[16] *Ibid.* 5 r-v; 6 r-v.
[17] *Ibid.* 5, 13 v-14 r.

case of 1833 he stated that the education of bannermen should be in horsemanship and archery, that they should be kept simple and straight and not exposed to weakening influences.[18] Similar decrees abound. Book learning was not for the Manchus, it would mean "leaving fallow their main occupation,"[19] and, the Emperor asked rhetorically, "in what way would they differ from Chinese officials?"[20]

As in other dynasties, the Emperor needed an ideologically uncommitted group.[21] In Manchu times, however, he did not have to go beyond the limits of status and frontier and enlist the services of eunuchs and foreigners for these tasks. It was his own men, the Banners, from whose ranks they were chosen. Chinese could react disdainfully, even militantly, toward a eunuch or a foreign mercenary, but no Chinese could dare to despise, or even to question the moral and social status of, these men. Chinese officials and Chinese philosophers alike had to learn how to cope with a situation in which the political process depended on the ideologically uncommitted.

The School of Sung Learning

We are not primarily concerned here with the attitudes the Chinese officials assumed under this set of circumstances. When we move into the world of the philosophers, however, we have to take into account, as stated, that they were frequently also officials and that political and intellectual concerns were bound to influence each other. This is particularly true for the representatives of the School of Sung Learning who found themselves conditioned by a system of doctrines which the Emperors utilized for political control. This, at least

---

[18] *Ibid.* 28, 13 v-14 r; see also *ibid.* 37, 3 v-4 v, where a Lieutenant-General is demoted for memorializing for support to establish an Academy at Urumchi, as this would mean taking light things seriously and serious things lightly.

[19] *Ibid.* 46, 4 v-5 v.

[20] *Ibid.* 31, 16 r; 17 r-v.

[21] See on this point Robert B. Crawford, "Eunuch Power in the Ming Dynasty" *T'oung Pao* 49, 3 (1961), esp. pp. 115-116.

partial, congruity of content should, however, not becloud the fact that their reasoning was activated by an entirely different set of motives. They fought for their intellectual cause with a degree of commitment which borders on the religious, and they took part in a living intellectual development, the trends of which they helped to shape.

We are confronted here with what Max Weber called the "ideological switchmen"[22] who, by constructing and upholding a conception of the world and of man's (the educated man's) place in the world, brought it about that officials willed to be the type of man they had to be, that they wholeheartedly and on their own accord entertained commitments which were so frequently contradictory to their personal interests. But we are also confronted with a group of men whose center of gravity rested with the intellectual tradition and not with the political interests for which this was exploited, and who, in this way, took part in shaping an intellectual flow, the course of which might have eventually led beyond the interests which the content of their thought was so shrewdly made to serve. It is the purpose of this paper to point out that even the Chu Hsi tradition, to which the philosophers of the School of Sung Learning adhered, was far from stagnant in Ch'ing times and that changes also within this current were incisive and approached being decisive. Their understanding of the traditional Confucianist task of "the cultivation of the personality" was well on the way toward what we today would call "self-realization." It amounted to a rediscovery of the human mind along psychological rather than philosophical lines and on this basis approached establishing the autonomy of the human mind within the framework of responsible orthodox thought.[23]

[22] See Hans Gerth, *From Max Weber*, New York 1946, pp. 63-64. Weber's phrase is: ". . . very frequently the 'world images' which have been created by ideas have, like switchmen, determined the tracks along which action has been pushed by the dynamics of interest." The term "ideological switchman" Weber picked up from Trotsky.

[23] For an evaluation of position and function of the human mind as seen by the Sung scholars and Wang Shou-jen, see Yu-Chung

It is worthy of note that the intellectual commitment of the philosophers of the Sung School frequently came about by a conversion or a sudden insight which at times resembled a sudden enlightenment of a Zenist nature. There was Lao Shih, who after having read Chu Hsi's *Chin-ssu-lu* several times, set up an altar and prostrated himself, saying: "This is my teacher. I consider him to be my fate bestowed on me by Heaven, just as a command issued by a ruler to an official or by a father to his son." There was Shao Tseng-k'o who one day, when reading the sentence in Meng-tzu: "Po I was the pure one among the sages,"[24] threw calligraphy and painting aside and concentrated on Sung studies. There was Ch'eng Tsai-jen, who once, taken to task by his teacher, did obeisance in a frightened state of mind, and after having been instructed in the *Chin-ssu-lu* got his inner enlightenment. There was Lo Yu-kao, in his youth an ardent reader of hero stories. After a lecture "sweat ran down his back, his tongue became numb and his limbs bent in a cramp. For a long time he could not regain his composure." Similar conversions are recorded for a number of other Sung scholars.[25]

A lack of congruity between the demands of a foreign court and the commitments of a Chu Hsi philosopher is particularly glaring in the first generation of the Ch'ing scholars of Sung learning. From these, four usually are singled out as the authoritative transmitters of the tradition: Lu Lung-chi (1630-1693), Chang Lü-hsiang (1611-1674), Lu Shih-i (1611-1672), and Chang Po-hsing (1652-1725).[26]

Lu Lung-chi[27] was strongly influenced by the thought, if not by the fate of Lü Liu-liang (1629-1683), a staunch sup-

---

Shih's "The Mind and the Moral Order," in *Mélanges Chinois et Bouddhiques* 10 (1955), pp. 347-364.

[24] *Meng-tzu* 5 B 1, Legge 371.

[25] On these cases see Chiang Fan, Sung-hsüeh yüan-yüan chi (in: *San-ch'ao hsüeh-an*, Shih-chieh, Shanghai 1936).

[26] Especially by T'ang Chien, *Hsüeh-an hsiao-shih*.

[27] *ECCP*, 547-548; T. Watters, *A Guide to the Tablets in the Temple of Confucius*, Shanghai 1879, pp. 240-243; A. Forke, *Geschichte der neueren chinesischen Philosophie* (Hamburg, 1938), pp. 489-492.

porter of Chu Hsi and implacable foe of Wang Yang-ming, and who, as will be recalled, shared the strongly anti-Manchu attitude of his period to the extent that he declined official service and even participation in the Po-hsüeh-hung-ju examination of 1679, retired into educational activities, and hid behind a Buddhist screen. Lü's consistent sniping against Manchu rule and Manchu customs has made him one of the most celebrated cases of literary inquisition in 1733, when his body was unearthed and dismembered, one of his sons executed, his grandsons banished, and many of his students involved in punishment.[28] In contradistinction to Lü, Lu remained within the official career but was rather unsuccessful in it[29] and thus also reverted to educational activities.

Lu's unquestioning reliance on Chu Hsi is expressed in the following quotation: "He who now-a-days discusses the doctrine has no other resort than reverence for Chu Hsi. Holding Chu Hsi in reverence is the correct (orthodox) doctrine, not holding Chu Hsi in reverence is not the correct doctrine." Lu's fierce battle against Wang Yang-ming and his influences was dictated by this attitude.

However, Lu made a rather narrow selection from the comprehensive system of Chu Hsi. Essentially there are only two among Chu Hsi's concepts which he emphasized: "abiding in reverence" and "exhausting the principles." What Lu lost in scope by this selection he gained in sophistication.

Reverence (*ching*) as the human attitude which directs all action was conceived by him primarily in psychological terms. He first of all analyzed his own psyche and investigated how it measured up to his own attitudes and actions. This need for trenchant and consistent self-analysis, self-reproach, and self-criticism led to the development of a number of psychological techniques which are at times reminiscent of a Xaverian discipline. One of these techniques was the keeping of a self-reproaching diary in which one's own attitudes and ac-

[28] *ECCP*, 581-582; L. C. Goodrich, *The Literary Inquisition of Ch'ien Lung* (1935), *passim*.

[29] He was sentenced to banishment for his opposition to the sale of offices during the Galdan campaign.

tions were daily examined and criticized, and guiding maxims were set down which might be quotes from the Classics, winged words of teachers and friends, or of one's own formulation. It became the custom to show these self-revealing diaries around among friends and have them add their criticism to one's own. Lu was the first Ch'ing scholar to keep such a diary; many others are in existence, frequently with marginal notes by friends.

Another one of these disciplinary techniques was the reading list. The establishment of such a list and the rigid adherence to such readings was not meant primarily as a help to convey certain factual or intellectual contents; they were, rather, designed to immerse oneself in, and become impregnated by, the spirit of prescribed parts of the Classics and the literature. Already here a purposive working on the unconscious mind can be perceived. Less purposive techniques were added to these, such as daily exercises in composition and calligraphy, again not primarily aimed at the development of literary or artistic craftsmanship but at disciplining both the conscious and the unconscious mind. Eventually meditation exercises (the art of sitting quiet) became more and more generally accepted as a supporting technique.[30]

All these techniques, the conscious submission to criticism and self-criticism as well as the subtler methods to influence oneself, were undertaken with the aim of conquering (or overcoming) one's individuality (*k'o-chi*). In the writings of the Sung School scholars of early Ch'ing this endeavor does not lack the aspects of a forced exertion, either negatively (eradicating the evil in oneself) or positively (imposing or implanting, at best developing, the good). What was to be considered evil and what good remained a more or less unasked question. Gradually and perhaps unconsciously, however, these men did reach out for a standard of good and evil which would transcend the tradition and could not be derived from the literature, but only from the deeper reaches of the self. Tech-

---

[30] This started already with Chang Po-hsing. "Sitting still" was a discipline long advocated by Chu Hsi philosophers, especially emphasized in Ming times.

niques devised to mold the self at the same time constituted the initial steps toward opening it. That the Sung School scholars of early Ch'ing would have been horrified by such an idea is shown by the violence of their opposition toward Wang Yang-ming and his school. As far as actual school configurations are concerned, this opposition amounted to flailing a dead horse. Its violence can only be explained by imputing to the Sung School scholars a vague sense of the "danger" which they themselves were approaching.[31] And then, attitudes toward ideas of Wang Yang-ming were subsequently modified even among Sung School scholars.

In the meantime the cultivation of the personality was carried on under the heading "abiding in reverence." This heading included more; it encompassed the entire universe of the Sung School Confucianist. As Lu Lung-chi put it in his *Essay on the Supreme Ultimate*: "If one is able to practise reverence he will be able to be void (*hsü*) in rest and straight in action, and the Supreme Ultimate in his person is really at its height. Even though the words of former Confucianists exhaust every loftiness and are the acme of profundity, if you boil down their meaning, then what they are really after is nothing but the *cultivation of the personality for the sake of the government of the world and the state.*" (emphasis mine)

[31] As an example of this, a passage from Lu Lung-chi's *Essay on the Supreme Ultimate* may serve: "To discuss the Supreme Ultimate does not consist in elucidating the Supreme Ultimate of Heaven and Earth, but in elucidating the Supreme Ultimate of the individual. If the Supreme Ultimate of the individual is elucidated, the Supreme Ultimate of Heaven and Earth is embodied therein. It is true that former Confucianists, when discussing the Supreme Ultimate, started their talks with the principles of yin and yang, the Five Active Essences, Heaven and Earth, and the living beings; but as I am afraid that people will not understand the basis of this principle, I attempt to speak about it by tracing its origin. . . . Therefore, for those who want to discuss ably the Supreme Ultimate, it is better to trace it in what is near than to trace it in what is far; it is better to trace it in what is real and can be followed than to trace it in what is empty and difficult to grasp." The man who wrote this at the same time wrote violent essays against Wang Yang-ming!

This emphatic repetition of a general Confucian norm by an early Sung School Confucianist has to be understood against the background of a period in which his world was a phantom world and his state a state governed by foreigners. The field of education appeared to provide the only practical outlet for creative activities. This emphasis on education remained with the Sung School all through Ch'ing times, and the circumstances under which this school rose determined the direction in which it developed, even through times during which these initial circumstances had changed radically.

It is important that the discipline the Sung School Confucianist underwent was self-imposed. The sternness with which one corrected his own mind was his justification in applying the same degree of sternness to others.[32] Education (or rather indoctrination) to him meant the same thing it meant to the Manchu Emperors, to correct people's minds: "Of the ways of the Holy Kings to govern the world, none is better than to correct people's minds. When people's minds are corrected, the political institutions can work; when the political institutions work, the government of the world can be achieved."

It remained for Chang Lü-hsiang[33] and Lu Shih-i[34] to elaborate upon educational principles and educational techniques. These cannot be gone into here. It has to be stressed, however, that they both proceed from the principle of "abiding in reverence" which they applied to themselves to an almost self-effacing degree before they applied it to others. Thus Chang states: "The whole day, from the time I get into my clothes until the time I get out of my clothes, in whatever I

[32] Lu Lung-chi seems to have been an unusually stern personality. Once he records in his diary, in this instance without the slightest pang of conscience, how he refused to give financial assistance to a close friend in need, and at another occasion he recounts how he scolded and had cudgelled a stranger whom he caught buying in the market four or five pounds of meat in order to entertain guests. The same degree of severity was not exhibited by all of the early Sung School scholars. Chang Lü-hsiang in particular seems to have been an amiable personality who was able to maintain the same principles in a much more palatable way.

[33] *ECCP*, pp. 45-46; Watters, pp. 232-236; Forke, pp. 520-522.
[34] *ECCP*, pp. 548-549; Watters, pp. 229-232; Forke, pp. 510-520.

say or do, I have to be aware of the number of mistakes I make. The whole night, from the time I get out of my clothes until the time I get into my clothes, in whatever I think or worry about, I have to be aware of the number of my depravities. Then only can I correct them."

Or more pragmatically:

"What the students have to be shown:
   Love of one's person,
   Cultivation of one's personality,
   Ardent studies,
   Attachment to worthies.

These four, if in actual practice conditioned by a sense of duty, are all contained in the love of one's own person. The cultivation of virtues is done on account of the love of one's own person, ardent studying is done on account of the cultivation of virtues, attachment to worthies is done in order to complete one's studies . . ."

"What the students have to be shown:
   Making distinct the motivations,
   Understanding the principles of Sung philosophy,
   Keeping in control nature and emotions.

These three (presuppose) reverence in order to straighten out the affairs of the within.
   Assuming correct postures,
   Application of care in one's speech,
   Devotion to caution in one's actions.

These three (presuppose) a sense of duty in order to square the affairs of the without."

Analysis of the correspondences in this statement will show the sophistication with which Chu Hsi's basic dualism is applied here.

Lu Shih-i, on the other hand, had the following to say: "Just to mention the one word reverence makes one perceive one's personal actions and undertakings as if in a clear mirror." And: "The emphasis on reverence has to be developed from the point of fear to the point of spontaneity. Fear is the core of the rules of social conduct, spontaneity is the emotional nature of music. To be based on the rules of social conduct and to reach perfection in music means nothing but to teach people from beginning to end to perfect the one word reverence."

The second concept which the Sung School scholars of early Ch'ing picked from the storehouse of Chu Hsi was "exhausting the principles" (*ch'iung-li*). Already from what has been said above it will be clear how much more limited their *li*-concept was in comparison with Chu Hsi's. They were not concerned with Chu Hsi's encyclopedic "investigation of things" nor with his metaphysical imagery in which principles of the phenomenal world arrived at through this investigation were expressed.[35] In both instances they participated in the trend toward the practical and pragmatic which was a general symptom of that period. Their *li*-concept is also much more man-centered. They needed it to uphold the dualistic tension of Chu Hsi which afforded vitality to their system, but they changed its key to adapt it to the aspect of human relationships with which they were concerned. In the words of Lu Lung-chi: "If you exhaust the principles without abiding in reverence, you will toy with reality, damage your intentions, and get lost in trifles. If you abide in reverence without exhausting the principles, you will sweep away your perceptions and will be unfounded in your moral judgments. It will be rare that in this way you will not fall prey to Buddhism and Taoism or even teach your mind to function by itself, resulting in madness and licentiousness."

And in the words of Lu Shih-i: "The main body of Chu Hsi's doctrines consists in exhausting the principles in order to complete one's knowledge and then revert humbly to practising their gist and thus to found oneself on abiding in reverence. This method is basic and the only correct rule for all the thousands of Saints and Sages."

[35] The defense of metaphysics was left to the lone wolves, such as Chang Erh-ch'i (1612-1678) (*ECCP*, pp. 34-35; H. Wilhelm, "Um die Metaphysik" in *Sinologische Arbeiten* I, pp. 136-152) who, interestingly enough, cannot be classified as either Sung or Han School scholar, and who somehow anticipated trends later prevalent in the New Text School.

It is interesting to note what social and political attitudes were derived from this new constellation of concepts at a period when it was still out of gear with the political constellation. Rigid criticism and mind-molding led Lu Lung-chi to a direct and openly stated divestiture of the self-assurance of the gentry as a social and political group, in contradistinction to the philosophers who remained for him the arbiters of human affairs. In the case of Lu Shih-i it led, conversely, to a strengthening of the solidarity of the gentry as a group of corrected (and correcting) individuals, a solidarity which was expressed in his founding of literary associations and study groups as well as in his demand for local self-government.

The congruence between the spheres of politics and philosophy, still lacking during the first generation, was implemented during the second. The Emperors, particularly the K'ang-hsi Emperor, did play up to the scholars to bring them back into the fold again,[36] since, in the words of Max Weber, "constitutionally, the Emperor could rule only by using certified literati as official; classically, he could rule only by using orthodox Confucian officials."[37] In 1724, Lu Lung-chi was included in official worship by being designated one of the nineteen leading Confucianists of all times,[38] and the career of the fourth of the great masters of the Sung School, Chang Po-hsing,[39] was smooth due to direct Imperial intercession, and led him to the highest honors.

The scope and the direction of the Ch'ing School of Sung Learning had, however, at that time already been fixed. It had been formed in early Manchu times under circumstances of utter social and psychological insecurity and could at that time be stayed only by a strong reliance on orthodox tradition. Its ensuing birthmarks came to the fore again when, after a

[36] On this point see: H. Wilhelm "The Po-hsüeh hung-ju examination of 1679" in *Journal of the American Oriental Society* [*JAOS*] 71 (1951), pp. 60-66.

[37] Hans H. Gerth, tr., *The Religions of China*, Glencoe 1951, p. 141.

[38] Chang Lü-hsiang, Lu Shih-i, and Chang Po-hsing achieved comparable honors in 1871, 1875, and 1878 respectively.

[39] *ECCP*, pp. 51-52; Watters, pp. 254-259.

period of complacency which could and did borrow the Emperor's thunder in support of its positions, it was called upon to perform and to provide solutions in another crisis.

The leading philosopher of the Sung School in the early nineteenth century was T'ang Chien (1776?-1861). His predominant position in that period is shown by the fact that figures like Wo-jen, Wu T'ing-tung, and Tseng Kuo-fan revered him as their teacher; nobody in his time had a stronger influence than he on the ideology of officialdom and the attitudes of officials.

T'ang continued consciously and directly the trends of early Ch'ing times. To Wo-jen he once said: "Learning should take abiding in reverence and exhausting the principles as guiding principles. Everything else is heresy." And to Tseng Kuo-fan he said: "The science of statesmanship is contained in the principles of Sung philosophy."

The passage of time and the specific contingencies of his period are, however, reflected in an evolution of the teachings of the earlier masters. He was aware of the fact that the times were out of joint and he unflinchingly accepted the responsibility of the philosopher to provide the remedy. Thus one part of his system is subsumed under the caption "maintain the tradition in order to save the time (*shou tao chiu shih*)." The change of key is again observable: the tradition which had then been used as a prop to stay the philosophical system in the face of threatening personal insecurities was now used to stay the Imperial system with which his school had in the meantime completely identified itself.

The insecurities nevertheless remained with the Sung School, also in T'ang's time. Thus a second part of his teachings is treated under the caption "the cultivation of the personality."[40] All the ideas and techniques of the earlier masters are developed here. The diary technique as a means of introspection and self-criticism was developed in his hands into an

[40] Benjamin Schwartz translated this term "self-realization" (in his introduction to Immanuel Hsü's translation mentioned in note 49). This translation appears to me permissible only if the term is stripped of all the connotations with which it is used in recent psychology.

"Introverted Breviary" (*Hsing-shen jih-ch'eng*) which is to an even stronger degree expressive of personal fears and doubts. The following passages will serve as examples:

"Know the fine points and you will know the apparent, but without and within know fear. Be doubtful at the outset and you will have final success, but fear should cover end and beginning."

"He who knows fate will cultivate the Way; he who relies on fate will do harm to the Way."

"Even if all your affairs are rooted in the Way, you will probably not lose your character; even if all your deliberations are rooted in the principle you will probably not lose your mental independence. The Book of Changes says: 'What need has the world of thoughts and care?'[41] Thus the mind is in a position to know."

"The word reverence comprises within and without, it penetrates end and beginning. With regard to a wooden figure you cannot speak of reverence."

"In matters of merit and reputation you may give in to people, in matters of morals you may not; in matters of gain and loss you may obey orders; in matters of right and wrong you may not."

"If the principles are exhaustively applied until they reach the point of essential oneness, humaneness is extended and the sense of duty is extended; if human nature is nurtured until it reaches the state of central harmony, joy is moderated and anger is moderated."

"If you know yourself and know people, humaneness and indulgence will come naturally; if you do away with your ego and do away with things, voidness and justice will come naturally."

"If, in the affairs of the state, the foreign affairs are taken seriously, then the internal affairs will be taken lightly; if

[41] See Wilhelm-Baynes, vol. i, p. 362.

internal affairs are taken seriously, then foreign affairs will be taken lightly. It is the same thing with the mind and the body. The gentleman in his affairs will therefore not set apart the within from the without."

"To move without losing substance is possible only if within movement there is rest. To rest without losing function is possible only if within rest there is movement."

"To strengthen oneself without ceasing, this is the invigorating aspect of the creative principle (of the Book of Changes); to bear the things with ample virtue, this is the compliant aspect of the receptive principle. If one starts from here to think about learning, then reverence cannot be said to be at its goal, unless it is capable of concentrated brilliance,[42] sincerity cannot be called to be at its acme, unless it is capable of the completion of things."

In the political sphere, T'ang's attitudes were fiercely traditionalist and staunchly conservative. No solutions for the ailments of the time could be provided on this basis, not even when "emperorology"[43] was added to the armory of the Sung Confucianists. This was done by T'ang Chien's disciple Wo-jen (1804-1871),[44] whose political attitudes, particularly his stand in the so-called T'ung-wen-kuan controversy, have been dealt with repeatedly in recent literature.[45] In his attempt to lay down the law for the emperor, Wo-jen followed wittingly in the footsteps of Tung Chung-shu of Han, who was not

---

[42] A quote from the Wen-wang ode. The translation of the term follows Erwin Reifler's suggestion. "Ever think of your ancestors" in: *Monumenta Serica* 14 (1949-1955), pp. 340-373.

[43] *Ti wang-hsüeh*. The term was coined by Fumoto Yasutake; see his "Shin dai shichō jō ni okeru Wa Bun Tan Kō no chii" ("Wo-jen, His man and his influence to the cultural world of China [sic]") in *Tōyō gakuhō* 32, 1 (Sept. 1948), pp. 92-107.

[44] *ECCP*, pp. 861-863.

[45] See Teng-Fairbank, *China's Response to the West* (Cambridge, 1954), pp. 75-77; Mary Clabaugh Wright, *The Last Stand of Chinese Conservatism* (Stanford, 1957), pp. 224-246 and passim; Chang Hao "The anti-foreignist role of Wo-jen" in *Papers on China* 14 (1960), pp. 1-29.

otherwise a hero of the Sung School, and unwittingly in those of people like Huang Tsung-hsi of early Ch'ing, conscious association with whom every good Sung scholar would have shunned.[46] Attempts of this kind were of course utopian. They show, however, into which fields of intellectual endeavor and into whose intellectual company even the Sung scholar was eventually led by his intellectual antecedents and by the autonomous development of his intellectual system.

T'ang Chien's personal philosophy however, his oscillating (theoretical) insecurity, his focus on man in search of himself, and particularly his attempt to overcome the dualism between the world of within and the world of without[47] carry a strangely modern ring. Circumstances did not provide the time for ideas like these to mature.

It is worthy of note that these developments occurred within the ranks of the orthodox, that is to say of those who were committed to the maintenance of the correct tradition as well as of the fundamental vocation of the Confucianist. They could not afford the irresponsible pride of the utopian who, as a heretic or semi-heretic, is free to let his mind wander in supreme disregard of these commitments. Thus even those of their statements which come close to formulations of Wang Yang-ming assume a very different place within their system, as this system was arrived at under a very different set of responsibilities. It is furthermore worthy of note that the intellectual endeavors of the Sung School philosophers proceeded with an uncanny, if undefined, knowledge of the unconscious reaches of the self.

This confrontation of the ego with the self was still conceived by them within the framework of the tenet "overcome your self." They had, however, already achieved in their probings the point of intellectual insecurity where attitudes, also intellectual attitudes, were fundamentally determined by fear. This dissolution into the irrational of the very root of

[46] However, already Yao Nai (see below) had dabbled in emperor-ology, see his *Han-lin lun*. Influenced by Wo-jen, the young Tseng Kuo-fan indulged in similar discourses.

[47] On this point see H. Wilhelm, "The Problem of Within and Without," *Journal of the History of Ideas* 12 (1951), pp. 48-60.

their thinking and being brought them very close to a realization of the nature of the self and with it to a realization of how and to what extent it could be overcome. In other words, they were not far any more from an understanding of the autonomy of the self and together with it of the autonomy of the human mind.

Attitudes prevailing among officialdom and among the educated in general weighed heavily in the circumstances which precluded this (speculative) intellectual breakthrough. These attitudes were not exclusively, not even primarily, determined by the progress of philosophy but by more pragmatic considerations. They were also determined by a non-philosophical school which tied together a great number of the intellectually and politically active. I am referring to the T'ung-ch'eng School, which owed its renown to its sophistication in the field of literature (more precisely: in the field of artistic prose), but which also sported an abbreviated and vulgarized, but none the less militant, Chu Hsi creed. Rising into dominance in a period when the political sphere tolerated nothing but the compliant, the school provided the medium of escape for all individualisms and creative urges. Particularly Yao Nai (1732-1815)[48] succeeded in creating a cohesive school spirit among the T'ung-ch'eng scholars who then dictated attitudes which became fashionable beyond the world of literature. That these attitudes included a belligerent conservatism justified by a sloganized Chu Hsi went a long way toward impeding those ideas within a developed Chu Hsi system which might have become germinating points of modernization.

The School of Han Learning

From among the schools of Ch'ing Confucianism, the School of Han Learning is by far the best known and most talked about.[49] The term is actually a misnomer and, strictly speaking, it should be applied only to the school of Hui Tung

[48] *ECCP*, pp. 900-901.
[49] Liang Ch'i-ch'ao's book *Intellectual Trends in the Ch'ing Period*, Immanuel Hsü tr. (Cambridge, 1959), deals in its premodern part almost exclusively with the concerns of this school.

(1697-1758)[50] in which it was coined. The alternative term, "School of Empirical Research," however, covers only one aspect of the intellectual concerns of the people loosely grouped together under this label. As the inaugurators of this movement, the great masters of early Ch'ing, such as Ku Yen-Wu,[51] Huang Tsung-hsi[52] and others are claimed. These, too, had lived in the period when intellectual (inner) exile had been the order of the day. Their influence and the influence of their attitudes, which were at least in part determined by the political situation of their life, was certainly strong and it grew as time went on.

We can dispense here with the problem which gave the movement its name, the concern with textual tradition and textual interpretation, even though this particular aspect of the movement is an indispensable link in its system of ideas and attitudes. It brought into play within this movement contact with ideas and personalities of a non-orthodox character and helped recreate a place for scholarship and research within the Confucian value system. The first sentence of the Analects was in this way brought into life again: "To learn and at due times to repeat what one has learned, is that after all not a pleasure?"[53] This place, once established, had to be acknowledged even by rivalling schools; and in the early nineteenth century this aspect of the school overshadowed all others, to the extent that the philosopher of the movement, Tai Chen (1724-1777)[54] was almost exclusively known for

[50] *ECCP*, pp. 357-358.

[51] See H. Wilhelm, *Gu Ting Lin, der Ethiker* (Darmstadt, 1932); de Bary ed., *Sources of Chinese Tradition* (New York, 1960), pp. 607-612.

[52] See several publications of Theodore de Bary, most conveniently in *Sources of Chinese Tradition*, pp. 585-597.

[53] Waley's translation. Waley implies that the "after all" means "even though one does not hold office." See Benjamin Schwartz's introduction to Liang, *op.cit.* on the problem of the place of scholarship in Ch'ing China.

[54] *ECCP*, pp. 695-700; Richard Wilhelm, "Der Philosoph Dai Dschen" in *Chinesisch-deutscher Almanach* 1932, pp. 6-13; Mansfield Freeman, "The Philosophy of Tai Tung-yüan" in *Journal of the North China Branch, Royal Asiatic Society* 64 (1933), pp. 50-71.

the new foundations he gave to scientific endeavors, and not for his philosophy.

Tai's philosophical stand is indebted in several respects to Huang Tsung-hsi. He inherited from him the partisan strength and determination of a philosophical warrior. And particularly he inherited from him the arguments to battle Chu Hsi's dualistic system. His battle was for the truth (or what he considered to be the truth) and this led him to an unbiased acknowledgement of those aspects of human nature which had been suppressed or banished into the world of the shadows. A few quotes will show this:

"What in antiquity was called the principle was sought out in accordance with human emotions and desires. If these two were rendered flawless, then that was called the principles. What today is called the principle is sought out without reference to human emotions and desires. If these are suppressed and disregarded, then that is called the principle. This split between the principle and desires is apt to transform all the people of the world into hypocrites."[55]

"Everybody who has vitality[56] and intelligence has at the same time desires. (Human) nature manifests itself in the desires in that through the sounds, the colors, the smells, and the tastes, likes and dislikes are (naturally) differentiated. If there are desires, then there are also emotions. (Human) nature manifests itself in the emotions in that through pleasure and displeasure, sadness and joy, excitement and calm are (naturally) differentiated. If there are desires and emotions, then there are skill and wisdom. (Human) nature manifests itself in skill and wisdom in that through the beautiful and the ugly, the right and the wrong, love and hatred are naturally differentiated. The Way of begetting and bearing is included in the desires. The Way of mutual understanding is included in the emotions. If the two spontaneously fit together, then the actions of the world are completely covered.

[55] *Meng-tzu tzu-i shu-cheng* 1, 12 r. This is adapted from Freeman's translation.

[56] *hsüeh-ch'i*, a key concept in Tai's system.

To treat exhaustively the acme of the beautiful and the ugly is included in skill. *Governmental powers originate here.* (emphasis mine) To treat exhaustively the acme of right and wrong is included in wisdom. The moral force of the sages and saints is prepared here. If the two also spontaneously fit together and are refined by subsuming them under the necessary, then the potentialities of the world are completely covered."[57]

"The science of the men of old consisted in acting, in understanding the people's desires and in substantiating the people's emotions. Therefore, if their science was complete, the people could rely on it for their living. The later Confucianists exacted the law of reason from their mind, and their keeping the people in bondage with the help of the law of reason was more severe than the law (*fa*) of the Lord of Shang and Han-fei-tzu. Therefore, if their science was complete, the emotions of the people remained unknown."[58]

We encounter here a self-assertion of the human personality which in its strength is reminiscent of the anthropocentrism of Wang T'ung of T'ang and Ch'en Liang of Sung. Tai's sophistication added to their position his concept of the wholeness and indivisibility of an integrated individual.

The same degree of self-assertion is also found in Hui Tung. His ideas and scholarly endeavors can more easily be traced back to Ku Yen-wu from whom he inherited the aristocratic spirit and the status-mindedness. (It has been said that Hui was out for the old rather than for the truth.) Combined, however, the warrior and the aristocrat added much to restore the self-reliance and pride of the scholar, personally and as the member of a status group, an attitude that was based on private accomplishments and social standing and not on official rank.[59] This attitude persisted through to

[57] *Yüan-shan*, I, 4 v.

[58] Letter to Somebody, *Wen-chi* 9, 12 v.

[59] Neither Tai nor Hui ever held official positions, if the short period is discarded during which Tai served on the Ssu-k'u Commission, engaged in scholarly and not in administrative work.

the times when the creative activities of this group were moving entirely along lines of "empirical research" (of a wide variety, to be sure), and it added contrast and vitality to intellectual exchange; but the intellectual current of the group it carried had run dry so that it stood in the way rather than enhancing probing sallies into the unexplored, sallies which might have prepared the Chinese mind for its encounter with the modern world.

The New Text School

There are certain links between Han School and the latest and last offshoot from the trunk of Confucianism, the New Text School. Of interest here is the figure of Ch'eng En-tse,[60] a great friend of Juan Yüan (1764-1849),[61] an author of a sound piece of empirical research,[62] and an influential tutor of a number of New Text scholars. Generally speaking, however, the New Texters did not stress this link. They maintained a rather neutral, "not Han, not Sung" attitude in the battle of the schools and drew whatever guidance they enjoyed from the New Text position in the Han controversy and, at a later stage of their development, from Wang Fu-chih (1619-1692),[63] his passionate nationalism, his unconventional conceptions about society, and his dynamic interpretation of the Book of Changes.

We can again discard here a discussion of the problems of textual criticism which gave the school its name. However, already about the founder of this school, Chuang Ts'un-yü (1719-1788),[64] Juan Yüan once said: "He alone grasps the subtleties and the great meaning of the Saint by reading between the lines." The grasp of the subtleties and the great meaning and the arriving there by reading between the lines

[60] On him see *Chung-ho yüeh-k'an* 2, 1 (Jan. 1941), pp. 3-16; 2, 5 (May 1941), pp. 59-80.

[61] *ECCP*, pp. 399-402; Wolfgang Franke, "Juan Yüan" in *Monumenta Serica* 9 (1944), pp. 59-80.

[62] The *Kuo-ts'e ti-ming k'ao.*

[63] *ECCP*, pp. 817-819; *Sources of Chinese Tradition*, pp. 597-606.

[64] *ECCP*, pp. 206-208.

then became established traditions within this school. The subtleties and the great meaning were, however, not grasped in the abstract. They were linked to the demands of the time. It was they who invented the practice of "advocating reform under the cloak of antiquity," and this candidly reformist attitude eventually outshone their scholarly pursuits.

This is not to say that their scholarship was not considerable, but they pursued it in an entirely new spirit. As Kung Tzu-chen (1792-1841)[65] once put it: "The affairs of scholarship are thus: striving after it has to be toilsome; grasping it has to be inventive; proving it has to be broad; expounding it has to be terse; it should not ail from being vague; it should not ail from being petty. If striving after it is not toilsome, it will be unrefined; if grasping it is not inventive, it will be plagiaristic; if proving it is not broad, it will be unreliable; if expounding it is not terse, it will not hit the point; if it ails from vagueness or pettiness it will not be complete. Its relation to the human character is thus: as it is the acme of pure archaism, it is also the acme of unadorned simplicity; as it is the acme of unadorned simplicity, it is also the acme of yielding and conceding; as it is the acme of yielding and conceding, it is also the acme of thoughtful deliberation; as it is the acme of thoughtful deliberation, it is also the acme of perfect compactness; as it is the acme of perfect compactness, it is also the acme of all-inclusive concern; as it is the acme of all-inclusive concern, it is also the acme of the minute essence. The affairs of philology and the deeds of humaneness, love, piety and brotherliness have an all-pervading unity."[66]

The all-pervading unity of man, human affairs, and the entire world of human relationships was a concept which the New Texters got from the Book of Changes. In addition to certain evolutionary concepts drawn from the Kung-yang tradition, the Book of Changes and writings about the Book of Changes were their most important source of inspiration. From here they derived their concept of change and, as they

[65] *ECCP*, pp. 431-434.
[66] From his *Hsiao-pao lun*. The last phrase is a quote from the famous *Lun-yü* passage 15, 2, Legge 295.

did not conceive of change as merely cyclical, the justification for their reformist attitude. They shared with Tung Chung-shu and Wang Fu-chih insight into the necessity of development and change in the world of thought, the world of art, the social world, and the world of political institutions. The intricate interrelationships between changes in these different worlds, which on the one hand depend on autonomous developments of the world in which they take place, but on the other hand mutually interlink, they took from their Classic, to be sure, but then developed them to a point of sophistication entirely their own. This was also true for their concept of timeliness, according to which man-induced change must hit the proper moment within the flow of spontaneous change in order to be effective. The application of this concept to the interrelationship of social (spontaneous) and institutional (man-induced) change is of particular interest.

The New Text School owes much of its sophistication to the poets in its ranks, Yün Ching (1757-1817)[67] and Chang Hui-yen (1761-1802).[68] Both are not usually considered philosophers, but are better known as the cofounders of another school of artistic prose, the Yang-hu School. Chang was also a founder of a new school of classical songs (*tz'u*). The relationships between the Yang-hu scholars and the New Text scholars are, however, intimate. They cannot be traced here in detail. Their mutual influence was definitely incisive, and both shared a stock of common conceptions and a common spirit. Chang wrote most extensively on the Book of Changes, but it may be that in Yün Ching, the change concept of the New Texters achieved its highest refinement. He brought to bear on this concept his familiarity with the creative process in the field of art, how it works in topics, in form, in the unity of both, and in the influence of one on the other. In a fascinating passage he once described how social change comes spontaneously and offers the idea of institutional change. He who grasps this offer at a time when

[67] *ECCP*, pp. 959-960.
[68] *ECCP*, pp. 42-43.

CHAPTER IX

Western and Indigenous Elements in Modern Indian Thought: The Case of Rammohun Roy

STEPHEN N. HAY

ALL through the non-Western world in recent centuries the pace of change has been vastly accelerated by contact and conflict with the expanding society and culture of the modern West. Although anthropologists have devoted a good deal of attention to the conceptual analysis of social and cultural change among tribal and peasant groups forced to respond to the intrusions of Westerners and the novel things, ways, and ideas they brought with them, historians are just beginning to attempt similar analyses of the far more complicated interactions among Western and indigenous elements in the high cultures of non-Western civilizations.

What terms and concepts has the historian of non-Western cultural change at hand to serve as his tools of analysis? Unfortunately, they are few in number, and rudely fashioned at that. Generally they are posed as contrasting opposites. That ancient pair, "the East and the West," still dodder on, and have recently been celebrated by the humorist-historian C. Northcote Parkinson.[1] A somewhat sprightlier couple, "the impact of the West" and "the response" of a given non-Western civilization, have been popularized by the writings of Arnold J. Toynbee, in the context of his treatment of "encounters between civilizations."[2] This terminology certainly

[1] *The East and the West* (New York: Houghton, 1963).

[2] *A Study of History*, vol. 8 (London: Oxford University Press, 1954), 198ff. deals with "The Modern West and the Hindu World." Although Toynbee has made an important contribution in this work by differentiating the "Zealot" from the "Herodian" responses to an "assault" on the "soul" of a given civilization (*ibid.*, pp. 580-623), he has elsewhere explicitly denied the contention (which it is one

marks an improvement upon the old East-West notion by
breaking up the supposedly unchangeable East into a number
of distinct civilizations, and by crediting them with at least
a measure of vitality.

The most recent pair of concepts to gain wide currency, the
"traditional" versus the "modern," shift the perspective on
change from a geographical plane to a time-dimension in
which some societies are seen to have progressed, or "modernized," more rapidly than others.[3] Although this new
emphasis on modernization comes as a welcome relief from
the Western-centricity implicit in the concept of Westernization (and has therefore been readily adopted by intellectuals
in non-Western countries), it tends to obscure two other
basic considerations. One is that a great many of the changes
taking place in non-Western societies during the past century
or more have either been imported directly from the West
or have been the work of Westerners themselves. Thus, while
the newer concept of "modernization" does improve upon
the older term "Westernization," it cannot replace it entirely;
ideally, both should be retained and integrated into a more
complex analytical framework than either now provides. The
other shortcoming of the term modernization is that, in its
current usage, it tends to relegate older traditions (whether
Western or non-Western) to passive or obstructive roles,
inhibiting change at every step of the way. Yet when we look
around us, we see that many cultural traditions in Asia and
Africa are thriving today as never before, albeit in novel
forms. If Europe had her artistic renaissance and her religious
reformation, so too have India, Japan, and Egypt. Clearly
the role of reinterpreted and reinvigorated traditions deserves
a prominent place in any comprehensive analysis of social
and cultural change in the non-Western world.

---

purpose of the present essay to demonstrate) that a viable distinction
can be drawn between "Western" and "modern" (see his *The Present
Experiment in Western Civilization* [London: Oxford University
Press, 1962], pp. 24ff.).

[3] See for example Daniel Lerner, *The Passing of Traditional Society: Modernizing the Middle East* (Glencoe, Illinois: Free Press,
1958).

Our problem, then, is to create and refine a conceptual framework for the study of change in non-Western civilizations, within which indigenous and Western, traditional and modern elements can be analyzed and meaningfully related to each other.

Although this problem can be posed in the study of any non-Western civilization, it is centrally important to the understanding of cultural or intellectual change in modern India. Harboring a great variety of regional and religious cultural traditions, Indian society has also been subjected to intensive and prolonged exposure to Western cultural influences during the past century and a half. Nowhere in India were Western influences stronger, and Indian "responses" more vigorous, than in the region where the British planted their capital: Bengal, the rich alluvial plain lying athwart the trade routes linking the Bay of Bengal with the populous hinterland of the Gangetic river basin. Interest in Western culture was initially confined to the Hindu gentry of Bengal, the high-caste *bhadralok,* many of whom the great expansion of trade and the permanent settlement of the land revenue had enriched and reconciled to British rule. (Although Bengal contained a large Muslim population, it lived mainly in remote eastern Bengal, and was composed for the most part of uneducated peasants, boatmen, and fishermen. Cultured Bengali Muslims, even those supported by the government-run Calcutta Madrasa, remained for many decades absorbed in traditional Islamic scholarship.) And among the Hindu gentry, it was members of the Brahmin caste, traditionally the custodians of higher learning, who first showed an interest in the cultural traditions of their new rulers.

Given these historical circumstances, it is not surprising that the first Indian intellectual seriously to study the civilization of the West should have been a West Bengal Brahmin of the most aristocratic lineage. He was Rammohun Roy, who was born probably in 1772 and died in 1833. Now known to his countrymen as "the father of modern India," Rammohun expressed in his writings the fundamental ideas on the nature and relationship of Indian and Western society and culture whose implications have been worked out by a succession of later thinkers and reformers, and are still being worked out today. The case of Rammohun Roy thus offers us a unique opportunity for studying on a microscopic level, and at a significantly early period, the nature and relationship of indigenous and Western, traditional and modern elements in nineteenth and twentieth century Indian thought.[4]

The first thing that impresses us about Rammohun is the broad and deep knowledge he acquired of the major cultural traditions then alive in northern India. Although some details of his early life are still in dispute,[5] we know that the first classical languages he was set to study were Persian (which remained until 1837 the official language of government), and Arabic. His father only wished to prepare his gifted second son for the family profession of land revenue administration, but Rammohun's studies (which included reading in Arabic the Qur'an, Euclid, and Aristotle, and in Persian Sufi writings) carried him deep into religious questions, and he soon became a convinced monotheist and a skilled logician. At the behest of his mother (whose forefathers had been Shakta priests), he next studied Sanskrit, probably in Benares. Here again his classical studies (which must have included Vedanta philosophy and probably familiarized him with the Nyaya school of logic) seem to have stimulated his

[4] The fullest and most authoritative biography of Rammohun is Sophia Dobson Collet, *The Life and Letters of Raja Rammohun Roy*, ed. Dilip Kumar Biswas and Prabhat Chandra Ganguli (3rd rev. ed.; Calcutta: Sadharan Brahmo Samaj, 1963). The most complete collection of Rammohun's English writings is *English Works of Raja Rammohun Roy*, ed. Kalidas Nag and Debajyoti Burman (7 parts; Calcutta: Sadharan Brahmo Samaj, 1945-1958). His Bengali writings (which are devoted almost entirely to theological questions and cover about one-half as many pages as his English writings) are collected in *Rāmmohan-granthābalī*, ed. Brajendranāth Bandhyopādhyāý and Sajanīkānta Dās (7 parts; Calcutta: Bangīya Sāhitya Parishat, n.d. [c. 1950]).

[5] Arguments and evidence discrediting various accounts of Rammohun's early life are summarized in Sushil Kumar De, *Bengali Literature in the Nineteenth Century* (2nd rev. ed.; Calcutta: Firma K. L. Mukhopadhyay, 1962), pp. 500ff.

search for religious truth, for at about the age of fifteen he composed an essay "calling in question the validity of the idolatrous system of the Hindus."[6] After arguing vehemently with his father over his heterodox views, Rammohun left home to spend several years travelling in India, and apparently also in Tibet, where he is said to have engaged the worshippers of the Dalai Lama in theological disputations which almost cost him his life.[7]

Exposed to this multiplicity of intellectual traditions—Sufi theocentric humanism, Qur'anic monotheism, Aristotelian logic, Nyaya logic, Shakta worship, Vedanta philosophy, and Tibetan Buddhism—Rammohun formulated the results of his study of comparative religions in a short tract which he very likely published when he was in his mid or late twenties, that is, some time in or after 1797, the year he first took up residence in Calcutta. Just as the young Gibbon, returning from his studies on the continent, had sought at twenty-four to establish himself in the literary world by bringing out a small

[6] "Original Papers. Biographical Sketch of Rajah Rammohun Roy," *The Athenaeum* (London), No. 310 (Oct. 5, 1833), p. 666. *The Athenaeum* notes (p. 666): "We have been favoured with the Sketch by Mr. Sandford Arnot. . . . The first part is a letter from the Rajah himself." Arnot appended to the letter "a few particulars in illustration of the above sketch, by one who was for years in habits of daily confidential communication with him. . . ." (*ibid.*). Miss Collet, whose biography is not free of errors, and who considered Arnot (p. 323 of her *Life*) "a low, cunning parasite," dismissed the sketch (*ibid.*, p. 496) as "spurious," without giving the evidence or reasoning on which she based this conclusion. Biswas and Ganguli (*ibid.*, p. 496) tend to accept the sketch as genuine. So do I, in view of the above facts, the style of the letter, and its contents, which corroborate rather than contradict established details of Rammohun's life.

[7] Collet, pp. 7-8, quoting Lant Carpenter, *A Review of the Labours, Opinions, and Character of Rajah Rammohun Roy* (London: Rowland Hunter, 1833), pp. 101-102. Carpenter (p. 120n.) says that he twice heard Rammohun mention in private conversations this visit to Tibet. It is also alluded to in his autobiographical sketch, in the book by his French friend, Garcin de Tassy, *Histoire de la littérature hindoui et hindoustani*, 2 vols. (1st ed.; Paris: The Oriental Translation Committee of Great Britain and Ireland, 1839), 1, 414, and in the opening sentence of Rammohun's first known publication (see n. 8 below).

book in French, so Rammohun seems to have sought fame at a similar point in his career by publishing his religious views in a Persian essay with an Arabic preface, the *Tuhfat-al-Muwahhidīn,* or "gift to believers in the unity of God."[8] His argument, although expounded in traditional Islamic philosophical terms, has a quite modern ring to it. Traditions as such carried little weight with him, for he asserted that "the inclination of each sect of mankind toward the worship of a particular god or gods . . . and toward certain peculiar forms of worship or devotion, is an extraneous attribute

[8] No copy of the original printing of this important tract seems to have survived the heat and moisture of Bengal, the omnivorousness of silverworms, and the indifference of men. The earliest printing of the Arabic-Persian text preserved in the British Museum was lithographed at Azimabad-Patna in 1898. An English translation, *Tuhfatul Muwahhiddin* [sic], *Or a Gift to Theists* was made by Maulavi Obaidullah El Obaide, published in Calcutta by the Adi Brahmo Samaj in 1884, and reprinted in Calcutta in 1949 by the Adi Brahmo Samaj, which in 1950 republished the Arabic-Persian text under the title *Tuhfatu'l-muwahhidīn.*
    The exact date of the *Tuhfat* is uncertain, but the accepted tradition assigns it to 1803-1804, the period when Rammohun is known to have been employed at Murshidabad, a predominantly Muslim city. The fact that Rammohun declared at the end of the work that he was having it printed (*tab' āvardam*) makes it likely that it was published in Calcutta, for printing in Bengal was unknown outside the Calcutta area in those days and few fonts of Persian type existed. (A. K. Priolkar, *The Printing Press in India. Its Beginnings and Early Development* [Bombay: Marathi Samshodhana Mandala, 1958], pp. 55, 63, 68, 112.) An earlier date for the tract than 1803-1804 seems likely in view of Rammohun's statement in 1820 that he had "not only renounced idolatry at a very early period in his life, but published at that time a treatise in Arabic and Persian against that system. . . ." (*Appeal to the Christian Public in Defence of the Precepts of Jesus,* in *English Works,* part 5, p. 58.) Since Rammohun was probably born in 1772 (or 1774 according to a conflicting tradition [see Collet, pp. 1, 23]) he would have been 31 or 32 (29 or 30) in 1803-1804—not what he would have called "a very early period" on looking back on it in 1820 at the age of 48 (or 46). This earlier dating is significant in corroborating what is already evident in the content and wording of the *Tuhfat* itself: namely, that Rammohun arrived at his rationalist position independently of European enlightenment influences on his thinking.

resulting from habits and education." The one form of worship acceptable to the Creator consisted, he declared, in "uniting the hearts of men without regard to their appearance or color, and without inspecting their beliefs and creeds."[9] As his favorite verse from the Persian poet Sa'di put it: "The true way of serving God is to do good to man."[10]

The remainder of Rammohun's long and useful life can be interpreted as but the implementation of this conviction. There is no need to detail here the many ways in which he served his own people—as a religious and social reformer, diplomat, journalist, philanthropist, grammarian, prose stylist, and as the most eminent political and intellectual leader of his day in India. What seems critically important to our search for an analytical framework for the study of intellectual change is the *method* by which Rammohun selected, reinterpreted, and combined elements from the most diverse sources in order to achieve his objectives. We have already noticed his dismissal of orthodox religious traditions, and his adoption of Sufi values, combined with logical reasoning derived from Greco-Islamic, and perhaps also from Hindu, sources. Let us now examine his treatment of those intellectual traditions to which he was exposed by his contact with Westerners and their civilization.

Rammohun is said to have begun his study of the English language in 1796.[11] A year later we find him lending a rather large sum to one of the East India Company's servants in Benares. Our knowledge of his activities for the next eighteen years is scanty, but it appears that he was chiefly engaged in amassing a small private fortune through commercial dealings in land and money-lending in Bengal, at Patna, and at Benares. He seems to have continued his philosophical studies,

[9] *Tuḥfatu'l-muwaḥḥidīn*, pp. iii, 13. I am grateful to Prof. Muhsin Mahdi for translating the first passage from the Arabic text, and to Mr. M. Asaad Nezami-Nav for translating the second from the Persian.

[10] [Sandford Arnot], "Original Papers," *Athenaeum*, Oct. 5, 1833, p. 668.

[11] Collet, pp. 23-24.

however, and by working as assistant to several officials of the Company at intervals between 1803 and 1815 was able to perfect his English and begin his study of Western culture. By 1815 he had acquired sufficient wealth to retire from business and devote himself entirely to philosophical and philanthropic pursuits as a private citizen of Calcutta—the political, commercial, and intellectual nerve-center of the British dominions in India.

Although Rammohun had felt during his youthful *Wanderjahre* during the late 1780's "great aversion to the establishment of the British power in India," his personal contacts with individual Britons produced in him a change of heart. "Finding them generally more intelligent, more steady, and moderate in their conduct," he reminisced many years later, "I gave up my prejudices against them, and became inclined in their favour, feeling persuaded that their rule, though a foreign yoke, would lead most speedily and surely to the amelioration of the native inhabitants."[12] The Western elements which Rammohun wished to import to facilitate this process of amelioration (which some would call India's modernization), can be examined under three headings: political, educational, and religious.

Once he had come to understand its underlying principles, Rammohun heartily welcomed the political system introduced by the British in India. In concluding a theological treatise in 1823 he went so far as to offer up "thanks to the Supreme Disposer of the events of this universe, for having unexpectedly delivered this country from the long-continued tyranny of its former Rulers, and placed it under the government of the English—a nation who not only are blessed with the enjoyment of civil and political liberty, but also interest themselves in promoting liberty and social happiness, as well as free inquiry into literary and religious subjects, among those nations to which their influence extends."[13]

[12] *Athenaeum*, Oct. 5, 1833, p. 666.
[13] Rammohun Roy, *Final Appeal to the Christian Public in Defence of "The Precepts of Jesus,"* in *English Works*, part 7, pp. 177-178.

Although he recognized British rule as the most effective agent for transmitting to India the traditions of political liberty and social and intellectual improvement developed in the West, Rammohun foresaw that a day might come when the foreign agent might turn from fostering to obstructing the flowering of these traditions on Indian soil. When this day came, the traditions of liberty and enlightenment would lead Indians to oppose the continuance of Western rule in India. As Rammohun wrote to a London correspondent in 1828: "Supposing that some 100 years hence the Native character becomes elevated from constant intercourse with Europeans and the acquirements of general and political knowledge as well as of modern arts and sciences, is it possible that they [the Indian people] will not have the spirit as well as the inclination to resist effectually any unjust and oppressive measures serving to degrade them in the scale of society?"[14]

It is clear from the two previous quotations that Rammohun viewed the progress of education, embracing the acquisition both of modern knowledge and of modern methods of inquiry, as one of the chief benefits to India of British rule. This being so, he could not refrain from writing an eloquent protest when in 1823 he heard that the government was proposing to establish a college in Calcutta that would promote the traditional Sanskritic system of education. Although himself an able Sanskrit scholar, he ridiculed the "imaginary learning" of the pandits and urged his British rulers to adopt "the glorious ambition of planting in Asia the Arts and Sciences of modern Europe."

To emphasize the superiority of modern over medieval systems of learning, he noted the progress of knowledge made since the time of Francis Bacon. "If it had been intended to keep the British nation in ignorance of real knowledge the Baconian philosophy would not have been allowed to displace the system of the schoolmen, which was best calculated to

[14] Rammohun Roy to J. Crawford, August 18, 1828, quoted in Collet, p. 267.

perpetuate ignorance. In the same manner the Sangscrit system of education would be best calculated to keep this country in darkness, if such had been the policy of the British Legislature. But as the improvement of the native population is the object of the Government, it will consequently promote a more liberal and enlightened system of instruction, embracing mathematics, natural philosophy, chemistry and anatomy with other useful sciences."[15]

As in the realm of politics, so in the realm of education, it can fairly be said that Rammohun favored Westernization, or the direct importation of existing modern Western traditions, not as an end in itself, but as the most efficient means to achieve his objective, which he variously defined as the "enlightenment," "amelioration," "improvement," "benefit," and "happiness" of his fellow men.

In the realm of religion, which seems always to have been closest to his heart, Rammohun similarly welcomed Western influences to the extent that they served his philanthropic purposes. In this instance, however, he went to great lengths to distinguish between those Western traditions he considered useful for Indians to adopt, and those he considered erroneous or harmful. As early as 1817 he declared his conviction that the teachings of Jesus were "more conducive to moral principles, and better adapted for the use of rational beings, than any others which have come to my knowledge."[16] Three years later he published a book in English entitled *The Precepts of Jesus, The Guide to Peace and Happiness*, comprising his selection of the ethical and spiritual teachings found in the four Gospels, deliberately omitting what he called the "miraculous relations" concerning Jesus, since he considered these "much less wonderful than the fabricated tales handed down to the natives of Asia, and consequently

[15] Rammohun Roy to the Rt. Hon. William Pitt, Lord Amherst, December 11, 1823, in *English Works*, part 4, pp. 106, 108.

[16] Rammohun Roy to William Digby (1816-1817), quoted in Collet, p. 71.

... apt ... to carry little weight with them."[17] Several missionaries in the Calcutta area, unimpressed by Rammohun's espousal of Christian ethics, were scandalized by his rejection of the doctrine of Christ's divinity. A three-year controversy ensued during which Rammohun wrote three lengthy *Appeals to the Christian Public* in defense of his selection of the precepts of Jesus, and learned sufficient Greek and Hebrew to refute Trinitarian interpretations of Biblical passages. Intellectually superior to his self-appointed opponents in theological resasoning, he argued his case so convincingly that one Baptist missionary was converted to his Unitarian point of view.

In this particular instance the concepts of Western impact and Indian response do not jibe with the evidence; instead we have an Indian initiative producing a Western response in the field of religious thought. To be sure, it was through the British that Rammohun came to know the Judaic and Christian scriptures, but his study of these scriptures convinced him that the Westerners were misinterpreting them.[18] His writings on Christian doctrines can therefore be seen as an attempt to enlighten his fellow men—both Western and Indian—by sorting out truth from falsehood in the contemporary interpretation of ancient religious texts. In one sense he was seeking to de-Westernize Christianity; indeed he once stressed the point that "almost all the ancient prophets and patriarchs venerated by Christians, nay even Jesus Christ himself ... the *founder* of the Christian Faith, were ASIATICS."[19] At a more fundamental level, his method of rational comparison, selection, and reinterpretation may be thought of as an ex-

[17] Rammohun Roy, *The Precepts of Jesus, The Guide to Peace and Happiness*, in *English Works*, part 5, p. 4.

[18] Marshall G. S. Hodgson, an authority on medieval Islam, has suggested to me that Rammohun's Islamic studies would have made him aware of criticisms of Christian Trinitarianism even before he gained the opportunity of studying the Christian scriptures themselves.

[19] Ram Doss [Rammohun Roy], *A Vindication of the Incarnation of the Deity, as the Common Basis of Hindooism and Christianity*, in *English Works*, part 4, p. 72.

ample of the method by which ancient traditions can be renovated or "modernized" in order to maximize their usefulness under modern conditions.

We find an equally clear example of this method in Rammohun's treatment of Hindu traditions. He had little patience with the beliefs and practices of his fellow Hindus, and declared that he found them "in general more superstitious and miserable, both in the performance of their religious rites, and in their domestic concerns, than the rest of the known nations on the earth."[20] Their belief in many gods, their worship of idols, and their custom of burning widows in order to help them join their husbands in heaven, he castigated as contrary to the most authoritative teachings of the ancient Hindus. To acquaint his contemporaries with these teachings he published in Sanskrit (with Bengali, English, and in some cases Hindustani translations) selected Vedic and Vedantic texts, arguing that these manifested "the real spirit of the Hindoo Scriptures, which is but the declaration of the unity of God."[21] As with his selections from the New Testament, his choice and interpretation of these texts aroused a storm of protest among the orthodox and involved him in prolonged theological debates. "The ground which I took in all my controversies," Rammohun later explained, "was not that of opposition to Brahmanism, but to a perversion of it; and I endeavoured to show that the idolatry of the Brahmans was contrary to the practice of their ancestors, and the principles of the ancient books and authorities, which they profess to revere and obey."[22]

This skeletal outline of Rammohun's scholarly and practical work suggests several conclusions relevant to the problem

[20] Roy to Digby, quoted in Collet, p. 71.

[21] Rammohun Roy, *Translation of the Cena Upanishad,* in *English Works,* part 2, p. 13. The fullest exposition of Rammohun's arguments against Hindu idolatry and for a theistic interpretation of Hindu scripture can be found in *Dialogue between a Theist and an Idolater (Brāhma pauttalik samvād), An 1820 Tract Probably by Rammohun Roy,* ed. Stephen N. Hay (Calcutta: Firma K. L. Mukhopadhyay, 1963).

[22] *Athenaeum,* Oct. 5, 1833, p. 666.

which was our starting point: the nature and relationship of indigenous and Western, traditional and modern elements in the thought of non-Western intellectuals during the past century and more. To begin with, the evidence justifies dispensing once and for all with the shibboleth of an East and a West eternally opposed to one another. The concepts of Western "challenge" and the "response" of a given non-Western civilization still seem meaningful, however, providing we think of them in the plural number and bear in mind that a myriad of Western impacts or influences, varying in nature and degree from one time and place to another, have affected the thinking of a great variety of Indian intellectuals and have produced a multiplicity of "responses" during the past 150 years (of which more will be said presently).

Even though much of what Rammohun thought and did would have taken a very different form if Western influences had never impinged on his life, it seems clear nonetheless that the historian depicting his ideas and actions only as responses to Western impacts would be drawing the merest caricature of what really happened. As we have seen, even before modern Western ideas could have affected his thinking he had shown a keen interest in religious reform, and a strong reliance on reason as a guide to such reform. Moreover, his early studies in Persian and Arabic had given him an appreciation of Hellenic logical reasoning and Judaic monotheism —traditions central to the development of modern European civilization. The very warmth with which he welcomed the introduction by the British of these great traditions, in the forms in which they had been developed in the modern West, also suggests his prior adoption of them.

The concept of "Western" and "indigenous" elements counterposed against each other, useful as it may be for less complex confrontations, thus seems too simplistic a framework to serve as our sole guide to understanding the case of Rammohun Roy. The "indigenous" elements are too diverse (the most important of them being domesticated in India centuries after their genesis in Greece, Palestine, Arabia, and Iran), and several of the "Western" ones turn out on inspection to be recent developments of traditions brought earlier to India in a less-developed form.

When we add to the Western-indigenous polarity a second, intersecting one, the concept of a movement in history from "traditional" to "modern" modes of society and culture, we have a somewhat more flexible framework within which to analyze Rammohun's ideas and activities, although these terms, as currently used, require some redefinition. First of all, "tradition" cannot be taken simply as the opposite of "modernity," for the two terms denote different kinds of things. Every society, whether "modern" or "non-modern," depends for its continuity on the persistence and development of certain traditions. Much depends on the nature of the traditions, and the purposes for which they are used. Some traditions, like the use of logical reasoning, may be conducive to modernization, while others may not be, and even the use of reason may inhibit change if it is employed only to defend and justify the status quo. The valid opposite of "modernity" is therefore not "tradition" as such, but what is often called "traditionalism," or the rigid adherence to a particular set of existing traditions in a manner which prevents or inhibits change.

Rammohun's active selection and reinterpretation of traditions mark him as an anti-traditionalist, but in what sense can he be called a modernizer? The word "modernize" currently has two basic and overlapping connotations: to change to a more recent form, and to improve. A concept of modernization as a process of change which includes and depends on the persistence and development of certain traditions stresses the notion of improvement more than that of recentness. Rammohun's writings contain frequent references to the desirability of improving, or ameliorating, his society; in his 1823 letter on educational policy he used "improvement" no less than five times.[23] More precisely, the standard by which

---

[23] Roy to Lord Amherst, *English Works*, part 4, pp. 106-108. In this same letter, Rammohun also used "improve" twice and "improved" once, making a total of eight references to the concept of improvement.

Rammohun gauged improvement appears to have been a twofold one: one aspect was intellectual improvement, or the adoption of "enlightened" ideas; the other was social and material improvement, or the achievement of individual and social well-being through the systematic application of reason to the solution of human problems.[24] If modernization is defined as a continuing process of improvement directed toward the achievement of this-worldly enlightenment and well-being through the sustained and systematic application of reason, then Rammohun may justly be called a modernizer.[25]

An intellectual leader like Rammohun wishing to move his society from traditionalism to modernization must take into account the concrete historical situation of that society, and most particularly its relationship to other, more modernized, societies. We have seen how Rammohun championed the political and educational traditions obtaining in Britain during his lifetime, not because they were Western but because they were more conducive to enlightenment and well-being than those obtaining in India at that time. We have also seen how

[24] Rammohun's strong emphasis on intellectual improvement, both for its own sake and for its practical results, is evident throughout the above-mentioned letter, in which he makes a total of twenty-one references to "knowledge," "learning," "instruction," "education," "teaching," "science," and "valuable information"; five references to "useful," "use," and "utility"; two references to "enlightened"; two to "benefit" and "beneficial," and so on. His ideal of education is put most explicitly in the sentence (*ibid.*, p. 106) in which he declares: "the efforts made to promote it should be guided by the most enlightened principles, so that the stream of intelligence may flow into the most useful channels."

[25] It is now common practice in Bengal to refer to Rammohun in this way. See for example Jogananda Das, *Rammohun Roy, The Modernizer* (Calcutta: Sadharan Brahmo Samaj, 1958). Das acknowledges his intellectual debt to P. Kodanda Rao, who distinguished modernization from Westernization in his *East versus West, A Denial of Contrast* (London: George Allen and Unwin, 1939). Other references to Rammohun's contributions to the making of "modern" India may be found in *The Father of Modern India. Commemoration Volume of the Rammohun Roy Centenary Celebrations, 1933*, ed. Satis Chandra Chakravarti (Calcutta: Rammohun Roy Centenary Committee, 1935).

he sought to renovate both the Christian and the Hindu traditionalisms of his day by selecting and reinterpreting traditions found in the ancient scriptures cherished by the followers of these religions. His selections and reinterpretations, however, were neither eclectic nor based on a predilection for either Western or indigenous traditions, but were guided by the application of reason to the problem of increasing the enlightenment and well-being of the members of his society.

Unfortunately but perhaps inevitably, this indifference to the "native" or "foreign" character of traditions was gradually obliterated in the minds of both Britishers and Indians in the century after his death in 1833. This was so for a variety of reasons. Most important of all was the gradual erosion of the conviction, held by Britishers of the generation of Munro, Elphinstone, and Macaulay, that British rule was only a temporary means by which the "improvement" or "progress" of the Indian people would be promoted, complete self-government being the natural outcome of this period of tutelage.[26] Bitter memories of the 1857 Rebellion in northern India widened the racial estrangement between Indians and Britishers, and in the latter half of the nineteenth century, Westerners in India were further encouraged to believe in their racial superiority by the rapid advances being made in science, technology, and the arts in the modern West. It was in this period that progress (in our terms, modernization) was identified with the West, and resistance to change (or traditionalism) with the "unchanging East."

Faced with an intensifying challenge to their most cherished beliefs, many Hindu and Muslim leaders felt compelled to emphasize the validity—if not the superiority—of indigenous traditions over Western ones. They continued the process of selection and reinterpretation of traditions in which Rammohun had pioneered, but their horizons were usually more

[26] For statements to this effect by Munro and Macaulay, see Reginald Coupland, *India, A Re-statement* (London: Humphrey Milford, Oxford University Press, 1945), pp. 291-292. For Elphinstone's views, see Kenneth Ballhatchet, *Social Policy and Social Change in Western India, 1817-1830* (London: Oxford University Press, 1957), pp. 249-250.

limited, their knowledge of both "Western" and "indigenous" traditions more superficial, and their use of reason more often rationalizing than dispassionate. By the end of the nineteenth century what one observer called "the full defence of the old religions" was everywhere in evidence.[27]

The first half of the twentieth century witnessed the fusion of these "nativistic," "revivalist," or "archaizing" ideas with the modern Western concept of the independent nation-state governed by elected representatives of the people. Gandhi, the foremost leader of the nationalist movement, skillfully employed reinterpreted Hindu, Jain, and Christian traditions of non-violence, asceticism, and courage in his campaign to achieve freedom for his people.[28] Unfortunately his religious ideas appealed more to his fellow-Hindus than to India's Muslims, whose own revivalist movements (encouraged by Gandhi himself during the Khilafat agitation of the 1920's) culminated in 1940-1947 in the successful campaign for the creation of a separate Muslim state, Pakistan.

In the perspective afforded by our analysis of the case of Rammohun Roy, these twentieth century movements for political independence can be seen as examples of political modernization, accompanied by cultural revivalism. On the one hand, in forcing the British to terminate their rule, they secured for the Indian people greater well-being by removing what Rammohun called "unjust and oppressive measures serving to degrade them in the scale of society." On the other hand, the appeals to traditionalist or revivalist religious sentiment which gave these movements against Western rule such widespread popular support also retarded the achievement of this-worldly enlightenment through the sustained and systematic use of reason.[29] Not only that, the spread of revivalist or archaizing attitudes among Hindus and Muslims produced a

[27] J. N. Farquhar. *Modern Religious Movements in India* (New York: The Macmillan Company, 1918), pp. 186-353.

[28] For a convincing analysis of Gandhi's reinterpretation of Indian traditions of courage, see Susanne Hoeber Rudolph, "The New Courage: An Essay on Gandhi's Psychology," *World Politics*, 16 (October, 1963), pp. 98-117.

[29] The contrast between Asian countries under Western rule, where

deep fissure between the two major religious communities of the subcontinent, and consequently a costly antagonism between independent India and Pakistan which is detrimental to the well-being of the citizens of both republics.

The withdrawal of Western rule has given a new impetus to modernization in the cultural as well as the social and material aspects of life in both India and Pakistan, for it is again clear that improvements in these spheres need not be modelled on those already adopted in the modern West, and must in fact make use of reinterpreted traditions, both indigenous and Western. The new security against total Westernization now enjoyed by the people of South Asia also makes possible more dispassionate evaluations of Hindu and Islamic traditions and the ways in which they may be renovated to maximize their contributions to the achievement of this-worldly enlightenment and well-being.

In the six centuries just prior to the imposition of Western rule, the intermingling of these two great streams of tradition had enriched the thinking of many creative individuals, of whom Rammohun Roy may be considered the last and one of the greatest. The intrusion of the modern West interrupted this interaction, threw each community back upon its own cultural resources, and so exacerbated the divisions between them. Westerners, however, brought to South Asia traditions of modernization which have transformed the views of Hindu and Muslim intellectuals toward their own traditions, making it impossible for them to return to their pre-modern, or traditionalist, orthodoxies. It is perhaps only a question of time until creative individuals come forward to continue the work pioneered by Rammohun Roy of selecting, reinterpreting, and integrating traditions from many civilizations, within the framework neither of traditionalism, nor of revivalism, but of continuing cultural modernization.

---

resistance to modern Western values was great, and those retaining independence, where such resistance was less, has been noted by Nikki Keddie in "Western Rule versus Western Values: Suggestions for Comparative Study in Asian Intellectual History," *Diogenes*, 26 (Summer, 1959), pp. 71-96.

PART FIVE

The New Values and the Old

The discussion so far has been limited largely to the formation of attitudes toward modernization; the acceptance, whole or partial, of the "new" on the part of men rooted in the "old." For the first generation of Japanese modernizers, the men of the Meiji era, the overriding urgency of national survival and independence sufficed to a large extent to answer questions about priorities within goals. But already some members of the first generation, and many more members of the second and third generations, found it necessary to look at the "old" from the perspective of the "new"; as citizens of the modern world they asked questions about the ideology of the family state, and as Japanese they sought some new way of integrating their present with their past.

Some of this was inevitable and not uniquely Japanese. The modernization process has brought strains and tensions throughout the world; even in Western Europe, where the transition came gradually and where the ideas and technology which transformed the traditional belief and society came from within that tradition, there were nevertheless dislocations and stresses of many sorts. In Japan, however, as in other non-Western countries more recently, the elements of change could be seen as external to the native tradition and destructive of its integrity, and the whole process was telescoped into a much shorter time span. The sense of dislocation and discontinuity that resulted was consequently far greater. Once the initial sense of crisis had passed, the nature of attitudes toward the Japanese past and tradition therefore came to the fore much more than it had in the early decades of the Meiji period.

The fact that the modern changes had been made in the name of tradition more ancient than the feudal order they supplanted could not, after all, obscure the numerous contradictions between that archaic order and the facts of the modern age. The traditions that had been revived also gained a momentum of their own, becoming increasingly rigid and compulsory with the pervasive influence of the education system and the restrictive nationalist orthodoxy that it fostered. Nor were the issues purely, or even predominantly, intellectual. Social discord that accompanied the growth of industrialization and the rush to the cities seemed to the conservative upper class an alarming lapse from the willingness to put country first that had, as they thought, characterized their own response to the nineteenth century emergencies, and required new emphasis on traditional values of loyalty, service, and cooperation. In the process, the content and thrust of slogans once put forward to secure change were altered; they now came to serve a new conservatism. For the next generation of Japanese the really new dynamics came gradually to be sought less in national than in individual appropriation and reward.

As was to be expected, problems involved in the relationship between the individual conscience and the inherited and the transplanted came to focus most immediately and directly among the first generation of Christian leaders who are the subject of the essay by John F. Howes. Their willingness to accept the full measure of what seemed to them Western values, and their consequent separation from much of the convention of their day meant that their relation with their Western preceptors would be charged with emotion. But it was not that they failed to share in the basic devotion to national independence of their contemporaries; as will be seen, they came to terms with these problems in their own way. Uchimura Kanzō, one of their number, faced the problems involved in the most direct and individual manner, and struggled to resist at once the claims of state, conformity of contemporaries, and control of foreign missionaries.

Uchimura's case is therefore central for the studies of the modern historian, Ienaga Saburō, the subject of the chapter by Robert N. Bellah. Ienaga's search for meaning in modern Japan, like his active role in postwar political discussions, grows out of the conviction that the failure of the Japanese tradition to provide more examples of "negation" on the basis of universal and transcendent values has had a direct and costly effect on Japan's modern history. As the essay makes clear, Ienaga's examination of the Japanese past is an expression of his consciousness, as a modern man, of the need for a new integration of values, without which the technical and material gains of modernization will be meaningless.

The sweep of Japanese history which is shown in the discussion of Ienaga's works comes to more specific and functional focus in Professor Katō's discussion of the relationship between three modern Japanese authors and their society. The writers, sensitive observers of and participants in their generation's experience, reflected most acutely and movingly the contradictions and inadequacies of Japan's modern synthesis, and their works mirror the conflicts of cultural values and individual standards.

Herbert Passin's discussion of the intellectuals reminds us that the issues involved in the diffusion of these and other misgivings in twentieth century Japan were by no means purely intellectual. The growing compartmentalization of life in Japan as bureaucracies proliferated, and the rise in number of and decrease in rewards for the educated provided ample grounds for the *bunkajin*, "men of letters," to wonder about the justice and stability of their social order. Extraordinary balance of a resurrected antiquity and a compartmentalized, selective modernity, of a god-king become constitutional monarch, of modern industry intertwined with traditional handicrafts and staffed by the practices of nineteenth century labor management, twentieth century Japan was indeed a country in need of external crises and challenges to maintain its ideological unity.

With this the wheel comes full cycle, as the discussion returns to the level of values and the relationship between individual appropriation of obligation and declaration of conscience which, as John Hall's description of the Hakone discussions makes clear, Japanese participants saw as an essential aspect to successful modernization. Professor Maruyama, in a paper which he developed immediately after the 1962 seminar, attempts to relate and bridge several of these concerns and positions by offering a conceptual scheme for the relation between the modernization process and predominant types of political and social response. In this he has made allowance for both "traditional" and "modern" political apathy in Japan, and for the loneliness of the crowd in the largest metropolis of the modern world.

CHAPTER X

Japanese Christians and American Missionaries

JOHN F. HOWES

AMONG the many new ways of thinking that flowed into Japan as part of its modernization, few were more at variance with existing tradition or have been more successful than Christianity. For Christianity when the first missionaries arrived in 1859 was not new to Japan. On the contrary, more than two hundred years earlier at least as high a percentage of Japanese had been Christians as at any time subsequently, and the faith had been ruthlessly suppressed since the mid-seventeenth century. Westerners arriving in 1859 reported that a Japanese instinctively moved his hand to his throat to indicate the extent and nature of the danger if the subject was brought up.

In spite of this very negative image one hundred years ago, Christianity now is an accepted part of the Japanese scene with an influence far beyond the comparative few who have become members in established churches. During the 1880's it seemed that a large segment of the population might become Christians, and the missionaries as well as the Japanese converts had a role in the nation not subsequently again equalled. Increasing sophistication with things Western led the Japanese to realize that there was disagreement within Christendom as well as many persons who had little interest in Christianity. The result was that subsequent development was slower, more widespread, and much more difficult to evaluate.

The story of this development has been told a number of times both on the basis of Japanese and missionary records. In this chapter I am not so much interested in it, important as it is in the consideration of modernization, as I am in another aspect of the modernization process about which the history of Christianity in Japan also has much to tell us. This is the psychological influence of the Christian message and those who brought it upon those who became Christians. It is a study of the changing attitudes of the converts, and the subject bears upon the particular history of Christianity in Japan as well as the general study of personality development in relation to the process of modernization.

The point in personality development with which this study deals is that of self-abasement, a subject which has been mentioned elsewhere in this volume. The general pattern in developing a feeling of self-abasement is for the individual who realizes his nation is in need of immediate modernization to feel that his countrymen are of a lower nature or state than those of more modern nations. At the personal level he is prone to feel that he is less worthy or able than individual foreigners. As modernization proceeds and the individual learns more about these strangers, he gradually sees himself as a better person and grows out of this self-abasement.

The first generation of Christian leaders in modern Japan went through a development of this sort in their relations with Western missionaries and other Westerners. The missionaries were the direct agents of their spiritual rebirth; in later contacts the missionaries faced the temptation of continuing to treat their converts as their spiritual children. They also proved a measure against which the developing young Japanese Christians judged their progress.

In this study I should like to look at some specific historical examples to see how this general phenomenon worked out within the nexus of individual lives. Before introducing these individuals, however, let us look briefly at the general historical setting.

The reintroduction of Christianity into Japan in 1859 came just as Japan's officials were starting to consider seriously the changes needed for modernization. Christianity arrived as an unwelcome guest, one which seemed determined to stay. The Westerners desired to see their religion taught in Japan, and they believed that it formed the spiritual basis of the modern world. Japan would have to become Christian, they felt, to achieve a position of international equality.

The Japanese could frustrate the desire of the Westerners to propagate their faith; this in part they did. They could not so easily deal with the confidence of the Westerners that the Japanese would ultimately have to adopt Christianity. As long as Westerners seemed superior to themselves, the Japanese could not avoid the lingering doubt that perhaps the Westerners were correct in their assumption. Philosophical exercises attempting to prove the contrary could overcome this doubt only when the West ceased to appear in fact superior. The Japanese nation sought material equality; the Japanese personally looked for the self-confidence that they as individuals were equal to other individuals. It is one of the assumptions of this study that modernization in terms of individual self-image meant the achievement of such personal self-confidence.

Not all individuals felt insecure; perhaps the majority did not. But individuals were liable to such feelings to the extent that they knew the West intimately. They might upon contact find there only inferior ways of thinking or acting and so reply to its obvious material superiority with an assertion of spiritual superiority. But this could not succeed too well, for the arts of philosophical defense which might have presented their case convincingly were no more equal to the emergency than were the defenses of Tokyo Bay equal to the emergency posed by Perry's gunboats. Knowledge of the West ultimately bred insecurity about themselves.

One possible solution in the face of this difficulty was to become Christians individually and to attempt to make other Japanese Christian. A small proportion of the people did this. They had problems of self-image but in one significant aspect their problem of this sort differed markedly from that of their fellows: they constantly dealt with foreigners and so the question of whether they were equal arose repeatedly and intensely. Most of their countrymen knew the West only through books. The Christians, almost alone in Japan, had

339

the opportunity to judge the West by means of its men as well as its writings.

Dramatis Personae

Out of the numerous biographies and histories of the early Christian movement the names of five Japanese and five Americans appear with great regularity. They were the leaders in bringing Christianity to Japan and spreading it among Japan's people. Individual choices would vary, but any list of the most important ten missionaries or converts would include these two groups of five.

Although each of the ten is remembered as an individual, characteristics they share in common also reflect the general nature of the American Protestant mission movement as it is remembered in Japan and the general nature of the Christian leadership within Japan. Through these ten men, therefore, we may obtain a picture of the whole movement. Before discussing them individually we will point out some of the things they had in common.

Both the Americans and the Japanese came from religiously conservative groups who felt themselves losing status in their home lands. They met at least in part because of decisions arising out of these circumstances. The American Christian message was new and very different from the Japanese point of view, but by the standards of the Americans it was traditional and an attempt to reinvigorate the past. The Japanese seemed to the Americans anxious to seek what differed from their own heritage, but in their own minds they also were trying to enliven the best in their past.

The Americans appear to have come from groups with long roots in American soil. James Curtis Hepburn, James Hamilton Ballagh, Leroy Janes, William Smith Clark and Jerome Davis: their names indicate they came from Puritan America, from the rural society that had dominated the early days of the nation. The members of this society found themselves during the nineteenth century losing influence to the cities which teemed with immigrants and spawned new poverty and new wealth. The social unit of the village with its white painted church and town meeting which served as the center for the farms in the neighborhood remained static; the cities with their ways threatened to usurp control of all society.

Economic loss accompanied decreased political influence in the countryside. With the opening of new lands in the Western Reserve many of the best and most ambitious young men moved to soil that would produce more with less effort. But when they went they took their societies with them so that although New England itself lost population and affluence, a new New England sprang up to the west. The Americans we are studying came from little towns in this area of larger New England. The very names of these towns seem to recall the attitudes of their society: Ashfield, Massachusetts; Milton, Pennsylvania; Lake Odell, New York; New Philadelphia, Ohio.

Intellectual leadership remained in New England though economic and political influence waned. The new towns sent their best men east for college, and these men returned often to found colleges of their own which looked back to New Haven and Cambridge. From the point of view of New England, then, it looked as if increased intellectual and spiritual influence might compensate for economic and political decline. New England was springing up renewed, like a Phoenix, in distant parts of America. Might it not also spring up renewed in the lands of the Orient? This was a dream that brought new spiritual vitality to Christians in the area and produced their dedication to societies organized to support mission effort.[1]

The established small colleges of the east and their new counterparts in the midwest gave the Americans we are studying their higher education before the Civil War. Hepburn, by any count the most cosmopolitan of the Americans, studied at Princeton and took a medical degree at the University of Pennsylvania. Clark, the only other one with a cos-

---

[1] A good summary of this subject as it applied to evangelization in Japan is contained in Ikado Fujio's "Toa dendō to seikyōtō seishin," *Shūkyō kenkyū,* XXXIV, 1, 164 (Sept. 30, 1960), pp. 50-83.

mopolitan background of sorts, was graduated from Amherst and took a doctorate from Göttingen. Janes attended West Point; Ballagh studied at Rutgers; and Davis was graduated in the tenth year of Beloit's existence and took theological training in the University of Chicago. These institutions of higher learning produced the men that went half way around the world to share their faith and to try to recreate in Japan the world they had known at home.

Though they travelled widely in their lives, they do not seem to have acquired the intellectual breadth one usually associates with such travel. Hepburn was again the exception; he had served in a mission hospital in Amoy and had a prosperous practice for a number of years in New York before going to Japan. He also seems to have been more influenced by what went on around him than were the others. One can not be sure on this point, but the short sojourns of Clark and Janes and their intense relations with their students must have precluded their learning very much about Japan itself or its culture, and the impression that Ballagh and Davis gave to the Japanese did not indicate that their life abroad had changed their basic orientation. For the most part the Americans took small-town New England attitudes with them and seem to have retained these while in Japan.

Of these five, it is Clark and Janes that come most to life in Japanese records. Though sharing the religious conservatism of the others, they understood students and knew how to respond to the eager attention of Japanese students. Clark, though a trained scientist, enjoyed contacts with people and expansive administrative schemes more than his laboratory. In Sapporo he took his boys on long hikes through the country, sang lustily along with them and imparted a deep sense of piety. His parting words, "Boys, be ambitious," were unnecessary; few groups of "boys" have ever been more ambitious. The words live on in Japan to commemorate a happy coincidence of attitudes.[2]

---

[2] Biographical material for these sketches comes from numerous sources. Rather than list all attributions, I shall give the major source or sources in each case. The best biography of Clark, painstakingly

Janes had a commanding physique. His training as an artillery officer had equipped him to handle horses well, so that he was a "beautiful sight" on horseback and entered Kumamoto "like a victorious shogun" to take up his job.[3] Once there he took advantage of the opportunity offered him to organize the schools as he desired. Unlike Clark, he did not evangelize the students in the beginning but waited almost until they asked him to teach them about Christianity. Clark died soon after he returned home, so we can not know how they might have felt toward him personally as they matured. Janes continued to be revered by those whom he had taught, however, and, when in his old age he was hard pressed for funds to operate his little chicken farm in California, they helped him with a loan of seven hundred dollars.[4]

Hepburn came to Japan first of the five, was the oldest, and had the highest opinion of Japanese abilities. When he first arrived, Americans going to live in Japan could not get life insurance and the sight of samurai striding down the streets with their two swords recalled this fact to their minds frequently; Hepburn's decision to go required considerable courage. In addition to this courage, Hepburn had long experience in his profession of medicine and commanded considerable language skills; he is remembered in Japan both for an eye medicine which is attributed to him and for the system of romanization which bears his name. But he earned the respect of the Japanese who knew him best by his recognition of their achievements. In 1872 before returning to America on furlough he sold his medical instruments, announcing that the Japanese were already producing good physicians and had no further need of him. Twenty-one

---

pieced together from scant material, is Ōsaka Shingo, *Kurāku Sensei hyōden* (Sapporo: *Kurāku Sensei Hyōden Kankōkai*, 1956).

[3] Watase Tsunekichi, *Ebina Danjō Sensei* (Tokyo, 1938), p. 76. This is the best biography; Ebina Danjō, *Kirisutokyō Gairon Mikankō, waga shinkyō no yurai to keika* (Tokyo, 1937), gives interesting sidelights into Ebina's childhood.

[4] Kozaki Hiromichi, *Nanajū nen no kaiko* (Tokyo, 1927), pp. 199-203. An excellent autobiography; the best source on Kozaki.

years later when he left Japan to retire, he announced that he was going home because Japan had now produced many evangelists of good calibre and did not need foreigners in that capacity either. A true Christian gentleman, he could implement the Christian ethic of service without requiring servility in return.[5]

Ballagh and Davis both spent almost their entire professional lives as ministers and evangelists in Japan. Ballagh went to Japan while in his twenties and worked in the Kanto for fifty years. One of four siblings to become missionaries under the influence of their mother, he is remembered for his piety and sympathetic love, though it was occasionally mixed with intolerance and emotional excesses. A photograph shows him in his later years with a white goatee kneeling behind a low pulpit set on *tatami*. This technique in itself must have been difficult to master and shows the lengths to which he went to set an atmosphere which he felt would make his audience receptive to his words.[6]

Davis spent his life working in the Kansai, first in straight evangelism and then with Niijima Jō in Dōshisha College in Kyoto. He composed one of the first evangelical tracts; it sold a total of over one hundred thousand copies. He was conscientious and worked hard, but as we shall have an opportunity to observe, he did not understand the temperament of the Japanese Christians. Little is available about his person in Japanese sources, perhaps because he appears there primarily as an adversary.[7]

These five men brought a specific kind of faith with them. It had grown originally in New England and was spreading rapidly in the American west. It emphasized personal conver-

[5] Saba Wataru, *Uemura Masahisa to sono jidai* (6 vols., Tokyo, 1937-1941), I, *passim*, has good sections on Hepburn. Saba's collection of primary sources in six volumes is an indispensable tool for studying the Protestant Christian movement. Takaya Michio, *The Letters of Dr. J. C. Hepburn* (Tokyo, 1955), though poorly proofread, makes available a large part of Hepburn's correspondence.

[6] Saba, *op.cit.*, I, pp. 349-351.

[7] J. Merle Davis, *Davis—Soldier, Missionary* (Boston, 1916), is the primary source.

sion, implicit faith in the Bible, moral rigor, and a sense of mission. Conversion, it held, was an intense personal matter, an experience which only the individual could identify but which was unmistakable when it occurred. It required the assistance of no other person. Intelligent reading of the Bible could lead the individual to it through the medium of divine grace and individual reason. Here was a faith well suited to the conditions both of the American frontier and of the spiritual desert in which many Japanese young men felt themselves. On the American frontier professional men of religion were scarce, and the Bible, which was often the only book, had to take their place.

In Japan there was no such physical separation, but there was spiritual isolation of one person from another. Young intellectuals who were particularly capable and alert often felt themselves cut off from their fellows in a way which seemed almost as complete as physical isolation. They had been torn from their social and psychological moorings by the effects of the Restoration and felt themselves unable to communicate with their fellow Japanese. They did not seek solace in religion, but on the contrary opposed religion because they could not abide the degraded state into which Buddhism had fallen. They felt consequently as lonely as a prospector in the Rockies. As the prospector turned to the Bible in his loneliness, so these men could turn to the Bible for consolation. And reading it as the missionaries taught them to read it, word for word, differed but slightly in form from the way they had been taught to read the Chinese classics. The emphasis on the individual and on the printed word fitted in well with the needs of such students.

Another feature of this faith was its rigorous moral demands upon the individual. Strict sexual ethics, abstinence from the use of liquor and tobacco, care in the observance of the Sabbath, and a sense of stewardship: all formed part of the ethical code. Strict rules by which to govern conduct seem to have an appeal to young people in general, but the Japanese acceptance of the moral code went far beyond that. Perhaps they accepted it in order to set themselves apart from other Japanese. More likely they conformed to it because it seemed to complement or to fulfill the best in the ethical world of their past. Buddhism and Confucianism were in disrepute, but their ethical imperatives remained clear for those who wanted to read about them. Contact with men who in their own lives seemed to live up to an ethic equally demanding had an attraction to young men whose own families held similar codes in esteem.

One example of a similarity in attitudes concerned liquor. Several of the Christians we are studying mention in their autobiographies that they had no trouble with the abstinence demanded of them because they had been brought up in families where there was no drinking. One of them became very disillusioned when he discovered that Ballagh kept wine in the house. Ballagh, flustered when it was discovered, explained that it was a health tonic, and the student took Ballagh's displeasure at its discovery as a sign of insincerity—an even greater sin than drinking.

The last contribution of the Americans was a strong sense of mission. We may smile at some of their ways, but they had a sense of this cardinal element in Christianity which commands our respect; and they managed to impart it to the young Japanese students. The later friction between them and the Japanese Christians resulted from their inability to recognize the capabilities of the Japanese as they matured. The missionaries erred by assuming that the Japanese could not do as well as they themselves. This in fact reflected faulty judgment but not necessarily the lack of respect. The Japanese, however, consumed as they were with the desire to be respected, could interpret it in no other terms than disrespect.

The young men to whom the missionaries brought the faith had backgrounds remarkably similar to their own. In the first place, they also came from a social group which was painfully adjusting to a change in status. All of them came from samurai families in domains which had backed the shogunate until near the end of the war of the Restoration. Their fathers, most of whom had been in the scholar-bureaucrat tradition of the samurai, had been at loose ends as their sons grew up; and we hear of strong mothers who seemed to carry more than their normal share of family responsibilities and instilled into their sons great ambition. Like the missionaries from America, these students had grown up in families whose members felt that history might be passing them by. And by going to learn of the West through foreigners they hoped to improve their position in the new society.

All of the students but one also came from the provinces, though not from small towns but from *jōkamachi*, provincial capitals which had long histories as regional centers. After they became Christians they moved to Tokyo where they spent most of their adult lives as national leaders in education and religion. They achieved their purpose of rising in the world through their new education, and as adults they had middle class tastes and attitudes. They also all travelled abroad at least once, so that they moved in a steady progression from provincials to cosmopolites.

The Japanese students also shared an attitude which corresponded to the missionaries' desire to reinvigorate the New England spirit. Like the motivation of the missionaries, this was not explicit at the time and is perhaps more apparent to the historian than it was to them. In essence, they hoped to give new relevance to the Confucian tradition through their interpretations of Christianity. They did not concern themselves with Buddhism since it did not live in their own personal backgrounds, but they were concerned about the Confucian tradition in their past. At first everything in Christianity seemed opposed to things Confucian, just as everything Japanese seemed different from everything Western. Later on similarities became apparent, however, and Christianity seemed to be the fulfillment of Confucianism. This is, of course, a complex subject, and one that we can only mention here. Further study will show, I believe, that these Japanese as they matured tried as the occasion demanded to forge a link between their new faith and their Confucian background. Their attitudes had much in common with those of the American missionaries who were attempting by an extension of their values abroad to reinvigorate the tradition at home upon which the values were based.

The five Japanese who were led by these missionaries to Christianity are Ebina Danjō, Kozaki Hiromichi, Honda Yōichi, Uemura Masahisa, and Uchimura Kanzō. Ebina and Kozaki came from Yanagawa and Kumamoto, respectively, domains in Kyushu near the great clans of Satsuma and Chōshū. Yanagawa and Kumamoto felt as if they were not getting their just share of the achievements of the Restoration, and Kumamoto hired Janes to establish a school of Western learning to improve their chances for the future. Ebina and Kozaki both went on to positions of leadership within the Japanese equivalent of the Congregational Church. Both had terms as presidents of Dōshisha, and both at other times had large churches in Tokyo. Kozaki's congregation included many government leaders, and business and professional men formed the majority in Ebina's. Beginning in his youth Ebina wore a beard which turned white as he aged and gave him a patriarchal air.[8]

Honda came from Hirosaki in what is now Aomori Prefecture. He went to Yokohama with the intention of going abroad, but remained to study in the English school there and later to come under the influence of Ballagh. Although originally converted a Presbyterian, he became a Methodist when he returned to Hirosaki because the missionary with whom he worked there was a Methodist. Later he became the president of Aoyama Gakuin and the first Japanese Methodist bishop. His change in denomination reflects the relatively casual attitude that the Japanese Protestants had toward sects. Their primary social and intellectual contacts remained with other Japanese Christians who were not so interested in denominational problems, and they had comparatively few relaxed contacts with the foreign missionaries who felt denominational distinctions more acutely.[9]

Uemura spent his first eleven years in Edo. Then with the downfall of the shogunate his family lost its wealth, and it

---

[8] Watase and Kozaki, *passim*.

[9] Okada Tetsuzō, *Honda Yōichi den* (Tokyo, 1935), p. 57.

moved to Yokohama where he and his father raised pigs. Another convert of Ballagh, he went on to become the leader of the Presbyterian tradition in Japan as well as a prolific translator and writer. He had a massive square head set atop sloping shoulders. As he aged his hairline receded on either side of his forehead and he wore a crew cut with the result that the exposed portion of his forehead looked like horns. This combined with the massiveness of his head gave him a taurine appearance which comported well with his stolid and capable personality.[10]

Uchimura was born in Edo but moved with his family several times as a boy to Takasaki and the Tōhoku. His father was a personal secretary to the daimyo. Converted under the influence of Clark, Uchimura early gained a deep respect for and identification with New England. A natural bent for language found expression in both Japanese- and English-language prose of remarkable vigor. Photographs of him in his twenties portray a young man, the corners of whose mouth droop in a scowl parallel to his string bow tie.[11]

These, then, were the ten men who came together in Japan in the 1870's.

Rebirth and Maturation

Through the contact the students found a spiritual rebirth. At the same time they found themselves in a kind of spiritual dependence upon the missionaries who had converted them. For the succeeding thirty years they grappled with the problems of growing out of this relationship; most of them achieved their independence at about the same time as their nation achieved recognition as a modern state.

The students met Christianity and Western society for the

---

[10] Saba, *op.cit.*, 1, pp. 615ff. has very good biographical material, and Aofusa Katsuhisa, *Uemura Masahisa den* (Tokyo, 1935), is the standard biography.

[11] *How I Became a Christian: Uchimura Kanzō zenshū* (20 vols., Tokyo, 1932-1937), xv, pp. 1-169, is an autobiography of his first twenty-eight years; Masaike Megumu, *Uchimura Kanzō* (Tokyo, 1953), is at present the best biography.

first time when they entered the schools of the missionaries; they were completely overawed. As one of them recalled later, any argument could be won at that time if you attributed your position to foreigners; and he blushed when he remembered how a chance but pointed remark by Mrs. Ballagh had made him change to wearing long underwear even in the summer.[12]

The students were in an impressionable position emotionally. At the age when the mind seems most open to influence, they were away from home for the first time and under powerful new guidance. They concentrated on their studies, finding in their English less disturbing ways to deal with topics which bothered them, so that Ebina, who could not abide the word *"inori,"* found himself able to deal with the subject calmly by using the English equivalent "prayer,"[13] and Uchimura referred to girls as "W matters."[14]

At this time when they were so defenseless, they found themselves the objects of great care and interest by men on the average twenty-five years their senior whom they suspected of wanting to convert them. Even though flattered, they felt that they must guard themselves against this interest lest they be led unwittingly into the new faith. Some vowed not to become Christians without consulting the others; another dared not confess his leanings toward Christianity for fear of ridicule; and Uchimura's conversion may have resulted from a similar psychological state working in reverse. He later recorded that he had been forced into Christianity by the upperclassmen at the school, all of whom themselves had been converted and did not want their faith threatened by disunity.

In the recollections of the others on the process of their conversion, two factors are frequently listed. The first is the intellectual training which they received. The Western ideas they learned at the school did not in general conflict with what they had learned in their earlier Confucian training. The supernatural elements in Christianity presented the

[12] Matsumura Kaiseki, *Shinkō gojū-nen shi* (Tokyo, 1926), p. 20.
[13] Ebina, *op.cit.*, p. 56.
[14] Letters to Miyabe Kingo *et al.*, 1883-1884; *zenshū* (Tokyo, 1932-1937), xx, pp. 67ff.

greatest difficulty, yet the science courses proved capable of overcoming that difficulty. Western science made it easier rather than more difficult to adopt Christianity.

The other factor important in conversion was the personality of the missionaries. Conversion almost always results from individual contacts, and these students had ample opportunity to get to know the missionaries well. Their teaching methods and their family life seemed to prove their contention that Christianity was the source of Western strength. More than anything else, however, the sight of the missionaries praying impressed the Japanese. Conversion occurred during prayer sessions in a number of instances. One evening, Ebina recalls, Janes asked them to stand and join him in prayer as part of a Bible-study group. Ebina hesitated, though the others rose. Janes continued to talk, telling them it was their duty (*shokubun*) to God to thank Him. The call to duty struck a responsive chord, and Ebina recalls that he stood at once, "for even a Confucian" would pray if it were his duty. As he stood he realized that God was his creator and entered into his new faith.[15]

The young men who like Ebina had been through this experience turned with great energy to the conversion of their countrymen. Their story commands respect. Trips out into the countryside to sell Bibles or to lecture before hostile groups trained them in the techniques of evangelism and taught them patience. A new church organized by students in Sapporo thrust them immediately into the problems of ecclesiastical organization. For all their energy and ambition, however, these new men were still young and disinclined to condone standards lower than their own. The rift between the converts from Kumamoto and Davis which was to have tragic consequences has its origins here.

Ebina and Kozaki went with the others who had been converted by Janes to the little school, later to become Dōshisha University, that Niijima Jō had established in Kyoto. Davis had charge of Bible training for the students. He felt chal-

[15] Ebina, *op.cit.*, p. 57.

lenged by them and put great study into preparing for his lectures. He tried to deliver them in Japanese, for he felt that the students needed training in expressing their new faith in their own tongue. He misjudged their ambition and abilities from the outset. They had done all their work under Janes in English and shortly began writing numerous theological tracts in Japanese. Davis's halting efforts caused him to lose control of the class so that the course on the harmony of the gospels turned into "disharmony." He suffered at the hands of the students, but he seems to have brought the trouble on himself.[16]

For the time being, however, the differences between the students and the missionaries did not loom large. The young Christians from the various schools gravitated toward Tokyo where they became warm friends and started a number of enterprises; all of them aimed at spreading their new faith and introducing the new culture they had come to know. They continued to work in harmony with the foreigners until the end of the 1880's when they had matured as individuals and when the enthusiasm in Japan for everything Western had cooled considerably. This enthusiasm had reached its greatest height a few years earlier; it had encouraged an uncritical acceptance of Christianity which led to mass apostasy as the tides of public favor and government policy brought things Western and Christian once more under suspicion.

Both the foreigners and the Japanese interested in evangelism turned to answer the challenge that this shift posed to their work. The clashes which resulted arose from differences over the course which should be adopted to meet these changed conditions. The missionaries favored an increase in the intensity of the Christian point of view, or a more direct witness, as they called it. The Japanese, faced now with the difficult problem of proving their loyalty both to their nation and to their faith, adopted a position that appeared to be less Christian. They attempted to reduce dependence on the outward forms of Christian practice and to emphasize instead

[16] Watase, *op.cit.*, p. 137.

inner spiritual development; this would assist the individual equally but would not antagonize those around him.

These points of view both represented logical reactions to the situation as the two groups understood it. The Japanese wanted to do without the Western elements unnecessary to the faith. The missionaries wanted to increase the visible elements which were unmistakably Christian and to uphold their theological position. They acted consistently by their lights. American Protestantism at the time emphasized the need for demonstrating at every opportunity how much one's faith meant to him. Street-corner preaching and meetings where individuals described their experience were the most obvious expressions of this; public prayers and hymn singing indirectly served the same ends and were so common they formed an important part of social life.

Theological conservatism accompanied this emphasis on witness. The conservatives wanted to maintain the position that the Bible was the literal word of God. Science under the influence of Darwin attacked this position, and new modernist theological interpretations which accepted these scientific findings came into Japan in the 1880's and appeared as one more threat to the missionaries. These differences between the Japanese and the missionary point of view came to the fore in decisions about educational policy. The missionaries had been most successful in education and relied upon it heavily as an evangelical tool. The Japanese people also highly valued education, but they looked with suspicion upon learning which would produce individuals who seemed so un-Japanese. They instead wanted to fashion education into a tool for making students aware of their own Japanese traditions. Like the New England movement which the missionaries represented, the Japanese position was conservative, but it harked back to a different tradition.

The Japanese Christians felt that if their schools were to survive in this atmosphere they would have to demonstrate that they could serve Japan and did not oppose national aims. Niijima and succeeding presidents of Dōshisha including Kozaki and Ebina conceived of their task in these terms. They called the schools which aimed primarily at conversion "mission schools," and differentiated sharply between them and schools like Dōshisha which offered "Christian education." This they defined as education of quality in surroundings which enabled students to see examples of the Christian life and did not discriminate against conversion.[17] It seemed to them a vital distinction.

Two examples will show how clashes developed between individuals holding these opposing views. The first arose at the Hokuetsu Gakkan in Niigata. The Hokuetsu Gakkan obtained its support from the prefectural government and was supposed by the Japanese not to be a mission school, though it had missionary teachers who taught English and were supported by their mission boards. Uchimura was employed to supervise instruction when he returned from study in the United States. Attempting to instill first in the students an appreciation for religion itself, he told them about religious men in their own past, and invited in a Nichiren priest to speak to them. The missionaries objected, and Uchimura left Niigata for Tokyo.[18]

Matsumura Kaiseki, similar to Uchimura in his convictions, replaced him at the Hokuetsu Gakkan. Matsumura went there on the condition that he have complete responsibility for educational policy. He preached at the church in town on Sundays but did not have public prayer or hymn singing in school meetings. He also maintained student discipline by what he called his "Ōyōmei" (Wang Yang-ming) method. This was to allow students to do anything they pleased as long as they acted in good conscience. The missionaries did not object to this method of discipline, but they could not long remain silent on the question of public witness. The break between Matsumura and them came on the occasion of a visit to the school by the members of the prefectural legislature. One of the missionaries suggested to Matsumura that he pray in the meeting and deliver an evangelical address. Matsumura refused. The missionaries left the school, and the

[17] Kozaki, *op.cit.*, p. 90.
[18] Letter to D. C. Bell, Sept. 26, 1890, *zenshū*, xx, pp. 198-199.

affair confirmed in Matsumura his conviction that foreigners could not work with Japanese.[19]

The second case concerns Dōshisha itself. It was the pride both of the Japanese Christians and the American Board of Commissioners for Foreign Missions. From the beginning it was frankly modeled on Amherst and other New England colleges. Niijima and his successors tried to keep it in line both with Christian teaching and Japanese requirements, while the co-founder Davis and his colleagues considered it as an extension of the New England ideal. The problem inherent in the differing points of view came out into the open a few years after Niijima died and was succeeded by Kozaki. Niijima had been able to keep the factions together by the strength of his personality; with the passing of this personal link went the mutual confidence that it had bred. The first clash resulted when the students invited Janes to come for an address. He was teaching in a government school in Kyoto and had become an advocate of the new scientific interpretation of the Bible. The missionaries hotly opposed his coming, and the administration used the objections by a part of the students as an excuse to cancel the invitation. Kozaki was not present in Kyoto when this happened, but he was responsible and resigned because of this and other problems of a similar nature.[20]

His successor, the son of Yokoi Shōnan, had the much more difficult task of trying to maintain the spirit of Dōshisha as a Christian institution while complying with a new government regulation that students in specifically Christian educational institutions could not gain exemption from military conscription. He and Ebina along with other Dōshisha trustees decided to delete from the charter both the clauses which stated that Dōshisha was a Christian institution and that the charter should never in the future be changed. A lawyer on the Dōshisha board had suggested this novel way of dealing with the former clause; if left in the charter, it would have made students ineligible for exemption. The Americans

19 Matsumura, *op.cit.*, pp. 130-142.
20 Kozaki, *op.cit.*, p. 102.

considered the action of the board to mean that the school would no longer be Christian. Yokoi and the others defended their action on the basis of expediency, stating that they had no intention of changing anything in the school but did of course need students to continue operation. There is no doubt that this was their intention. It was an unfortunate decision, however, for in changing the charter this way they had both broken the letter of the original agreement and had violated its spirit at that point where the missionaries were most concerned. Kozaki and most other Christians agreed that the decision was wrong because it confirmed the missionaries in their mistrust and for a while strengthened them in positions of increased influence.[21]

Davis won the argument because of the disagreement among the Japanese Christians and because the American Board threatened to take the case to the civil courts. His opponents were the same men who had created disharmony in his class almost twenty years earlier, and he seems to have considered them still as students. They were in fact responsible leaders in their society, liable to mistaken judgments like anyone else, but deserving the respect of adults. Davis, perhaps because of their previous association, does not seem to have shown them this respect.

The histories of Christianity in Japan contain a number of examples of this sort, not many in the light of the numbers of persons involved perhaps, but sufficient to attract attention. Our purpose here is not to emphasize their existence but rather to estimate their significance in studying the process of modernization. The young men who had gained spiritual rebirth at the hands of these missionaries were now at the stage where they felt confidence in their abilities but were not confident enough to make a complete break. In the secular society around them most of the foreign specialists had by 1890 completed their work and left the Japanese to gain further experience themselves. The question of missionaries was much more difficult. The Japanese Christians shared with them a deep sense of mission to convert Japan, and it re-

[21] *Ibid.*, pp. 162ff.

quired a greater degree of confidence to assume that burden than secular endeavors required. Until the Russo-Japanese War, therefore, they adopted intermediate positions, either pleading for understanding or relying on mediating individual differences.

Kozaki represented the former point of view. He had become convinced that the Japanese must have control of their own Christian movement even before the Janes affair and was absent from Dōshisha at that time expressly to plead for an understanding of the Japanese Christians before the First World Parliament of Religions which was being held in Chicago. He gave two addresses, one before a plenary session and the other before a smaller group that was interested in Christian missions. In the first one he emphasized the vigor of the Japanese leadership and the necessity that it control its own affairs. In the second address he told the missionary group that they must understand those among whom they go, have faith and sympathy with them, and be willing to work along with others.[22] That he felt it necessary to state his case in these terms reflects both his attitudes toward the Western mission movement and his feeling that the Japanese Christian movement was not yet sufficiently mature to make stronger representations.

Later on a visit to New York, Kozaki asked the secretary of the American Board if it would not send teachers who could answer better the intellectual problems of the Japanese young people. He felt Japan needed teachers versed in the critical approach to the Bible, in philosophy, and in science. The secretary replied by asking whether Davis was not his man. Kozaki was hurt that the secretary neither seemed to understand his request nor knew of anyone else that might be better suited than Davis.[23] He returned home shaken in his confidence that an appeal to Americans for understanding would solve the problem, and his retirement from Dōshisha removed him from the arena of direct conflict.

Honda's attitude toward working with the foreigners re-

[22] *Ibid.*, pp. 425-455.
[23] *Ibid.*, p. 130.

veals similar self-confidence in his own judgment coupled with a lack of confidence that the foreigners could be made to understand him. Early in his term as president of Aoyama Gakuin the question of science versus the Bible became an issue, and a number of young faculty members appealed directly to the mission board headquarters in New York. Honda was in New York when the letter arrived. He was consulted and tried his best to inform the leaders there of conditions in Japan. In a long letter to the dissidents in Tokyo he explained how he had failed and counseled submission to the will of the foreigners on the basis of devotion to a common task.[24] This represents the position upheld by Honda during the remainder of his life, at what cost to himself we do not know, although the constant strain of acting as a middleman may have been a factor in his comparatively early death. The final remark in the letter is revealing. After his numerous appeals to the teachers to bear with the missionaries, Honda concludes with the reminder that the individual who has troubled them the most will be going home the following year.[25] Honda recognized that time was on the side of those who worked in their own home environment.

The positions of both Kozaki and Honda reflect their confidence that mutually acceptable solutions would result if they sought to gain understanding through rational explanation. If we explain, they seem to be saying, they will be moved by our reasoning to agree with us. It is a good position, one that would seem very suitable to a person trained in the Confucian tradition. But there are times when the other party does not respond to such reasoning. He is not necessarily motivated by reason. The idea of mission itself is often not rational. For this contingency Kozaki's and Honda's position at this time had no answer. They could only respond at the expense of their self-image and their self-confidence. Before they could feel self-reliant they had to have a solution to this final aspect of the problem.

This answer developed out of the events of the following

[24] Okada, *op.cit.*, p. 79.
[25] *Ibid.*, p. 81.

decade. The Sino-Japanese and Russo-Japanese wars and the Anglo-Japanese Alliance increased Japanese prestige abroad and gave the nation as a whole the assurance that they had arrived at their goal of modernization. In the terms of our analogy, they had arrived at adulthood. A parallel development occurred in the relationships between the Japanese Christians and the missionaries. The Japanese at Dōshisha managed to get control to their own satisfaction late in the 1890's, and about the end of the Russo-Japanese War the Japanese counterpart of the Presbyterian Church arrived at a solution.

The solution worked out by the Presbyterians eventuated in removing the missionaries from influence in policy. They did this through a change in the rules under which the General Assembly, the chief governing body of the church, operated. Up until that time the missionaries and pastors of all the churches had voices and votes in the General Assembly. They represented two very different kinds of congregations, however. One group had ministers of the caliber of Uemura himself. These churches were self-sustaining and free of mission control. The other group consisted of churches on the fringes of Christian growth; missionaries supported them until they grew to support themselves. Uemura contended that such churches were immature and unworthy of representation in church government. To deprive these congregations of voting rights would also mean, however, that the missionaries would lose their votes, since they worked only in such churches. The proposal came up in 1904 for the first time but was finally voted down, apparently because of an impassioned plea by the aged Ballagh. The next year it was passed by a comfortable majority.[26] A way had been found for solving the disputes between foreigners and Japanese whereby both parties were bound by their respect for church government, one of the bases of their work together. In effect the

[26] "Dai jūhakkai daikai gijiroku furoku," Saba, *op.cit.*, IV, 501; "Kyōkai jiji mondai," *Fukuin shimpō,* 521 (June 22, 1908), Saba *op.cit.*, p. 523. It is not certain that Uemura wrote this, but it appeared in his magazine without a byline, and Saba indicates that it is Uemura's.

missionaries were reduced to their powers of persuasion alone. The position of Kozaki and Honda was reversed. Uemura had power on his side in a form that both sides respected. Where reliance on negotiation and reason had failed, he invoked church law; and by so doing he shifted from Confucian to traditional Christian means.

The controversy over this question moved Uemura to consider the problems of the missionaries. He set down his conclusions in a number of articles during the years shortly after the Russo-Japanese War. They show the result of long thought. Missionaries are no longer a novelty in Japan, he says, and their words no longer have influence just because they say them. "They have become equal to Japanese"[27] and reduced to handling administrative and reportorial details. They often use native helpers to speak for them, and this leads to their own spiritual decay. Look at their libraries; this will show that they suffer intellectual malnutrition.[28]

Uemura went on to discuss the thorny problem of gifts that one does not want to receive. Many people from abroad wanted to help. How should the Japanese respond to their offer of money or service? and what should they do with the aged missionaries who were rounding out years of devotion? There was no objection to receiving money, he said, from any source. But one should always be sure that such funds did more good than harm. As for persons who wanted to help with their personal service, they could be happy only if they mingled directly with the Japanese, got to know them as individuals, shared their problems, and shared their way of life. But there was little chance that this would happen, and so the mission boards should be encouraged not to send further persons. Perhaps it seemed cruel to speak so frankly, but such persons would be happier in the long run if addressed this way at the outset.[29]

The old missionaries had served the cause of Japan well by introducing Christianity to it; they should be treated with

[27] *Ibid.*, p. 523.
[28] *Ibid.*, p. 524.
[29] *Ibid.*, pp. 521-522.

all respect before they retired, or as he put it in a graceful classical phrase, "clothed in brocade and returned to their native villages."[30] Uemura exemplified this attitude in his own actions. He treated the missionaries he had known as a young man with respect, and the articles about them and their work which he published in his magazine form one of the best sources for the early history of Christianity in Japan.

This reasoned statement marks the end of the period of apprenticeship for Japanese Christianity. Uemura treats a most difficult subject involving sensitive emotional problems judiciously. He does not write in English and appeal to the foreigners. Instead he makes what he says available to that small circle who read his magazine regularly. We do not know if it was ever translated or referred to in English. Uemura was apparently not concerned that foreigners read it; and this lack of concern for what foreigners thought, seen in the context of a nation that had a history of intense concern for what such persons thought, demonstrated his maturity. Although there were to be many more individual differences between missionaries and Japanese Christians, these differences were interpreted increasingly less in terms of culture than of individual variation. With this development the Christians of Japan had become modern men.

The Slow Maturer

One among the Japanese Christians disagreed with Uemura and the others. Yet he is the one who is today best remembered, and it is through him that Christianity has made the most direct impression on the secular intellectual world. He is Uchimura, the doubter who did not solve the problems that adoption of Christianity posed for the individual for fifteen years after Uemura solved them. Uchimura's experience parallels that of the sensitive youth whose scruples prevent him from taking on the responsibilities of manhood until long after his fellows.

[30] "Gaikoku senkyōshi," *Fukuin shimpō*, 591 (Oct. 25, 1906), Saba, *op.cit.*, p. 535.

From Niigata, where we last saw him, Uchimura went to Tokyo where he made history and precipitated a long debate by his refusal to bow before the Imperial Rescript on Education. The issue was whether the state should inculcate ethical attitudes through education. He next went into journalism and had attained a position as one of the most respected editors in the nation when his scruples forced him into another dramatic move: he resigned his post right before the Russo-Japanese War because he had become a convinced pacifist and felt he should not write for a paper that disagreed with his views. He then retired to editing a monthly magazine on Bible study and teaching a few selected students. He was joined to the world by omnivorous reading and extensive correspondence, but met his peers only infrequently. This life of comparative quiet was interrupted toward the end of World War I when he joined a group of millenarianists in predicting the impending end of the world. Travelling widely, he lectured extensively on the subject for a few years and then gradually lost interest, confiding in his son that one would go insane if he continued to believe in the imminent Second Coming for too long. He spent the remaining years until his death in 1930 in a relaxed mood, completed his greatest exegetical work, and mixed much more freely with other people.

The calm of Uchimura's final years contrasts strangely with the restlessness and sense of contingency which characterized his life before World War I. His works and his personality influenced different persons in different ways, but most men who came into contact with him seem to have reacted strongly either for or against him. Although many interpretations for this differing influence are possible, the one that seems most plausible is that Uchimura affects those who read him because he deals at a subtle level with the problem of the self-image of the person who is converted to Christianity. In a larger sense it is the relation between the claims of the nation and culture into which one is born, and those of the religion which he adopts of his own free will.

In his autobiography Uchimura states that his reason for

going to the United States was *"to be a* MAN *first, and then a* PATRIOT."*[31]* He achieved his aim completely only with his loss of interest in the Second Coming Movement almost forty years later. His standards were incredibly high, and he responded to any situation involving his conscience with a deadly seriousness—so much so that one is often tempted to laugh at him or consider him mentally ill. But as Erik Erikson points out in his *Young Man Luther*, this characteristic appears in both the mentally ill and those who are mentally too healthy, who cannot take themselves other than seriously because they feel to a heightened degree problems spared other men by common sense. Men like Luther have no common sense, but rather a heightened sensitivity which makes impossible the compromises which assist others to live more relaxedly. Uchimura was such a person.

He gradually achieved his aim of becoming a man by refusing to compromise his principles, even though this led him to a life of comparative seclusion and little direct influence. He had much more difficulty becoming a patriot, because to be a patriot he had to have a country of group morality sufficiently high for him to feel he could tender it his loyalty. To expect any nation to live up to his uncompromising standards was to seek the impossible, but it took Uchimura a long time to realize this. He tried for a number of years to persuade Japan through his criticism to live up to his ideals for it. Finally he gave up and let his spiritual loyalties instead remain with his second home, the United States. He recalls late in life that he considered July Fourth his own national holiday for many years, and he built up an elaborate illusion about the United States which enabled him to keep faith in it while recognizing that not all its citizens lived up to its ideals.

The ideals Uchimura ascribed to America were the same ideals that the missionaries had come to give to Japan: the ideals of rural New England. While studying in the United States Uchimura had met some men who represented

---

[31] *How I Became a Christian; zenshū,* xv, 78.

the final stages of this tradition. These men were respected in their professions and are still remembered today. Uchimura's compelling sincerity and ability led him to the best intellectual leaders of his day both while he was abroad and after he returned to Japan. In Japan he could not meet his American friends personally but instead corresponded frequently. His first two English-language works were translated and published in numerous European languages so that he was well known there; he remains better known there than in the English-speaking world. He met the best representatives of Christendom through his writings, while other Japanese Christians met Western Christians who were cut off from major spiritual developments in their homeland—the missionaries or mission board administrators. Uchimura maintained his image of the remnant who were loyal to the best of Christian ideals by dismissing Westerners who did not live up to his interpretation of those ideals, and by maintaining a friendship through correspondence with those who did live up to them.

These people whom he saw as loyal to the old conservative ideals were, in his view, the ones upon whom Japan had to depend for religious guidance. They were the only ones who could teach her in the subjects where she lacked most: the bases of the Christian life. Japan did not understand this message completely; she had to be taught. The small remnant in the West loyal to the Puritan tradition could and would teach her.

Here was an illusory world that fitted Uchimura's particular need. Long after Uemura and the others accepted themselves as equal to other men, Uchimura demanded that Japanese be treated as equals but felt in his heart that they were still inferior. Disturbing as this admission of inferiority was, it was not as disturbing as the prospect of complete responsibility that would devolve upon Japan if she recognized that no one could teach her. For if there was no one who could teach her, Japan must be equal to any task; Uchimura could not accept Japan as equal to any task because of its obvious defections from his ideal for it.

This whole extended mental framework rested on one slim assumption: the existence of a small group in the West and particularly the United States who stood intermediate between Japan and God. The First World War shattered this assumption as it shattered many other assumptions but Uchimura reacted differently to this than did others. Most thinkers saw in it the end of Western claims to cultural superiority. Not so Uchimura. He reacted to America's entry into the war by concluding that the United States had thereby disqualified itself as Japan's religious teacher.[32] So great was his preoccupation with Japan's spiritual problems that he interpreted even this catastrophe of world importance in its parochial terms.

This proved the beginning of the end. A few months later Uchimura went to Nikkō. One day while walking over the plain above the Kegon falls he suddenly became convinced that the war heralded the coming of Christ in the near future. This led him to start a series of lectures on the Second Coming. His most loyal disciples could not understand why he acted as he did. In terms of the peculiar psychological position into which he had worked himself, however, it appears clear that he was here subconsciously finding another intermediary between his nation and God. If the United States could not act as intermediary, Christ himself would.

Uchimura's lectures in the Second Coming Movement were not as irrational as one might have expected them to be. They were calm, clear expositions of a point of view in Christianity that appears and disappears repeatedly. They represented rational thought, and it was the rational mind of Uchimura that slowly led him away from the position. A number of his fellows in the movement were American missionaries. They became increasingly interested in maintaining orthodoxy against the claims of science, and Uchimura lost interest in them and their movement. The issue of science versus Christianity had never bothered him, and the reports of the Scopes

[32] "Beikoku no sansen," *Seisho no kenkyū*, 202 (May 10, 1917), p. 221.

trial which he read indicated the extremes to which the position could be taken. As a result he left the millenarians.

His way of life changed little, but he was a different person. He had arrived at a position, similar to that which Uemura had achieved some fifteen years earlier, in which he calmly accepted himself and his nation. Uchimura seemed then to be more content: he made friends more easily; he felt neither such extremes of anger toward nor of dependence upon foreigners; and his occasional English-language essays were not pleas for understanding or assistance but little gems of Christian thought; they covered a wide range of topics common to the problems of all men, not just Japanese.

New objectivity about Japan accompanied the universality apparent in these essays. He accepted Japan as equal to other nations. He found its Bible-centered Christianity as good as the expressions of Christianity in other lands. And when he lectured on the passages in *Romans* enjoining Christians to obey constituted authority, he remarked that this injunction caused Japanese no difficulty since their government was at least as good as that of any other nation.[33] At last he could accept Japan and had become, even by his uncompromising standards, a patriot.

The intellectual climate within Japan in the 1920's encouraged relaxed acceptance of Japan as a Western nation. Uchimura died in 1930. Many persons have speculated on what his attitude would have been had he lived through the Second World War. We cannot know except through the attitudes of his disciples. They demonstrated their objections to the war at least as effectively as any other group. Since the war, they have gone back to Uchimura's earlier prophetic writings in which he foresaw such a war if Japan did not become Christian. They have not also returned to his earlier position of seeking help in the West. Even the shambles of the Second World War could not shake their basic confidence that Japan could handle its own problems as well as anyone else could.

[33] "Seifu to kokka ni taisuru gimu," *Seisho no kenkyū*, 266 (Sept. 10, 1922), p. 406.

Conclusion

The experience of the Japanese Christians in achieving a self-image of equality with Westerners provides us with some interesting clues to understanding both the history of Christianity in Japan and the psychological mechanism that accompanies acceptance of a new philosophy as a part of modernization.

One of the big questions in the history of modern Christianity in Japan has been why such exceptionally capable persons were attracted to it when it was first introduced. Converts in other countries of Asia have generally come from the lower classes who were attracted by Christianity's egalitarian teachings or from those who were already committed to lives as religious leaders. In the case of Japan the converts came from families who had traditionally served in government; some of them gave up political careers to continue in positions of Christian leadership. It is true that they were attracted at first partially by the new Western culture the missionaries represented. This seems an insufficient reason for such later activity. Had it been the main reason, they would have left Christianity as soon as everything Western lost favor. More important than the attraction of Westernism was the sense of dedication to spiritual reform which the young men found expressed in the action and teaching of the missionaries. The backgrounds from which the young men came provided them with a sense of need for spiritual reform, and the spirit of the missionaries coupled with the contents of the faith itself led them to dedicate their lives to such reform.

A second point concerns the "nationalism" of the Japanese Christians. It is often held that the churches were very nationalistic in their desire for independence and control of their own destinies. Of course the Japanese Christians were nationalists in the sense that they loved their country. But they were neither jingoistic nor anti-foreign. They deeply desired the respect of others as well as themselves. They found as they matured into responsible positions that they had to free themselves of foreign control, real or imagined, in order to do their jobs adequately. Their actions appeared unduly nationalistic only when the Americans misinterpreted their sincere attempts to meet the problems their society presented them.

The third point about Japanese Christian history concerns Uchimura's legacy and postwar concern over responsibility for the war. The majority of the Protestants, precisely because they had accepted the state and had been so integrated into the mainstream of Japanese society, could not stand outside that stream and judge their nation's actions. Uchimura's more tentative acceptance of the Japanese state gave his followers a sense of responsibility to transcend their nationality if the state did not live up to their ideals. To this can be traced their record of greater opposition to the Second World War and their greater concern with maintaining the peace since the war. In their forthright criticism of the state they have provided good examples for those interested in the responsibilities of citizenship everywhere.

Finally we must consider the effect of this sort of encounter upon those who come in the role of modernizers. The self-image of those who receive will be one of inferiority coupled with an ardent desire for self-respect. The one who comes to modernize must always be on his guard lest his desire to help be corrupted by this sense of inferiority into feelings of condescension. Above all he must be humble and, at least while working in matters of the spirit, prepared to "be clothed in brocade and sent back to his native village" when those among whom he has gone to work feel that the time is ripe.

CHAPTER XI

Ienaga Saburō and the Search for Meaning in Modern Japan

ROBERT N. BELLAH

MODERNIZATION is usually discussed in economic or political terms. Certainly the major "impact" of the West on Asian countries has been economic and political, and the "response" has had to deal centrally with economic and political problems. Yet it is generally recognized that cultural problems are also involved and that attempts at modernization, successful or not, involve a cultural dimension, even though this dimension has as yet been much less carefully studied than the political and economic dimensions. Central to what I am calling the cultural dimension of modernization is the problem of meaning. How do the people and more especially how do the intellectuals, those especially responsible for interpreting the meaning of the world, make sense out of what is happening? The situation in which modernizing nations find themselves is often interpreted in slogan-like phrases: "imperialism," "national essence," "socialism," "capitalism." Behind these phrases lie more or less coherent political ideologies, formulated out of traditional, Western, and newly created elements by the intellectuals. For most people, including most intellectuals, the problems of meaning raised by the Western impact and the consequent attempts at modernization are answered by one or other of the popular ideologies of the day, ideologies which are heavily political in vocabulary and explicit concern.

But behind the popular ideologies, implicit or in some cases explicit in them, lie deeper problems of meaning, problems of a historical, philosophical, and even religious nature. The traditional culture had its own view of the world and of man; the modern West has quite a different view. Can the two be reconciled? If so how? What must be given up, what changed? The problem of how to act in a given historical situation leads to the deeper problems of what is true, what is good. Conscious concern with such problems has not been widespread or typical, though the degree to which unconscious concern with them has goaded leaders or even large groups remains an open question. But in most of the modernizing nations there have been a few men who have grappled with such problems in more than a superficial way. For one who is interested in cultural change, and who believes that although it operates on a longer time scale than economic and political change, it is even more profoundly important in human history, such men are of the greatest significance. It is an interest in this sort of problem which has led me to study the work of Ienaga Saburō.

Ienaga is a specialist in the history of Japanese thought, and in recent years he has become widely known as a political ideologist. Yet it is not as an ideologist that I wish to study him, rather I wish to deal with his deep concern with the moral, philosophical, and religious issues underlying Japanese modernization. The relation between the two sides of Ienaga's work cannot be neglected, but this study claims to be relatively complete only with respect to Ienaga's more philosophical thought. This means that his work before 1952 will receive the most attention even though the popular image of him both in Japan and the West is largely based on his post-1952 activities.

Though I have said Ienaga has been concerned with the moral, philosophical, and religious issues of Japanese modernization (a concern which makes him relatively unique among modern Japanese intellectuals—I am not at all claiming that he is typical), he is not a philosopher or theologian, but rather he is a historian of thought. His approach then is always through history. In his search for answers to what are clearly existential questions for him he has been led to peruse the whole course of Japanese history and subject it—ancient, medieval and modern—to a series of stimulating reevaluations. It is with these reevaluations that I am concerned and I will bring in only so much biography as is necessary to understand them. It is the ideas, representing as I think they do, cultural mutations, in which I am chiefly interested. Therefore I have relied on Ienaga's own work for my data. The biographical details are derived mainly from his own reminiscences and have not been checked with other sources. They represent therefore largely Ienaga's own view of himself. As for the thought, that exists in his writings and it is against those writings that my interpretations must ultimately be checked.

The Young Ienaga and His World (1913-1935)

Born in 1913, Ienaga spans three major periods of modern Japanese history: Taishō Democracy; the Nationalist Period from the Manchurian Incident of 1931 to the end of the Second World War; and the new Japan which has emerged subsequently. Known primarily as a student of ancient and medieval Buddhism who after the war became "progressive" and took up the study of modern intellectual history, Ienaga's early grounding in the Taishō spirit is sometimes overlooked or forgotten. But the events and influences of those early years were in many respects decisive and it is there that we must look first if we are to understand him.

The "pre-historic period"[1] in his intellectual life begins with his enjoyment of historical stories told by his mother and read in grammar school, but takes on more serious significance in Middle School where he first read Natsume Sōseki's *Botchan* and became a partisan of his.[2] At the same time he noticed among his elder brother's college textbooks a copy of Minobe Tatsukichi's (1873-1948) *Kempō satsuyō* (Constitutional Outlines) and read it.[3] This book made a great impression on him and remained a favorite for many years. Because of its "clear logic" Ienaga was attracted to the study of law and at this time read such abstruse things as a

---

[1] "Watakushi no dokusho henreki," in *Rekishi no kiki ni menshite* (1954), p. 241.

[2] He would later write an important essay on Sōseki.

[3] This was of course before the attack on Minobe's theories which developed in the 1930's.

book on the Japanese penal code and the *Collected Statutes* (*Roppō zensho*). Also while in Middle School he was intro- duced to the scientific study of Japan's ancient history through Nishimura Shinji's *Yamato jidaishi*.[4]

In First Higher School Ienaga underwent a decisive experi- ence which is best described in his own words: "When I entered Higher School in the spring of 1931, just before the Manchurian incident, Marxism was still at its zenith. In the year I entered school there were two strikes arising from questions of student thought. Facing that atmosphere for the first time in my life and seeing that the nationalist morality (*kokka dōtoku*) which had been poured into me at home and at school was without authority, I felt that the ground on which I stood had crumbled. Seeking for something on which my spirit could rely I took hold of philosophy. After the orthodox morality which had no basis outside of the historical tradition of the past had slipped from the seat of my heart, philosophy, which speaks of 'what one ought to do' had for me a fresh fascination. Throwing away many years of educational precepts I was spiritually reborn. This is an incident which can be called the Copernican Revolution (*tenkai*) in my spiritual life."[5]

The book in which he discovered his solution was Tanabe Hajime's *Kagaku gairon*.[6] In it he was introduced to the "value philosophy" of the Southwest German school of Neo- Kantian thought, of which Windelband and Rickert were the leading figures. For him the idea of "value" which is not "existence" or "value which ought to be" independently of "existence" offered the only way out when the notion of "*kokutai*," namely that "Japan is a country blessed with a single line of emperors for ten thousand generations from most ancient times,"[7] had collapsed. While in Higher School, besides German Neo-Kantian and Japanese Kyoto School philosophy, Ienaga was also reading books on Marxism and

[4] *Ibid.*, pp. 240-241.

[5] "Waga chojutsu to shisaku o kataru," in *ibid.*, pp. 231-232.

[6] *Ibid.*, p. 241. The book was first published by Iwanami in 1918.

[7] Private communication, July 9, 1961. The date was 1932 or 1933.

Christianity,[8] as well as Buddhism. Among the latter was the early biography of Shotoku Taishi, *Jōgū Shōtoku Hōō teisetsu*,[9] and Shinran's *Tannishō*.[10] Ienaga relates his reactions to the changing situation in Japan at this time in a passage that directly follows the one quoted above: "After I had begun to think in this way in my own mind, the Japanese thought world gradually underwent a drastic change in the direction of fanaticism. After I had tasted the forbidden fruit called liberty, an unbearable atmosphere became pervasive. Not yet having a place of discussion in the body of students, I sought an outlet for my unexpressed indignation in the magazine *Dai ichi* put out by the alumni association of my Middle School. In the November 1935 issue of *Dai ichi* I published an article concerning the problem of the 'organ theory' of the emperor which I concluded with the following sentence: 'Doesn't one feel that the whole Japanese thought world generally has gone mad since the Manchurian incident? The most important admonition for our people is exhausted in the one sentence 'Keep your feet on the ground.' "[11]

Most of the major themes of Ienaga's later work were foreshadowed in interests of his Middle and Higher School years, as they have just been outlined. The rest of the chapter will involve a working out of these themes. But here we must pause to consider some of the implications of his "Copernican Revolution." This is an example of the kind of experience which many Japanese have been going through ever since the opening of the country (and in a sense some Japanese went through long before that). It involves the replacement of the traditional social system, defined in narrower or broader terms, by a set of universal principles, as the ultimate locus of value. In the traditional view there is a harmony between the natural order, the moral order and the actual social order.

---

[8] Private conversation, 1961.

[9] According to an article by Ienaga in *Shūkan dokusho*, May 5, 1961.

[10] In the preface, dated November 1941, of his *Jōdai Bukkyō shisōshi* (1942), later reissued more correctly as *Jōdai Bukkyō shisōshi kenkyū*, he said he read the *Tannishō* "about ten years ago."

[11] *Rekishi no kiki ni menshite*, p. 232.

Maruyama Masao, in the second chapter of his *Studies in the History of Japanese Political Thought* (*Nihon seiji shisōshi kenkyū*), has described this undifferentiated conception of order as it existed in orthodox Confucian thought in the Tokugawa period. Ishida Takeshi in the first part of his *Studies in the History of Meiji Political Thought* (*Meiji seiji shisōshi kenkyū*) has described the formation of the "family state" concept in the late Meiji period which may be seen as the adaptation to new circumstances of virtually the same tradition of thought which Maruyama described for the earlier period. It was this new orthodoxy[12] centering around the concept of *kokutai* (national body) with the imperial line at its heart, against which Ienaga was reacting.

The set of universal principles which for many has broken through the "inherited conglomerate" (to borrow Gilbert Murray's phrase from another context) has probably in most cases in modern Japan been provided by Christianity or Marxism, but secular Western philosophy has also played its part. But in the latter case it has perhaps usually been the more radical French or British philosophies as in the case of early Meiji utilitarians (e.g., Fukuzawa Yukichi) or the non-Christian *Jiyū minken undō* (Freedom and Peoples' Rights Movement) leaders (e.g., Nakae Chōmin). In the case of Ienaga, though Marxism clearly played a role destructive to his traditional ideas, and Christianity may have been in the background, it was German Neo-Kantianism which provided the basis for a new way of thought.[13] At any rate what

[12] Maruyama has said that Japan never had an "orthodoxy." This is true in the sense that what was ultimately sacred was always a system of social relations rather than a system of ideas. But the word "ortho-relational" is too barbarous to use. See *Nihon no shisō* (Tokyo, 1961).

[13] Ienaga himself has pointed out (private conversation) that what most of the followers of Neo-Kantianism in Japan picked up was its cultural historical emphasis, not the theory of value which interested him. Nevertheless one should perhaps be cautious in assigning German idealism or the Kyoto School to the category of "establishment" philosophy. Actually one might make out a case for inner break-down of "orthodox" philosophy in Modern Japan from Inoue Tetsu-jirō to Nishida Kitarō to Tanabe Hajime along lines quite analogous

374

is important is that henceforth for Ienaga "what is" could not automatically be identified with "what ought to be." His adoption of a transcendental morality put him in critical relation with his environment and must have, especially in the circumstances of those days, increased the tension between himself and his world. But at the same time, that philosophy of value provided him with the basis for a "spiritual rebirth." In it he found meaning when the "ground on which I stood" had crumbled and he was threatened with meaninglessness.

It is interesting that out of his spiritual crisis and his confrontation with the sharp change occurring in the intellectual world came an impulse to social action. The specific instance that we know about involved the constitutional theories of Minobe Tatsukichi (who was attacked for believing that the emperor was an organ of the state) whose work Ienaga had admired before his Higher School days, as we have seen.[14] His recent concern with constitutional and other social problems may appear strange to those who know only his writings on Buddhist thought before the end of the war. But it does not seem so once one knows of his early history. Though his attention soon turned rather exclusively to religious history this can be considered as a temporary shift in emphasis for both inner and outer reasons as will be con-

---

to that described by Maruyama for Tokugawa orthodox thought (*op.cit.*). The process involves the differentiation of previously undifferentiated elements in which the distinction between social order and moral order is central in both cases, though of course in quite different ways.

[14] Minobe's theories clearly had no revolutionary meaning for Ienaga when he first read them. They were attacked as being out of keeping with the *kokutai* in 1935 approximately 25 years after they had originally been enunciated. Part of the reason for this is that the *kokutai* notion itself was changing. The ultra-nationalism of the 1930's may in a sense have been "implied" in the Meiji family state notion but it was not there in all its virulence. On the special characteristics of this ultra-nationalism see Maruyama Masao: "Chōkokkashugi no ronri to shinri," in *Gendai seiji no shisō to kōdō*, Vol. I, (1956), pp. 7-24. This essay has been translated by Ivan Morris as "Theory and Psychology of Ultra-Nationalism." *Thought and Behaviour in Modern Japanese Politics* (Oxford, 1963).

sidered below, rather than a radical shift in ideology (*tenkō*). There is no evidence in any of his writings before 1945 for any support for statism or ultra-nationalism or the *kokutai* or "Imperial Way" ideologies. Indeed, even when not being specifically political Ienaga was sufficiently out of step with the spirit of the times to have his first scholarly article, arguing for Buddhist influence on an important passage of the *Nihon shoki*, pulled at the last minute by the editors of *Rekishi chiri* on grounds that the sale of the issue might be banned if it contained such an article.[15] At any rate it should be clear that Ienaga, while still in his student years, participated in the major trends of thought associated with the period of "Taishō Democracy" (even though in these early Shōwa years it was in its twilight stage) and was profoundly shaped by them. This is the indispensable precondition for understanding his later work.

In his first year in Tokyo Imperial University (1934) Ienaga underwent a new spiritual crisis, this time of a religious nature. "At that time for various reasons I was beaten in mind and body (*shin-shin tomo ni uchinomesarete ita*)," he wrote of this experience in 1961. He had great anxieties about his own abilities in facing the choice of a special field which would determine his whole life. "The dry and lifeless university lectures without any real thought in them" could not save him from a feeling of despair. On top of that Ienaga who had never from childhood been physically strong was afflicted by a turn for the worse in his physical condition. In this situation he understood existentially for the first time the meaning of Shōtoku Taishi's words "The world is empty and false; only the Buddha is true," which he had already read in Higher School.[16] In this statement he found support in the midst of despair and partly through reflecting on it he kept his balance in the "dark valley" of the years of frenzied nationalism which

[15] "Watakushi no shojo shuppan," in *Rekishi no kiki ni menshite,* p. 235. The incident occurred in the summer of 1937.
[16] This paragraph is based on Ienaga's article in *Shūkan dokushojin,* July 15, 1961.

lay immediately ahead. It seems likely[17] that a deeper knowledge of Shinran's thought also contributed to his emergence from this spiritual crisis. It is certainly around Shinran that his subsequent studies of Buddhism revolve.

In a sense the university crisis and its solution involve a deepening of the problems of the earlier crisis in Higher School: the shift is from the realm of morality to that of religion. This implies a further differentiation. Whereas the earlier crisis had led to the differentiation of social system and morality in his thought, this second one led to the differentiation of morality and religion. A concern for the moral nature of man continues to be very important for Ienaga and is deepened by his religious experience. But during the period of greatest concern with religious problems there is almost complete withdrawal from concern with social and political action. This withdrawal must be explained in terms both of inner preoccupations and the outer pressures of the period. There is a further shift involved in the university experience which is worth noting. This is a shift from primary concern with modern thought (constitutionalism, German idealism) which is Western in origin to ancient (Shōtoku Taishi) and medieval (Shinran) thought which is Japanese.[18] Thus at the same time that he has moved to the level of the ultimate problems of meaning (religion) he has moved to a consideration of his own historical heritage. The choice then of ancient and medieval Japanese Buddhist thought as his field of scholarly specialization was not fortuitous but came directly out of his own experience and as he would say "practical" concerns. This is a characteristic of Ienaga in all his work.[19]

[17] On the basis of the preface to *Jōdai Bukkyō shisōshi kenkyū* mentioned above it is probable that the thought of Shinran also became central at this time. He says that it was the reading of the *Tannishō* (which undoubtedly first occurred in Higher School) which drew his interest to the practice and thought of Buddhism and determined his scholarly interest in this field.

[18] Though I believe there were Christian elements directly or indirectly in the background, for reasons which will become clear later.

[19] A number of elements in Ienaga's early experience are not unrelated to some of those described for post-war Japanese youth by

THE SEARCH FOR MEANING

The "Logic of Negation" and the History of Japanese Thought (1934-1945)

After his graduation from the university in 1937 Ienaga was affiliated with the Tokyo University Shiryō Hensanjo (Institute for the Compilation of Historical Materials), taught for a while at the Niigata Higher School and eventually became a professor at the Tokyo University of Education. From his university days until the end of the war his research was almost exclusively directed to the history of Buddhist thought. He published a series of important books on this subject from 1940 to 1947.[20] In his first book Ienaga lays out his general interpretation of Japanese thought focusing around the problem of the development of the "logic of negation" in Japanese Buddhism. All of the other studies are developments of various parts of the schema of the first book. It is to the analysis of that general schema that we must now turn.

The Development of the Logic of Negation in the History of Japanese Thought is a small but remarkable book. It shows Ienaga at the age of 27 already at the height of his powers as a scholar. Although the terminology of the book, beginning with the notion of the "logic of negation" itself, certainly smacks of the Kyōto School,[21] the terms take on a special

Robert Jay Lifton in his article "Youth and History: Individual Change in Postwar Japan" (*Daedalus,* Winter 1962, pp. 172-197).

[20] The major books are *Nihon shisōshi ni okeru hitei no ronri no hattatsu* (The Development of the Logic of Negation in the History of Japanese Thought) (1940) ; *Jōdai Bukkyō shisōshi kenkyū* (Studies in Ancient Buddhist Thought) (1942) ; *Nihon shisōshi ni okeru shūkyōteki shizenkan no tenkai* (The Development of the Religious View of Nature in the History of Japanese Thought) (1944) ; and *Chūsei Bukkyō shisōshi kenkyū* (Studies in Medieval Buddhist Thought) (1947, enlarged edition 1955). In the same period he published several works on ancient Japanese painting (of which the most important was *Yamatoe zenshi* published in 1946) but these fall outside the central concern of this paper.

[21] The last quote in the book (p. 116) is from Nishida Kitarō's *Tetsugaku no kompon mondai,* p. 90, where he is cited as saying that for a new philosophy of negation "there must be a basic change in logic." See also Tanabe Hajime, *Tetsugaku tsūron* (1933), Chapter

378

meaning in the context of Ienaga's analysis which is always historical rather than abstract. The distinctiveness of Ienaga's position relative to the Kyōto School and the basis for the difference will perhaps appear most clearly after the contents of the book are summarized.

1. The first chapter traces the development of the logic of negation (*hitei* can also be translated as "denial") in the West as a background for the clarification of the Japanese material. Ancient Greek philosophy, says Ienaga, had no category of negation. It was based on a theory of being (*u*) rather than non-being (*mu*). From this point of view the ideal is a fulfillment of the real, not a negation of it, and the ideal god is a fulfillment of the human. Plato proceeds in an unbroken line from this-worldly goods to the Good. Only in their tragic drama did the Greeks express the logic of negation. In the tragedies men must submit to fate—their free will is crushed when they struggle with divine authority. In this relation of opposition and contradiction between gods and men, "god" is not an idea or *eidos*. So among the Greeks the logic of negation can be recognized, but it is not expressed as such in philosophy.

   In Hebrew and Christian thought, however, the logic of negation is openly expressed. Value resides in God not in man. God is not an ideal man. Salvation comes from God alone and not by human effort. Christian *agape* comes first from God and differs from the *eros* of Greek philosophy.

2. As in the West the most ancient Japanese thought did not know of the logic of negation. Just as Christianity brought this logic to the West so Buddhism brought it to Japan. However, at first it was only an imported idea. The present book is an attempt to describe the process whereby the Japanese people only gradually and through their own experience grasped the meaning of the logic of negation.

2, section 8, pp. 170-236, for a discussion of dialectical method in which many of the terms in Ienaga's book appear.

Pre-Buddhist thought in Japan was entirely affirmative (*kōteiteki*, the opposite of *hiteiteki*). Its optimistic view of man emphasized purity from contamination rather than salvation from sin. Its notion of "other worlds" (*takama-gahara, yomi no kuni*, etc.) was simply one of other places not essentially different from this world and even at certain points spatially connected. For the early Japanese these "other worlds" are much like this one for, since they did not deny this world, they had no wish for an ideal other world.

3. Shōtoku Taishi was the first Japanese to understand Buddhism. Buddhism's basic dialectical movement is the absolute denial of the actual (*genjitsu*) and as a result of that denial the return to an absolute affirmation on another plane. This Buddhist "logic of negation" Shōtoku Taishi clearly understood when he said, "The world is empty and false; only the Buddha is true."

In the Seventeen Article Constitution Shōtoku criticized the individual and social evils of the Japanese society of his day—for example, party spirit, flattery, envy, covetousness, bribery, oppressing peasants, disorder between ruler and people, lack of loyalty to ruler and lack of benevolence to people—on the basis of Confucian ethics. But he says ethics is not enough: we cannot expect the final solution by human effort alone, but must rely on the three treasures of Buddhism.[22] There is only one way to escape from this world and that is by thoroughly denying it. For evil and suffering are not discrete phenomena but the essence of the human world; this is a world of fire and there is no one who does not suffer. But through the experience of absolute denial of this world one can attain the other shore, the pure land, which as the denial of the denial is the Buddha world of absolute affirmation. The core of Shōtoku's teaching is the idea of turning (*ten*), that is, turning from illusion to truth.

[22] Here Ienaga attributes to Shōtoku Taishi the same series of differentiations—of morality from social system and religion from morality—which we posited he experienced in his own development.

Shōtoku of course transcended his time. In the general consciousness the Buddhist logic of negation was not grasped but Buddhism was used instead as a magical power for obtaining recovery from illness or protection of the state. But even there the absoluteness of Buddhism was recognized and there was at least not the simple optimism of earlier days. The *Manyōshū* reflects a quite new feeling of human limitation, transience and consciousness of death. But on the whole, social conditions in this ancient period had not yet mediated the consciousness of the logic of negation. Shōtoku's understanding may have been partly motivated by anxiety aroused by the collapse of the old clan (*uji*) system, but this was not enough to bring about his consciousness of the need for absolute negation. This consciousness was rather mediated by his extraordinary soul.

4. The Nara court was not particularly conducive to the development of *hitei* thought and the early Heian court was even less so. The latter saw a reversal of the earlier pro-Buddhist policy and its replacement by an emphasis on Confucian morality with its reliance on human this-worldly effort. Buddhism was rigidly controlled and the court favored Hinayana legalism. Saichō's life and work were a protest against these new policies but later Tendai thought and Kūkai's Shingon sect compromised with the *kōtei* tendencies of the court. The esoteric sects propagated the idea that everything is a Buddha and that denial of the world is not necessary. In practice the esoteric sects simply catered to the satisfaction of worldly desires through magical means.

But in the disturbed conditions of the late Heian period a situation arose in which the essence of human life and the logic of negation could be more deeply grasped. Although they lived in the midst of pleasure the aristocrats had begun to grasp its limits. But they were not ready for the absolute denial of this world: they preferred to place the Pure Land or its artistic illusion in the midst of this world (e.g., the Byōdōin) and enjoy it. By encouraging self-power methods (such as contemplating statues and pictures of Amida) they retained the tie between this and the other world which existed from of old in Japan and hindered the full realization of *hitei* thought.

5. The late Heian aristocrats wanted to pray for an after-world so that they could continue to enjoy their pleasures in it, not in order to make a basic turn (*ten*) away from actuality. In order to break out of this superficial and primitive optimism to a deeper and more concrete world-view there had to be an absolutely negative experience which could mediate the consciousness of the logic of negation. The collapse of Heian life in the Heike and Genji wars provided just such an experience. The fall of the aristoc-racy was a great moment in the history of Japanese thought for it provided the basis for the thorough grasping of the logic of negation.

6. But probably the contradictions of suffering could not be felt in their deepest sense by the aristocrats. The latter at their best sought for a real, sudden enlightenment. How-ever, suffering which can be solved by one sudden enlight-enment is not real suffering and consequently a turn toward salvation whose aim is such an overcoming of suffering cannot be a truly dialectical absolute turn. Only in facing a truly impossible antinomy is absolute nega-tivity realized. Consequently it was not the nobles but those whose very way of life necessarily bound them to the wheel of Karma and who had no hope of salvation, such as warriors, hunters, monks who had broken their vows, prostitutes and the like, who felt the extreme of suffering, and who became conscious of their inescapably evil nature.

7. Already in Genshin there was a tendency to equate this world with hell, but the tendency was not yet complete. By Kamakura times the recognition that this world is hell was fully expressed. The conditions for the fulfillment of the development of the logic of negation were complete. Shinran's doctrine is its fullest expression.

In Shinran with his deep sense of sin the recognition of the inescapable nature of human evil becomes dialectically the positive basis for salvation. It is on these grounds that Shinran could say "If the good are saved, how much more the wicked." For in the recognition of his own inescapable sinfulness the sinner casts away all self-power and so it is possible for him to attain salvation through absolute other-power. In connection with the exegesis of Shinran's views Ienaga quotes Romans 3.10: "None is righteous, no, not one," and refers to Karl Barth's discussion in his Commentary on Romans.[23]

Zen Buddhism attacked the main premises of the Pure Land view and reasserted self-power, yet it still participated in the currents of the age (e.g., Dōgen's rejection of the world).

8. The absolute denial of Kamakura Buddhism also contained an absolute affirmation. After the Kamakura experience in the Muromachi age the affirmation could be more freely expressed, but it was not the naive affirmation of ancient times. It had the quality of "not having to deny all human life as a dream but viewing this dream as a dream and expressing the feeling of living quietly alongside it" (p. 108). This was the ideal of "*wabi*," not to avoid suffering but to live quietly in its midst. What would be denied by most people is affirmed as it is by the man of *wabi* (*wabibito*). Just because the world has no fixity it is splendid. Is this not perhaps the highest stage of the logic of denial? The Muromachi period was also a time of great disturbances and turmoil for which this was an appropriate way of thinking. A free heaven and earth could be maintained in spite of external travail.

But this absolute affirmation of the Muromachi age cannot be traced back simply to the earlier absolute denial of the Kamakura Age alone. There is an element of fusion with the old Japanese idea of a limitlessly amiable world. Deep suffering dissolves into sentiment and so deep

---

[23] Elsewhere Ienaga asserts the essential similarity of the views of Paul and Shinran. See "Nihon Bukkyō no kongo no seimei" in *Chūsei Bukkyō shisōshi kenkyū*, p. 229. Other aspects of Ienaga's evaluation of Christianity will appear below.

thought gradually is made shallow. The resurgence of the ancient affirmative feeling and amiable view of the world destroys the dialectical opposition which existed in Kamakura Buddhism. This tendency is related to the fact that Zen thought replaced Pure Land thought in the center of cultural life. Zen denies the opposition and asserts a simple unity, though it has a latent dialectic within it.

But the element of negation is still at the base of Muromachi culture, for example in Seami's conception of *yūgen* (mystery) as the essence of the Nō drama. In the tea ceremony the starting point is absolute negation as is also the case in the arts of garden building and flower arrangement. All these arts start from the dialectical basis of seeing the greatest by making themselves into the least. We cannot deny that these arts had a negative character partly as a result of external pressures arising from the disorders of the day. But we must remember their paradoxical structure in that in an important sense this external defeat meant an inner victory. In the smallest things the Muromachi artists saw the largest, and through one stick or one stone they saw the whole world. Without saying that these Muromachi arts had no connection with the ancient Japanese spirit we can say that they are chiefly understandable as having arisen in a world of high affirmation which had just passed through the depths of denial.

9. However, from late Muromachi times things changed greatly. The dictators beginning with Oda Nobunaga destroyed medieval feudalism and established absolutism. The dictators relied on military and economic power and placed no reliance on anything metaphysical. Their position drove them to self-deification and both Nobunaga and Hideyoshi planned to have themselves worshipped as gods.

In subsequent years Bashō and a few others kept the tradition of *hitei* alive but most people lost it. The common people became swallowed up in commercial interests and the rulers were absorbed in a this-worldly Confucianism. However, to the extent that the realism (*genjitsushugi*) of the Tokugawa period is a product of the middle ages it differs from ancient realism. In Tokugawa literature there is expressed a thorough respect for the actual which sees as absolute the wealth and pleasure of "today." But such respect for the actual is premised unconsciously on a bottomless uneasiness about the limitations of "today" because of the limitless darkness between today and tomorrow. Everywhere in Tokugawa culture the logic of negation is vanquished, yet everywhere it shows unquenchable remnants even though these do not eventuate in a positive view of man but are rather controlled by quite other elements.

For 300 years there has been a loss of connection with the logic of negation. In this respect the modern period is continuous with the Tokugawa period. The enlightenment philosophy and later Neo-Kantianism just continued, though outwardly different in form, the Tokugawa respect for this world. But now partly due to Western influence there is a chance to create a new philosophy of negation, which will require a new logic of negation, as Nishida Kitarō has indicated.[24]

Even from this inadequate summary I think it will be recognized that Ienaga's *The Development of the Logic of Negation* is from a number of points of view a remarkable construction. It is very clear that Ienaga's turn to religion did not mean the renunciation of his critical intelligence. He was able "dialectically" to utilize his own partly externally forced withdrawal from more immediate problems for the purpose of a deeply critical analysis of some of the most basic problems of his own and Western culture. Just how critical the book is (even to the point of political implications) will become clear when we reflect that it was published in the year 1940 when the Japanese market was being deluged with eulogistic histories of the "Japanese spirit." In the face of this flood Ienaga published a book which was almost a complete denial of the Japanese tradition, or at least it was

---

[24] In the above highly condensed summary I have tried to maintain as much of the flavor of the original as possible and many phrases are direct translations.

a denial of every element in the tradition which was not itself premised on denial. In it Shintō and the ancient Yamato spirit are dismissed as "primitive and superficial," Confucianism is rejected as "shallow and this-worldly" and the *kokutai* and the emperor are not even mentioned. Of course it can be argued that Ienaga was not writing a general history of Japanese thought but only trying to follow up one strand, but it is nonetheless true that by implication this is the strand he considered to be really valuable, which had real universality and which could contribute to a positive solution of present and future problems.[25] Such a position could only imply an intensely negative evaluation of the prevailing intellectual currents.

Ienaga's essential structure is simple, even somewhat somber, but it only gains in suggestive power on those accounts. At the beginning stands Shōtoku Taishi, the first hero, who foreshadows in his own person what is to come, but remains an isolated figure, rising above the limitations of his time. Then through a process of ever more drastic experiences with social disruption the logic of negation which was grasped already by Shōtoku Taishi is gradually borne in on the Japanese people. Out of the recognition in the Kamakura period that "the world is hell" the Japanese people finally came to understand Buddhism themselves and their experience was most rigorously expressed in Shinran, the second hero, who stands at the climax of the story. The apparent fruits of the great age of denial in the Zen inspired Muromachi culture, however, turn to an early decay and the process from there on is a steady falling away mitigated only by an occasional Bashō and by the knowledge that the experience of negation has only been repressed and remains hauntingly in the unconscious. At the end there is no third hero and the reader is left alone to face himself.[26]

[25] We shall discuss below other elements in the Japanese tradition which receive positive evaluation from Ienaga in his work after the war, but these do not of course include Shintō, Confucianism, the *kokutai*, or even any of the schools of Buddhism except those in the Pure Land tradition.

[26] If there is a third hero for Ienaga, taking the whole of his work and not just this one book, it would probably be Uchimura Kanzō.

It is interesting that in this first book the notion of "modern" (*kindai*) which will later play such an important part in his thought receives only a negative evaluation. Modern thought like that of Tokugawa Japan suffers from an unbroken this-worldliness. It may seem natural in this period when in Japan "modern" was a bad word and something to be "overcome" that Ienaga would not evaluate it highly. Yet this judgment seems to come from other roots. It certainly has no relation to the prevailing judgment that what is "Japanese" is good as against what is Western, for his criticism of the modern spirit is in precisely the same terms that he criticizes the characteristic Japanese affirmativeness. And it is especially worthy of note that while "modern" is negatively evaluated "Western" is not. It is worth taking a closer look at the place of Western references in *The Development of the Logic of Negation*.

References to the West enter at three points in the book, at the beginning, at the climax and at the end. Ienaga actually sets his case by discussing the relations of Greek and Christian thought and posits the *same* relation between Japanese and Buddhist thought. For all the concern for what is specifically Japanese in the book, the comparative setting gives the discussion a strong note of universalism. This note is again reinforced by the introduction of references to the New Testament and to Karl Barth during the climactic discussion of Shinran, where again there is the strong sense of similarity between something central in the Christian tradition and the product of Japan's most creative religious mind. Finally at the end there is the suggestion that Western influences may help in the solution of the problem of reviving the logic of denial.

The position of the Kyōto School of philosophy was similar and yet I feel a certain difference in Ienaga. Tatsuo Arima has recently argued that what Nishida Kitarō was trying to do was to find a logical (Western) structure for Japanese thought rather than to synthesize East and West.[27] Ienaga

[27] Tatsuo Arima, *The Failure of Freedom: An Intellectual Portrait of Taishō Japan*, doctoral dissertation, Department of Government, Harvard University, 1961, p. 16.

is trying to do neither. He finds a profound point of linkage in the fundamentally similar experience of Paul and Shinran, but this involves neither synthesis nor the assertion of essential difference, nor the superiority of either side. It is a ground from which problems can be commonly viewed. The difference from Nishida probably resides mainly in what they took to be basic in the Japanese tradition. For Nishida it was Zen, which must always perhaps remain mysterious from the point of view of Western thought and transcend its categories. Thus Nishida's philosophy has the quality of "capping" or "completing" or adding a missing quality to Western thought. But Ienaga has always been profoundly mistrustful of Zen and unconvinced of its claims. Because he bases himself on Shinran's sense of sin and proclamation of salvation through faith alone, coming to terms with Christian categories almost ceases to be a problem for him. Perhaps this difference is also related to Ienaga's deeper concern with social problems than has been characteristic of the Kyōto School. Zen tends to go "beyond good and evil" to a realm of "pure experience" in which the individual and the absolute are united. But Shinran could not forget evil and sin any more than could Luther. Perhaps this helped provide Ienaga with a greater moral realism than Zen did for Nishida. But of course the Lutheran analogy indicates all too clearly the weaknesses of Shinran's position as a basis for social action. Other things obviously had to enter Ienaga's thought in order to produce his later social concern.

In two subsequent books, *Studies in Ancient Buddhist Thought* and *Studies in Medieval Buddhist Thought* (both of these refer exclusively to *Japanese* Buddhism), Ienaga spelled out in much greater detail some of the essential ideas contained in *The Development of the Logic of Negation*.[28]

---

[28] The former book deals with aspects of the thought of Shōtoku Taishi (including his Pure Land thought) and of Nara and Heian Buddhism. The latter book is especially interesting in that it presents a new way of thinking about Kamakura Buddhism. Ienaga vigorously opposes the tendency to view Hōnen, Shinran, Nichiren and Dōgen as simply parallel "great religious leaders" without carefully analyzing the relations between them and their different positions relative to

But in his long essay "The Development of the Religious View of Nature in the History of Japanese Thought,"[29] he expands and supplements the over-all scheme of *The Development of the Logic of Negation*, and he suggests that the two be read together. In intrinsic interest this essay rivals Ienaga's

---

earlier Japanese Buddhism. Ienaga reserves the notion of Kamakura Buddhism as a "new" Buddhism exclusively to the Pure Land tradition. For him Hōnen represents a drastic break with previous tradition, a rejection of the earlier eclecticism and the formulation of a powerful and radical religious insight. This is carried to thorough completion in Shinran with his "absolute faith alone" position. But the various "old" Buddhist sects did not simply remain passive or merely react with a negative persecution of the "new" Buddhism, though they attempted the latter. They instituted a series of reforms and doctrinal innovations in every case, Ienaga argues, *derived from the influence of the "new" Buddhism* but with the aim of combating it. There were such movements not only within Tendai and Shingon but also in the Nara sects, which were more vigorous by far in the Kamakura period than they had been since ancient times or ever were again. This even included a revival in the Ritsu (Precepts) Sect and an outburst of enthusiasm for adhering to the Hinayana rules for monks. Nichiren is treated as the most powerful of these "counter-reformation" leaders, but one so deeply influenced by the new Buddhism that he actually breaks out of the forms of the old, even of the Tendai which he so dearly loved. But, while attaining many of the insights of the "new" Buddhism (even though derivatively, Ienaga feels) Nichiren was not "thorough." Many magical elements which were purged by Shinran remain in his system, such as the magical use of prayer. Further, he continues the old *honjisuijaku* theory of the relation of the Buddhas and the Shintō deities, rather than radically eliminating any syncretism with Shintō as the Pure Land thinkers did. Ienaga traces the nationalistic and contentious spirit of Nichiren to this lack of thoroughness even though he does not deny to Nichiren a real participation in the universalism of the "new" Buddhism.

Ienaga treats Kamakura Zen Buddhism and its greatest exponent Dōgen in somewhat different terms. However radical the new Kamakura Buddhism of Hōnen and Shinran was, it grew entirely out of the inner dialectic of *Japanese* Buddhism, as did of course the "counter-reformation" movements which defined themselves relative to it. Zen on the other hand in Kamakura times was something absolutely out of the blue. It was the latest import from China without roots or historical relevance to the Japanese situation. Nonetheless, once entering the Japanese scene, it could not but be influenced by it. Ienaga contrasts the eclecticism of Eisai for whom Zen was perhaps merely

first book, but within the confines of this chapter it must receive briefer treatment. The concern for nature has been a pervasive one in much modern Japanese thought.[30] The idea that there is something specifically Japanese about finding an ultimate answer in or through nature is not original with Ienaga. But given his urge in these years to come to terms critically with the whole of his tradition, it was natural that he would attempt a systematic analysis of a position which is in some ways similar to "the logic of negation" but also differs significantly from it. Probably the book remains the most ambitious attempt to develop a critical analysis of this strand in Japanese thought and as such is another of Ienaga's major scholarly contributions.

The "dialectical" element in Ienaga's approach is illustrated throughout though we must confine ourselves here to only a few examples. From the outset Ienaga draws a sharp distinction between what he is calling the religious view of nature and primitive animism.[31] The religious view of nature in Ienaga's sense develops only after the influence of continental culture when nature is seen as something *different from* human life, something with which one can esthetically and consciously commune. Animism is precisely a state of

---

one more embellishment in his stock of esoteric practices to the single-mindedness of Dōgen for whom *zazen* (Zen meditation) became the *only way*. In this latter point Ienaga sees the influence of the new Buddhism on Dōgen (and cites texts to prove it). But for Ienaga Zen lacks thoroughness since *zazen* must after all be practiced in the meditation hall and not in the midst of the actualities of life. While highly appreciating Dōgen (whom he likes much more than Nichiren, I feel) he must conclude that there remains about him a monkish smell when compared with Shinran.

It of course remains to be seen to what extent future research will validate this scheme, but it illustrates the suggestive power of Ienaga's scholarship in bringing a new level of order to a great deal of complex material and thus suggesting the directions which future research can most fruitfully take.

[29] Published together with three other essays in the book which bears the same title in 1944.

[30] See Tatsuo Arima, *op.cit., passim.*

[31] *Shūkyōteki shizenkan no tenkai,* pp. 4-6.

primitive undifferentiation of consciousness in which nature as nature is not known. He quotes Motoori Norinaga on the indiscrimination with which the ancients worshipped natural objects. It was their inherent power alone which mattered and considerations of good or bad, respect-worthy or despicable, and even beautiful or ugly were quite beside the point. The earliest Japanese poetry is about love, war, and hunting and not nature, and when nature does emerge as an important theme, as in the *Manyōshū*, the treatment of it betrays continental cultural influences. It seems to me that this initial point serves two functions besides that of being an empirical generalization. It indicates that Ienaga is not talking about the mysterious Japanese folk-soul which goes back for ages. And it brings in right at the beginning an element of brokenness, of tension and negation, which must be present if the religious view of nature is to interest Ienaga. If he felt that the religious view of nature were simply the celebration of the harmonious union of the Japanese with nature it seems to me unlikely that the subject would have ever received his consideration.

The treatment of the development of the religious view of nature is quite parallel to the treatment of the logic of negation. Both depend on contact with foreign culture for their initiation, but both develop and deepen only through becoming part of the actual experience of the Japanese people themselves.[32] From being a temporary consolation nature gradually becomes an absolute savior. This realization is made apparent through the same process of deepening social disruption that was described in the earlier book. Similarly it is the Kamakura period which sees the fulfillment of this tendency. It was gradually realized that temporary visits to natural sites were not enough and so the ideal of the *yamazato* (mountain retreat) as a permanent dwelling place developed.[33] It was this *yamazato* ideal which reached its fulfillment in Saigyō

[32] Unlike the logic of negation the religious view of nature is treated as being unique in its Japanese form. In the last analysis, however, this for Ienaga is perhaps more of a liability than an asset.

[33] *Op.cit.*, pp. 20ff.

and Kamo no Chōmei in Kamakura times. In this ideal there is the sharpest antagonism between the world of men and the world of nature. Only by fleeing to the bosom of nature can one escape the contaminations and sufferings of human troubles. Thus there is involved here too a type of logic of negation.

However, and this Ienaga believes to be specifically Japanese, the *yamazato* which was supposed to be a realm of escape from suffering turns out to have its own kind of suffering, the suffering of loneliness, which he illustrates with a wealth of poetic citations.[34] Japanese being people of strong human feelings and close human ties cannot easily give up human companionship and in fact can be miserably unhappy in its absence. Consequently the *yamazato* hermit longs to see a human face and may even wistfully dream of the happy bustle of city life. But of course a return to the city and its complexities could only make things worse. In this situation the *yamazato* hermit has reached an absolute impasse analogous to that of Shinran's sinner. "At this point he reaches an insoluble difficulty. However, this contradiction is broken not by neutralizing it but rather by a seemingly paradoxical accepting the contradiction as a contradiction in a higher frame of mind. That is to say, an absolute contradiction causes the self to open up through absolute negation. To explain more concretely, a special frame of mind opens up in which the loneliness (*sabishisa*) of the *yamazato* in its loneliness itself is conversely the highest joy and becomes the salvation of the spirit. After all, the sadness and misery (*kanashisa, wabishisa*) which nature contains differ from the suffering arising from human difficulties and are linked to a quality which one feels as a difficult to define consolation within the sadness and misery."[35]

Ienaga discusses another strand of the *yamazato* tradition represented first clearly by Fujiwara Teika and some of his fellow *Shinkokinshū* poets. Unlike Saigyō and Chōmei these court nobles did not actually go themselves to dwell in nature,

[34] *Ibid.*, pp. 48ff.
[35] *Ibid.*, pp. 60-61.

and so to that extent were not as thorough. But in their poetry they developed a symbolic nature which, though different from real nature, had the same function as a savior. Ienaga sees this symbolic *yamazato* tradition as one of the ingredients (besides the Zen cultural influences from China) which went into the highly symbolic Muromachi culture in which nature (in the tea house [*chashitsu*] with its accompanying arts of flower arrangement, gardening, ink painting and so on) plays a central role.[36]

In Bashō the *yamazato* tradition finds a late embodiment: "So finally the decisive reason that Bashō is the true heir of the *yamazato* spirit is that he experiences an unlimited religious ecstasy in the loneliness (*sabishisa*) of loneliness as loneliness itself and that sphere of paradoxical salvation of the *yamazato* actually finds in him its most typical, even its most thorough expression."[37]

On the whole the Edo period was not conducive to this kind of experience, but after all the religious view of nature has never died out and remains alive in modern Japan, as quotations from Nagai Kafū and Natsume Sōseki indicate. Ienaga argues that the history of Japanese religion is not fully encompassed by the categories of "Shintō," "Buddhism" and "Christianity." "Did not Saigyō and Bashō, who could not be saved by Buddhism, experience tranquility for the first time when they were embraced in nature's bosom?"[38] Thus any history of Japanese religion which leaves out the religious view of nature will be distorted.

In this book written in the midst of the war (1944) and more concerned with the Japaneseness of the Japanese than are any other of Ienaga's writings, he even toys (in quotations from others, not directly in his own words) with the idea that the religious view of nature is an element of superiority which the Japanese have over the West.[39] But this mood is quickly dispelled in the question which opens the penultimate

[36] *Ibid.*, pp. 43-47, 74-78. The complexities of Ienaga's argument are only suggested here.
[37] *Ibid.*, p. 80.
[38] *Ibid.*, p. 85.
[39] *Ibid.*, p. 84.

section of the essay: Was this salvation after all an absolute salvation? "Nature has certainly come to be a great salvation for the spiritual sufferings of the Japanese. But was this salvation after all an absolute salvation? Does the *yamazato* ambiance have the capacity to dispel all human illusion? Here I think there is in this special Japanese religious sphere an insurmountable limitation."[40]

Ienaga cites the long tradition of criticism of the *yamazato* tradition which also existed in Japan, especially the criticism from the Pure Land point of view, namely that the *yamazato* is not a real "other shore" but a part of this transient world and subject to its contaminations. "If we press this far an entirely new road opens up. If the *yamazato* is after all part of this sad world and is not therefore a place of absolute repose, is it necessary to seek salvation by fleeing from men into the mountains and hating the world? Rather salvation comes not through fleeing from the troubles of this dirty world, but by facing them head on and seeking it in committing oneself in the midst of them."[41] Here Ienaga returns to the theme of *The Logic of Negation*. One enters the dirty world as it is. One does not flee from sin but uses it as an opportunity for salvation. Indeed, for Shinran, man's finitude is a positive precondition for salvation and this is why he spoke of the "remembrance of sin." This way of salvation is entirely different from that of Saigyō and Chōmei.[42]

But the essay closes by attacking those who criticize the religious view of nature as escapist from a purely this-worldly point of view, whether in Tokugawa or modern times. He argues that this experience is apt to be permanently meaningful to the Japanese people.[43]

Before summarizing the religious position which Ienaga had reached by 1945 we must consider one more important essay: "Natsume Sōseki as a Thinker and His Historical Position."[44] This, it might be noted, is the only study in all

[40] *Ibid.*, p. 84.

[41] *Ibid.*, pp. 87-88.

[42] *Ibid.*, p. 88.

[43] *Ibid.*, pp. 89-90.

[44] "Shisōka to shite no Natsume Sōseki, narabi ni sono shiteki ichi," in *Nihon shisōshi ni okeru shūkyōteki shizenkan no tenkai*, pp. 149-221.

of Ienaga's work before the end of the war which is primarily concerned with a modern figure. He chooses to treat Sōseki as a "thinker" because of the deep moral and religious concern which pervaded the whole of his work. But in interpreting Sōseki's thought Ienaga opposes two current conceptions of it, which might be called the historical materialist and the religious pantheist. He recognizes that there is in Sōseki's work, especially the early work, an element of social criticism, both of feudalism and feudal remnants and of the excesses of capitalism. At the same time his criticism lacked any clear theoretical basis or guiding principle so that while "liberating from the fetters of the old morality" his work contains no new positive morality to take its place and often ends up simply in indignation.[45] While recognizing that Sōseki's later work turns away from direct social criticism, Ienaga refuses to see in this a religious escapism or simply an expression of "the agony of 'egoistic liberals at the end of Meiji,'" as a powerful current of interpretation among Japanese intellectuals who make the "social viewpoint" primary would have it.[46] On the contrary, according to Ienaga it is not that Sōseki's moral and ethical concern did not continue to the end—it did strongly—but that in the early work he was concerned with discerning good and bad people whereas later he was concerned with the basic human structure. All men, he came to see, are untrustworthy sinners. Having come to understand the fundamental evil of the human condition he could no longer simply judge the relative good and evil in social life. But this does not mean a rejection of the moral problem; rather it led to a profounder understanding of it.[47]

If Ienaga rejects the historical materialist interpretation of Sōseki and positively evaluates the later religious preoccupations, he also opposes a common interpretation of Sōseki's religious position, one which would assert that he found final consolation in the spirit of Zen and haiku. Here Ienaga is on more delicate ground, for Sōseki was all his life devoted to Zen and haiku. But Ienaga believes that through a careful

[45] *Ibid.*, p. 158.
[46] *Ibid.*, Note 3, pp. 198-199, 220.
[47] *Ibid.*, p. 162.

analysis of Sōseki's novels it can be discerned that he actually attained a somewhat different position. Ienaga interprets the Zen-inspired euphoric pantheism of such early novels as *Kusamakura* and the poetry which he wrote throughout his life as merely the starting point of Sōseki's spiritual quest, one which would eventually be found wanting. Similarly he interprets the ecstatic religious experience of 1910 as stemming from primarily physical conditions brought on by illness and exhaustion.[48] So he turns to a step by step analysis of the later novels in order to discover Sōseki's final religious position.

According to Ienaga, around 1909, with *Sore kara* as the watershed, Sōseki's style underwent a great change. From the elegant optimism of the *Kusamakura* period Sōseki's mood becomes more somber and his style more direct. The shift is something like that from late Heian aristocratic Buddhism to Kamakura Buddhism, says Ienaga. The sufferings and limitations of the *petit bourgeois* life, which had not previously occupied Sōseki's attention, come increasingly into the subject matter of the later novels—first notably in *Mon*. But the thing which chiefly attracts Ienaga's attention in *Mon* is the failure of the hero to attain any solution to his problems through Zen meditation. For the hero, Sōsuke, the "gate" of Zen is closed. The situation reminds Ienaga of Hōnen in tears because he had failed at the practices of the Shōdō (Holy Way, with the implication of salvation through works).[49]

In the next three novels, *Higan sugi made*, *Kōjin*, and *Kokoro*, the gloomy mood in which *Mon* ended is successively deepened. The scholar hero of *Kōjin* fails in the attempt at Zen meditation as completely as the *petit bourgeois* hero of *Mon* had before him. He finds himself with but three choices: to die, to go mad, or to enter religion. The novel closes with-

[48] *Ibid.*, p. 197. It will be remembered that in *The Logic of Negation* Ienaga had said that the suffering which can be solved by sudden enlightenment is not real suffering.

[49] *Ibid.*, pp. 175-183. Once again the subtleties of Ienaga's argument suffer from the extreme compression of the summary.

out a solution. *Kokoro* represents a kind of end of the road for Sōseki. In it "Sensei" has arrived at a completely negative view of human life and has no alternative but to commit suicide. Ienaga's account of Sōseki's religious development as seen through the novels now reaches its climax: "The thunder roars and the lightning falls. As the effort of the whole life of a human being is not worth a hair before God, all human sin is buried beneath the avalanche in the valley. But isn't it just at the moment when the sin which it is so hard to rise above is buried at the bottom of the abyss of death that one meets anew the call of the 'God of love'? The little human soul which died with the death of the hero of *Kokoro* was completely buried in absolute negation, but a great selfless love is resurrected from the blood of the cross. The new life thus arisen from the depths of death became concretized in the novel *Michigusa* of 1915."[50]

For Ienaga it is only in *Michigusa* and *Meian* that Sōseki indicates that he has attained his early aim of "overcoming life and death." And that he sees as happening not through any cosmic euphoria or sudden enlightenment, but only through a profound confrontation of the fundamental sinfulness of human life.

According to Ienaga, Sōseki virtually identified religion with Zen. He implies that this was natural for an intellectual of his day. Thus whenever Sōseki speaks of religion objectively in his essays he is using Zen categories. His philosophy of *sokuten kyoshi* (to model oneself on heaven and depart from the self)[51] Sōseki defined as *kenshō jōbutsu* (attaining enlightenment and becoming a Buddha),[52] using Zen terminology. But Ienaga feels that Sōseki's actual religious experience as expressed in the novels transcended his conscious categories. He stresses the limited knowledge which Sōseki had of the Japanese tradition in contrast with his thorough

---

[50] *Ibid.*, p. 186.

[51] For this translation I am indebted to Valdo Viglielmo's *The Later Natsume Sōseki*, Doctoral Dissertation, Department of Far Eastern Languages, Harvard, 1955, p. 12.

[52] Viglielmo, p. 212.

knowledge of the West, with the implication that Sōseki was not aware of the full meaning of the Japanese Pure Land tradition. But for Ienaga, of course, the important thing is that he attained the insight, not the words he used to express it.

At the end of the essay Ienaga returns to the first point and to those who would interpret Sōseki entirely in terms of the "crisis of the age." He says: "To me Sōseki's deeper historic meaning lies in the fact that he was a great religious thinker who pointed out the way to understand and overcome the permanent human crisis which is mediated to men by the 'agony of the age' but always transcends it."[53]

We have now completed a review of the major writings of Ienaga before 1945 which bear on the problem of meaning. It seems evident that in the years 1935 to 1945 he worked out a religious position of great cogency which not only allowed him to maintain his own stability in those years which were indeed a "dark valley" for any sensitive Japanese intellectual, but also from which he was able to develop a critical interpretation of the Japanese tradition in its religious aspects. Rejecting completely those parts of the tradition (Shintō, Confucianism) which were too simply affirmations of a traditional social system, Ienaga turned to Buddhism with its more complex dialectic. Here he found a correspondence between his own experience and the "logic of negation" of Shōtoku Taishi and Shinran. Salvation comes not through fleeing from the world but through "facing it head on" and recognizing its sinful and suffering nature. This position, as he wrote of Sōseki's, does not reject the problem of morality but treats it from a deeper level. For Ienaga religion does not dissolve the tension between the real and the ideal—it offers no resolution at all on this level—but insists on remaining acutely conscious of it. Salvation comes not through any kind of "solution" but "through accepting the contradiction as a contradiction." This is about as anti-magical as a religious position can get. This highly critical, realistic character of

[53] *Ibid.*, p. 220.

the position together with the seriousness with which it takes human suffering and sin, perhaps help us to understand its relation to the more directly socially conscious earlier and later Ienaga.

From this position it is easy to understand his evaluation of Zen Buddhism and the religious view of nature. Both are attractive to him for both have something of the dialectical quality of the "logic of negation." But both are in the last analysis unsatisfactory for they tend easily either toward a retreat from the merciless nature of reality into the mountains or the meditation hall, or they offer too easy a salvation which ends in an unbroken acceptance of the given. Christianity, on the other hand, while it is to be criticized for its retention of mythical forms and for its theism, is nevertheless deeply congenial in its symbolism as the almost unconscious use of it in the passage describing Sōseki's attainment of religious insight ("God of love," "blood of the cross," etc.) indicates.[54]

[54] In "The Future of Japanese Buddhism" (in *Chūsei Bukkyō shisōshi kenkyū*, expanded edition, 1955) Ienaga makes his criticism of Christianity only after the most extensive demolition job of religious self-criticism the writer has seen outside of the Christian West. Not only does almost every aspect of traditional Buddhism go down the drain, but Amida and the Pure Land itself are found to be meaningless in the present age (p. 230). Only the recognition of human sinfulness and the understanding that salvation can come in no other way than through that recognition remain. It is at this point that Ienaga turns to Christianity to note that its apprehension of the same truth is blurred by its own mythical forms and its theism. Actually Ienaga is only pointing to something of which a number of contemporary Christian theologians are aware, Rudolph Bultmann and Paul Tillich being examples. In conversation with Ienaga I questioned him about his use of Christian references to explain the thought of Shinran. He said that he had been criticized for this but that he felt this was perfectly defensible and that in fact in the modern period Shinran had become understood only after the impact of Christian theology—in Tokugawa times Nembutsu thought had been understood only magically. Ienaga's criticism of Christian theism in this conversation (1961) was, as I understand it, as follows: Theism makes an illegitimate initial affirmation which does not arise out of the experience of absolute negation and may actually prevent the attainment of that experience. Ienaga

Ienaga's religious position gave him a place to stand in relation to his world, his cultural tradition, and that of the West. Perhaps it is not unrelated, in a paradoxical sort of way, to the fact that it was precisely during the midst of the war itself that Ienaga began to turn away from the problems of ancient Japanese religion and to face "head on" the problem of modernization.

The Modern Spirit and Its Limitations (1942-1952)

It would perhaps be best to let Ienaga describe the next major phase of his development in his own words:

"I don't remember today exactly when I first put my hand to the study of the history of modern thought. But since my first essay concerning this area, 'Opposition to Tendencies Favoring the Revival of the Past in the Tokugawa Period,' was published in the magazine *Rekishi chiri* in March of 1943 it was probably around the beginning of the Pacific War. In that atmosphere which was like being in an oppressive prison I began to study the ABC's of the history of Meiji thought. I still remember vividly my feelings at that time—when one had to read currently only material which lacked any sane meaning —how moving were many of the passages in [Meiji magazines such as] *Kokumin no tomo* and *Rikugo zasshi* which I was perusing in the Meiji Newspaper and Magazine Library.

"Until the end of the Pacific War I was concerned only to preserve my own conscience; I lacked the leeway to reflect upon others. Also, until that time, because my responsibilities were light, I thought that to get through with that would be doing well enough. But, from the time of the war's final debacle I became unable to con-

---

also discusses Christianity in a long essay on Buddhist-Christian controversy in Japan ("Waga kuni ni okeru Bukki ryōkyō ronsō no tetsugakushiteki kōsatsu," in *Chūsei Bukkyō shisōshi kenkyū*, pp. 111-180) in the last section of which he discusses views of Tanabe Hajime which are probably not far from his own.

tinue indefinitely with that attitude. I had, in my family, in my place of work, and finally in regard to society to grapple with the problem of modernization. The question of modern thought was not simply an object of scholastic concern, rather it became an urgent problem pressing in on me, one that I could not refuse. [Therefore] I, who until then had taken ancient or at best medieval Japanese intellectual history as my field of study, was forced, completely by the above spiritual considerations, to throw myself into the study of modern intellectual history."[55]

It is important to keep in mind how long the shift described above actually took. Ienaga first turned to the study of modern thought around 1942. It was not until ten years later, in July 1952, that he first became involved publicly in political action. The changes are with respect to fields of study and types of political and social action, not with respect to basic political thought itself, which we have reason to believe remained fairly stable ever since his Higher School days.[56] Nevertheless the shift from the "old liberal" position of constitutional monarchy to the more "progressive" position of principled rejection of the emperor system, the most dramatic aspect of his change of political views, is in the Japanese context of considerable symbolic significance.

[55] From the preface to *Nihon kindai shisōshi kenkyū* (1953) dated September 30, 1953. The article referred to in the first paragraph above, "Kinsei ni okeru hanfukkosh[u]gi shichō," was reprinted in *Nihon shisōshi ni okeru shūkyōteki shizenkan no tenkai* (1944), pp. 122-147. One result of his wartime labors was his *Essay on the History of the Reception of Foreign Culture* (*Gairai bunka sesshushi ron*, 1948) subtitled, "An Intellectual Historical Investigation into the Reception of Modern Western Culture." In the preface to this book he says that he began the research for it around the beginning of 1942 and completed the manuscript in March of 1945. Due to difficulties in obtaining materials at that time, illness, and the external pressures of the atmosphere, Ienaga states that he is not entirely satisfied with this work (Preface, pp. 3-4). It consists largely of copious quotations illustrating various reactions of Tokugawa and early Meiji figures to foreign culture. There is also a section devoted to the earlier reception of Buddhism and Chinese culture.

[56] Personal communication, July 9, 1961.

The thing which recalled Ienaga from his preoccupation with religious studies to research on more contemporary problems was the "strengthening of Fascism" which occurred with Japan's entry into the war. Though he did not cooperate at all with Fascism and so had a clean conscience on that score, the fact that he did not openly oppose the war became a matter of later self-reproach.[57] As we have seen, he was actually at that time trying to get a clearer picture of the beginnings of Japanese modernization, the reception of modern Western culture, and what this has meant for Japanese society. For these purposes the Meiji period is particularly strategic and it is to this period that his empirical researches have been largely confined almost until the present time.[58] The loss of the war and the beginning of the American occupation, which precipitated a rush to the standard of "democracy" in the Japanese intellectual world, had no such effect on Ienaga. He "felt a certain inability to trust in the sudden popularity of 'democracy,'" and held aloof from the nearly uniform propaganda in its favor which appeared to him something like the reverse side of Fascism.[59] This attitude earned for Ienaga the sobriquet of "reactionary" in the years just after the war. It was the threat to the constitution arising from the "reverse

[57] *Rekishi no kiki ni menshite*, pp. 233-234.

[58] In his most recent, as yet unpublished, work he is turning to a consideration of the thought of "Taishō Democracy." He has published a few brief studies on Tokugawa thinkers (most of which appear in *Nihon kindai shisōshi kenkyū*) and a number of brief complete histories of Japan, but his monographic publications since the war are exclusively on Meiji figures.

[59] *Rekishi no kiki ni menshite*, p. 234. Also personal communication of July 9, 1961. In this respect Ienaga probably stood close to the position of Tsuda Sōkichi whom he quotes as saying not long after the war that the absolute uniformity of all that he reads and hears reminds him of the absolute uniformity of what he read and heard during the war and makes him think that the situation in Japan has not changed. ("Tsuda shigaku no shisōshiteki kōsatsu" in *Nihon no kindai shigaku*, 1957, p. 154. This article was first published in June 1953.) At the time he published this article, however, Ienaga was already critical of this attitude in Tsuda and presumably in his own past.

course" (*gyaku-kōsu*) policy of the occupation in the last years of the decade of the 1940's which precipitated Ienaga's move into the political arena in defense, as he believed, of liberty and democracy in Japan. But, as is indicated in the quotation at the beginning of this section, this was the result of his experiences in home and place of work with the concrete problems of modernization in Japanese society, even before the political currents changed, and so was not merely a change in ideology.[60]

It should be evident from this review that Ienaga's shift to concern with contemporary problems and political activism, while of course related to changes going on in Japanese society, proceeded gradually. When we come to consider the book which stands at the end of this period of transition and summarizes eight years of reflection on the problems of Japanese modernization, namely *The Modern Spirit and its Limitations* (1950), the essential continuity in his development should become even more clear. But first we must consider some of the problems of theory and method which occupied Ienaga more in the years 1945-1950 than before or after.

Methodological problems must have come to a head for Ienaga in these years partly because of the great currency of the Marxist approach to history, in relation to which he must have had to define his own position, but also because of the need to secure a firmer theoretical grounding in his approach to the understanding of modernization. In an article on the "New Conception of Intellectual History"[61] he says that intellectual history understands thought "above history" and at the same time historically. Proper method starts with the first task, that is to understand the thought as it is in itself in its own inner meaning, and is completed by a consideration of the thought in relation to other thought and to non-ideational historical elements. Further, since all thought is conditioned by society in its historical development, it is ulti-

[60] *Ibid.*, and personal communication of July 9, 1961.
[61] "Atarashii shisōshi no kōsō" in *Kokumin no rekishi*, vol. 2, no. 9 (1948), pp. 14-18.

mately necessary to understand the whole course of Japanese society from primitive times to the present day if one is to understand a single Japanese thinker.

In another longer essay of the same year he amplifies these ideas while reflecting on "The Past and Present of Japanese Intellectual Historiography."[62] Here he asserts that Japanese intellectual history was virtually founded by two men: Muraoka Tsunetsugu (1884-1946), and Tsuda Sōkichi (1873-1961). These men, he asserts, "complete" tendencies already discernible in the work of two men in the Tokugawa period who foreshadowed the scientific study of intellectual history: Motoori Norinaga (1730-1801), to whom he links Muraoka, and Tominaga Nakamoto (1715-1746), to whom he links Tsuda. The strong point of the former pair is that they grasp the inner meaning of the thought as it is. Motoori was the first to penetrate deeply into the world-view of the ancient Japanese classics. Muraoka, of course, lacks the non-scientific overtones of Motoori and so fulfills the possibilities of this approach. Muraoka's weakness, however, is that, while dealing sensitively with particular works and writers, he does not relate them to the social context or see them in the sweep of historical development. The strong point of the latter pair is precisely that they do see the social context and the historical development. Ienaga considers Tsuda's *A Study of Our National Thought as it Was Expressed in Literature* (*Bungaku ni arawaretaru waga kokumin shisō no kenkyū*, 4 vols., 1916-1921) to be the greatest single work in the field and the starting point for future work. Nevertheless he feels that Tsuda fails to appreciate certain writers and movements and sometimes makes value judgments from present concerns which distort the original thought. These are defects even though critical appraisal of past thought from the point of view of present needs is not in principle bad.

In an essay published in 1949 Ienaga takes the issues sketched out above to the philosophical level.[63] Here he faces

---

[62] "Nihon shisōshigaku no kako to shōrai" in *Nihon shisōshi no shomondai* (1948), pp. 149-239.

[63] "Shisōshigaku no tachiba" reprinted in *Nihon no kindai shigaku* (1957), pp. 24-44.

the Marxist position head on. Basing himself on the general position of Nicolai Hartmann he argues that "while the sub-structure conditions the superstructure there are elements in the superstructure which cannot be understood in terms of the substructure."[64] For example Shinran's thought may have been conditioned by the society and economy of 13th century Japan, but it is not explained by it. It is not a necessary product of that society and economy nor is its meaning exhausted only by considering its function in that society. According to Ienaga the self-conscious subject has an essential, if conditioned, freedom. Consequently his thought can never be reduced simply to a reflection of the substructure. In the case of Shinran it was his "meticulous reflection on human reality and thorough criticism of previous Jōdo thought arising from his highly developed consciousness" which allowed him to arrive at his radical religious conclusions. These conclusions were not "necessary" or "externally determined" consequences of any social process.[65]

Ienaga admits that in the historical process thought is, compared to substructural elements, "weak." But this is from the point of view of cause and effect relations. From the point of view of value what is weak, i.e., thought, has high value and what is strong has low value.[66] Finally he turns to the problem of the categories to be used in intellectual history. He notes that they can be drawn from the conditioning social structure (e.g., the thought of slave society, feudal society, capitalist society) or from the structure of the thought itself (e.g., Shintō thought, Buddhist thought, Confucian thought). He notes that either of these alone is inadequate and that what is needed is a way of putting together meaningful categories which will take account of both types of factors.[67]

As recently as 1957 Ienaga has reiterated his position on the point of the relative independence and value of culture in relation to social structure. We may quote from an essay first published in that year: "Finally and most importantly is

---

[64] *Ibid.*, p. 29.   [65] *Ibid.*, pp. 32-33.   [66] *Ibid.*, p. 40.
[67] *Ibid.*, pp. 41-44.

the fact that there is sometimes in culture accompanying its character as the product of its age and its class character, something which may be called its pan-human character which transcends its period and class character, or may there not even be something which transcends its pan-human character?" He suggests that Jesus' Sermon on the Mount or the faith of Shinran as expressed in the *Tannishō* may be recognized as having this sort of character.[68]

In these writings we can discern the same basic Neo-Kantian position, with its distinction between "existence" and "value," which Ienaga adopted in his higher school days. Since Ienaga's primary concern is with value there is always a strong practical (in the Kantian sense) element in his work. This has led to the evaluation of his work as "subjective." He says that relative to the Academic empiricists, the historical materialists, and the students of Max Weber—each in their own way "objective"—there is indeed a "subjective" character to his work which makes him somewhat isolated in the scholarly world.[69] It is of course this "practical" character in all his work from beginning to end which allows us to treat him as a thinker as well as a historian of thought.

We must now turn to the first book in which Ienaga's general approach to modernization becomes clearly discernible. The book is entitled, significantly, *The Modern Spirit and its Limitations* (1950). The work consists of four separate but not unrelated studies: "The Modern Bourgeois Spirit in Kitamura Tōkoku," "The Modern Spirit and its Limitations —An Intellectual Historical Examination of Uchimura Kanzō," "The Class Consciousness of Fukuzawa Yukichi," and "The 'Sociology' of Taguchi Ukichi."

The figure of Fukuzawa Yukichi (1835-1901) broods over the whole book. From the outset it is stated that whereas many figures represent various aspects of the modern spirit in Japan, Fukuzawa does so completely.[70] References to Fukuzawa form a kind of counterpoint in the essays on the other

[68] "Bunkashi to bunka isan no mondai," in *ibid.*, p. 15.
[69] Personal communication, July 9, 1961.
[70] *Kindai seishin to sono genkai*, p. 9.

men who are constantly being compared to and measured against him. Fukuzawa was the great stalwart in the struggle against feudalism. He was the champion of independence for the individual, freedom and equality in human relationships, a democratic family ideal, and so on. But at the same time that he provides an ideal type of the modern spirit he also provides an ideal type of its limitations. The essay on Fukuzawa's class consciousness is largely concerned with pointing these out.

The basic limitation for Fukuzawa is that "modernization" meant "establishing capitalism." Consequently when he was for freedom and equality it meant basically the freedom of enterprise and the equality of the middle classes. It did not mean a thoroughly free and equal society. Though his opposition to feudalism may have been based on universal human feelings originally, from the time he first came into contact with the capitalist spirit of Europe and America in Bakumatsu times it was indissolubly linked to the advancement of capitalism.[71] It was because of this basic limitation that Fukuzawa was never able to sympathize with the poor or the working classes. He attributed poverty and bad living conditions to the lack of energy or even the criminality of the people concerned, and he did not feel there was any social responsibility to remedy the situation. Nevertheless the fact that Fukuzawa favored capitalism does not mean that his thought is of low value, for that was "an extremely progressive attitude" for that time.[72] But this does not mean we should overlook its limitations.

Finally Ienaga asks the question of why Fukuzawa, who had such a sharp social understanding, could never be a friend of the proletariat. He does not feel satisfied with an explanation purely in terms of Fukuzawa's own class identity. He was not after all himself a capitalist. Ienaga suggests that the reason is bound up with the utilitarianism and pragmatism which formed the essence of his thought. Consequently, says Ienaga, Fukuzawa lacked the Kantian principle of "act so as

[71] *Ibid.*, pp. 173-174.
[72] *Ibid.*, pp. 202-203.

to treat every man as an end, never merely as a means."
Since for Fukuzawa a strong economy is a necessary means
for an independent nation and the concentration of capital is
a necessary means for a strong economy both the capitalist
class and the working class are means. Consequently, it is
hard to see how the poor as ends in themselves could have
much meaning for him. But Uchimura Kanzō, who was
similar to Fukuzawa in that he fought feudalism and could
not espouse socialism, was quite different from him in his
idealistic spirit.[73]

Since it is Uchimura who emerges in the final paragraph
of the essay on Fukuzawa as a possible alternative to the
latter's limitations, let us turn to the essay on Uchimura, by
far the longest in the book. In a sustained passage of about
26 pages Ienaga builds up a picture of Uchimura as struggling
for many of the values that Fukuzawa espoused.[74] First there
is his openness to the world, his bitter attack on the "closed
country" (*sakoku*) idea. He opposed a parochial "Japanese"
point of view and insisted on viewing matters from a world-
wide perspective. His position was based on his Christian
universalism. Men are basically citizens of the kingdom of
heaven and this comes before their being Japanese or Western.
Unlike the bureaucrats who favored "Europeanization," Uchimura stood for a universal position which was above "Eu-
ropeanism" as well as "Japanese purism."[75]

Secondly, Uchimura favored the development of public
spirit and a public morality against the purely private nature
of traditional Japanese morality as he viewed it. According
to Uchimura, loyalty and filial piety (*chū* and *kō*) are based
on personal relations and so are personal obligations. As
opposed to personal obligation (*giri*) he supported duty
(*gimu*) which he defined as having a universal moral character. In sociological terms Uchimura advocated a universalistic
ethic in place of a particularistic one.[76]

[73] *Ibid.*, pp. 204-205.   [74] *Ibid.*, pp. 60-84.   [75] *Ibid.*, pp. 60-64.
[76] *Ibid.*, pp. 65-67. Maruyama Masao has argued what seems to be
the opposite position, namely that there was no sphere of *private*
morality in traditional Japanese thinking (*Gendai seiji no shisō to*

Thirdly Uchimura opposes the respect for empty forms which characterizes traditional Japanese feudal society, and advocates a greater degree of naturalness and directness. Fourthly he opposes the negative retrogressive side of feudalism which revered tradition above change. As against the feudal dislike of the new and untraditional, Uchimura argues for advance, progress, change. Nothing in the society is sacred to him because it is old. As against the feudal "negative morality" of abstaining from doing evil he urges a positive morality which tries to fulfill its ideals in practice.[77]

Fifthly Uchimura, like Fukuzawa, vigorously attacked the traditional family system. He favored monogamy, opposing the traditional double standard and degradation of women. He opposed the patriarchal family and argued that love, not authority, should be the basis of family relations. While remaining traditional to the extent of stressing obligations of children to parents, he nonetheless argued for the small nuclear family as the ideal type of family structure.[78]

Sixthly Uchimura opposed the feudal status system and its survival in Meiji times. Like Fukuzawa he favored a system of formal equality for all citizens, but unlike him his ultimate reason was that in Christ all distinctions of class between men are overcome. And seventhly Uchimura was a stalwart fighter for freedom, democracy, and peoples' rights. In fact his position on questions of political democracy was more thorough than most of the leaders of the Movement for Freedom and Peoples' Rights.[79]

In conclusion, then, Ienaga argues, contrary to the opin-

---

kōdō, vol. 1, pp. 11-12). This, however, does not seem to be a real contradiction for what both Uchimura and Maruyama are pointing to is the *undifferentiated* nature of the traditional point of view. This becomes clear I think when we take the concrete example of the "family-state concept" described by Ishida Takeshi (*op.cit.*). From Uchimura's point of view this is a pervasively private concept which leaves no room for a universalistic public ethic. From Maruyama's point of view it is a pervasively public morality which allows no moral legitimacy to the private sphere. These are two sides of the same coin.

[77] *Ibid.*, pp. 69-73.   [78] *Ibid.*, pp. 73-79.   [79] *Ibid.*, pp. 79-86.

ion of Masamune Hakucho (that Uchimura's thought was not as "advanced" as Fukuzawa's), that Uchimura was actually more advanced and thorough than Fukuzawa even on the issues where Fukuzawa himself made his main contribution. And on a number of other issues where Fukuzawa was not so clear Uchimura was far beyond him. For example he criticized as false a civilization (*bummei*) which has more respect for battleships than for human beings, and as empty a democracy which exists in names and forms only. While, like Fukuzawa, he favored capitalism, he wanted free productive enterprise and opposed monopoly. Unlike Fukuzawa he wanted some controls on absolutely free competition when this competition had destructive social consequences. He argued for respect for labor and the laborer, as against Fukuzawa's contempt for the lower classes. Again, unlike Fukuzawa, he bitterly opposed the "rich nation, strong army" idea. He was patriotic and a nationalist, but he always held the nation to be the instrument of higher ideals, never an end in itself. One of the duties of the patriot, he felt, was to criticize his country vigorously when it required criticism. He never apologized for an oppressive statism, as Fukuzawa on occasion did. He was one of the first to speak out against imperialism in Japan, even before Kōtoku Shūsui.[80] If Uchimura opposed his epoch, it was not because he was behind it, but because he was ahead of it. "It cannot be doubted that he was the most splendid embodiment of the Meiji modern spirit," says Ienaga.[81]

But the thing which makes Ienaga evaluate Uchimura so highly is more than his stand on particular issues. It is the special kind of individualism for which he stood. Of course this special individualism is based on Uchimura's Christianity. Uchimura wrote, "The individual is the basis of church and the foundation of the state. God dwells in the spirit of the individual before he dwells in the church, he faces the spirit of the individual before he faces the nation." Individual conscience should be beyond any coercion, according to Uchimura. Not only should pressure from ruling powers above

80 *Ibid.*, pp. 86-117.
81 *Ibid.*, p. 103.

be resisted, but pressure from the power of the masses below should also be resisted. "However good a principle, it cannot fail to be a bad principle if it is enforced from without," he said.[82] Christ alone is the basis from which the individual can fight all the powers of the world.

In summing up Ienaga says: "Individualism is an essential element in the modern spirit, an inescapable component of it. But the Meiji enlightenment thinkers (*keimōshisōka*) were apt to run in the direction of a utilitarianism which makes the individual's pleasure his highest value. They were unable to establish an ethical individualism which makes individual moral duty its absolutely highest thing. So even after modernization advanced successively in the Taishō and Shōwa periods, as before there did not appear a firm individual self-consciousness but only a vacillating tendency to follow blindly whatever opinion was current. If we reflect on this situation, the intellectual historical meaning of Uchimura's unique individualism is that it showed for a Japanese a remarkably rare height."[83]

It was from his position of ethical individualism with its ultimately religious basis that Uchimura could make his profound criticism of not only the traditional Japanese society but the modern spirit itself. He criticized the false modern individualism which would deify the self,[84] just as he criticized any tendency to deify progress, or the state, or socialism. "How many people besides Uchimura," says Ienaga, "would we find among all the Japanese thinkers since Meiji who truly reached the foundation of the modern spirit, stood there and broke through its limitations?"[85]

[82] *Ibid.*, p. 112.   [83] *Ibid.*, p. 114.   [84] *Ibid.*, p. 130.

[85] *Ibid.*, p. 136. Ienaga highly appreciates Uchimura's views on religion, starting from the point that this world is not its own end but exists for the sake of eternity. But also he notes the fact that Uchimura was as critical of the church as anything else. He quotes Uchimura as saying, "Heresy, heresy, they say. But truly there is nothing as honorable in the world as heresy. Just because there is heresy in the world there is progress. The prophets were heretics. Jesus was a heretic. Paul was a heretic. Luther was a heretic" (p. 110). Similarly Uchimura was no biblical fundamentalist. He wrote, "I do not say this

Finally Ienaga turns to the problem of the latter years of Uchimura and his apparent turn to conservatism. He points out that to some degree Uchimura's progressive attitudes continued to the end, and quotes some sharp critical comments from the early and late 1920's. Further, some of his anti-progressive tendencies are only seemingly so. For example his praise of Bushidō is not to be taken literally. It is not Bushidō as it actually was but an idealized Kantian Bushidō in which the element of selfless duty has been extricated from the particular nexus of feudal relationships. Even when all this has been said Ienaga admits that there really was a retrogressive tendency and proceeds relentlessly to document it. What most of all Ienaga finds difficult to forgive is Uchimura's backtracking on the family ethic, which he takes as a kind of touchstone of modernization.[86] But, finally, Ienaga denies that the later retrogression can detract from the "high historical meaning carried by his early thought."[87] (Any more than the conservatism of the aging Luther can dim the achievements of his early years.) And even in his "betrayal" of his own progressive past Uchimura maintained his integrity, says Ienaga. Such betrayal has been common enough in Japan, but usually it has been carried out in a group and under some kind of group pressure. Not so with Uchimura.

---

is the truth because it is in the Bible. I say it is the truth because it is the truth. I study the Bible. I don't blindly follow the Bible" (p. 123). Ienaga also emphasizes the positive side of Uchimura's doctrine of "no church," namely that all mankind is the church. He notes Uchimura's openness to other religions, and cites these interesting words of Uchimura: "My friends are Hōnen rather than Wesley, Shinran rather than Moody. Those of the same religion do not necessarily have the same direction of faith. The heart with which I turn to Jesus is like the heart with which Hōnen and Shinran relied on Amida. It is not like the heart with which English and Americans believe in Christ" (p. 123).

[86] *Ibid.*, pp. 137-166. Ienaga returns to this theme in the essay "Historical Reflections on Anti-Modernism," in *Nihon kindai shisōshi kenkyū* (1953) where Uchimura is one of the prime examples, but this does not represent a revision of his earlier analysis.

[87] *Ibid.*, p. 166.

Even his "betrayal" manifested the quality of his individualism for he carried it out at his own time, for his own reasons, in his own way.[88]

Since the essays on Taguchi and Kitamura only supplement themes already sketched out in the Fukuzawa and Uchimura essays, we may turn to a general estimate of the significance of *The Modern Spirit and its Limitations* as a work which summarizes a nearly ten-year period in Ienaga's development.[89] The most impressive thing to me about this book of 1950 is its essential continuity with his earlier work on religious history, a continuity considerably greater than one might have expected from reading the quotation with which we began this section. There is in this book a shift in basic interest from religion to what I shall call the moral level. But there is no indication of a rejection of earlier positions most

[88] *Ibid.*, p. 167.

[89] The essay on Taguchi is an appreciation of his early contribution to an economic and social interpretation of history such as had already been hinted at in Fukuzawa. Kitamura Tōkoku, on the other hand, occupies a position similar to that of Uchimura in Ienaga's view. He shared many of the anti-feudal and liberal values of Fukuzawa (pp. 13-23) but like Uchimura he went beyond that to criticize the utilitarian and non-transcendent side of the modern spirit itself (though Ienaga sees the self-criticism of the modern spirit as itself in a sense truly modern), also on the basis of a Christian position. One of his contributions somewhat different from Uchimura was his "romantic" spirit which stressed the emotional and expressive side of human life and opposed an exclusively intellectualist or scientific preoccupation (pp. 24-44). Ienaga's final estimate is as follows: "Even though he cannot escape the criticism that he was weak in the power of judging social reality and, fleeing to the world of art, lost a broad social view, nevertheless not only did he fulfill a historical mission in giving an important spiritual backing to one side of the development of modern society, but he left behind an eternally imperishable heritage in grasping the essence of the human condition" (p. 45). Kitamura came to his understanding of life through his own suffering, and discovered its essence to be suffering. Since he thought that the true meaning of human life was in suffering itself he rejected "enlightenment" (*gedatsu, satori*) as an escape from the truth (pp. 46-48). Here we see a very close approximation to "the logic of negation" though Ienaga does not use the term. Through Kitamura Ienaga even seems to be repeating his old antipathy to a Zen type mysticism.

of which are directly or indirectly reaffirmed. Of course the shift in primary concern is itself of the highest significance. In the earlier work on religion it is remarkable that the moral problem is almost completely ignored. It was salvation through the logic of denial which had interested Ienaga, not any implications about human moral action. But on the other hand Ienaga had never denied the possibility of moral implications, and indeed by insisting on keeping the religious man so firmly in this world and resisting any tendency to escape from the actualities of human existence, he seemed actually to be setting the stage for a working out of those implications.

Ienaga's attitude to the modern (*kindai*) is itself a test case of what I call his continuity. We saw at the end of *The Development of the Logic of Negation* a basically negative evaluation of the modern, whereas by 1950 he was a firm supporter of modernization. But this is no mere reversal. The essential grounds on which he had criticized the modern spirit in 1940, namely its utilitarian and non-transcendent aspect, are reaffirmed in 1950, and indeed again in 1960.[90] It is not that Ienaga has become a utilitarian or a materialist. While remaining faithful to his own basic religious and philosophical commitments he has nonetheless changed his evaluation of the possibility of realizing those commitments in modern society. The modern is good precisely because it more fully expresses the values which Ienaga had long held. Relative to traditional "feudal" society the modern society and culture have greater "universality" (*fuhensei*) and give a fuller and more adequate expression of human capacities. This is the constant theme of Ienaga's evaluation of "progressive" tendencies. In this respect it is clear that, within the realm of the modern, Ienaga feels that socialism is a fuller expression of human universality than capitalism, and consequently though it is good to favor capitalism relative to feudalism it is even more progressive to favor socialism relative to capitalism. But there is nothing in the sphere of the modern, including socialism, which is not subject to criticism from a value position. Ienaga never collapses his early distinction between what

[90] *Ueki Emori kenkyū*, pp. 401-403.

is and what ought to be. He never deifies history or idolizes the modern.

In this connection it might be well to consider another statement by Ienaga which shows his attitude toward the relation of Western culture and modernization and what this means for Japan:

> "It is already clear that Western culture is not the only human culture. Besides Europe and America there are various different societies and cultures and consequently besides Western history there exist the histories of a number of peoples and regions. But, since the West's modern culture having a world universality and power of diffusion has swept the globe, it has come to be thought that the Western culture which is the womb of that culture is a model form for world history.
>
> "Formerly as some people of narrow thought have supposed, Western culture is materialistic and Eastern culture is spiritual and much superior to Western culture and such like. That is not to be believed. Modern culture which had its source in Europe and America does not simply belong to Westerners only, now it is the world's culture and no one can overlook that. Pre-modern oriental classical culture does not have the power to replace this modern culture. However, if you say that modern culture is complete and has no lacks that is not at all so. It must not be forgotten that it contains not a few contradictions and lacks deriving from its womb. . . .
>
> "It cannot be that Japan can fail to feel the suffering coming from the contradictions and lacks mentioned above. Now the Japanese together with the other peoples of the world are facing the great task of overcoming the contradictions and lacks of modern culture. Today may be said to be the age of the labor pains of giving birth to a new future."[91]

The essentially new element in the period under discussion is the working out of Ienaga's moral position, bringing with it a

[91] *Shin Nihonshi*, pp. 306-307.

heightened sense of moral responsibility, as indicated in the opening quotation in this section. The core of his ethical position is an ethical individualism of which Uchimura is the paradigm. (Ienaga indicated to me in 1961 that Uchimura remains for him the most significant modern Japanese.) This is an individualism which accepts the duty to be oneself, which refuses to renounce that responsibility through dependence on any group, but which avoids self-deification and finds its highest realization in an unshakable loyalty to values which transcend the self. It is in this context of working out his moral position that I think we can understand Ienaga's refusal to plunge into the political struggle right after the end of the war. He had genuinely to appropriate a position that would really be his own, and that took time and could not be rushed. As was his habit, he worked these problems through by defining himself in relation to paradigmatic figures in the past. By 1950 he had added Uchimura Kanzō to the figures of Shōtoku Taishi and Shinran as the third hero. Having moved back from the religious sphere to the moral, not through renouncing the religious but through working out its implications in relation to human actuality, he was now in a position to answer the call to social responsibility.

Facing Historical Crisis (1950-   )

If we can characterize the preceding period as one in which Ienaga moved from primarily religious to primarily moral concern, this most recent phase of his development can be seen as still a further shift in emphasis from the moral to the social institutional level, but of course with the same proviso as above, that the shift did not mean abandonment of earlier positions. In addition to the conditions in family and place of work which aroused his social concern it was the "reverse course" policy of the late 1940's which seemed to involve a recession from the democratic reforms of the early occupation years, and threatened to make the constitution "empty words" which stimulated Ienaga to become involved in political matters. A very strong motive was the desire not to have to repent a second time for having failed openly to oppose the reactionary elements in Japanese society.[92]

From March 1952 Ienaga has been a regular contributor to popular newspapers and magazines on topical political matters. The first paragraph of the first of these articles, "University Self-government" (*Asahi Shimbun*, March 4, 1952), gives an example of the motives which prompted him to take this step: "It is said that very recently the idea that university presidents be chosen by the government is being talked about, but this is a matter which ought to surprise us. The supporters of this idea say that even in the case of the university there is no freedom to cause social anxiety. But is it after all the university which is causing social anxiety? Or is it indeed the policy of those people who, overlooking the clear wording of the constitution, want to strengthen 'war power' and reduce 'the freedom of assembly, association, speech, publication and all other forms of expression'? A wise nation will not make a mistake in judging [the answer to these questions]."[93]

His topical articles have been collected in three volumes so far, *Facing Historical Crisis* (1954), *History and Education* (1956) and *History and Today* (1959). They contain articles dealing with a wide variety of subjects but mainly centering around questions of educational and political policy and above all the defense of the constitution. Another volume which should perhaps be mentioned at this point is his *Criticism of the Courts* (*Saiban hihan*) (1959) which is an independent essay discussing the legitimacy and appropriate limits to public criticism of the judicial process. The legal emphasis in this most recent period should not surprise us when we remember Ienaga's fascination with constitutional and legal matters from Middle School days. Also we must remember the 1935 article published in his Middle School alumni magazine on the question of the "organ theory" of the emperor.

In addition to vigorous journalistic activity Ienaga has also been active in a number of movements in defense of the con-

[92] *Rekishi no kiki ni menshite*, p. 234.
[93] Reprinted in *Rekishi no kiki ni menshite*, p. 115.

stitution and liberal causes. He was very active in the opposition to the security treaty of 1960. In response to criticisms which say that the scholar's duty is to scholarship and, besides voting, he ought not to bother with politics, Ienaga made this defense in the preface to *History and Education*: "Firstly, a scholar must be a member of society before he is a scholar. Is it permissible for him, while fulfilling his occupation as a scholar, to renounce his duty as a member of society? Just as it is natural that the scholar, being a member of a family should fulfill his moral obligations to the family, is it not also natural that he, as a member of larger social groups, should positively cooperate in the running of those social groups to which he belongs? Since in a democratic country all the people bear a responsibility for the management of the country, it is not a matter of asking about occupation. It cannot be said that the scholar alone is exempted from that responsibility."

At any rate it is clear that Ienaga has not allowed his concern for social and political issues to divert him from his professional activities for he has continued to publish with amazing frequency during this most recent period. Here we can only review briefly the major categories of his recent work.

During the decade of the 1950's Ienaga wrote several historical surveys of which the most important are *A History of Japanese Moral Thought* (through Meiji) (1954), and *A History of Japanese Culture* (through the Tokugawa period) (1959).[94] In these books Ienaga returns to an overview of the development of Japanese thought and culture such as he had not undertaken since *The Development of the Logic of Negation* and *The Development of the Religious View of Nature*, but they are very different in character from the

[94] Besides these he published a high school textbook, *Shin Nihonshi* (I have the fourth printing of 1961 and have not been able to ascertain the date of the first edition. From the following book which is a supplement to the *Shin Nihonshi* for more advanced students I surmise the date to be 1949 or 1950), *Shinkokushi gaisetsu* (1950), *History of Japan* (in English, Tourist Library Series, 1953, but too condensed to be very revealing about Ienaga), and *Kokumin no Nihonshi* (1959, a revised edition of *Shin Nihonshi* not for textbook use).

earlier books. Unlike the earlier books which drew their categories from the sphere of thought itself, these books utilize categories that are drawn mainly from the "substructure," such as for example: the moral thought of the nobility, of the warriors, of the townsmen, of the peasants, of the bourgeois.[95] One of the most interesting chapters in the *History of Japanese Moral Thought* is on the moral thought of the monks, which is not exactly a "substructural" category though it is in a sense a social category. Since Ienaga's work always has its "practical" aspect, it is probably not illegitimate to ask what is the function of these books in the context of Ienaga's most recent concerns. Here it seems to me that they serve the function of providing a historical grounding in the Japanese tradition for a modern democratic Japan. Given the almost complete lack of an explicit democratic tradition, this means that a great deal of weight has to be given to the relatively inarticulate "peoples' struggles" down through the centuries and the occasional unorthodox thinker, like Andō Shōeki (who receives more pages of discussion in the *History of Japanese Culture* than any other figure in all Japanese history).

While the treatment is as always rich in illustration and often subtle in analysis, the writer cannot help but entertain a certain feeling of dissatisfaction with these books compared with the rest of Ienaga's work. Though in no orthodox sense Marxist, they do at times seem to have a mechanical quality. This is especially evident it seems to me in the case of the treatment of feudal society. In the *History of Japanese Moral Thought*, for example, while the treatment of the aristocrats and monks on the one hand and of the Meiji bourgeois on the other seems to be insightful, the discussion of the warriors (*bushi*), townsmen (*chōnin*) and peasants seems to be one-sided. For example it is hard for me to accept the characterization of the warrior ethic as "utilitarian" (chapter 7) or the townsmen and peasants as quite as progressive as Ienaga

[95] In this respect the *Nihon dōtoku shisōshi* is reminiscent of the great work of Tsuda Sōkichi, to whom Ienaga acknowledges a great debt (p. 276).

would seem to have it (chapters 8 and 9). Ienaga's treatment is perhaps understandable. The Japanese tradition of "feudalism" is still too strongly alive, not only in the massive weight of reactionary survivals, but within the soul of even progressive individuals, for most Japanese intellectuals yet to be able to assess it entirely objectively. Yet I cannot help but feel that here is one of the few points at which Ienaga's "practical" primacy has distorted his objective analysis. Part of the difficulty, however, is the inevitable schematization which arises from a brief treatment of a very large subject. In this respect the hundred page treatment of Meiji thought in the first volume of *A Symposium on Modern Japanese Intellectual History* (1959), since it involves a smaller time span on a broader canvas, is a more richly suggestive discussion.

Perhaps even more closely related to the constitutional and political concerns of the decade of the 1950's is Ienaga's preoccupation with the figure of Ueki Emori (1857-1892).[96] Ueki is important for Ienaga as a leading thinker in the Movement for Freedom and Peoples' Rights and as an early constitutionalist. In attempting to establish the Japanese democratic tradition in modern times Ueki is a key figure. These interests are continuing in his most recent as yet unpublished work where he is turning to Minobe Tatsukichi (1873-1948) and Taishō democratic thought, coming back in a sense to the point where his own intellectual development began.

In this most recent period Ienaga's problem is not primarily religious or moral. It is the problem of how to *institutionalize* democracy securely in Japan. It is natural, therefore, that legal and constitutional matters should figure prominently in his concerns. Much of Ienaga's political writing seems Marxist, at least to an American,[97] but this reflects mainly the

[96] First in the article on Ueki's thought in *Nihon kindai shisōshi kenkyū* (1953), then in the small Iwanami Shinsho volume on him called *A Pioneer of Revolutionary Thought* (*Kakumei shisō no senkusha*, 1955) and finally in the compendious *Ueki Emori kenkyū* (1960), 792 pp.

[97] This was the writer's initial impression.

current political vocabulary in Japan. In the case of Ienaga the reader soon discovers the basically liberal and democratic values beneath the vocabulary.

But if political concerns have had primacy in this most recent period, Ienaga's moral and religious concerns have not gone unexpressed. A small book on Taoka Reiun (1870-1912)[98] seems to represent what we have called Ienaga's moral concern, for Taoka was not a political leader but a somewhat "contradictory" literary critic whom Ienaga appreciates chiefly because of his "sense of justice and his love of humanity."[99] On the religious side, in 1961 Ienaga published a brief article in *Shūkan dokushojin* reaffirming the significance to him of Shōtoku Taishi's statement, "The world is empty and false; only the Buddha is true," though stating that it is the first phrase that continues to have meaning for him. Perhaps even more interesting is Ienaga's criticism in 1960 of Ueki for the latter's tendency to self-deification, which he finds responsible for his singular lack of self-criticism.[100] In the course of this discussion he raises again his old objections to utilitarianism, the philosophy of "limitless progress," and the idea of making the human being ultimate (*ningenshi-jōshugi*). Finally in answer to the question as to what was lacking in Ueki's philosophy of human ultimacy and limitless progress he answers, "the logic of negation" (*hitei no ronri*).[101]

Epilogue

Ienaga Saburō like all men is the product of his age. But unlike most he has been acutely sensitive to its pressures and has made its problems his own. The three main phases in his thought broadly conform to three main phases of modern Japanese history: Taishō Democracy, the Nationalist Period,

[98] *Sūki naru shisōka no shōgai*, Iwanami Shinsho (1955).

[99] *Ibid.*, p. 192.

[100] *Ueki Emori kenkyū*, pp. 396-403. In a note (p. 406) he points out the parallel lack of self-criticism in the Japanese communist militants up to 1955. It is clear that Ienaga would see in the recognition of Stalin's evil the beginning of wisdom.

[101] *Ibid.*, p. 403.

and the postwar period. But though always in dialogue with his epoch he has been capable of saying no to it as well as yes. In fact in spite of the clearly definable stages in his thought reflecting different sorts of external pressure, there is an equally clear continuity and cumulativeness. In dealing with the cultural problems of his day he has made his own synthesis, drawing from such diverse sources as Buddhism and Christianity, Liberalism and Marxism. It is not that Ienaga has or claims to have solved the problems of Japan's cultural modernization. But he has clearly discerned what some of them are and uncovered some of the cultural resources which may be used in their solution.

Ienaga notes that in all his reading of Ueki's writings, including his journals, he never came across a single instance of self-doubt. This he says is not unique to Ueki but is a characteristic of his generation. Fukuzawa Yukichi (1835-1901), Nakamura Keiu (1832-1891), Katō Hiroyuki (1836-1916), and we could probably add Nishimura Shigeki (1828-1902), were the same. How different, he notes is the next generation of people like Kitamura Tōkoku (1869-1894) and Uchimura Kanzō (1861-1930), with their deep inner conflicts and doubts. It is interesting that the generation of the great enlighteners grew up in Tokugawa times. Those men all came to know who they were when the traditional order was intact. This provided the fundamental personality stability which carried them through all the vicissitudes of later years. They became heroes of Japan's social, political, economic, and scientific modernization. But the next generation, already growing up in a broken world, never knew the personality security of their elders. For them modernization implied the "spiritual breakdown"[102] which Natsume Sōseki spoke of as following the impact of Western culture. But nevertheless that generation produced the first heroes of the "modernization of the soul" if such a phrase is permissible. Kitamura, who committed suicide, and Uchimura, who retrogressed in his later years, are nonetheless heroes for Ienaga. The strain on them of their own inner revolution was too great to be

[102] Arima, *op.cit.*

borne and they were unable to actualize all of its possibilities. But, in a sense, what they have done does not need to be done again in quite the same way. They do not save succeeding generations from working out their own solutions, as the life of Ienaga itself shows. But they make it more likely that that working through will be successful. And of course Ienaga and men like him become examples for those who follow in the task of gradually creating a new cultural tradition for Japan.

CHAPTER XII

Japanese Writers and Modernization

SHŪICHI KATŌ

AT THE beginning were the *"Kurofune."* Then came the awakening of a small nation suddenly realizing that it had to be reorganized in order to cope with the danger from the outside. The nation was unanimous about the goal it was to achieve: *fukoku-kyōhei,* a "wealthy state with a strong army." Not all were agreed on the method, or on the manner and extent of popular participation in the political process in achieving this aim. There were partisans of *minken* (the rights of the people) and partisans of *kokken* (the rights of the state); some emphasized the independence of the individual, and others emphasized the subordination of individual rights in order to maintain national independence. This was the major controversy in the Meiji society throughout the whole period. But at least during the first fifteen years after the Meiji reform the interrelation between the rights of the people and the claims of the state was widely recognized by both sides.

In the early years of the Meiji era, for instance, there were two leaders who had a very clear insight into the importance of general education and argued that modern institutions should be run only by modernized people, and that these could be provided only as a result of modern education. One of them was Mori Arinori, the first Minister of Education; the other, who was outside the administration, was Fukuzawa Yukichi, the founder of Keiō University. Mori made it clear in his explanation of the new educational system, which he himself had forged, that education at any level should find its ultimate aim in serving the state, whereas Fukuzawa never tired of emphasizing, in all his writings and speeches, his famous "independence of the individual." It is to be noted, however, that Mori introduced liberal ideas into his national universities by encouraging individual initiative in higher education,[1] and that Fukuzawa was perfectly aware of the need, not only of a "wealthy nation" but also of a "strong army."[2] In other words they at first had some common ground—the realization of the interrelationship between *minken* and *kokken*. But during the 1890's this common ground was lost.

The period between the Sino-Japanese War and the Russo-Japanese War may be characterized by a definite split between the protagonists of *kokken* and those of *minken*. Nationalists on the side of the government, largely supported by the masses, concerned themselves mainly with what they considered to be national interests which should be advanced even at the expense of civil rights. Liberal intellectuals, who were put in a position of defending civil rights, apparently had no time to take into consideration the national interests during crises affecting Japan's relations with the outside world. In this period between the two wars the common ground between the government and the opposition was diminished, and the possibility of dialogue was lessened. Under such circumstances in most countries the opposition becomes more and more radical, and the government responds with more and more restrictions on civil rights. This is what happened in Japan.

The main effect of the Russo-Japanese War was to accentuate this separation of the rights of the state from those of the people. After the victory, the state was triumphant; sure of its achievement of *fukoku-kyōhei*, it now wanted more. An authoritarian bureaucracy developed, while the liberal intellectuals (and also the early anarchists and socialists) became more conscious of the miseries of the people in mines, factories, and villages. The war had been won at the expense

[1] Nagai Michio: "Chishiki-jin no seisan ruuto," *Kindai Nihon shisō shi kōza*, vol. 4 (Tokyo, 1959).

[2] See, for example, his *Bummei-ron no gairyaku*, and also *Fukuō jiden*. On the nationalistic arguments by the *minken* newspapers about foreign policy a very good résumé is found in Oka Yoshitake, "Meiji shoki no jiyū-minken ronja no me ni eijitaru tōji no kokusai jōsei," *Meiji-shi kenkyū sōsho*, vol. 4 (Tokyo, 1957).

of the welfare of the common people, yet the popular sacrifice was not recompensed by the much acclaimed military success. Giving up reliance on legal attempts to ameliorate the situation, the opposition exploded in hopeless revolt against the ruling political power and social order.

The year 1910 saw the Kōtoku Shūsui incident. The government discovered the alleged plot, suppressed it, and executed Kōtoku.[3] This affair shook Japanese intellectuals at the time, from Mori Ōgai to Ishikawa Takuboku, from Nagai Kafū to anonymous university students. In fact, nothing between the Meiji reform and the unconditional surrender of 1945 exerted the influence on the Japanese intellectual world that the Russo-Japanese War and the Kōtoku incident did. These were touchstones which revealed the fundamental attitudes of many writers toward the general modernization of the country. In fact, the most revealing accounts of modern Japan to be found in literature belong mostly to the period between the beginning of the Russo-Japanese War and the end of the First World War. Four writers of this period may be selected as representing different attitudes of intellectuals toward the modernization of Japan: Mori Ōgai (1862-1922), Natsume Sōseki (1867-1916), Nagai Kafū (1879-1959), and Uchimura Kanzō (1861-1930).

The contrast between Mori Ōgai and Natsume Sōseki may

[3] In late May and early June in 1910 the police discovered a plot to assassinate the Emperor Meiji; they arrested a few people who were supposed to be under the influence of Kōtoku Shūsui, an anarchist-socialist. The Katsura Government also arrested hundreds of socialists all over the country. After six months of a secret trial, the Supreme Court decreed the death sentence for twelve, including Kōtoku, with life sentences for the other twelve accused. Witnesses presented by the defendants were not allowed to testify in court. The executions of the twelve were carried out immediately after the sentence was declared. Press reports about the affair were extremely vague under a strict censorship imposed by the Government. A detailed account of the affair can be found in Shioda Shōbei and Watanabe Junzō (eds.), *Hiroku taigyaku jiken*, 2 vols. (Tokyo, 1959). On the reactions of writers to the incident, see, for example, Usui Yoshimi: "Taishō. Taishō Tenki. Futatsu no jiken," *Gendai Nihon bungaku shi, Gendai Nihon bungaku zenshū*, Supplement, vol. 1 (Tokyo, 1959).

be compared with that between Mori Arinori and Fukuzawa Yukichi. Ōgai, a medical officer of high rank in the Imperial Army, engaged in all kinds of literary and cultural activities at the same time that he worked in the administration. His objective was the enlightenment of the intellectual public, taking into account both national traditions and Western ideas. Sōseki, on the contrary, was never in government, and even resigned from his professorship at the Imperial University, living on his writings. As a novelist his major concern was individual ethics, but he was perfectly aware of the problems of society at large.

In the Russo-Japanese War Ōgai participated as a medical officer in battles in Manchuria, and at the time of the Kōtoku incident he began to study how the regime could cope with the problems raised by the anarchists and socialists. He concluded with much insight that suppression by force would not solve these problems and that the regime, if it wanted to attain social stability, should be prepared to work out its own answers to the labor problem; perhaps through a program of extended social legislation.[4] Thus he was doing his best to serve the state, whether in war or in the crisis posed by the radical movement, both as medical officer and as one of the most powerful ideological writers of his time.

The case of Sōseki was different. Two wars led him to bitter disillusionment about the Meiji state, and also to individualism as the last stronghold of moral values. What, he asked, is the relationship between the rights of the state and those of the individual? In a state crisis such as the Russo-Japanese War, he argued, the rights of the individual could be reasonably restricted. In ordinary times, as in Japan during the First World War, civil rights should be respected to the maximum. He cited the case of Britain, which adopted

[4] Ideas of this kind were expressed by Mori Ōgai in his short stories, e.g., "Kano yōni" (1912), "Fujidana" (1912), and "Ōshio Heihachirō" (1914). His protest against censorship is to be found in "Chin moku no tō" (1910). His later writings about the subject are: "Furui techō kara" and the letter of December 24th, 1919, addressed to Kako Kakusho. All works and letters of Mori Ōgai may be found in *Ōgai Zenshū*, 53 vols. (Tokyo, 1951-1956).

compulsory military service only on the outbreak of the war in contrast to Germany, whose institutions had been militaristic even during peace time.[5] But his analysis did not go farther on this point, and he did not analyze the case of Japanese militarism in detail.

There were two kinds of opposition to the Russo-Japanese War: that of Yosano Akiko, and that of Uchimura Kanzō. Yosano Akiko (1878-1942) expressed her pacifist feeling in her famous poems. Compared with her brother's life, she wrote, it was not at all important whether Port Arthur fell or not.[6] But of course, if Port Arthur had not fallen, Japan would have lost the war; if the war had been lost, there would have been no guarantee that the country would not have been occupied by Tsarist Russia. We do not know whether the poet was really prepared to accept all these possible results. She was against the war, but she did not show any alternative to it.

Uchimura's stand was much more far-reaching: he was not only against the Russo-Japanese War, but against all wars. Differing from Natsume Sōseki's relative freedom of the individual as well as from Yosano's sentimental pacifism, Uchimura's cause could be defended at both levels—that of the individual and that of the state. In fact, he did not see any difference between the individual's obligations and the duties of the state in the international arena. The same principle of moral and absolute pacifism was to be applied either to any individual or to any state, at any time or place in the world. What would happen then, if you do not resist your enemy? The enemy would destroy you. Uchimura said: then die as a martyr.[7] In other words, his was a logic of martyr-

---

[5] "Watakushi no kojinshugi" (1915); all works and writings of Natsume Sōseki quoted in this paper are found in *Sōseki zenshū*, 34 vols. (Tokyo, 1956-1957).

[6] "Kimi shinitamo koto nakare," *Myōjō*, September 1904.

[7] "Heiwa no fukuin" (1903) with the subtitle "Zettai heiwa shugi." Referring to St. Matthew, Chap. 26, Verse 52, Uchimura argues here that freedom cannot be gained by conquering the enemy of freedom, but can be restored after one has been killed by the enemy. This was the year before the Russo-Japanese War. A year after the victory he wrote

dom. This argument is perfectly cohesive and valid. But one thing is certain: no state in history has ever been prepared to die voluntarily, and Meiji Japan was certainly the last of all countries which would have accepted that. Uchimura opposed the government from his stand of absolute pacifism, but he did not propose any concrete alternative to the government's policy. The barrier which separated the opposition from the government remained insurmountable.

The Kōtoku affair, in its turn, deepened the gap between the ruling political power and the politically conscious intellectuals. Kōtoku Shūsui died, but in death he inspired more than he had in life, as Mori Ōgai had foreseen. Many young people were becoming more and more dissatisfied with the government during the last years of Meiji. Ishikawa Takuboku (1886-1912) may be taken as typical of these young people. While still in his twenties Ishikawa Takuboku was working on a newspaper in sickness and poverty. He was much impressed by Kōtoku and his friends and he collected available documents about the case, and began to think that the anarchists had been right in many respects.[8] However, he died of tuberculosis not long after the affair, so we cannot know the direction his thoughts would have taken had he lived.

Nagai Kafū, who had come back from Europe after a long absence from Japan, reacted in a different way to the incident.

---

in "Nichi-Ro sensō yori yo ga ukeshi rieki" (1906) : "The war is fought for the sake of the war; there has never been the war really for the sake of peace. The Chinese-Japanese War, fought in the name of peace in the Orient, caused the greater Russo-Japanese War. This war is also supposed to have been fought for the sake of peace in the Orient. I think it will cause another much greater war for the sake of peace in the Orient again." As we know now, Uchimura was perfectly right. All quotations of writings of Uchimura are taken from *Uchimura Kanzō chosaku shū*, 21 vols. (Tokyo, 1955).

[8] "Editor's Notes" (written in January 1911 for a collection of documents about the affair compiled by Ishikawa himself) ; "Iwayuru kondo no koto" (written probably in summer 1910, otherwise in January 1911). Ishikawa's view of Meiji society was formulated in: "Jidai heisoku no genjō" (1910), *Takuboku hyōron shū, shimpen Ishikawa Takuboku senshū*, vol. 4 (Tokyo, 1961). See also some letters in *Takuboku shokan shū* in vol. 6, same series.

He realized that he could not defend the cause of Kōtoku in the way Zola fought for Dreyfus, and that Meiji society was not like French society at the time of Zola. In Japan, he concluded, the business of writers had always been, and could still be, concerned only with love, pleasure, sake, and geisha, but not with national politics.[9] Kafū's general attitude toward Meiji society had, to be sure, developed earlier. It was one of evasion, and his reaction to the Kōtoku affair is symptomatic of it.[10] Ishikawa Takuboku died young, Nagai Kafū lived long.

Among the four men under discussion, only Mori Ōgai collaborated with the state: Natsume Sōseki minimized it; Uchimura Kanzō criticized it; and Nagai Kafū escaped from it. The divorce of the rights of the state and those of the individual was accomplished at the level of ideas. But it does not follow that these men ignored national problems. On the contrary, they had at the very center of their intellectual worlds one national problem—the problem of cultural modernization.

Cultural and social modernization was for them a confrontation of two different cultures, the Western and the traditionally Japanese. The two cultures were different first of all in their economic background; before the First World War the industrialization of Japan was still far behind that of the Western powers. Secondly, they differed in their historical backgrounds; Christian versus Shintō-Buddhist worlds, and Greek versus Confucian ideas. All four writers had lived abroad and observed Western cultures with their own eyes: Mori Ōgai in Germany; Natsume Sōseki in England; Nagai Kafū in France; and Uchimura Kanzō in America.[11] All

---

[9] "Hanabi," *Kaizō*, December 1919. Also in *Nagai Kafū zenshū*, 24 vols. (Tokyo, 1948-1953).

[10] It is only partly correct to attribute Kafū's evasion to his disillusionment with Meiji society after his return to Japan, and it is absolutely wrong to see in his reaction to the Kōtoku affair not a symptom but the cause of his evasion. Discussion in detail can be found in Katō Shūichi, "Kafū to yū genshō," *Sekai*, June, July, August 1960.

[11] Mori Ōgai, as a medical officer of the Imperial Army, in Ger-

noticed profound contradictions in Japanese modernization, which seemed both desirable and undesirable, when they came back to their country. What they had all understood abroad was that Western culture could not be separated from Western history—in other words, that culture is fundamentally conditioned by history. Naturally enough they observed in Tokyo a sharp contrast between the unfinished (Mori Ōgai),[12] and the superficial (Natsume Sōseki),[13] the false (Nagai Kafū),[14] the distorted imitations of Western culture (Uchi-

---

many from October 1884 to July 1888; Natsume Sōseki, as a student of English literature, in England from October 1900 until the end of 1902; Nagai Kafū, with financial support from his father, in America from October 1903 to July 1907, then in France from July 1907 to July 1908; Uchimura Kanzō, as a private visitor, in America from the end of 1884 until May 1888. None of them went abroad again after their return to Japan, except for Mori Ōgai's military service in Manchuria during the Russo-Japanese War.

[12] See, for example, "Fushin chū" (1910): "Japan is Yet in Construction." Also "Mōsō" (1911): "It was not without regret that I returned to a country which does not yet afford necessary conditions for exploration of new fields in science,—I say 'not yet.' . . . I say 'not yet,' because I do not think that there is no hope for Japanese race . . ." *Ōgai zenshū, op.cit.*

[13] See, for example, "Gendai Nihon no kaika" (a lecture in 1911). "What we are doing now is not a result of our own development, but of the influences from outside. In one word, the modernization of contemporary Japan can be summed up as a superficial one. I am not saying all of it must be superficial. On such a complicated problem we should refrain from any sweeping generalization. Yet I cannot help admitting that the large part of our modernization is at its best like this. My point is not that we should stop it, but that we actually have no choice, however sad it may be, other than to go on with this superficial way." *Sōseki zenshū, op.cit.*

[14] The complete works of Nagai Kafū are full of remarks of this kind. Some examples follow. "This is not reform, not progress, not construction. Meiji means nothing but destruction: the beauty of old aspects was destroyed only to be replaced by a confusion of all bad qualities produced in one night." ("Shin kichōsha no nikki," 1909. *Nagai Kafū zenshū, op.cit.*) "There may be no country where you can do so many things so easily as in present day Japan. If you refuse, however, to live in such a way, you have to give place to others and retire." "I take back streets, walk alone in alleyways." ("Hiyori geta," 1915. *Nagai Kafū zenshū, op.cit.*)

mura Kanzō),[15] and the finished, solid, genuine, self-sufficient traditions of Japanese culture.

The modernization of a country on Western models cannot, in principle, be confined to the purely technological field. Sooner or later all ideas, fashions, and customs will flow in, so that many of the traditional ideas and values will be lost. Given the fact that the culture to be imported is history-bound, and that Japanese history is different from that of Western countries, the imported culture can hardly become deeply rooted in the Japanese soil. Thus the early stage of modernization cannot avoid the danger of simply replacing a genuine traditional culture by superficial imitations of the alien culture. All these writers were aware of this controversy, but their approaches to the same controversy were different because they understood Western culture in different ways. For Mori Ōgai the West symbolized science and a logical, systematic way of thinking;[16] for Natsume Sōseki, it was a sort of individualism and internalized moral values;[17] for Nagai Kafū, sensitive forms in which a historical culture was incarnated;[18] and for Uchimura Kanzō, of course, the Christian faith.[19]

[15] See, for example, "Jisei no kansatsu" (1896). "Ancient Jews described hypocrites by the words 'whited sepulcher'; 'white painted house' may be the best word to call present Japanese." Also "Shitsubō to kibō" (1903) : "The perishing of Japan is not a mere fantasy. A liar like Count Ōkuma is leading a big political party; a horde of evil men under him are playing around with national politics. It is only natural that nothing can be expected from political Japan." Uchimura even argued in the same article: "The present corruption of Japan is a sign of her resurrection. Now we are seeing that what should die is dying." *Uchimura zenshū, op.cit.*

[16] See "Doitsu nikki" (Ōgai's Diary compiled in Germany). Also "Yōgaku no seisui o ronzu" (1902) ; "Mōsō" (1911), and many other works. On Ōgai's attitude toward medicine, the following books are valuable: Nakano Shigeharu; *Ōgai sono sokumen* (Tokyo, 1952) ; and Oimatsu Keizō; *Mori Ōgai* (Tokyo, 1958).

[17] See, for example, "Watakushi no kojin shugi," *op.cit.*

[18] "Amerika monogatari" (1908) and "Furansu monogatari" (1909) are undoubtedly the most valuable; a part of his diary (*Danchōtei nichijō*) is concerned with his life abroad.

[19] To be more exact, in the case of Uchimura, the West symbolized Christian faith only historically; the very core of his faith was beyond

433

In other words, Mori Ōgai thought in terms of science, Natsume Sōseki in terms of morality, Nagai Kafū in terms of esthetics, Uchimura Kanzō in terms of faith. Now science is not history-bound, its principles transcend history. Christian faith also transcends history. But ethics and esthetics are different: both are closely connected with a concrete historical national culture. These differences were of primary importance because the controversy in question derived from different historical backgrounds and would be solved, if it could be solved at all, only in terms of principles which are somehow wider than that history.

Having come back from the leading medical laboratories of Germany at the end of the 1880's, Mori Ōgai argued vigorously that there was but a single real medicine and that one could not speak of such things as "Western" or "traditional Japanese" medicines.[20] He then proceeded to stress the importance of cultivating the "seeds of science" instead of being satisfied with taking from outside the "fruits of science."[21] So far as science was concerned, Mori Ōgai's arguments were clear and cogent. There was no doubt at all about the possibility of introducing scientific methods. But of course Western culture meant for Mori Ōgai not only science but also literature, philosophy, ethics, and way of life. All these were closely connected with history, and Mori Ōgai's attitude toward the indiscriminate introduction of Western ideas was very ambivalent. He thought that the cultural traditions of Japan should be respected as much as possible in any program of reform. The food of Japanese soldiers should be based on traditional food; cities should have covered sewers, but the construction of high stone buildings should be avoided;[22]

---

any historical culture, either of the West or of Japan. That is why he later condemned the churches in the West as well as in Japan. An excellent work on this point is: Mori Arimasa: "Uchimura Kanzō" in *Fukuzawa Yukichi, Uchimura Kanzō, Okakura Tenshin shū*, (*Gendai Nihon bungaku zenshū*, vol. 51) (Tokyo, 1958).

[20] Nakano Shigeharu, *op.cit.*
[21] "Yōgaku no seisui o ronzu," *op.cit.*
[22] Ōgai summed up his attitude on this matter in "Mōsō," *op.cit.*

literature should, by contrast with the Edo novels, cope with serious ideals in human life, but those ideals should be largely based on the national tradition, particularly those of the samurai.[23] Not without a certain resignation, not without detached patience, Mori Ōgai seems to have thought that the only practical solution to the problems raised by Japan's accelerated modernization was the encouragement of the scientific spirit, combined with a sort of traditionalism in creative arts and literature, and in morals and social reforms. As for himself, he engaged more and more in the study of the late Edo scholars, elaborating at the same time his own prose style, the quality of which has been thus far unsurpassed.[24]

What Natsume Sōseki observed in Meiji society can be reduced to three major points. First, as we have seen, moral values can be maintained by the individual since the state has not much to do with them. Secondly, all that was Western in the Tokyo of the late Meiji was superficial. Thirdly, what could be done then? Nothing.[25] Modernization is inevitable and so once that process is started, it cannot be confined to a chosen particular field. Pessimistic though he was, Sōseki explored his inner world to the point where the universal

---

[23] The whole series of Ōgai's historical stories, which were started just after General Nogi's suicide in 1912, can be regarded as Ōgai's appreciation as well as criticism of samurai ethics of loyalty, self-sacrifice, self-discipline, will-power, etc.

[24] Notably "Shibue chusai" (1916) ; "Izawa Ranken" (1916-1917) ; "Hōjō Katei" (1917-1918), *Ōgai zenshū, op.cit.* These three biographies are great for three reasons. First, their style is the best in modern Japanese prose ; second, the form is original, almost a new genre, namely a "biography in process" in which the author describes not only the life of the persons concerned, but also the author's own intellectual process of writing a biography—his sorrow for lost documents, his joy at others discovered, his reasoning about available materials, his imagination, his insight ; third, the personalities involved are all alive through the facts and dates of their every day lives and are related to, in one way or another, the *Weltanschauung* of the author. On this subject, two works are to be noted. Ishikawa Jun, *Mori Ōgai* (Tokyo, 1941) ; and Katō Shūichi, "Mori Ōgai," *Asahi jiyaanaru*, May 5, 1963.

[25] "Gendai Nihon no kaika," *op.cit.*

character of human nature revealed itself finally in his last un-finished novel.[26] In more general terms, as we have noticed, Sōseki preached a sort of individualism, which was at his death only related to society, history, and the state. His stand was not based on any immediate universality of scientific principles transcending national culture and history, but rather on moral values which are inescapably determined by history. He had to live in a constant tension between traditional moral values and the individualism of the modern society.

Unlike Mori Ōgai, Uchimura Kanzō did not deal with the immediate universality of scientific principles; unlike Natsume Sōseki, he did establish the universality of moral values by the intermediacy of his absolute faith in the Christian God. Faith is to be valid beyond national borders and different historical backgrounds; so must be the ethics which derive from this transcendent faith. Above his Truth there was nothing—neither emperor, nor nation, nor national history.[27] Nor could there be anything above his moral standards. He was a formidable critic of Meiji society. From his point of view modernization could have a real meaning only if it led to the Christianization of the nation, and Christianization of any country was regarded by him as possible, at least in principle. In reality the overwhelming majority of the Japanese people have so far not accepted, and will not accept in the foreseeable future, his starting point, namely his faith. Consequently they have not accepted, and will not accept, his moral values for the individual and for the state either. Uchimura's stand was the most articulate and perhaps the most cohesive one, but undoubtedly the most isolated one of all.

When Nagai Kafū came back from Paris to Tokyo, he found the city ugly and was immediately convinced that the only reason for this ugliness was the modernization or West-ernization. For him Western civilization was the solid form in which the long span of Western history had crystallized itself. Without tradition there was no beauty; this was true

[26] "Meian," *Sōseki zenshū, op.cit.*
[27] This point is well developed in Mori Arimasa, *op.cit.*

of Paris, so should it be of Tokyo. Those things he found beautiful and genuine in Tokyo were all traditional—the remnant of Edo culture; what he found ugly, spurious and superficial were the imitations of Western buildings, costumes, fashions, and even literature.[28] He rejected the world of modernization. In the sequence of modernization of the human mind, the intelligence comes first; then perhaps follows a change of emotional reactions; and finally, if it comes at all, the modernization of the senses. But, Kafū's approach to the world was par excellence through his senses. In a Meiji society which was modernizing itself as quickly as possible and at any cost, the only possible choice for Nagai was evasion. But we should not forget that evasion implies detachment, and detachment sometimes makes possible very accurate observations of society as we know it—similar, for instance, to Montesquieu's Persian, who happened to be a formidable critic of eighteenth century France. As a matter of fact, in the 1930's it was Nagai Kafū who more than anybody else had a clear insight into the significance of the rise of Japanese militarism.[29]

During and after the First World War Japanese industrialization made extraordinary progress with the expansion of foreign trade. For the first time in Japanese history a large labor force was needed in factories, and at the same time there was a much closer integration of the national economy with the world market. Hence economic depressions produced unemployment, misery, and social insecurity in Japan just as in any other industrialized country at that time. On the other hand, the Wilsonian hope of permanent peace was in the air. Japan was cooperating in the League of Nations, naval disarmament was agreed upon, communications with the outside world were extended, and the country was, with many

[28] See, for example: "Shin kichōsha no nikki"; "Kōcha no ato" (1910-1911); "Hiyori geta"; "Chiru yanagi mado no yubae" (1914); "Shitaya sōwa" (1926).

[29] Katō Shūichi, "Kafū et la littérature française," *Bulletin Franco-Japonais*, No. 42, juin 1959; also "Sensō to chishiki-jin" in *Chishiki-jin no sensei to yakuwari*, (*Kindai Nihon shisō-shi kōza*, vol. 4) (Tokyo. 1959).

fewer restrictions, exposed to all kinds of Western ideas and fashions.

Against this background it is understandable that the governments of the 1920's, with the head of the majority party serving as Prime Minister, tolerated more or less liberal ideas, not only in foreign policies but also in internal policies: universal manhood suffrage, and relative freedom of expression, if not legally, at least in practice. Liberalism was encouraged in the academic world as well as in journalism. Yoshino Sakuzō (1878-1933), who, in academic work, journalism, and public meetings, led vigorous campaigns for universal suffrage, disarmament, democratic procedure in Parliament, and other liberal-democratic causes, was perhaps the most representative spokesman of liberal opinion. On the other hand, Yoshino did not ignore the defense of Japan's national interests in China, and tried to reconcile it with a sense of justice which he wanted to maintain in international relations as well as in internal affairs.[30]

If we can say that a dialogue was possible between the "People's rights" argument of Fukuzawa and the "State's rights" argument of Mori in the early Meiji era, we might now say that communication was beginning to become possible again between the "democracy" of Yoshino Sakuzō and the political ideas of, for instance, Prime Minister Hara Kei, who had been struggling against the army and the aristocratic political establishment of the Meiji *genrō*.[31] But in reality Yoshino could not carry with him the majority of intellectuals, let alone the general public, while the people in power were

[30] Important writings of Yoshino Sakuzō are collected in *Yoshino Sakuzō Hakase minshushugi rombun shū*, 8 vols. (Tokyo, 1948). See particularly: "Kensei no hongi o toite sono yūshū no bi o nasu no michi o ronzu" (1916); "Kokka seikatsu no isshin" (1910); "Taigai-teki ryōshin no hakki" (1919). A detailed survey of the life and ideas of Yoshino is to be found in Tanaka Sōgorō, *Yoshino Sakuzō* (Tokyo, 1958).

[31] See *Hara Kei nikki* (Tokyo, 1951, particularly during the decision of the Siberian Intervention [1917-1918]). On the role of Hara Kei in the Foreign Policy Committee, see also James William Morley, *The Japanese Thrust into Siberia* (New York, 1957).

preparing the means of counterattack against the "excessive" liberal trends which in their opinion prevailed in the 1920's. Yoshino Sakuzō strove for "democratization," and consequently for political modernization, in so far as the latter goes together with the former. He failed for two reasons: liberalism of his kind was first overwhelmed by Marxism; and then in the 1930's it was crushed by ultra-nationalism.

This is not the place to discuss in detail the reasons why Marxism became so popular in the 1920's among urban intellectuals. Several points, however, may be made. First, Marxism was quite popular in the late 1920's and early 1930's not only among Japanese intellectuals but also among many Western intellectuals.[32] The Japanese phenomenon was thus not an isolated one. Secondly, Japanese had, in contrast with the Europeans, no powerful tradition of socialistic thinking except Marxism with which to cope with the acute labor problems aggravated by depressions. Thirdly, urban intellectuals had no close links with the working mass, the majority of whom, whether on farms or in factories, were not organized.[33] Relatively isolated intellectuals were inclined to subscribe to radical political ideas.

One of the major concerns of the Marxists was to know exactly in what respects the economic structure of the country was modernized and in what respects not; what kind of basic "contradictions" were embodied in the "infra-structure" of Japanese society after the First World War, and what further developments were to be expected in the future. Noro Eitarō (1901-1934), for example, the most influential theoretician of the Marxist group of that time, pointed out the contrast between the modernized industries and the unmodernized agricultural sectors. In his terms this was the basic contradiction between the monopolistic stage of industrial-finance capital and the semi-feudal stage of agricultural production.

[32] To mention only a few examples: André Malraux, André Gide, Stephen Spender, Ignatio Silone.

[33] In 1930 less than 10 percent of the factory-workers were organized; and we must assume that non-organized workers had practically no contact whatever with any of the leftist intelligentsia.

439

Further, he predicted in 1930 the coming war, in which Japan would come into conflict with other capitalist countries in her demand for redistribution of colonies.[34]

Then the war came; starting in September 1931 in Manchuria, it spread to north China, then to the whole of China and finally to the whole of the Pacific. To be sure, Japan's leaders always used the argument of "haves" and "have nots," almost exactly as Noro had predicted. During the fifteen years of the war practically all Japanese writers were forced to support it, directly or indirectly. The attitudes not only of the writers but of all the intellectuals of the time can be divided roughly into three categories. First, some who were determinedly against the war had to keep silence, either in prison, or on country farms, or in sanatoria, or somewhere else. Second, some others were converted, on the contrary, to a sort of ultra-nationalism as a reaction to the Westernization drive and the liberalism of the 1920's. Third, most of the leading intellectuals of the time tried to justify the war not with fanaticism but in a somewhat rational manner.[35]

Thus the war made the intellectuals consider once again the role and meaning of Japanese culture as a whole in the international community. The discussions of two groups in 1942[36]

[34] Noro Eitarō, *Nihon shihon-shugi hattatsu shi,* Iwanami Bunko (Tokyo, 1954). As for the program of the Communist Party at that time, it was almost nothing but the demand for provisions included in the present Constitution: abolition of sovereignty of the Emperor; nationalization of large private lands without compensation; abolition of the House of Peers and Privy Council; abolition of the army; universal suffrage; freedom of expression, meeting, and assembly; eight-hour day labor; fixed minimum wage; social security; legal recognition of trade unions. If one put "abolition of the large landowner system" instead of "nationalization of large private lands without compensation," one would get almost exactly Japan's present democratic system. What the Communist Party wanted in the 1920's the American Occupation did in the 1940's.

[35] It is impossible here to enumerate the names of writers for each category. On the subject the following works are useful: Hirano Ken, "Shōwa," Chapter 3, "Shōwa Jūnen-dai," in *Gendai Nihon bungaku shi, op.cit.*; also Shisō no Kagaku Kenkyū Kai (ed.): *Tenkō,* Heibonsha (Tokyo, 1959).

[36] *Kindai no chōkoku* (Tokyo, 1943). Participants in this symposium

—the philosophers of Kyoto University on one hand, and a group of writers of the *Bungakkai* on the other—may be the most representative of this type of intellectual reaction to the war. The points made in these discussions can be summed up as follows. First, Japan's historic mission was to be a leader of the Asian countries. This point was not new. All the nationalism of the Meiji period had again and again preached the same ideal. Second, Japan's cultural mission was not to modernize itself, but to go beyond modern civilization, because modern civilization was now becoming decadent in its very core. This new point of view on modernization was called the theory of "overcoming modern civilization." For the first time after the Meiji Restoration Japanese intellectuals were aware of the serious difficulties which may be inherent in modern civilization itself. Unfortunately, this new point of view was introduced during the war and under the very strong pressures toward chauvinism of the militaristic regime. Inevitably, the new point of view did not serve accurately to illuminate the problems of modernization, but rather to falsify the picture of the imperialistic war. Because of the war the theory of "overcoming modern civilization" was doomed to become a tool of militant anti-western nationalists.

So it was not until the end of the Second World War that the modernization of the country as a whole became once again one of the major concerns of Japanese intellectuals and writers. As in the Meiji period, modernization is again identified with Westernization, or more recently, at least to some extent, with Americanization. Under the Occupation most of the modernization of institutions was based on American models and the modernization of most of the industries was also effected by the introduction of American technology. Japanese society and traditions were all put on trial not by the Americans but by the Japanese themselves in terms of

---

were Kamei Katsuichirō, Nishitani Keiji, Moroi Saburō, Yoshimitsu Yoshihiko, Hayashi Fusao, Shimomura Toratarō, Tsumura Hideo, Miyoshi Tatsuji, Kikuchi Masashi, Nakamura Mitsuo, Kawakami Tetsutarō, Suzuki Shigetaka, Kobayashi Hideo.

democracy. Historians separated Japanese history from the myth of the origins of the Imperial line to reveal to the astonished public the objective images of the nation's past.[37] Political scientists explained for the first time in scientific terms the mechanism of Japanese fascism and traced its course from the Manchurian invasion to the surrender.[38] Sociologists pointed out the predominance of small communities in Japanese society and particularly the institution of the patriarchal family.[39] Students of foreign literature, having regained contact with the outside world, argued that the Japanese writers had been far behind the Westerners in new ideas and techniques.[40] All this demonstrated a widespread realization of Japan's backwardness. This backwardness was now to be overcome by a new wave of modernization; this was a sort of second *kaikoku* or opening of the country. On the level of ideas this can be explained to some extent also as a sort of reaction to the "overcoming modern civilization" myth during the war.

In the last decade, however, this renewed drive toward Westernization has slowed down. One cause of this is revived nationalism which has not been accompanied, as have previous upsurges of nationalism, by anti-Westernism. Rather, it is marked by the introduction of new points of view which separate modernization from Westernization.

First of all, modernization is no longer seen as a phenomenon peculiar to Japan, but the major concern of most Asian nations. As most of those nations are former colonies and their nationalism is tied closely with anti-colonialism, mod-

[37] This is most obvious when we compare the textbooks of Japanese history before and after the last war. See Karasawa Tomitarō: *Kyōkasho no rekishi* (Tokyo, 1956). Also Kindai Nihon Kyōiku Seido Shiryō Hensan Kai (ed.): *Kindai Nihon kyōiku seido shiryō*, 33 vols. (Tokyo, 1956-1958).

[38] For example, Maruyama Masao, *Gendai seiji no shisō to kodō*, 2 vols. (Tokyo, 1957).

[39] For example, Kawashima Takeyoshi, *Nihon shakai no kazokuteki kōsei* (Tokyo, 1948).

[40] For example, Nakamura Mitsuo, *Fūzoku shōsetsu ron* (Tokyo, 1950).

ernization as a national aim in those countries cannot be identified with Westernization, at least in aspiration. This change of international environment has given a strong impulse to the students of Japanese modernization. Writers, like Takeuchi Yoshimi,[41] are inclined to reconsider the whole process of Japanese modernization in the context of the modernization of Asia as a whole. This trend in my opinion cannot be regarded as a revival of the old conception of "Japan as a leader of Asia" because these writers are prepared rather to learn from other nations' experiences than to look down on the backwardness of these neighbors. They advocate no more modernization for *fukoku kyōhei*, but instead modernization combined with anti-colonialism.

Secondly, at the national level, democratic institutions after the war and industrial prosperity in the 1950's have altogether changed the way of urban, and even of rural, life in Japan. Most of the troubles and unsolved problems are now no longer mainly due to a low but to a high degree of modernization. From traffic jams to juvenile delinquency, from mass communications to protective policies for agriculture, from abstract art to electronic music, these are not to be found in non-modernized countries, but are found everywhere in modernized countries. From this situation retrospectively, for instance, Umezao Tadao[42] argues that there is no significant difference between Japanese and Western societies, in contrast with all other Asian countries, and that the modernization of Japan has been not the process of Westernization but a process which happened to be parallel to that of the West. Exaggerated though it may be, this view goes together with the academic trends in Japan and abroad which emphasize the influence of internal rather than external factors on the process of modernization, and particularly stress the preconditions for the whole process present in Tokugawa Japan.

In her modern history Japan has seen three periods in

[41] Takeuchi Yoshimi, "Nihon to Ajiya," in *Sekai no naka no Nihon*, (*Kindai Nihon shisōshi kōza*, vol. 8) (Tokyo, 1961).

[42] Umezao Tadao, "Bummei no seitai shikan josetsu," *Chūō kōron*, February 1957.

which the country was very receptive to Western ideas. Each of the three periods followed immediately upon a great change in society: first, the Meiji Reform; second, the First World War; third, the Second World War. Each of them continued roughly for ten or fifteen years. Each was succeeded by a period of nationalism, in which the country was rather closed to Western ideas, ethical and political. In other words, there has been an alternating cycle of the periods of two different inclinations, toward the West and toward the Japanese traditions.

The views of the most representative Japanese writers about modernization and its implications, as reviewed briefly in this paper, should be understood against this background of the alternating cycle. The period of inclination toward the West is marked by liberal political trends with a special emphasis on civil rights; the period of nationalism, in contrast, manifests conservative political trends with an emphasis on the overriding importance of the state. During the first liberal period the arguments for the "rights of the people" and for the "rights of the state" were bridged by a compromise on both sides. Then they were divided once for all during the following period of nationalism which culminated with the Japanese military victory over Tsarist Russia. With the exception of Mori Ōgai, perhaps most writers thereafter took the stand of tolerating or ignoring the state, as did Natsume Sōseki or Nagai Kafū. In the 1920's, during the second liberal period, there was an attempt, for instance by Yoshino Sakuzō, to reconcile the "rights of the people" and the "rights of the state"—liberalism within and national interests abroad. But the war which started in the early 1930's quickly overwhelmed any kind of liberalism before it could get a solid foundation. Then came the third drive for Westernization under the Occupation, followed by the recent nationalist reactions. Today it is a matter for speculation whether the old controversy of the rights of the people and of the state is going to be reconciled in the near future. There are some signs that this may occur, but other evidence is to the contrary. In my opinion, in the foreseeable future, the majority of writers

444

will remain in opposition to the political power of the state. As for the cultural modernization, the situation has largely changed in the last decade; it is now regarded rather as achieved than as a goal to be achieved, more as an inevitable process than as a kind of national aspiration.

CHAPTER XIII

Modernization and the Japanese Intellectual: Some Comparative Observations

HERBERT PASSIN

A MODERN society requires a modern intellectual class. In one sense, this is a circular statement, because "presence of a modern intellectual class" is one of the constitutive, defining elements of "modern society." The intellectual is both the subject and the object of modernization. He is its initiator (or one of its important initiators), if only in the sense that without the presence of some intellectuals with at least some elements of modernity of outlook or aspiration the process can scarcely get under way. And he is also one of its characteristic products. Once a society enters the cycle of modernization, it commits itself, wittingly or not, to dependence on a many-sided class of modern intellectuals.

It was perhaps de Tocqueville who first pointed out the significance of intellectuals in post-1789 revolutions: the intellectuals turn against the *ancien régime*, and what had hitherto been abstract speculation among a narrow class of literati and educated people, more or less isolated from the centers of power, becomes a driving force in national politics. ". . . [Why] was it," he asks, "that men of letters [read 'intellectuals'—HP], men without wealth, social eminence, responsibilities, or official status, became in practice the leading politicians of the age, since despite the fact that others held the reins of government, they alone spoke with accents of authority?"[1] ". . . [Our] writers now became the leaders of public opinion and played for a while the part which normally, in free countries, falls to the professional politi-

[1] Alexis de Tocqueville, *The Old Régime and the French Revolution* (Garden City, New York, Doubleday and Co., Doubleday Anchor Books, 1955), pp. 139-140.

447

cian."[2] "Never before had the entire political education of a great nation been the work of its men of letters and it was this peculiarity that perhaps did most to give the French Revolution its exceptional character and the regime that followed it the form we are familiar with."[3]

What for de Tocqueville had been a "peculiarity" of the French Revolution has become the common characteristic of all modernizing movements since that time, whether revolutions or independence movements. The intellectuals spread discontent and give systematic form to criticism and alternative possibilities; they take a leading part in the work of transformation and modernization; and once the new institutions are created, they often take a leading part in their operation.

But while in the Western world these developments emerge more or less organically, as it were, from the pre-existing matrix of culture, institutions, and ideas, the development in the non-Western world appears more discontinuous, a more drastic break with pre-existing institutions. It is possible to exaggerate both the continuity in the Western world and the discontinuity in the non-Western world. From a certain point of view the Western world of today is as different from the Western world of, say, the year 1600 as the modernizing non-Western society is from its own immediate past,[4] and in much the same way. The Western past was also a traditional society, with its domination of sacred over secular elements,[5] its low

[2] *Ibid.*, p. 142.   [3] *Ibid.*, p. 146.

[4] The urbanization of peasant or isolated farming communities in the West is, in principle, a similar process. Even in the United States we have many enclaves of "folk" society, in the Deep South, in the Ozarks, etc. What has been happening to them, a process thoroughly documented by rural sociologists and local historians, is strictly comparable to what is happening in the non-Western world: the breaking open of isolated organic societies, which are relatively self-sufficient, through the expansion of communications and transportation, the spread of education, and the penetration of a money economy to replace traditional systems of barter and local exchange. The social and psychological changes are no less drastic and unsettling.

[5] Takeyama Michio has even argued that secularization, in the modern sense, began earlier in Japan than in the Western world.

mobility and hierarchy, its preference for stability and order rather than change. To the pre-Cartesian Western world, the notion of "progress" could have been no less alien than it first appeared to the peoples of the Far East; but in the West it seems to emerge from within, while in the East it arrives with a foreign label. New elements are injected, radioactively tagged, as it were, into the bloodstream of the traditional societies; as they circulate, wreaking their changes, their foreign (that is their Western) provenience cannot be forgotten. The change from traditional to modern society, therefore, requires in principle as thorough-going a transformation of ideas, ideals, and institutions in the West as in the East. But while the West has been making this transition over centuries, non-Western peoples have had to accomplish it within one or two generations under conditions of implicit or explicit pressure.

To speak of "intellectuals" and their "influence" obliges us to give some idea, however inconclusive, of what we mean by these terms. It would be useless to linger too long over the exact delimitation of the class of intellectuals, or whether they are truly a "class," a "stratum," or a "functional group." The definitions we use will ultimately be normative, and this implies either a point of view or a particular problem in mind.

Perhaps the most useful for our purposes will be the distinction between "intelligentsia" and "intellectuals." Historically, "intelligentsia" has always implied a critical posture toward authority, traditional culture, and the Establishment. This distinction is undoubtedly a useful one for countries like Russia, and we shall also find an important strand of "intelligentsia" in the history of the intellectual classes in Japan. It is also a useful term to distinguish the great intellectual figures of late Tokugawa and early Meiji days, who esteemed general knowledge and culture and devoted themselves to the cultivation of a world view, from mere technical specialists.

Another criterion commonly proposed is that of "true" creativity, or "true" intellectual quality, or as it might otherwise be phrased, between "real intellectuals" and "technicians"

449

—the primary, creative producers of ideas and intellectual products and the diffusers and consumers of these products. There is nothing wrong with this definition for the elucidation of particular problems. What is difficult is defining the qualities that it implies—how able is able? how wise is wise?— and its degrees. While the extremes are always clear, the borderlines are usually blurred. Most people would probably agree that teachers are in some sense intellectuals. But where do we draw the line? University professors?—with some reservations, most people would accept their inclusion among intellectuals. But what about university students? Perhaps we can call them "incipient" intellectuals. Then what about those who lie on the borderline—the graduate students, students engaged in advanced research, just-employed junior lecturers? Or, to move down another line, should we include high school teachers, or only those in advanced positions, or only those who clearly evince intellectual interests and pre-occupations? Then, what about elementary school teachers?

In many countries the elementary school teacher is undoubtedly an intellectual and an extremely important, often self-conscious, modernizing force. This is particularly the case in the early stages of modern development, and it remains true even today in many Japanese villages, where the school teacher and the doctor are the local intellectuals. But once the higher ranks of the intellectuals have differentiated themselves and produced some achievements, the elementary school teachers are no longer so important. It may be that this is a function of the stage of modernization of the society. In the transitional and early modern period, the class of intellectuals is small. In the extremest cases, as in certain African countries, it can be described as any and everyone having any degree of modern education. But with the growth of modern institutions and the increase in the number of educated persons, the educated class differentiates and even stratifies. Elements that were once important become less so; new elements, or new types of intellectuals that were unimportant or that may not even have existed before, now become important. Standing at this point in time, we are often too far from the modernizing generation to see its composition clearly. Our tendency is to project backwards in time the present composition that we see before us. A rather remote example may perhaps illustrate this point.

Recently I spent a few weeks revisiting the Tarahumara Indians of Mexico after an absence of 20 years. What struck me most was the appearance of what, with all due misgiving, can only be called the beginnings of a Tarahumara "intelligentsia," that is, somewhat Mexicanized young people, educated in local schools, able to speak Spanish, teaching school, serving government authorities as interpreters, self-conscious mediators (between their people and the government) and leaders of their people on the path of "civilization." It is true that their education rarely goes beyond four years of fairly crude schooling, that the Spanish they speak is poor, and that they can scarcely be said to have been deeply touched by modern ideas (few of them read anything at all), but for all that they are still a new elite in the process of taking over leadership from the traditional authorities. Are they "intellectuals"? By Tarahumara standards they are, and in the view of the Mexicans they are at least "incipient intellectuals." What is important is that these semi-educated school teachers —for most of them are or were such—are going to transform their people. I do not like the kind of transformation that is going to take place—I think it will be a de-Indianization rather than a real Mexicanization. But this lowest of all possible low-grade "intellectuals" will be responsible for doing it.

The Soviets draw the lines simply: "workers of brain" as against "workers of hand."[6] The "toiling intelligentsia," by this definition, would automatically include the entire class of white-collar workers, businessmen, managers, bankers, etc. This, I think, would be going too far, for any purposes. There are certainly individuals and groups among white-collar

[6] Joseph Stalin, *Problems of Leninism* (Moscow, Foreign Languages Publishing House), pp. 559-560, 638-640; also see Leopold Labedz, "The Structure of the Soviet Intelligentsia," in Richard Pipes (ed.), *The Russian Intelligentsia* (New York, Columbia University Press, 1961).

workers, businessmen, and even the military who should properly be included among the intellectuals on the basis of certain normative criteria, but not all.

A useful working definition would have to make some reference to the element of self-awareness and self-consciousness. In Japan the saying goes that intellectuals are those who read (or carry about) the *sōgō-zasshi* or opinion magazines. Although I do not agree with this, it does touch on the element of self-awareness, which if not fully definitive, at least distinguishes between whatever we may try to express by the notion of a "higher" and a "lower" intellectual class. This is not the place to settle the problem of definition, but I would offer the proposal that we consider the intellectuals a self-aware body of educated persons who by vocation, interest, or disposition deal with or are concerned with general ideas and issues that go beyond purely technical and professional matters. Some—perhaps a growing number—will make their living from intellectual activity; but others may not.

The problem of "influence" also requires a brief comment. Depending upon one's premises, it is as easy to argue that intellectuals are isolated and ineffectual as that they are profoundly influential and powerful, that they are "rootless" as that they are functionally important. The Russian Bolsheviks expended a prodigious exegetical energy to prove the *petit-bourgeois* nature—and therefore, by implication, the insignificance and ineffectiveness—of intellectuals, when it was these very intellectuals who were forming Lenin's vanguard. Each such proposition, however it appears to contradict another equally plausible one, can be defended under certain circumstances. The reason is that they derive from the particular problem we are dealing with or from our view of the nature of power in society and upon just exactly what we mean by such terms as "influence" and "importance." "How many divisions has the Pope?" is not always the final answer to the question of influence. If we are speaking of direct influence, let us say, on the number of votes cast for a particular party or policy, we might conclude, as many people do all too easily, that intellectuals have no effect. But is this the best measure of influence? American businessmen, we are told, generally support the Republican Party, and presumably put all their weight behind it. Yet this has not always prevented the Democrats from winning national elections. Does this mean that businessmen have no influence, that they are isolated, ineffective, etc.?

Another chain of reasoning runs somewhat as follows: intellectuals have their own political aims; these are not achieved in the form they urge; *therefore* intellectuals have no influence. In Japan, for example, most intellectuals favor neutralism, etc., but in spite of their articulateness, it is the "real" powerholders who decide; *therefore* Japanese intellectuals have no influence. This, it seems to me, is a demonstrably naïve argument. Quite obviously what we need is a more pluralistic conception of power and influence, perhaps one that permits us to see "degree" of influence or the actual outcome as the complex emergent of many competing forces. In this view, we should have no trouble demonstrating that intellectuals are, in fact, very important. Moreover, the specific weight of the intellectuals in the power constellation or in the balance of power, varies from country to country. It therefore does have significance—and tells us much about the nature of particular power structures—that in Japan and France, for example, intellectuals are very influential, while in the United States, to accept for the moment the conventional argument,[7] they are not.

Antecedents

If we take the Tarahumara Indians at one end and Japan at the other, it is apparent that "non-Western" societies differ conspicuously in their readiness for producing a modern intellectual class. To take a less extreme example—Africa— although there are undoubtedly some antecedents of an intel-

[7] Personally I think the "ineffectuality" of intellectuals in the United States is very often overstated. See, for example, Seymour Martin Lipset, "American Intellectuals: Their Politics and Status," *Daedalus*, Summer 1959.

lectual class—perhaps among priests, chiefs, diviners, minstrels, artists, musicians, etc.—a true modern intellectual class has had to be created virtually *de novo* from among young people exposed to the metropolitan civilization, whether in the metropolis itself or in the local schools. The worst case among the existing states, the Belgian Congo, seems now, in many respects, to have been hardly better prepared for modern life than the Tarahumara Indians.

But when we come to the great non-Western civilizations, such as Japan, China, India, the Islamic world, and Southeast Asia, the starting point for modernization is entirely different. They all have at the outset a fairly numerous and differentiated intellectual class, and a powerful literate tradition in the arts, literature, religion, and speculative philosophy.[8] From the standpoint of modernization, it should be noted, this is not all advantage. An adaptable intellectual class can exert more leadership and modernize more easily; however, as against this, the weight of tradition, which has its own structure, canons, and vested interests, can interfere with the acceptance of new elements.

Japan in this respect was perhaps the most advanced, the most "ready." Pre-Meiji Japan could pride itself on a rather considerable panoply of intellectual life. By the end of Tokugawa there were about 17,000 schools of all types, from the high-level Shogunal and fief institutions, through private schools, to the extensive network of *terakoya* (parish schools) and other types of elementary schools. Recent analyses suggest the conclusion that early Meiji Japan may have started out with something over 40 percent male literacy. The large numbers of educated people of all classes provided the arena for a very considerable intellectual life. Intellectual career lines were definable, and large numbers of people found it possible to carry on the life of the intellectual, the poet, the writer, and the artist, and were even able to make their living at it.

At the base of intellectual life was the school system, which

[8] I have discussed this problem at some length in "Writer and Journalist in Transitional Society," in Lucian Pye (ed.) *Communication and Political Development* (Princeton, Princeton University Press, 1963).

expanded rapidly in the second half of the Tokugawa period.

SCHOOLS OF VARIOUS TYPES, BY DATE OF ESTABLISHMENT[a]

	Domain Schools (hankō[b])	Semi-official Local Schools (gōgaku[c])	Parish Schools (terakoya[d])	Private Academies (shijuku[e])
Before 1750	31	0	141	?
After 1750	223	568	11,199	1,500

[a] These data are taken without correction from standard Japanese sources. For a discussion of how seriously they underestimate the actual situation, see Chapter 2 and Appendix III of my *Society and Education in Japan* (New York, Columbia University, Teachers College, 1964). Apart from the underestimation in the listed categories, a number of school types, such as military-training (especially fencing) schools, are left out entirely.

[b] From Ishikawa Ken: *Kinsei no gakkō* (Tokyo, 1957), p. 264.

[c] Summarized from *ibid.*, pp. 267-268.

[d] These are summarized from an earlier estimate by Ishikawa Ken, in his *Nihon shomin kyōiku-shi.* (Tokyo, 1929). His later estimates, as given in *Kinsei shomin kyōiku-shi,* are somewhat below this.

[e] My own general summary from various sources.

The most substantial component of the intellectual classes of Tokugawa Japan was the samurai. It would not be far wrong to say that virtually all samurai males had received some education and, increasingly toward the end of the era, one that went well beyond the elementary levels. The most important centers for their training were the *hankō* (fief schools) and the higher institutions established by the Bakufu. However, samurai education was carried on in other types of school as well. Many, for example, studied in the private academies (*shijuku*) that were found throughout the country. In some cases students started their education in lower-level *shijuku* and then went on to *hankō* or one of the shogunal schools. In other cases education started first in the *hankō*, after which a more ambitious or intellectually curious student went to one of the more advanced *shijuku*. Following the sharp increase of officially sponsored schools for commoners (*gōgaku*), starting in the 1850's, many samurai boys, particularly in remoter areas distant from the castle towns and the *hankō*, attended them for at least part of their education, often alongside commoners. In the final decades of the Tokugawa period samurai children were even beginning to attend *terakoya*. Nor should we overlook the fact that rather large numbers received part or all of their schooling from private tutors at home and that many, at one stage or another of their careers, attended military-training schools, particularly the fencing academies, where the curriculum was not limited to military subjects. Although samurai women did not usually attend schools, there can be no question that a fairly high degree of literacy was not uncommon among them. Most of this education would have been acquired through private tutors.

But weighty as the samurai element was in the educated classes of immediate pre-Meiji Japan, it was not the only one. Although the court nobility (*kuge*) was small in numbers, in general it attained rather high levels of education. Far more numerous were the clerics. In the many monasteries and temples, with their thousands of monks, their libraries, their patronage of the arts, intellectual life of a kind was also carried on. However, by contrast with the Muromachi period, clerical intellectual life of the late Tokugawa period was no longer the main channel but rather a relatively quiet backwater.

Perhaps the most significant development of late Tokugawa was the emergence of the lower feudal orders. This was manifested in the enormous growth of commoner schooling, particularly in the *terakoya* and the *gōgaku*. In the more advanced metropolises of Edo, Osaka, and Kyoto, as well as in the leading commercial cities, the end of the Tokugawa period saw a majority, at least of the upper strata, of the merchant class (*shōnin*) acquiring some education, and very often of a rather high level. A substantial proportion of students in the private academies were of merchant origin, and in some cases they constituted a majority. Already in 1680 Itō Jinsai's Kyoto school, one of the most important of the *shijuku*, had many *shōnin* students. The *kokugaku* (Japanese learning) school of Motoori, who was himself of *shōnin* origin, had some 500 pupils, almost all of them from merchant families. The growing aspirations and needs of the *shōnin* class brought about the establishment of schools specifically for their needs.

Although it was usually considered that the higher realms of Confucianism and philosophy were only for those destined for political rule—the samurai—the *shōnin* schools were not limited to practical studies for the successful merchant. Some of them, as in the case of the Kaidoku-dō of Osaka, were based on the adaptation of Confucianism to the needs and role of the merchant class, a kind of *shōnin* Confucianism. *Shingaku*, and perhaps even *Hōtoku-kyō*, can in one aspect be understood in this way—the application of Confucian ethics to the daily life of the common people: self-training *and* the accumulation of wealth; honesty, frugality, obedience to the laws, proper control of the family, and the morality of earning and spending money.

The *gōgaku*, and related types of officially supported schools, were originally designed to provide a higher level of training, with greater emphasis on virtue, for the village notable class, the *shōya*, *toshiyori*, and *kumi-gashira*, than was available in the *terakoya*. Soon these schools began to have mixed attendance of upper peasants, samurai, *gōshi* (rural samurai), and merchants. And many of the *terakoya* themselves, particularly in the more advanced urban and even rural areas, began to provide a richer curriculum for peasant children than the three R's (or, more accurately, two R's, because arithmetic was much less commonly given). As a result of these developments, better-educated members of the merchant classes, the *gōshi*, and the upper peasant strata increasingly manifested a style and intellectual activities similar to those of the educated samurai.

A considerable part of intellectual life was also carried on by groups not clearly identified with the well-defined classes of Tokugawa Japan—scholars, doctors, artists, Nagasaki interpreters, actors, calligraphers, musicians.[9] In some cases they may have sprung from samurai or, more likely, *rōnin* families, but in the course of time they came to constitute a kind of hereditary intellectual class. By the end of the Toku-

[9] See John Hall's illuminating picture of the life of the intellectual during the Tokugawa period in his "The Confucian Teacher in Tokugawa Japan," in David S. Nivison and Arthur F. Wright (eds.), *Confucianism in Action* (Stamford University Press, 1959).

gawa era, these traditional intellectuals who did not fit clearly into the official niches of the legal class structure were very numerous. The higher and more esteemed branches were accorded a samurai-like treatment and status. In the case of the (officially employed) *goyō-gakusha*, or even of favored and patronized artists and scholars not retained in official employment, rice stipends at roughly the ranges of the lower and middle samurai were granted.[10] But the significant point —because it is so "modern"—is that large numbers were able to live from their own writing, teaching, and other services.

If we include artistic life, as I think we should in order to understand the development of a modern intellectual class in Japan, it will be clear that there was a very broad base for intellectual life. Perhaps most artists came from samurai families, but there were many who came from merchant or even lower origins, and many "schools" and "families" that had their own tradition, quite independent of the official classes. The schools of great painters, sculptors, potters, calligraphers, etc. form to some extent a social entity of their own, a stratum that does not fit precisely into the traditional *shi-nō-kō-shō* (warriors-farmers-craftsmen-merchants) division. Musicians showed a complete range from those in official employment in the courts (imperial, shogunal, and domainal), temples and shrines, established schools and families, down to itinerant minstrels and strolling players. While the upper levels were treated on the same level as officials, the lower ranks, often shifting in composition, were even from time to time classified among the outcaste *hinin*.[11] (The borderline between "art" and "entertainment" has never been entirely clear.)

The problem of the writers was much more complex. Certainly by Genroku Japan had developed many of the charac-

---

[10] See Hall, *ibid.*, on the stipends of the *jusha* and *juin*.

[11] The *hinin* were officially designated as a special group in late Tokugawa times, although they were often spoken of together with the *eta* as the *eta-hinin*. While the *eta* were a relatively stable caste, the *hinin* consisted of floaters of many kinds—criminal elements, itinerant actors, musicians, prostitutes, etc. A similar distinction between stable and floating outcaste elements is made, by the way, in Korea also. (See my "The Paekchōng: A Brief Social History," *Monumenta Nipponica*, 1956.)

teristics of modern literary life: free-lance writers able to make their living from the sale of their work; a well-developed and organized publishing and distribution industry; a sizable audience of high literacy and taste. While many of the writers were of samurai origin, they turned themselves primarily to the tastes and interests of the growing commercial and urban sector, which often made them, even if only by implication, critical of official society. In the theatre as well, a very considerable body of actors was able to sustain itself through public support, not only official patronage.

It would be a useful exercise to try to estimate the numbers of these intellectuals (whatever the criteria we use) in the immediate pre-Meiji period. I think we would be surprised by both their amplitude and their "modernity."

In spite of the many different elements going into the composition of the educated classes of late Tokugawa times, it was, by and large, the samurai and their preoccupations that gave form to its intellectual life. The most representative type were the *jusha*, the professional Confucians. They dominated the centers of orthodoxy, led in the training of the future leaders, and were close to the councils of government. Nevertheless, their position was increasingly challenged by new elements. These have been so well described by intellectual historians of the period that it would be presumptuous to repeat the details here. Very briefly, however, the various schools of thought were potentially—and more and more, as time went on, actually—in conflict with each other. Orthodox Chu Hsi thought itself was subject to different interpretations and different weights and emphasis could be assigned to its several components. One could emphasize learning for rulership or for self-training; the study of first principles (virtue and ethics) or of natural phenomena (*kyūri*). The Wang Yang-ming version of Confucianism emphasized, even more explicitly, the importance of objective knowledge and practical learning. *Kokugaku* ("national scholarship") not only offered a basis for the potential subversion of the legitimacy of the Bakufu, but in Motoori's version argued that learning—including poetry and history—could be pursued for its own sake, not only in the interests of political rule. *Ran-*

gaku ("Dutch" learning) was potentially the most subversive. But in the famous formula of Sakuma Shōzan's *"Tōyō no dōtoku, seiyō no gei"* (Eastern morality, Western skills), it was partially domesticated.

The *rangaku* of independent scholars—of doctors and language students—became an official *rangaku*. Shogun Yoshimune had already given the warrant by holding that *yōgaku* (Western learning) was practical learning that might benefit the country, and that it need not be an obstacle to the "old learning." This was the basis for the willingness of the Bakufu to support Siebold's school, which was attended not only by private students but by Bakufu officials as well. The relative emphasis on practical learning and traditional ethics by different *rangaku* specialists varied subtly, but I leave the analysis of this problem to the intellectual historian. Suffice it to say, the line was a hard one to draw, and officials were prepared to crack down hard when it was overstepped. Watanabe Kazan and the other *rangakusha* were arrested in 1839 not because anyone questioned the practical benefits of Western learning but because they appeared to be on the verge of moving over to open political criticism. The Bakufu continued to support Western studies on an increasing scale after that, in 1856 establishing the crucially important *Bansho torishirabe-sho,* and *rangaku* spread rapidly throughout the domain schools and private academies and even as far down as some of the more advanced *terakoya*.

Until Perry's arrival (or, as some might argue, until the Tempō reforms) these debates were by and large theoretical. From then on, however, the issues become real, they become central to the expanding political struggle. The vague dissatisfactions now found their object—the new issues facing the country: financial reform, the control of prices, the presence of the foreigners, the threat of the West, the need for modernizing national defense, the apparent weaknesses of government structure.

By the end of the first half of the nineteenth century it is apparent that there was a large body of critical, ideologically orientated intellectuals, discontented with the condition of their own society, extremely responsive to new ideas and seeking new solutions. They constituted, in the sense of the Russian usage, a true intelligentsia. What affected this internal differentiation of the intellectual classes, who until this time had been more or less in accord with official society, was the challenge of the West. It was activated and given form not so much by the specific content of Western ideas as by its mere *présence*. It presented itself to them in a variety of ways, and a highly differentiated reaction began to take place. Some response had to be made, whether it was direct or indirect, accepting, reactive, or resistant. Suddenly the level of criticism and political thought began to rise. People were increasingly willing to debate the "conventional wisdom," whether to attack it, defend it, or revise it.

In this development the *rangaku* scholars started from a much more pro-Western position than the national scholars. But the national scholars too were responding to the West, seeking a solution in their own terms to the problems created by the West. Even Confucianists were making major adjustments. All, that is to say, whether we consider them "progressive" or "reactionary," were vitalized as it were, quickened by the growing awareness of the West, its power and ideas. The experience ended up somehow transforming, or at least touching, all. This dialogue, or dialectic, between the pre-existing body of Japanese ideas and the invading Western ideas, gave shape both to the reform and to the society that emerged after the reform.

There were very important elements of strength among the Japanese intelligentsia, in some cases strikingly different from their Russian counterparts of a slightly earlier period.[12] They had, first, as a result of their class origins, experience, and the pervasive Confucian ideas, a strong sense of public vocation. Whether in official employment or not, the concept of *meibun*—the duty of acting in accordance with one's status —led them to voice their criticism and propose their programs

[12] See the illuminating article by Martin Malia: "What is the Intelligentsia?", in Richard Pipes (ed.), *op.cit.*

openly, even at considerable personal risk.[13] Moreover, they showed a much greater readiness for practical work than do intelligentsia at corresponding stages of development in other countries. It is a refreshing contrast with the intellectuals of many "underdeveloped" countries today to see how many of them—and here the *yōgaku* schools are particularly important—devoted so much attention to practical matters, such as medicine, geography, economics, astronomy, zoology, national defense, coastal defense, armaments and ship design, as against genteel letters and moral commentary. Even orthodox Confucianism was willing to acknowledge—increasingly as we approach the Restoration itself—the importance of practical learning, however much it strained to confine it within permissible limits.

The modern intellectual classes in Japan, therefore, did not spring into existence full formed from the brow of Zeus but rather evolved from antecedent structures and situations that were highly elaborated. It was men educated in the traditional society who led the way across the vital gap of modernity.

The Beginnings of the Modern Intellectual Classes

It is from within this class that both the leaders and the intelligentsia of the Restoration period came. They carried through the Restoration and created and operated the institutions of the new Japan. The closing struggles during the Shogunate made manifest a latent division that was largely independent of previously-held doctrinal positions—the supporters of the Restoration, most characteristically the *shishi*, and the opponents, intellectuals who sided with, or felt bound to, the Shogunate. Among both groups there were advocates of Chu Hsi, Wang Yang-ming, *rangaku, kokugaku*, and the many other views taking part in the national debates.

But it was the *shishi*[14] who provided the real leadership

---

[13] The Seibold Affair of 1828, for example, when eleven *yōgaku* specialists were imprisoned; or the experience of Watanabe Kazan, Takano Chōei, and Takashima Shūhan in the 1840's.

[14] Marius Jansen's phrase. See his "Men of High Purpose" in *Sakamoto Ryoma and the Meiji Restoration*, Princeton, Princeton University

of the Restoration movement. Starting out as han samurai, they took part in han politics, sometimes in and sometimes out of office, winning over their han or being exiled from them, engaging in illegal activities and plots. In the end, they overthrew the Shogunate and became themselves the new modernizing bureaucrats of the Meiji government.

Closely associated with them were what might be called the Bakufu intellectuals, men who felt committed by feudal or personal bonds to the Tokugawa and therefore could not fully join the Restoration movement at the start. Most of them had been trained in the higher Bakufu institutions, particularly the Kaiseijo (the successor to the *Bansho torishirabe-sho*), and were extremely well-educated and knowledgeable about the West. In many respects they were probably better qualified than the *shishi*, who were men of a rather rougher cut, and although in general they supported the main aims of the Restoration, they tended to be somewhat critical of methods. Katō Hiroyuki, Nishi Amane, and Kanda Takahira were all examples of this type. Fukuzawa, who held himself aloof from the final Restoration battles, should perhaps be classified with them.

Another group consisted of samurai from Bakufu territories or from fiefs that did not join the Restoration side. In some cases restrained by the feeling that they could not serve two masters, in others simply excluded from the new councils of government, most of them were from the outset critical of the new government. It was from this group that many of the early journalists and teachers came, and it also provided many of the supporters of the out-of-office *shishi* who started the *jiyū minken* movement. The oppositionist tradition of Japanese journalism was thus very early entrenched, as was the "interventionism" that has characterized official attitudes toward education.

These were the principal groups forming the political

Press, 1961 and Albert Craig (*Chōshū in the Meiji Restoration*, Cambridge, Harvard University Press, 1961), as well as Thomas Smith's review, "The Discontented," *Journal of Asian Studies*, vol. 21, No. 2, February 1962.

leadership of the early Restoration period. In business and other areas of national life, different combinations were beginning to emerge, but for the early period it was the political elite that dominated the scene. Their character has left its imprint on the intellectual classes virtually down to modern times; it forms part of their tradition. First of all, most of them were of lower-samurai or equivalent origin. As samurai they counted themselves among the natural rulers of society. But as lowly samurai they felt themselves excluded from the higher positions of power and prestige. This gave their outlook a dual character that was in some respects unique among modernizing elites. Discontented, even alienated from the conditions of Bakumatsu society, they still remained deeply *engagé*. Yoshida Shōin's call for an uprising of the "unattached"—the *rōnin* and samurai detached from their feudal obligations—had to some extent been realized in practice. If the *shishi* best embodied Shōin's ideal, the others were not far behind in their strong sense of public vocation. Together they formed, in fact, a true political intelligentsia. They had not acted in the name of some well-formulated democratic revolutionary ideal of modern society, but in the end their struggle to rectify an unsatisfactory situation turned out to be more revolutionary than they might have intended.

Once the new government was established, most of them participated very closely in public affairs, whether by joining the government (or, very soon, the *minken* movement), or by their work in private schools, learned societies, and newspapers. Being out of office implied no lesser concern with public affairs than holding office. The oppositionist, from the wrong domain or active in a newspaper or small political association, had his mind on the same problems of state and society as government leaders and officials. When Fukuzawa Yukichi, for example, refused to take public office, he was not rejecting political obligations but on the contrary seeking a better platform for fulfilling them. The early debates on this question in the *Meirokusha* were not so much over the fun-

damental principle of the social responsibility of the intellectual as over the form in which it could best be expressed.

Samurai origin and the deep sense of public responsibility
also implied an elitist approach to problems. The educated
classes, whether samurai or non-samurai in origin, continued
to feel, as they had in feudal times, that it was for them to
lead and for the masses to follow. A large proportion of the
early school teachers were of samurai origin. Since teaching
had always been looked upon as *tenshoku* (heavenly calling),
it ranked along with government service, the police, and the
military as an honorable modern occupation for the natural
rulers of society. During the Edo period even commoner
teachers in the *terakoya* had been treated as samurai, and this
attitude continued into the early years of Meiji.

All of them were under the impress of the evident "superiority" of the West, its power, its science, its freedom of
speculative thought, its conspicuous achievements. They reacted differently, some by becoming worshipers of the West,
others by becoming implacable enemies; some by trying to
adjust Japan as much as necessary to be able to stand up to
the West, others by trying to restrain changes to the narrowest
limits consistent with national strength and growth. Although each separate response implied a different program
for Japan, the common element was the awareness of the
West, which weighed heavily upon them. It was necessary not
only to prevent Western domination but to pull level with the
West and win its respect. Therefore, they were concerned
with problems of "identity"—what is Japanese and what is
Western? are we as good as they?—preoccupations that manifest themselves over and over again in modern Japanese
history.

The leaders of early Meiji were public-spirited intellectuals, concerned with broad political and philosophical issues,
agitated by the problems of creating a "new Japanese man."
But this concept involved equal emphasis on both terms, the
"new" and the "Japanese." At the margins there were those
who rejected the "Japanese" part—extremely alienated, anti-

political intellectuals, many of whom became Christians, socialists, or advocates of particular Western cultures; and others who could see no solution but to reject the "new," or at least as much as did not appear to them absolutely necessary. This latter tendency found expression in the Saigō movement and in the growing "Japanism" which finally established itself firmly by the 1890's. The general reaction against the excesses of the "Western fever" was given form by it. Therefore many individuals who started out far on the pro-Western side ended up much more "conservative" and "pro-Japanist." The struggle was as much within individuals as among groups. But the main trend still remained, in general, the attempt to combine the two elements. Many of the political and intellectual differences that appeared reflected differences in the formula of accommodation rather than all-out advocacy of one or the other.

After the confusions of the immediate Restoration period, the first general policy that began to emerge was the *bummei kaika*. In 1873 Nishimura Shigeki, Mori Arinori, and Fukuzawa Yukichi, along with seven other leading intellectual figures, formed the *Meirokusha*. Almost all of them were of lower samurai origin and had been connected with the Bakufu's Kaiseijo, either as instructors or students. Although they were well grounded in the Chinese classics, most of them had had extensive contact with Western culture, through their substantive and language studies or through first-hand experience. They held leading positions in intellectual and public life, and at one time or another almost all of them held official positions in the government and were intimately associated with the political leaders. Therefore although most of them had not originally sided with the *shishi* and the Imperial Restorationists, they were committed to the new government and they played an active role in giving shape to the new ideas and institutions. *Bummei kaika* was pre-eminently their field. Their debates ranged over language problems, the role of the intellectual, the accommodation of Western ideas to the Japanese situation, and the institutional requirements of the new state. They wrote textbooks, as well as general works of enlightenment and information, and they carried on a vigorous public life, whether in or outside of office.

Other intellectuals, including educated provincial samurai, were equally active in their own way in the propagation of enlightenment and in shaping the outcome of debates over the new institutions. Many of them had become school teachers, and many who had been excluded from government office started a vigorous journalism, usually somewhat oppositionist. The early newspapers and journals were highly political and played an important part in the modern political education of the population.

But while these debates and movements were going on among the intellectual classes formed in Tokugawa times, Japan herself was undergoing changes. New political institutions were in formation; the economy was advancing along modern lines; and the new mass school system was gradually going into operation. The result was the beginning of important changes in the character of the intellectual classes, in their experience, and in the problems that confronted them. The new school system signaled the end of class education. While this had been underway in the closing years of the Bakufu, the '*gakusei*' (1872 Code of Education) made this an explicit part of official policy. The language of the new education, in the first flush of Western enthusiasm, was utilitarian, pragmatic, and almost individualistic. But it contained within itself several elements that began to make their importance felt later on—the notion of education as for the "sake of the country," and of the ruler sending his people to school. The Code had argued that education was so self-evidently in the interests of the people that they would spontaneously bear its burdens and take advantage of it. But Nishimura, after his 1877 survey of the school system, found it necessary to urge that the prestige of the government be used to *make* parents send their children to school.

The early response to the school system showed a differential readiness among the various elements of pre-Meiji society. The highest responsiveness was, as might have been expected, from the samurai and the higher merchant-class elements of the cities. As late as 1886,[15] for example, while 74 percent of samurai children in Mie Prefecture were attending school, only 53 percent of farm children and 37 percent of laborers' children were attending. In Saga Prefecture, in the same year, the corresponding proportions were: samurai, 62 percent; farmers, 39 percent; and laborers, 24 percent. Even more revealing than the gross rates of attendance was the internal composition of the school population. Of the samurai children attending school in Mie Prefecture, for example, 61 percent were in elementary schools, 34 percent in middle schools, and 5 percent in higher schools. For farmers' children, the corresponding proportions were 81, 18, and 1 ; for laborers' children, 85, 15, and 0.[16] The same differential readiness can be seen in the composition of the student body in higher educational institutions. In 1877 almost 80 percent of the students in the one and only university-level institution in the country, Tokyo Imperial, were of samurai origin.[17] By 1882 this percentage had gone down to 50 percent. (It should be remembered that samurai constituted approximately 5 percent of the total population.) In the next level of higher education, just below the university, we find a similar picture. A survey of 40 *shijuku* in Tokyo in 1873[18] revealed the following distribution:

samurai	80%
commoners	17
nobility	3

[15] Information in the next few sentences is summarized from Ministry of Education: *Dai-14 nenpo* (*Fourteenth Annual Report*) (Tokyo, 1886), p. 26.

[16] 0.15 per cent, to be exact. *Ibid.*

[17] Reported in a number of places, including, most recently, Ministry of Education, *Nihon no seichō to kyōiku* (*Japan's growth and education*) (Tokyo, 1962), p. 35.

[18] From a survey of private schools in Tokyo conducted in May 1873, cited in Tōyama Shigeki: "Ishin no henkaku to kindaiteki chishikijin no tanjō" ("The Restoration changes and the birth of the modern intellectual"), in *Kindai Nihon shisō-shi kōza* (*Lectures on the history of modern Japanese thought*), Vol. 4, *Chishikijin no seisei to yakuwari* (*The formation and role of intellectuals*) (Tokyo, Chikuma Shobo, 1959), p. 179.

In the normal schools,[19] which were early one of the important channels for attaining respectable social position, the overwhelming majority of the early students were of samurai origin. Of the 240 graduates of the Public School Division of the Tokyo Normal School between 1873 and 1878, 164 were samurai. Of the 12 graduating members of the Middle School Section of the same school in July 1878, 10 were samurai. The situation in the provincial normal schools was similar. In the Elementary School Course of the Kumamoto Normal School, for which we have relatively full data, we find the following:

COMPOSITION OF KUMAMOTO NORMAL SCHOOL STUDENT BODY[a]

Class Origin	1878-1887	1888-1897	1898-1907	1908-1917	1918-1927	1928-1932
Samurai	80	67	50	34	13	10
Commoner	20	33	50	66	87	90

[a] Summarized from data in Karasawa Tomitarō: *Kyōshi no rekishi* p. 86.

But by the 1880's, and particularly in the 1890's, the school system was increasingly successful in drawing in wider strata of the population. The popular resistance in certain areas, which in the 1870's had manifested itself in riots and school burnings, was over. Education was becoming self-evidently the pathway to success and attainment and was thereby bringing about changes in the composition of the educated classes.

Higher education became the channel for entering high position. For government, the main channel was the Imperial University (Tokyo was established in 1877, Kyoto in 1897). But higher education was also available in other institutions (although they were not accorded university status), such as the private academies, especially Keio and Waseda (established in 1882), the normal schools, and the military schools. Each opened the way to different careers and to different levels in the emergent status system. For graduates of the Imperial schools, high positions in government were

[19] The data in the remainder of this paragraph is taken from Karasawa Tomitarō: *Kyōshi no rekishi* (*The history of the teacher*) (Tokyo, Sōbun-sha, 1956), pp. 299, 86.

almost immediately available. Not only could they get high-paying government jobs, but until after the Sino-Japanese War, when Japanese industry made a major spurt forward, there was not much place for their skills outside of government. The private schools, particularly Keio, opened the way into business rather than government, but this too was a highly desired, if not quite so prestigious, career for the young men of early and middle Meiji. Although the normal schools appealed to the samurai for a period, they soon fell into disfavor as farm boys began to enter the field and as ex-samurai ambition stepped up to higher levels. The military schools began to draw upon ambitious local youth, particularly from rural areas, who could not afford or make the higher metropolitan institutions for one reason or another.

With the establishment of these elite training grounds for the bureaucracy, career possibilities increased enormously, but career lines became more fixed. The channels for entrance into government position or business came increasingly to be through these higher institutions, and large numbers of students went to school to prepare themselves for the new careers opened up by the modernization of the country.

This change in the class composition of the intellectuals was to have important consequences. Whereas the earlier intellectuals had all been of relatively high class origin, deeply imbued with a sense of public vocation, an increasing number began to come from non-samurai orders—merchants, the growing middle class, and landowning families in the countryside. We have already noted the similar change among elementary school teachers, those early bearers of modernity to the rural villages. While during the first period large numbers of samurai had gone into teaching as one of the honorable modern professions, once the system of normal schools was well under way, the teachers began to come increasingly from the countryside itself.

The unity of the intellectual classes began to break down in response to these new developments. Where formerly there had been close relations between intellectuals and politicians, now there were new combinations. On the one hand, the politicians found themselves closer to the bureaucrats, technicians, and the growing military; on the other, intellectuals were withdrawing further into the new academies, into their professions, and, for public expression, into the growing world of journalism. Politics was more stable and bureaucratized, and although there were still outlets in opposition movements, politics was becoming more professionalized and civil intellectuals were increasingly excluded. While politics remained a high preoccupation, a growing number of intellectuals found themselves outside of and even hostile to political activity. These included many technicians, professionals, engineers, and even writers and others in artistic fields. For intellectuals who wanted an outlet for their social and political views, a new world of small-scale journalism was growing up, of *dōjin-zasshi* ("small magazines"), literary magazines, and journals of comment. Later, around the time of the Russo-Japanese War when large-scale commercial journalism began to develop, this field offered important outlets for the educated.

The end of the heroic Restoration period then sees a new situation among the intellectuals and the educated classes. The *shishi*, the Bakufu intellectuals, the Kaiseijo generation, and the provincial samurai were no longer the only element on the scene. Graduates of the new higher schools, particularly of the Tokyo Imperial University, begin to enter the marketplace; although samurai children were still disproportionately represented, there was an increasing representation from the other pre-modern classes. There was less need for politicized intellectuals devoted to reform than for intellectuals obedient to authority and working quietly and earnestly to cultivate their disciplines and skills. Itō Hirobumi had already hinted at this as early as 1879, in his *Kyōiku-gi*.[20] Although it was primarily directed against Motoda Eifu and the neo-Confu-

[20] Written in 1879 in response to Motoda's *Kyōgaku taishi*. A copy will be found in Kokumin Seishin Bunka Kenkyūjo (ed.): *Kyōiku chokugo kanpatsu kankei shiryō-shū*, vol. 1 (Tokyo, 1949), pp. 5-9. On the *Kyōgaku taishi*, see Donald Shively: "Motoda Eifu: Confucian Lecturer to the Meiji Emperor," in *Confucianism in Action*.

cianists, Itō did note that one solution for the political turbulence of the youth was stricter discipline and devotion to studies. The country needs rather less of articulate political partisans, he suggested, than earnest and well-trained experts. The Restoration leaders had been an adventurous lot who did not put too fine an edge on legality and bureaucratic procedures. The emerging group, raised under their tutelage, were more law-abiding and bureaucratic and less adventurous. While the *shishi*-type leaders were no doubt convinced of the importance of rule by law, they saw it pragmatically as a device to achieve their goals. They were not overwhelmed by its transcendent character (after all, they themselves knew that laws were manmade) as was their successor generation. After the first adventurous period of importing Western learning, examining it, trying it out, and adapting it to Japanese conditions, scholarship differentiated itself, specialized, and settled down into academicism.

Already in 1888 Tokutomi Sohō had noted this loss of enthusiasm among the intellectuals, their settling down to routine and job.[21] This undoubtedly reflected both the shift of the center of gravity of the educated classes from the samurai to the commoners as well as the settling down of the new state into stabler molds. A large portion of the intellectuals were by now part of the Establishment, as bureaucrats, or somehow involved in the work of government and the state; the civil intellectuals divided among the established—those in academic positions or in stable employment with newspapers, businesses, societies, etc.—and a new intelligentsia, which was critical, progressive, often free-lance, and out of harmony with the established balance of modernity and Japanism.

To carry our story one step further, we shall find that when we enter the Taishō period, the educated classes, as a result of the operation of the six-year compulsory education system (since 1906) and the expansion of institutions of higher learning, have become very numerous indeed and much more

[21] Cited in Tōyama, *op.cit.*, p. 194.

plebeian in composition. While lower samurai and upper *sho-min* (common people) origin is still very important, new elements appear from the lower orders. Career routings are much more fixed, and the separation of the civil and the bureaucratic intellectuals is much sharper. Equally important, the intelligentsia element has become much larger and begins to take on its characteristic political form as a result of the influence of Marxism following the Russian Revolution, serious intellectual unemployment in the early 1920's and then during the Great Depression, and the spread of ultra-nationalist militarism.

The three strands distinguishable in the contemporary intellectual classes are already evident, then, by the late Meiji period: (1) the progressive, politically orientated intelligentsia, who can be traced approximately in a line from the discontented elements of the late Tokugawa period, through the *jiyū minken* movement, through the intellectuals outside the Establishment by late Meiji and early Taishō (including Christians, socialists, strongly alienated foreign-educated), those who began to come under Marxist influence at the same time that intellectual unemployment became a serious problem, the liberals and radicals of the thought-control period, down to the progressive intellectuals of today, who take the lead in intellectual, political journalism; (2) the established intellectuals, who work for the government or hold the stable positions of authority in universities, newspapers, and other intellectual institutions and feel more "responsible" than "critical"; and (3) the non-ideological intellectuals, both non-political *bunkajin* ("men of culture") and technicians, who regard their primary task as artistic and technical rather than as moral and political.[22]

The Intellectual, Modernization, and Society

Although we can say that the intellectual classes of Japan came under Western influence and went through the baptism of Western ideas, this does not mean that all were equally

---

[22] There is good reason to believe that this element is growing very rapidly today, but I cannot go into the matter here.

influenced or influenced in the same way. Once they had passed through this experience, they ended up in different positions on the other side of the great divide. The struggle to establish a consensus has been a continuing one. The shifting balance of pro-modernity and pro-Japanism has taken many forms—the Saigō reaction versus the oligarchy, the oligarchy versus the *minken*, representative versus oligarchical government, nationalism versus individualism, ultra-nationalism versus liberalism—and provides the main poles of the dialectic of Japanese intellectual development. It can be seen within specific fields, within institutions, within individuals themselves, not to speak of the nation as a whole. And the swings of the pendulum have been very rapid: the strong pro-Western sentiment of the early Meiji period was followed by a widespread reaction; this, in turn, gave way to another wave of pro-Western feeling, particularly a "pro-democratic" one around the time of the First World War and into the early 1920's; the reaction against this was severe and led into ultra-nationalistic military control and war.

Each class of intellectuals and each position among them has been differentially affected by these general swings of mood. The turn to an anti-Western mood throws the pro-Western, liberal elements into the opposition, in some cases so extreme as to constitute veritable alienation. A progressive shift brings them back into a more harmonious, accommodating position in regard to the existing Establishment.

This cycle is itself, in the manner of the Ptolemaic system, made up of smaller epi-cycles. It may even be more accurate to say that the major mood cycles we have been describing are the "resultant" of all the smaller sub-cycles.

Among these we can specify, very briefly, Japan's foreign relations; her internal growth and modern development; and what might be called the personal dialectic.

The subject of the psychological effects of Japan's relations with the outside world is a large one, and I should prefer to leave it to specialists. But it is quite obvious that the fearful and trembling Japan of the 1860's saw the world in a very different way from the triumphant Japan of the Russo-Japanese War. Her attitude toward the United States is not the same in the 1870's, when she feels that the United States has much to teach her, and at the turn of the century, when, on the basis of experience and growing knowledge of the world, she comes to feel that Europe provides more suitable models.

We often assume, when we speak of the confrontation of Japan and the West, that the protagonists remain frozen in position; it is always the same Japan that confronts the same West. This is clearly not so. At every given moment the character of this confrontation is different. Japan and the West, 1860 model, is very different from Japan and the West, 1940. Not only has the West been changing (empires rise and fall; the mighty are defeated and the weak exalted; science, the franchise, and education advance; internal and external tensions grow), but Japan herself is constantly changing. She becomes rapidly more modern and Westernized, she knows more and more about the West. Therefore her responses become more discriminating and differentiated. A stronger Japan can act with self-confidence, even aggressiveness, toward the West where a weak and humble Japan cannot. If she still needs Western knowledge, it is no longer the same knowledge. In the 1860's she might have been satisfied with the rudiments of elementary technology; but by the 1920's she is in need of the advanced ranges of scientific development. In 1870 Western academic art may have been new and exciting, but by 1920 it was already incorporated in the Japanese academy; for something new the Japanese artists had to turn to Dadaism and futurism.

The apposition is therefore not one of tradition and modernity in a simple sense. There have been approximately four generations between the first modernizing generation of Meiji and the present. Each generation seeks its "tradition" in its own immediate past, becoming in turn the traditional base for its successor. The present generation does not turn to a "pristine" Japanese past but to the preceding generation, which already incorporates in its *corpus* of ideas a substantial admixture of the modern and the Western. The point of departure for a Japanese writer, for example, is not the *Tales of Genji* or Saikaku, but the naturalists, proletarian writers, the *Shirakaba*, etc., who have already transmuted the "pure" tradition through the sieve of modern experiences.

If it is never the same "Japan" in contact with the West, neither is it the same West. "The West" is not and has never been univocal. It has always offered a range. Sometimes the West has meant liberalism and individualism, sometimes German conservative philosophy; sometimes Catholicism, sometimes Protestantism; Bulwer-Lytton or Tolstoy; "high culture" or mass culture; academic painting or Dadaism. The consequences of each of these is different, and often contradictory. What ultimately comes to be selected depends upon an intricate dialectic between felt needs at particular times, what was available in the West, and the particular West to which people were responding.

It is well known, for example, that there were great differences both in personal style and in ideology among overseas students (*ryūgakusei*) depending on the countries they went to. While for the American-educated the West meant liberalism, individualism, pragmatism, empiricism, enterprise, and more relaxed personal relations, for the German-educated it meant order, system, administration, comprehensive, deductive philosophies, and respect for hierarchy. Similarly, that the Japanese Army sent many officers for training to Germany may have had something to do with its authoritarian politics as against the relatively more liberal outlook of the Navy, which had historically always maintained closer relations with England.

And finally there is what we might call a personal cycle. The first reaction of people confronted by the enormous superiority of the West is self-abasement and over-admiration. This gives way, with growing self-confidence and reaction against the former self-abasement, to an over-rejection. And this, in turn, is followed by some attempt at synthesis. In some cases it is a continuing effort to balance different proportions of Japanese and Western elements, or to maintain a Japanese framework with Western content, or a Western form with Japanese content.[23] Another direction it can take is toward true cosmopolitanism, the assertion of a personal view and style, without regard for the origin of the particular elements. This kind of cycle, which has profound, if subtle, effects on the master cycles, has been very little studied. We can see it in general trends and in institutional growth, but more particularly in the life cycles of individuals: writers who start out passionately pro-Western and then become passionately anti-Western; *ryūgakusei* who return home scornful of Japan but end up appreciating the delights of the *tatami*, the Japanese bath, the geisha party, and the submissive Japanese housewife. Again, this dialectic was strongly influenced by personal contact with the West. For many who had lived or studied abroad, the greatest fruit of the experience was not so much their direct learning as the new insight it gave them into their own country. The dialogue of the directly-experienced and taken-for-granted with something radically different gave them, as it were, a new *optique* for seeing themselves. Like Hawthorne they could say: "I grew better acquainted with many of our national characteristics during those four years (in Europe) than in all my preceding life."[24] Nagai Kafū, for example, found many things he disliked about Japan when he returned from his long travels, particularly in France, but he saw the solution in a more organic development for Japan rather than in greater Westernization.[25]

[23] Although we cannot always be sure what is "Japanese" and what is "Western." To take a recent example that has been troubling me: is *wasabi* chewing gum Japanese or Western? Is it a perfect fusion, or is it the ultimate barbarity?

[24] Nathaniel Hawthorne, *Notes of Travel* (New York and Boston, Houghton Mifflin and Co., 1900), 4 vols.

[25] In a like vein, Tanizaki has speculated regretfully that under other circumstances Japan might have modernized herself without destroying the continuity of her character: if, for example, he writes, the fountain pen "had been invented by the ancient Chinese or Japanese, it would surely have had a tufted end like our writing brush. The ink would not have been this bluish color, but rather black, something like the India ink, and it would have been made to seep down from the handle into the brush. And since we would then have found it

In the best cases a higher, personal resolution is achieved, liberated from the chain of causation (as the Buddhists might say), autonomous (as the psychoanalysts might say), in short, cosmopolitan.

These cycles are strongly affected, if not fundamentally governed, by some kind of relation between the production of intellectuals within a society, through its schools and universities, and the outlets it provides for them in work, satisfaction, rewards, prestige, and status. Where there is a marked disproportion, there is difficulty. In countries where there are far more intellectuals than places for them, the intellectual is dissatisfied, alienated, resentful, and radical. Or, as is much more commonly the case, there may be discrepancies between the kinds of intellectuals produced and the kinds of outlets available at any given time: too many writers for the state of the publishing industry, or for the size of the literate, reading public; too many technicians for the stage of development of industry; or highly trained physicists, mathematicians, and aeronautical engineers without facilities for their work. Or, as we see in so many underdeveloped countries these days, too many trained in literature, law, humanities, and general studies, while what the society needs is more technically trained people. This incoordination often creates sectoral discontent and even, in extreme cases, alienation.

---

inconvenient to write on Western paper, something near Japanese paper—even under mass production, if you will—would have been most in demand. Foreign ink and pen would not be as popular as they are; the talk of discarding our system of writing for Roman letters would be less noisy. . . . But more than that: our thought and our literature might not be imitating the West as they are, they might have pushed forward into new regions quite on their own. An insignificant little piece of writing equipment, when one thinks of it, has had a vast, almost boundless, influence on our culture. . . . [Having] come this far we cannot turn back. . . . [But] . . . it is not impossible that we would one day have discovered our own substitute for the trolley, the radio, the airplane of today. They would have been no borrowed gadgets, they would have been the tools of our own culture, suited to us. . . ." (Quoted in Edward Seidensticker: "'In Praise of Shadows,' A Prose Elegy by Tanizaki," *Japan Quarterly*, vol. 1, no. 1, October-December 1954.)

Where, as in such golden ages as early Meiji Japan, there is more demand for intellectuals than supply, the intellectual is a member of the elite, smothered with rewards and perquisites far beyond those of ordinary mortals. In Burma, for example, there was at least until a few years ago, only one real university. The demands of the new welfare state for educated people was so great that the university professor there had an extremely privileged place in society. His housing was gratis and ample, his salary was in the upper brackets, he was securely fixed with retirement pensions, insurance, health services. As a member of the elite, he was a regular frequenter of "high society" and was able to lead a gracious existence. He was even able to afford an automobile, at a time when this was the perquisite only of wealthy people and high government officials. In nineteenth century Austria, it is said, the university professor held the honorary rank of colonel in the imperial army ;[26] the Burmese professors were at least the confrères of cabinet ministers and other high officials of government.

Contrast this with India, where intellectual under-employment is a permanent source of political instability. The hordes of semi-trained, resentful, restlessly ambitious young intellectuals,[27] with little or no hope of living the kind of life their books had taught them to look forward to, form a pool of seething resentment against existing society, a guarantee against stability. By starting its modern career with an excessive number of insufficiently prepared intellectuals and a rate of economic growth too slow to absorb them, India has built for herself severe political problems. Countries fortunate enough to start with the opposite combination are in a much happier position.

Japan was one of the more fortunate countries. In early Meiji, when the country was desperately modernizing, there was room for every intellectual who could be launched into society by the schools and by self-study. It was a time of

[26] Golo Mann: "The German Intellectuals," *Encounter*, June 1955.
[27] India has several hundred colleges grouped into about 40 universities with something over 1,500,000 students.

opportunity, when anyone with education or skills could rise to high office. Even an *ashigaru* ("foot soldier," the lowest ranking warrior), it was said, could become a *sangi* or a secretary of state. A high premium was paid for the skills and the knowledge of technicians, specialists, and persons familiar with Western thought, science, and languages. The expanding state found use for all of them. A graduate of Tokyo Imperial was automatically hired by the government and, for a period (between 1887 and 1893), without examination. His entering salary, which ran between 450 and 600 yen per month, was based entirely on his school grades. In terms of the price level of the period, this salary corresponds to between 1.0 and 1.5 million yen per month.[28] At that time it was just below ministerial and cabinet councillor salaries (800 and 500 yen per month, respectively). In this way their sense of public vocation and self-importance, as well as their skills, found some outlet in the government, in government-supported enterprises and activities, or in activities that opened up as a result of the government's modernizing policy. It is not surprising, therefore, that the early Meiji intellectuals had a high sense of national purpose, of obligation, of responsibility. There was a keenness, an enthusiasm, a zest for the adventure of modernization which made the intellectual a firmly wedded member of the leadership stratum.

With the constant growth in the numbers of the highly educated, two things happened. First, the individual intellectual no longer had as much prestige as when he was a member of a much smaller class. The big fish in the little pond was becoming the little fish in the big pond. Second, this intellectual inflation reduced his rewards in proportion to the rise of those of other elements, not only of the elite but of society in general. The lowest point in this process was reached, of course, during the late 1920's and 1930's, when there was large-scale intellectual unemployment, and in the first years after the Second World War. To take an example from the

[28] One *koku* of rice, which today sells for 10,000 yen, sold for six yen.

academic world, let us consider the "professor." In early Meiji he was an exalted being, about whom still clung the aura of the *sensei*, the master of esoteric knowledge of the earlier ages; but at the same time there was about him the suggestion of the modern expert, bringing salvation and prosperity to his country through his knowledge of Western science and learning. Today, he often feels, whether justifiably or not, that he is only one of many, with a salary just about equal to that of skilled workers or lower bureaucrats, scrabbling to make a living, out in the marketplace competing with others.[29]

We could, were there space, trace this process in detail. In the postwar period it has been particularly important because of the vast inflation of universities and the number of university students.[30] And since then the upthrust of the lower orders, as a result of the remarkable high level of economic growth and the strength of the trade unions, has extended the process even further. The evening out of living standards and the growth of equality are, to be sure, among the desiderata of the "progressive" intellectuals; but these do not help their status.

Old Tradition, Modern Intellectual

Just as "the West" is not univocal, neither is "the Japanese tradition" unequivocal in its promptings. To favor tradition does not mean a single, definable thing. The intellectual is able to be selective about the elements of the total received tradition that he rejects or accepts. He may accept underlying moral principles and ideals of family relations but reject the "absurd usages and customs" of the past, superstitions, things that demean personal dignity and individuality. Or he may favor the traditional arts but oppose obscurantism, religion, hierarchical ideas, etc. There is much to the widely

[29] The postwar educational reform increased the number of university teachers about ten times.

[30] The normal prewar number was about 70,000; the postwar figure now reaches about ten times that.

accepted proposition that traditional elements—authority, Confucian morality, and the family system—form a unified ideology. But it can be overstated. (Even in the West there are authoritarian husbands and submissive wives.)

Each area of traditional culture and each sector of the intellectual classes is differentially affected by the pressure of modernity and Westernism. Some, quite obviously, are extremely vulnerable—as, say, the study of science or industrial technology—but others are much less so. The calligrapher, for example, or the priest of the local shrine, is certainly not under the same compulsion to alter his methods as the professor of anatomy. The calligrapher *may* change, but that would be because of the slow, permeative changes in the climate of thought brought about by the growth of new ideas and institutions.[31] There is no inherent reason, at least in the early stages of modernization and contact with the West, why he *should* do so.

The argument is justly made that any single "culture-complex" from the West, even a material object or an industrial process, implies a whole supportive network of ideas, philosophy, social organization, etc. One cannot accept the one without, at least over a period of time, accepting the rest. Western science is, in this view, a kind of Trojan horse, from whose belly leap out the ideologies, philosophies, attitudes, and conflicts of Western society. For many areas of cultural life this is certainly true. The creation of industry inevitably meant a working class; and this in turn meant some form of class conflict. But whether this represented the simple unfolding of an immanent logic or can be explained in some other way is uncertain.

Modernization does not mean the complete and instant displacement of the traditional. The process is not uniform; it affects the separate cultural elements, areas of thought, and population groups that make up a nation in different ways. Certain elements of traditional culture may remain completely

---

[31] Some have been going in for an "abstract calligraphy" that is very influential and popular not only in Japan but among European artists as well.

unaltered as, for example, food habits, family relations, or religious beliefs, in spite of modern transportation and government bureaus. Because of the unevenness of the process certain groups—isolated peasants or clerics, for example—are less touched than city people or the upper classes. The result is that a modern sector grows up alongside the traditional one.

Although the modern sector tends to expand, it is by no means certain that the final culmination of this process is the complete obsolescence of the traditional. At the very least, for long periods they can co-exist side by side.

As (I think) Takeyama Michio once pointed out,[32] it is not always necessary to make an exclusive choice. One can enjoy both forms either at the same time or separately. In fact the introduction of Western elements may simply mean an extension of the cultural repertoire of a modern Japanese. He may have *misoshiru* (a soup made of fermented bean curd), rice, and tea for breakfast, or he may have toast, eggs, and coffee. He may even, in spite of the purists, have *misoshiru and* coffee; both are equally a part of the "culture" of modern Japan.

There is undoubtedly here a question of inherent concordance, or congruence, aside from questions of taste. The sensibility required for Western music, for example, is very different from that required for traditional Japanese music. The result is that there has grown up a complete separation of the two. Japanese music has its own traditions, performers, and audiences; Western music its own, and completely different ones. Many Western-style composers and performers, for example, refuse even to listen to Japanese-style music for fear that it will upset their delicately attuned ear. The tonalities, scales, and harmonic conceptions are too different. We shall have to leave it to musicologists to determine how incongruent they really are.

In the same way we find a sharp separation between the Western and the traditional in many of the arts, notably painting and the theater. This does not mean, of course, that the gap is entirely impermeable, but the tendency has been to

[32] In private conversation.

encapsulate the traditional, so that it continues relatively unchanged, while the modern expands along new lines.

This co-existence of traditional and modern sectors in intellectual life and in the arts has, it seems to me, far-reaching implications for understanding what is likely to happen in the present-day underdeveloped countries. Modern education, Western literature, and altered circumstances of life have made it impossible for many artists to express their modern sensibilities in traditional forms. Yet although there has been great change in the novel, we find less in poetry—at least from the standpoint of the volume of poetry published. Side by side with a very considerable modern poetry, such traditional forms as the *haiku* and *tanka* flourish. Scores of magazines are devoted to them, with millions of readers, and they publish several million new ones per year. It is true that some *haiku* are affected by modernity (as, for example, in the new *haiku* movements or the proletarian *tanka* movement of the 1920's) and that some modern poetry is affected by aesthetic conceptions and conventions of traditional Japanese poetry. But on the whole, it is fair to say that they co-exist rather than interpenetrate.

If we come to the character of the modern intellectuals, we find a very considerable persistence of tradition. I shall here suggest only a few brief examples. First, the *sensei* tradition. The venerated *sensei* of the past was no mere technician or expert. He was guide, leader, and master. To become his student, or more accurately his disciple, was to enter a special relationship that implied life-long obedience and respect. And yet we know that in spite of the transformation of the teacher into a paid employee, he still tends to remain the *sensei*. His student-disciple serves him faithfully and depends upon him for guidance and help throughout life. The system has profound effects on classroom performance, freedom of discussion, the acceptance of authority, initiative, and the student's getting ahead in the world. Professor Miyagi Otoya somewhere tells the story that in the medical school he attended so great was the dependence of the students and so profound their respect for the *sensei* that they were even willing to allow him to choose their marriage partners for them. When the *sensei* took up tennis, all his disciples took up tennis. (Today, presumably, they would take up golf.) If this still lingers on in the universities, the very citadels of Westernization, it is even more persistent in the traditional fields: the theater, calligraphy, pottery, art, and music.

However, here again it would be wrong to describe this simply as a "carry-over" of tradition into modern conditions. There are important contemporary pressures that—depending upon our choice of statement—sustain the traditional system or create it anew. The fact is that academic and professional life is extremely competitive and that many intellectual fields have been, at various times, over-crowded. It was therefore a practical necessity, not only an ideological preference for tradition, that sustained the system. In order to get ahead in certain fields, it was absolutely essential to have strong backing.

Another example often given of the persistence of traditional elements in modern intellectual life is the clique, the *batsu*. The individual faces the world not so much as an individual, with his personal talents and accomplishments, but as a member of a clique. These filiative networks, which extend through the universities, government, and business, exert a very considerable control over their members by virtue of their monopoly of certain posts. Although this has been changing in the past years, it remains sufficiently important to engage the attention of liberal intellectuals. A recent report[33] is still able to say: "A particular school has hegemony among the staff in certain offices or schools, who exclude graduates of other universities irrespective of their ability. This is a subtle revival of feudalism amidst the rationalistic forms of bureaucracy. These differences in quality, certainly in repute, among universities appear to be widening. These social and political forces penetrate the educational system,

[33] "International Study of University Admissions in Japan." Unpublished manuscript, prepared by a committee, including professors from Tokyo, Keio, Hiroshima, International Christian, and other universities, p. 238.

and they underlie the incessant clamor for reviving and strengthening the dual system."

In order to get ahead in certain fields it was necessary to belong to the right cliques; for certain posts in universities, civil service, or business it was essential to be supported by the clique that controlled it. Now, here again, we find a concordance of the new with the traditional. As institutions the *batsu* are new, but the ideas and dispositions on which they are based—cliquism, lord-vassal relations, *oyabun-kobun* relations—are certainly traditional. The system continues not only because it appeals to traditional feelings—although this is often important—but because it fulfills genuine needs in contemporary life and because it has become institutionalized through the rooting of vested interests.

One final example is what I have earlier called the sense of "public vocation" of the Japanese intellectuals. This can be traced, I think, to their samurai origin. The responsible samurai always had a feeling of public responsibility, a commitment to the national interest and welfare, whether he held office or not. This tradition was perpetuated even when the intellectual classes began to be drawn from non-samurai orders of society. Herein we may find part of the explanation of the special role of intellectuals in contemporary Japan. They conceive of themselves not merely as specialists but, in the words of Herbert Luethy, as "the moral guardians of the political republic."[34]

The conscious relation of the intellectual to his own tradition and to modernity is a more complicated problem. That he has, on the whole, been anti-traditional does not necessarily imply alienation or isolation. It may, in the event that he finds himself completely unable to live in his own country and develops a positive hate for it. But this is more likely to arise from his relations with the polity, rather than with "tradition" as a whole.

I do not intend to go into this subject here except to suggest that in order to make significant statements we must think

[34] Herbert Luethy, "The French Intellectuals," *Encounter*, August 1955.

in terms of multi-dimensional continua: tradition to modernity; nationalism to non-nationalism; liberalism to conservatism; pro- to anti-Establishment. The individual's attitude toward all four need not necessarily be in the same direction. Modernists may be liberal or conservative; traditionalists may be for or against the polity, depending upon the dominant consensus it represents.

In any event, it will be apparent that the Japanese experience is rich in suggestions, particularly for the contemporary "emergent nations" that are about to start out on their modern adventure.

CHAPTER XIV

Patterns of Individuation and the Case of Japan: A Conceptual Scheme

MASAO MARUYAMA

ONE of the questions raised at the Hakone Conference on "Modernization of Japan" in the summer of 1960 was whether we should incorporate such concepts as "democracy," "liberalism," and "socialism" into the conceptual framework with which to deal with the problems involved in modernization. In spite of—or rather because of—the polemical nature of the issue, the problem was never thoroughly discussed. The American participants, in their papers, hesitated to introduce any ideologically charged concepts into the definition of "modernization," the Japanese side in the main insisted that it would be meaningless to discuss modernization, especially that of Japan, without paying due consideration to these concepts. It would be an over-simplification to understand this difference in approach merely in terms of the "ideologists" opposing the "non-ideologists."

For example, naturally Professor J. Hall, in his capacity as chairman of the conference, doubted "whether in the tense political environment of the summer of demonstrations, these subjects could have been objectively discussed," and was worried about "the acrimony of debate over the question of 'what kind of democracy do you mean?' "[1] Apart from such practical considerations as Professor Hall's there was a more theoretical ground for the skepticism of the Americans, to which Professor Schwartz's paper gave the typical expression, with its emphasis on the "ambivalence" or rather "multivalence" of the consequences of what is called the modernization process, particularly in the cultural or political realms.[2]

[1] J. W. Hall, "Changing Conceptions of the Modernization of Japan." See above.

[2] B. I. Schwartz, "Modernization and Its Ambiguities," Hakone Conference Paper.

Undoubtedly, what lies behind this skepticism is the experience of a generation which witnessed irrational myths being combined with what Max Weber called *Zweckrationalität* in German Nazism and Japanese militarism. Moreover, there is the recognition that not only in the Soviet Union and Communist China but also in many developing areas rapid industrialization now under way is initiated by regimes which are neither liberal nor democratic in the traditional Western sense of the words.

There were two schools of thought on the Japanese side. The first, represented by Professors Ōuchi and Tōyama, is more or less derived from Marxism. The reason why they advocated introducing such concepts as "capitalism" and "bourgeois-democracy" into the definition of modernization is not that they are—at least primarily—interested in the problems of "ethos" and "ideologies," but that they believe above all in the validity and the necessity of limiting the notion of modernization to a particular historical process, i.e., the process from feudalism to capitalism. They could form a united front with certain American social scientists and historians in labeling as "subjectivists" or "idealists" those whose approach to the issues of modernization is based on the level of ethos or the value orientation of the individual.

Opposed to this group were those who argued against limiting the concept of modernization to a particular historical process, either from feudalism to capitalism or from absolutism to bourgeois-democracy. The Japanese scholars of this latter group are in agreement with most American scholars in using "modernization" as a wide conceptual framework with which to understand and analyze great transformations that are taking place in the world today, including the Soviet bloc and developing countries. What they criticized, however, in an examination of modernization, was the avoidance of the problems of individualism, democracy, communism, or fascism, on the grounds that such words are value-oriented. Not a little difference, however, existed even among the Japanese scholars of the second school in setting up the problems and the analytical processes. In any event, the problem was not so simple as to allow a clear distinction between the "fact-oriented" and "value-oriented." Therefore, if the Hakone Conference had not shelved the issues concerning "-isms," and if we had been given more time to discuss these matters, there might have appeared a more complex regrouping of arguments. Needless to say, I am not blaming anyone; rather, I am trying to clear up whatever misunderstanding there may have been.

The following attempt to schematize the modernization process is not at all unrelated to the results of the Hakone Conference; indeed, I hope to lead the problem of modernization into areas related to "ethos" or "ideology" questions, taking full account of the experience of the Hakone Conference. For this purpose, I should like to examine the influence modernization has on the members of a society with a view to showing the forms of reaction possible on the level of the attitude of the individual, rather than on the level of socio-political system or ideas proper.

In the following analysis there are two themes which the writer wishes to underscore. The first is the disparity between what is expected of modern institutions—legal, political, and economic—and the interpersonal relations which in fact are at work within the framework of such institutions. Of course in any country there are discrepancies between the theory and practice of institutions. However, it is beyond dispute that the degree of inconsistency in Japan, or in other non-Western countries where all modern institutions and ideas were imported from outside as "ready-made articles," is far greater than in the Western countries. The discrepancies are found both on the level of the individual and the group; moreover, in cases where the individual belongs to several groups at one time, inconsistencies also appear between his behavior in one group and that in another. Thus a political group standing for a liberal and democratic ideology might be composed of members among whom the "authoritarian" personality is predominant. On the other hand, it often happens that at the general meeting of a political party standing for collectivism, we find the rank and file to be much more independent

491

and free from authorities than those who belong to a political group boasting of its "respect for individuality." Or, to take another instance, the patterns of daily behavior of a person who is acknowledged to be an exponent of traditionalism might be remarkably individualistic, and, on the contrary, an advocate of "Westernization" might be a conformist in terms of traditional behavior patterns. Nor is it rare that one who entertains conservative political views is tolerant of the independent ideas of his wife at home, and that a radical progressive in social activities carries into execution the notorious "Absolutism of the Emperor System" in the microcosm of his own home.

However, it would be too hasty to declare a general mistrust of incorporating problems of ideologies into a consideration of modernization simply because there really exist such discrepancies; and we must not content ourselves with taking precautions not to confuse these levels of institutions, ideas, and attitudes with one another. What is important here is to examine how functionally related such discrepancies are with changes of the whole society and social sub-systems. Thus, the hypothesis in the scheme presented below is that the dominant personality type in any society experiencing modernization seems to have a definite interrelationship with the kind of political and social system the society develops; and that different patterns in the disintegration of "traditional" attitudes, as well as their variances from one social strata to another or from one generation to another, may be one of the crucial factors in determining the political dynamics of modernization.

The second problem in this analysis was actually suggested by Professor B. Schwartz's remarks, to which I have already referred, concerning the ambivalence of direction toward which modernization develops. The fact that political and economic development in Japan after Meiji did not always proceed in the direction of individualism, liberalism, and democracy does not, according to Professor Schwartz, justify the interpretation of history which states that the traditional authoritarianism or "feudal-absolutism" of Japan "distorted" or "delayed" modernization. He argues that we should pay due regard to the possibility that the so-called "feudal-mentality" might have been a spring board which made possible the rapid modernization of Japan. Thus, Schwartz concludes that "modernization" can be given a universal definition only with regard to the appropriate means by which man controls his physical and social environments; the aims for which the means are implemented vary greatly.

Although the present writer quite agrees with this suggestion, he feels that interesting problems about modernization in Japan may lie one step further. For example, it seems to have been impossible for the power elites of modern Japan to cut off entirely and over a long period of time various "subversive" counteractions which the technological modernization brought about, in the field of ideology or, in other words, in the field of "purpose." Besides a traditional ethos which has been valid for promoting modernization at a certain stage —for instance, the family principle in a business organization —might transform itself into fetters when further modernization becomes necessary at a later stage. These considerations will lead us to a very important point in understanding the success and failure of modern Japan. This is the problem of *limit* in highly purposeful and selective modernization. Furthermore, that modernization implies ambivalent possibilities in a cultural and political domain does not necessarily mean these possibilities are in fact *in*numerable. Given certain historical circumstances, it is practical and significant for us to eliminate some kinds of possibilities as being improbable, and to consider which among the remaining possibilities are highly probable; for example, a direction toward democracy or toward authoritarianism. The present paper, of course, is not designed to treat these problems comprehensively. The following attempt to schematize changes in various phases of modernization on the level of attitudes is motivated by a desire to answer, though from a limited viewpoint, the challenge given by the question of ambivalence in modernization.

Pattern of Individuation

My present analysis begins by observing the well-known historical experience that everywhere the process of "modernization" has been *in some sense* disruptive for the individual living in "traditional" society. He is "emancipated," willingly or unwillingly, from the communal ties which have hitherto bound him and which have prescribed to him certain traditional behavior, though, of course, the nature as well as the degree of this "emancipation" varies from one case to another. For the sake of convenience, I shall call this general phenomenon "individuation," as distinguished from the term "individualization," an explanation of which is given below.

Now I should like to suggest that there are four possible patterns of such an individuation process which can be distinguished according to the attitude of the person experiencing various phases of modernization, and which determine his sense of relationship with his community. These four are: INDIVIDUALIZATION, DEMOCRATIZATION, PRIVATIZATION, and ATOMIZATION. In order to indicate the interrelations and movements of each pattern in the simplest form possible, let us suppose that such differentiation in terms of individual attitudes takes place simultaneously in a community under the impact of modernization (which, of course, is improbable in the real world). We then get the opposite paradigm (Paradigm A).[3]

In this scheme, the horizontal axis represents the degree of the individual's distance from the focus of political authority, so that the further a person goes toward the left, the more the degree of centrifugality increases; i.e., the less he is interested in identifying himself with the center of decision-making. In this way, INDIVIDUALIZATION and PRIVATIZATION may be placed toward the left along the axis, in contrast to DEMOCRATIZATION and ATOMIZATION, both of which represent centripetal attitudes toward political authority. The vertical axis, on the other hand, may be made to represent the degree of association that individuals develop voluntarily with each other. Here as we go up the axis we get more associative

[3] For this scheme, the writer is indebted to the well-known paradigm of Lawrence Lowell concerning political opinions—liberal, conservative, radical and reactionary—although the motivations behind the present scheme and the terms applied herein are different. (Cf., A. L. Lowell, *Public Opinion in War and Peace*, 1923, Chapter 7.)

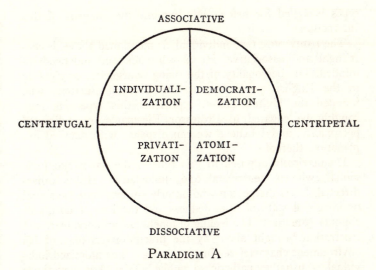

ASSOCIATIVE

INDIVIDUALI-
ZATION

DEMOCRATI-
ZATION

CENTRIFUGAL

CENTRIPETAL

PRIVATI-
ZATION

ATOMI-
ZATION

DISSOCIATIVE

PARADIGM A

individuals—those who are ready to associate themselves with their neighbors in order to attain various, not necessarily political, purposes. As we go down we get *dis*SOCIATIVE individuals whose sense of solidarity with their fellow men is comparatively weak. In this scheme INDIVIDUALIZATION and DEMOCRATIZATION must be placed higher along the axis, while PRIVATIZATION and ATOMIZATION will occupy lower positions. Thus, in short, individualization is centrifugal and yet associative; democratization is associative and centripetal; privatization is centrifugal and dissociative; finally, atomization is dissociative and yet centripetal. It is perhaps unnecessary to remark that these are merely suggested as ideal types of individual reactions to such modernizing processes as were summarized in Professor Hall's chapter above, i.e., *rationalization, mechanization,* and *bureaucratization.* Here I am not concerned with the static distinction between these categories, but rather with the interactions among these four different responses and their interrelationships with the political system. However, a brief explanation of each of these

495

types is called for before entering into the analysis of this interaction.

The INDIVIDUALIZED individual, as mentioned above, is centrifugal and associative. He is self-made and independent-minded. The personality of the rising bourgeoisie originating in the English yeomanry, or the Colonial Puritans who founded the United States, represents this type. He may roughly be equated to Professor Riesman's inner-directed personality, and I believe we can dispense with detailed explanation thereof.

Diametrically opposed to this type is the ATOMIZED individual, who is centripetal and dissociative. He is other-directed. He is the person who bitterly suffers from the actual or imagined state of uprootedness and the loss of norms of conduct (anomie). The feeling of loneliness, anxiety, fear, and frustration brought about by the precipitous change of his environment characterizes his psychology. The atomized individual is usually apathetic to public affairs, but sometimes this very apathy will turn abruptly into fanatic participation in politics. Just because he is concerned with escaping from loneliness and insecurity, he is inclined to identify himself totally with authoritarian leadership or to submerge himself into the mystical "whole" expressed in such ideas as national community, eternal racial culture, and so on. The eruption of this pattern of "individuation" is usually a phenomenon of the stage of high modernization, as was typically the case in pre-Hitlerite Germany. But we can also apply the category to the urbanized individuals in the early phase of modernization, for example, in many developing areas.[4]

[4] "The shift to a money, and often a one-crop, economy forced many peasants to go to work in the plantations and mines and in the factories of the growing cities. At present, these workers are frequently less than a generation removed from their ancestral villages and tribes where life, although—or because—extremely limited materially and intellectually, provided a high degree of security for the individual. Suddenly torn from the bonds of such a small, highly integrated society and thrown into the anonymity of life in an industrial plant and an urban slum, where not only the physical surroundings, but also many values and behaviour patterns, are utterly alien, the worker is

The DEMOCRATIZED individual occupies the middle position between the individualized type and the atomized type. Like the individualized individual, the democratized individual is associative; i.e., prone to form voluntary groups and associations. They are both rational in their individual choice between alternative courses of social action, and relatively free from a compulsive submission to authority. The democratized individual, however, is more centripetal and is oriented toward innovations by the central government, while the individualized type is more centrifugal and is concerned with local autonomy. While the latter is more interested in institutional guarantees of civil liberties, the former is more inclined to go farther in the direction of abolishing privileges or of broadening the base of political participation to include the largest number of people dealing with the widest range of public affairs. Thus the democratized is more prone to mass movement—in this sense he comes closer to the atomized person—than the individualized. Where democratization predominates, the emphasis is likely to be put on the ideal of equality rather than on that of liberty, to which the individualized person primarily commits himself. If we were to compare historically political modernization in the U.S. and Great Britain—both early modernizers—we might say roughly that in the U.S. democratization has traditionally predominated over individualization, while in Britain the reverse has been the case.[5]

The exact opposite of the democratized type is the PRIVATIZED individual. Like the atomized individual, the privatized one is also oriented toward the achievement of self-gratification rather than public goals. Both are dissociative in the sense that they shun taking the initiative in associating themselves

---

bound to be subject to maladjustments, tensions and frustrations of various kinds." (*Political Change in Underdeveloped Countries: Nationalism and Communism*. Ed. by John H. Kautsky, N.Y., 1962, p. 43.)

[5] A. de Tocqueville's study of American democracy is rich with examples of this relative difference in the dominant behavior patterns of his age.

with their neighbors. But in the case of privatization, the scope of interest is rather confined to one's "private" affairs and is not as floating as that of atomization. Though political apathy characterizes both types, the apathetic attitude of the privatized individual may be expressed as *withdrawal* rather than escape from his inner self. Thus, psychologically he is more stable than the atomized individual and comes closer to the individualized one. On the other hand, however, this withdrawal tends to "contain" his interest within the spheres of private consumption and entertainment, while the individualized is always prepared for political participation *because of* his concern with his private interests. The "retreatism" of the privatized person must not be confused with the "natural" indifference toward public affairs prevalent in traditional communities,[6] because the former represents a *conscious* reaction against the increasing bureaucratization of the system and against the complexities of the social and political process in which he finds himself involved.

These are the four possible types of individuation defined as the response to the process of modernization. Of course, it is rare that a particular individual inclusively and freely belongs to one of the four categories throughout his lifetime. Subsequently, real individuals are not distributed proportionately in the scheme: rather the density of concentration is high around center and becomes sparse as the areas become farther away from it. Further it is unlikely that a particular instance of modernization will produce all these types of individuals in equal proportions. That is, it is in fact impossible for both axes to go through the center of the circle. In accordance with the socio-cultural conditions and the different patterns of modernization process in different societies, and because of the difference in the successive stages of modernization even in the same society, one or two of the four types become predominant over the others. The primary

---

[6] "As the sun rises, we cultivate, and with the twilight we rest. What does the power of the Emperor have to do with me?" The attitude of the peasants in the ancient Chinese Empire, described in *Shih pa shih lüeh*, is a typical expression of this traditional indifference.

concern of this paper is the problem of interrelation between the socio-political system and the different patterns of predominance and their shifts. It is impossible, of course, to discuss inclusively all possible situations. Let us therefore set up some hypothetical cases by shifting the two axes respectively.

First, let us assume the associative-dissociative distribution to be constant, and change the ratio of centrifugal and centripetal attitudes. We will get two different types of situation. (Paradigm B)

i CENTRIFUGAL OR IP TYPE   ii CENTRIPETAL OR DA TYPE

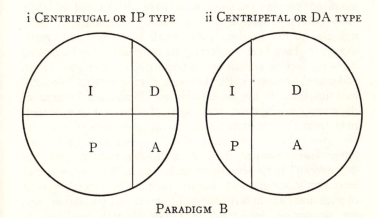

PARADIGM B

In the first type, centrifugality predominates over centripetality; in other words, individualization and privatization are predominant in the modernization process. In the second type, centripetality predominates over centrifugality; that is, democratized and atomized individuals are in the majority. The contrast between these two types of society is clear enough. The CENTRIPETAL or Democratization-Atomization (D A) type is more dynamic and revolutionary than the centrifugal or Individualization-Privatization (I P) type, the more so because both democratized and atomized individuals are prone to mass movements, though from different motivations. Thus, for example, in many developing areas where traditional rural communities are precipitously exposed to the destructive influences of urbanization and industrialization, the nationalist mass movement is often composed of such individuals. In most cases, the democratized type is found among lawyers, political journalists, university professors, and students—all of whom have received higher education either in the West or in the Westernized institutions of their own countries—and leaders of nationalist movements are usually recruited from this strata. But the rank and file who follow the movement consist not rarely of typically atomized people—peasants who were driven out of their native lands; industrial workers coming from different communities to live in slums; and small tradesmen and craftsmen, who have been constantly threatened by the increasing mass-production system or the import of cheaper goods from "advanced" countries. Furthermore, even emerging Westernized intellectuals are susceptible to atomization because of their underemployment; their sense of alienation or uprootedness from the common people, supposedly imbued with indigenous culture;[7] and more often than not, because of their bitter disillusionment with what "modernization" and "independence" have actually brought about. This accounts, at least partly, for the fact that the political and social systems of such areas are in a situation of "permanent revolution" and the democratic leadership is rather abruptly replaced by dictatorship either of the right or of the left. In any case, the predominance of D A type over I P type is functionally related to the rise of the labor movement as a political force, preceding or overstepping the liberal-constitutionalist reforms which characterized the early phase of political modernization in the West.[8]

[7] Cf., E. Schils' "The Intellectuals in the Political Development of the New States," in Kautsky, ed., *op.cit.*, pp. 215-216.

[8] It was with civic and material interest that the carriers of liberal constitutionalism in the West participated in politics, for they had the economic and occupational bases in their society. This kind of indigenous middle class usually does not grow in the underdeveloped countries where the intellectuals, free from occupational commitments,

It seems to be comparatively rare for the CENTRIFUGAL, i.e., I P type, to prevail in a society under rapid modernization. I P type society is witnessed in those cases where modernization proceeded slowly from within, without radically disturbing the prevailing value-system or where the initial stormy phase of modernization is slowing down. When modernization proceeds under a relatively moderate and stable oligarchy, this type of response tends to appear. British society in the eighteenth century, prior to the Industrial Revolution, is close to this type. Also the Soviet Union under Khrushchev appears to be approaching this type. In such a society, the concern with the social and legal protection of the security and happiness of individuals and local communities is strong, and the mass movement seldom takes place. Therefore, political changes initiated at the top-level are rather slow in reaching the bottom of the society and are not likely to be followed by a radical transformation of the whole system. On the other hand, however, the relative indifference to the problems of central government, common to I and P attitudes, tends to allow oligarchic-aristocratic forms of government to exist, thereby often causing political corruption at the top level.

Next, let us assume the centrifugal-centripetal distribution to be constant and consider changing the associative-dissociative axis. (Paradigm C)

In this ASSOCIATIVE type, individualized and democratized behavior becomes predominant with the process of modernization. Voluntary associations of every kind appear in great number, none of which ever engulfs the whole personality of its members. Extreme politicalization and over-centralization of the society are prevented by the feed-back role played by individualized persons, while the tendency toward political apathy is checked mainly by the activities of democratized types. This situation of equilibrium is often considered as

---

often devote their whole selves to political activities. This is one social condition that makes the growth of the Western-type liberal difficult, and encourages the prevalence of radical politicalization.

i Associative or ID type ii Dissociative or PA type

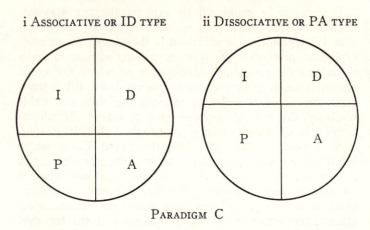

Paradigm C

the ideal state or the ultimate goal of any modernizing society, not only by Western liberals but also by many non-Western intellectuals—including those who are judged to be "radicals" according to Western standards. Whether it is ideal or not, it must not be confused with any existing society in which liberal democracy prevails as a political ideology, though certain phases of political development in the West might have proved to be most approximate to this type. With the advance of a high degree of technological modernization there emerges, also in the West, the possibility that the number of dissociative type may rise and apathetic attitudes either in the form of atomization or of privatization may cause various disturbances in the working of democratic institutions.

The DISSOCIATIVE, i.e., P A type, is likely to take root where, particularly under colonial or semi-colonial conditions, rapid and forced industrialization is carried out almost exclusively through foreign investment, often made possible by the alliance of traditional oligarchies with governments of "advanced" countries. Here, because of the lack of popular initiative and spontaneity, *social* stagnation often stands side by side with technological innovations introduced from above, or even with frequent *political* changes in the form of *coups d'état* (for example, Central and South America). In such types of society, also, sudden mass action occurs on the basis of atomized individuals. (Thus the political scene is here more dynamic than in the case of I P type). However, such actions may be called sporadic riots rather than organized mass movements with strong leadership. It is only when the hitherto privatized individuals move en masse in the direction either of INDIVIDUALIZATION or of ATOMIZATION, and the atomized individuals move toward DEMOCRATIZATION to some extent at least, that in these areas a continuous mass movement, nationalist or democratic, can develop.

Finally we may of course shift *both* axes, thus changing the relative distribution of the four different attitudes. In this case we will get four further types. (Paradigm D)

In the first type, INDIVIDUALIZATION is maximal and atomization minimal (the relation of D and P is indefinite). In the second, ATOMIZATION is maximal and individualization minimal. In the third, DEMOCRATIZATION is maximal and privatization is minimal. In the fourth, PRIVATIZATION is maximal and democratization is minimal.

The writer cannot enumerate here all possible implications of each case, nor does he have space enough to discuss in general the problem of shifts from one type to another within the same society during different stages of modernization. It is possible, however, to establish at least one formula. It is that the attitudinal changes are liable to take place from one type to its adjacent type, and less likely to proceed from one type to the diagonal type. This is because such a change to the diagonal type would involve crossing both axes at once; for example, I type has the ambivalent tendency to move to D if the centripetal tendency becomes strong, and to P if the associative tendency atrophies. But he is not likely to change himself *directly* into the atomized type without passing through either the stage of democratization or of privatization. This partially explains the fact that among countries in the West, those whose members' behavior pattern tends to be maximal in I are more immune to the totalitarian regimentation of society than those who tend to maximize D.

On the other hand, if we observe the attitudinal changes,

503

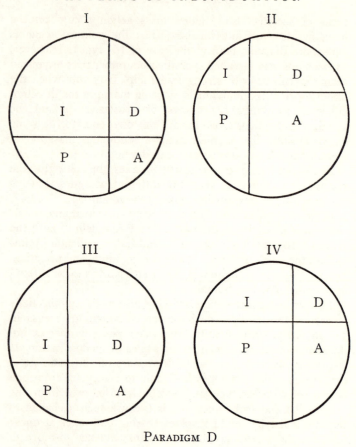

PARADIGM D

we realize that we should not too quickly despair of the possibility of creating the individualistic self in totalitarian regimes, under which modernization often proceeds in developing areas. For it is feasible that the unstable ATOMIZED individual may either change to the psychologically more stable, PRIVATIZED individual based on an assured way of life or to the DEMOCRATIZED individual conscious of horizontal solidarity, and lead to forming individuality. Whether a society in its behavior

pattern proceeds D→I→P or A→D→I, etc., depends on
the various historical conditions of the society. It also varies
from class to class within the same society. In either case the
examination of these shifting probabilities will prevent us from
falling into either excessive optimism, or fatalistic pessimism
concerning what modernization has in store for us.

The Case of Japan

It is beyond the scope of this paper to discuss generally and
inclusively the various forms and processes individuation has
assumed in modern Japan. The attempt here made is simply
to select as models two periods in which various types of individuation became predominant and to describe some of their
social consequences.

The periods chosen in this paper include, first, the years
from around 1900 to 1910, and then the years immediately
following the Great Earthquake of 1923. The Second World
War, of course, was one of the most cataclysmic events in
modern Japan's history, but so many changes have taken place
so drastically that the writer was forced to abandon his plan
to treat the postwar period as a "third case" in this paper.
Incidentally, we are here concerned with the range of attitudes
sufficiently wide to characterize the social climate of the
period, so that our observation will be directed not so much
to the personality types of the ruling elites as to the reaction
of the ordinary intellectuals, students, and common people.

It is, of course, possible to trace back the beginning of
modernization in Japan long before 1900, to the years of the
Meiji Restoration, or to the end of the Tokugawa period.
During the last years of the Tokugawa period, there were
certainly some enlightenment thinkers who insisted on the
value of individualism. We can consider the radicalism of the
lower ex-samurai in terms of the reaction formula of the up-
rooted, atomized intellectual. If we limit ourselves, however,
to the problem of response to such social transformations as
rationalization, mechanization, and bureaucratization referred
to earlier, it is only after the Sino-Japanese War, or only in
the late 1890's, that individuation takes a sharp focus. In this

periodization, the present writer's view is in full accord with Professor M. Jansen's, in his distinction between Meiji Japan and Imperial Japan.[9]

The contemporaries of this period were very much aware that theirs was the second turning point after the Restoration. For example, Takayama Chogyū wrote in 1899 in *New Japan*: "The Meiji Restoration was no more than the profound social changes that were to follow. . . . In my view, 'New Japan,' in its most proper sense is really starting its first chapter now.

"What is then the so-called New Japan? Internally, it is the Japan where the great figures at the beginning, *genrō*, are fading. It is the Japan where the new personalities, educated in the atmosphere of the new Japan, are taking hold of the reins in such areas as politics, law, literature, and religion. It is the Japan which tries to wipe out the family-system through the new Civil Code. It is the Japan where the idea of rights is replacing the traditional morality based on piety. It is the Japan where workers' unions in the industrial world are emerging. . . . It is the Japan which acknowledges its own national interests in the opening of the Siberian Railroad and the Nicaragua Canal. . . . It is the Japan which recognizes the immoral acquisition of the Philippine Islands by the United States for its own national interest."

And Chogyū goes on to appeal to the young people of his time: "I shall dare to ask the new people who are to become the backbone of this new Japan, what are their wishes, their hopes; what is their determination with which to manage the new Japan? The new Japan should bid farewell to the decrepit *genrō*. We can trust only the new people reared in this new Japan. What is your determination and aspiration?"[10]

Whether and how the young people responded to this appeal will be discussed below. Here suffice it to notice that Chogyū's remark: "the idea of rights is replacing the tradi-

[9] M. B. Jansen, "Changing Japanese Attitudes Toward Modernization." See above, Chapter II.

[10] *Chogyū zenshū*, vol. IV, 1915 Edition, pp. 410-414.

tional morality based on piety," corresponds to what the conventional Japanese history of literature describes as the "emergence of individualism," or the "awakening of individuality" (from "Myōjō-group" to shizenshugi, naturalism). Also, the proposition: "It is the Japan where the workers' unions in the industrial world are emerging," is supported by a series of events in this period. (1897: the establishment of the Association for the Formation of Labor Unions, and the Steel Workers Union; the publication of Rōdō sekai by Katayama Sen; 1890: the foundation of the Association for the Universal Enfranchisement; 1900: the promulgation of the Security-Police Act; 1901: the formation of the Japanese Social Democratic Party which was banned immediately; 1903: the publication of Heimin shimbun.) It is undeniably after this period that the incessant warnings and accusations by the conservative politicians, educators, and thinkers— "rampant individualism" and "frivolous and dangerous social thought"—came to appear.

Furthermore, what is noteworthy is that around the time of the Russo-Japanese War such expressions as "modern" ideas or "modern" women came to be used, instead of the conventional adjective "Western."[11] Yet, the question is whether and to what extent this new vogue of "individualism" or the emergence of labor unions reflected INDIVIDUALIZATION or DEMOCRATIZATION in terms of the attitudes prevalent among youths and industrial workers. The present author's conclusion is that the individuation of this stage meant the predominance of the PRIVATIZED and ATOMIZED type.

The "naturalist" novels which came to predominate the

---

[11] For example, Hasegawa Tenkei, a contemporary literary critic, writes in his essay, "Kindaiteki josei": "The term, modanizumu (modernism) has obviously become current in the society of men in general as well as in the world of Christianity. Moreover, 'modernism' can be seen even in the world of women. . . . It must be noted that although modern-type women are the last things to be managed, they may, at the same time, play an important part for the advancement of civilization. Whether they are useful or harmful for the society depends on those who supervise them, but it is more usual that 'modernism' brings forth injurious women." (Taiyō, vol. 13, 1908.)

literary scene after the Russo-Japanese War represent most clearly the trend of PRIVATIZATION. Even after the slogan of naturalism atrophied, its tradition long continued to serve as the orthodox pattern in modern Japanese literature with the symbolic title, *watakushi shōsetsu*. Its ideas were quite different from rising individualism in the European sense of the term. The expression (favored by Japanese naturalists), "the sorrow and disillusionment of exposing realities," well describes the hero in such a novel, who is neither a masculine individualist, facing the challenges of life with grand dreams for the future, nor the Nietzschean superman, courageously trampling over conventional moral restraints with the objective of *Umwertung aller Werte*. Such representative writers as Tayama Katai describes the hero, modeled after himself, in a tone of disgust and self-aversion; the hero, disillusioned by the social climate, confines himself to his own small room, delving into the rotten carnality of his own desire. Daisuke, the hero in Natsume Sōseki's *Sore kara*, or the hero of *Kusa-makura*, were other types representing the retreatism of the youth of this new era, even though Sōseki himself, who was in temperament close to the European individualists, violently opposed the naturalist literature. These protagonists evidenced precociously the feeling of dull and nihilistic boredom with life or the apathetic attitude of a mere onlooker of society —feelings and attitudes expressed in the "over-matured" culture of Western Europe after the First World War. Such a literary work could have a wide audience precisely because such types of people, if not predominant, were in fact emerging. The expressions *kōtō-yūmin* (educated loafers) or *hammon-seinen* (agonized youth), which were the fashionable words in the newspapers and magazines of the time, cleverly depicted the trend of PRIVATIZATION and ATOMIZATION of the rapidly expanding group of urbanized intellectuals.[12]

[12] The population of Tokyo grew in the decade after 1898 from 1,425,366 to 2,168,815 persons.

The report in 1913 made by Regimental-district commanders throughout Japan, concerning the conscription tests, contains interesting examples of how the "bad influences" rapid urbanization had on

Besides these *hammon-seinen* or *bungaku-seinen* (literary youth) who, escaping from *seken* (the world), indulged themselves in masochistic self-disclosure, there appeared another type of privatization at the end of Meiji. This type was named in those days *seikō-seinen*—a pursuer of success in life—and was much more vulgar and light-hearted than the *hammon-seinen* type. We cannot survey the journalism and publishing circles of this period without being astonished at the flood of books and articles which would tell either in a pompous or vulgar tone *"How to* succeed" or *"How to* earn." Here we must pay special attention to the fact that there is a difference in mentality between the enthusiastic pursuit of success in the 1900's and the dreams and aspirations for *risshi* (decision of purpose in life), and *yūhi* (a heroic leap in the world) which excited young men at the first half of Meiji. In the aspirations current in early Meiji, we can see the passions of youths who, only recently emerged from the stagnant atmosphere of an isolated country, found themselves freed of the suffocating hierarchies of social status.

It is indeed symbolic that the translated edition of *Self Help* written by Samuel Smiles, which was one of the best sellers immediately after the Meiji Restoration, should have been entitled *Saikoku risshi hen*. At the beginning of Meiji, *risshi*

---

the behavior of the youths, were a matter of anxiety for the military authorities. For instance, the commander of the Hiroshima district wrote: "Kure has rapidly developed in a short time and there we find many factories, naval officers and soldiers. The city looks like a new colony because factory laborers have immigrated here from almost every district of Japan, and even not a few outlaws can be seen. The air of the city appears to be very lively, but the mind of the people is full of frivolity and fraud, and they seem to be blinded by immediate profits. This lamentable tendency cannot but have a bad influence on the neighboring villages, and in fact good habits and simple customs of rural communities are gradually being destroyed."

Also the report from the commander of Ibaragi district includes an item *"kōtō-yumin"* and describes it as follows: "There are not a few of those educated at middle schools who . . . have no intention of being engaged in agrarian or commercial activities, thus becoming utterly useless loafers. There were 161 youths who were tested this year and considered no-good."

or *risshin* (rise in the world) substantially meant the new idea of independence and self-determination of individuals, being grafted on to the Confucian concept of raising the reputation of the family by pursuing learning. Moreover, it should be noted that in this case the *risshin* of an individual was psychologically linked with aspirations for national independence and self-determination. In contrast to this, running after "success in life," which came into fashion at the end of Meiji (even though it was used as a synonym for *risshin-shusse*), no longer implied either personally or nationally the norm of independence; rather, it suggested something like shrewdness in the art of living. As *shosei*, the old name for students and young intellectuals, evolved into *gakusei*, magnificent ambitions for grasping state-power or for engaging in extravagant activities on the continent were replaced by petty desires to get along skillfully in the network of bureaucratic organizations which were rapidly developing, or to earn enough money to enjoy a luxurious urban life. It seems only natural that this kind of enthusiasm for success at the end of Meiji was labeled "individualistic deviation" both by traditional conservatives and by early socialists who had inherited the traditions of *shishi*. One of the writers of the day said, "Now in the business world of Japan, individualism is going to be put into practice *much more violently than in England, America, Germany, and France* (!). Apart from times of national crisis, there are no people on earth who are more individualistic than the Japanese."[13] Yet the "individualism" referred to was in fact nothing but a naked egoism into which the *risshi* of the former days was transformed by privatization.

What is the historical background of the privatized pattern of individuation spreading among intelligentsia and the younger generation? There are various factors which promoted this tendency. The most decisive reason may be that after the victory of the Sino-Japanese War, and particularly after the Russo-Japanese War, people suddenly felt relieved of the heavy burden they had had to bear, in the name of

[13] Ukita Kazutami, *Shin-kokumin no shūyo* (1913).

Fukoku kyōhei, ever since the Restoration, and therefore, their crisis consciousness was rapidly on the ebb.

It is commonly observed that a sense of national security works toward turning people's interests and activities from a centripetal to a centrifugal direction vis-à-vis the central authority. But in the above-mentioned case, there was another factor—the problem of generation. It was particularly among the younger generation that such a decrease in crisis consciousness was most conspicuous. For those who arrived at manhood in the 1900's, the ferment of the democratic rights movement as well as of the civil wars, which the preceding generation had actually experienced, was already an old story. The Japan in which the younger generation lived was a country where a fundamental construction of the national state had almost been completed and social life had begun to be managed by routine.

In proportion to the development of bureaucracies, nationalism, too, was becoming ritualized. Yamaji Aizan, a contemporary critic and journalist, commented: "Japanese youths were to hear a gratuitous sermon on 'loyalty to the Emperor and patriotism' from a preacher called schoolmaster. At first, they received it in a dignified manner. As the edifying sermon was repeated, however, the students became bored to death. . . . Takayama Rinjiro (Chogyū), who was the brightest student in the Imperial University, advocated an 'aesthetic life' as soon as he graduated from it . . . and attacked the formalism of the moral code of Confucianism. This shows that students went so far as to revolt against the so-called étatist education. The loose and licentious tendency became more noticeable day by day; and finally, just at the middle of the Russo-Japanese War a writer of *Kokumin shimbun* was forced to complain that 'Some of the young are interested in the gossip of *sōshi*-drama rather than in the fierce battle fought at Liaoyang . . .' "[14]

Yamaji's remarks suggest that the privatization of the younger generation was one of the reactions against bureau-

[14] *Gendai nihon kyōkai shiron* (1906).

cratic nationalism. But it must be added that this reaction was not so much a rebellion against nationalism as a retreat from *both* loyalty and rebellion. It was not without reason that Tokutomi Sohō, another contemporary journalist, called the apathetic attitude toward war current among the youth in those days a "*non*-war attitude" which he clearly distinguished from the "*anti*-war attitude" adopted by socialists and some Christians.

On the other hand, there were gradually growing a small group of young intelligentsia who showed tendencies toward INDIVIDUALIZATION quite distinct from PRIVATIZATION. Ishikawa Takuboku was one of the members of this minority. Seen from his eyes, the "individualistic" tendency represented by "naturalism" did not at all imply a revolt against the authority of the Meiji system. Takuboku interpreted the naturalist literature as a reflection of the feelings found in "most of the comparatively cultured youths," i.e., the feeling that "the nation must be strong and great. We have not a single reason to hinder the growth of Japan. But *we* would rather be excused from lending aid to it." Thus he perceived with his keen insight that behind their declaration that "we have nothing to do with strong authority," behind such an "individualistic" tendency, there lay a kind of passive conformism.[15] Takuboku has usually been called a sympathizer with radical socialism or a sentimental romanticist; however, if we examine his ideas and behaviours thoroughly, we shall find his life attitude far closer to the ethos of open and associative individualism than were most of the contemporary advocates of the "emancipation of individuality."[16]

[15] Cf. Takuboku's *Jidai heisoku no genjō* (1911).

[16] The following passage is an example of what the present writer calls associative individualism: "Those who, having high ideals, are unable to confront the problems of their own actual life, are miserable persons. At the same time, poor are they who, overwhelmed by the realities of life, forget all the possibilities of man latent within himself. Today's Japan is full of deficiencies. But I am a Japanese, too; and I have my share in such deficiencies. In short, should I not strive to synchronize my effort to better my character and my life with that of improving Japan and the lives of the Japanese?" (Takuboku's letter to Ōshima Tsuneo, dated January 1910.)

So far we have been concerned mainly with the trend of PRIVATIZATION. Those who may be regarded as typically representative of ATOMIZATION in the 1900's were the workers in such mining industries as coal, copper, and silver, and in the ship-building and steel industries. The great increase in productive power in those industries—due to military necessities unmatched in other areas of industry and agriculture—forced them almost constantly to recruit additional labor. Whereas the recruitment of female workers in the textile industries depended heavily upon connections with their native places, the male workers in the mining and heavy industries were either picked up "at random" from among the multitudes of idle labor in the agricultural areas by the "collectors" each company had dispatched throughout the nation, or were taken from the vagrant population "voluntarily" flowing into these industries. One of the characteristics of labor relations in the early days of the industrial revolution in Japan, as distinguished from the period since the middle of Taishō, was that the employers, relying on the almost limitless number of available workers, were quite unprepared to maintain stable and continuous labor relations, and correspondingly, there was a high degree of migration of workers from one factory to another. This is not to be understood in terms of social mobility in the modern world, for the laborers had not yet constituted a social "class," but existed only as a great multitude of tramps or displaced persons. Moreover, labor conditions in these industries were unbelievably miserable; the *naya* institution of coal-mining workers is one obvious example.

What made matters still worse was the fact that the rapid expansion of industrial equipment just after the Russo-Japanese War resulted in the decrease of *oyabun*—workers who had hitherto kept personal, albeit patriarchal contact with the "inferior" laborers. Now a situation emerged in which the field officials, often representing the worst side of bureaucratic personality, came to supervise directly great numbers of workers who had already been deprived of every sort of protection. The strikes and riots that broke out frequently in large mines and armament factories soon after the war must be comprehended against such a background. Disturbances in an arsenal in Ōsaka and in a naval dockyard at Kure (both in 1906) and the famous riots in Ashio and Besshi copper mines (both in 1907) were chain reaction explosions giving vent to the pent-up grievances of the workers. Their huge destructive power, revealed in such outrages as arson, bomb explosions in buildings, and the assault on the official residence of supervisors, shook the government and company authorities and led to the summoning of troops. True, the contemporary socialists and anarchists were not a little encouraged by the successive uprisings, but these were in fact nothing more than the spasmodic fits of desperately atomized workers and not in any sense part of an organized labor movement. It is no wonder, then, that all such events were squelched very shortly, with small likelihood that they would continue to develop or to spread.

Then what kind of people were those early socialists who had been called by the symbolic name *Shugisha* ("Ists")? First, a very few were intellectual leaders who, inheriting the Confucian trait of self-sacrifice from the tradition of *shishi-jinjin*, were provided with high intelligence and noble character. Next came the mixed troops of malcontents and the *déclassé* originating from extremely multifarious occupational and social standing. In January 1906, when the *Nippon Shakaitō* was born as the first legal socialist party, Sakai Toshihiko applauded the fact that this small party of 200 members contained such a variety of people: rikisha-men, jerry vendors, factory workers, the unemployed, *isōrō* (hanger-on), privates, tenants and post-office clerks.[17] But among them were included "not a few rucks, *sunemono* (a kind of misanthropic cynic) and malcontents—in short, those who had dropped behind in the competitions of capitalist society," as Yamakata Hitoshi recollected in later years. The presence of such déclassé elements explains why the party's movements, for instance, the movement against the increase of street-car fares in 1906, easily degenerated into mob scenes in the streets. Thus the real basis of what was called "syndical-

[17] *Hikari*, No. 11.

ism" at that time consisted mainly of the activities of atomized individuals.

Surely the subscribers to the *Heimin shimbun* amounted to more than ten thousand persons; but the majority of them were students and especially those students who had much in common with the above-mentioned *kōtō-yumin* privatized type in that they were merely the admirers of a liberty which involved neither self-control nor responsibility. They constituted, as it were, a group of "fans," certainly not a very reliable element for the growth of the movement.

Of course we must not overlook the fact that also from among the "syndicalist" and socialist tendencies in late Meiji there appeared the faint gleam of the ASSOCIATIVE form of individuation, just as the trend toward INDIVIDUALIZATION was emerging even from the baptism of naturalism. Katayama Sen was at that time representative of such a direction on the level of individual attitudes; he warned tirelessly against overestimating the effects of demonstrations in the streets or the riots of workers which looked so spectacular on the surface, and he tried to develop the unpretentious but continuous labor movement in the factories throughout the country. It is interesting to note that even Kōtoku Shūsui, who was inclined heavily toward "syndicalism" in his later years, interpreted the title of his last journal, "Free Thought," as "an idea which recognizes the ultimate judge not in any traditional authority but solely in reason."

It was not long before members of a new intellectual élite, with strongly individualistic personalities, appeared from among the youths who had been brought up amidst the turmoil of early socialist activities—men such as Ōsugi Sakae and Arahata Kanson, who were destined to shoulder the movement in the following generation. After the Lèse-majesté Incident (elsewhere referred to as Kōtoku, or High Treason Incident), which resulted in stifling almost every sort of socialist activity, Ōsugi and others began to publish in 1912 a literary journal, significantly named "Modern Thought." While criticizing, on the one hand, the anti-social attitude latent in the pleas for "respect of individuality" that were in

515

vogue in the early Taishō period (including such variations as the "self-assertion" of the *Shirakaba* school or the *Persönlichkeitsidee* of Abe Jirō), Ōsugi was suspicious, on the other hand, of the authoritarian tendency which danced around the rising Bolshevist movement. He sought to plot the future course of the labor movement in the direction of "the simultaneous accomplishment of individual *and* social revolution."

Such a trend from P to I to D or from A to D was not only confined to the ideas and activities of a few intellectual élites. It was also awakening in the attitude of the rank and file in the labor movement that developed on a larger scale after the First World War. Since this problem falls outside the bounds of the period we have delineated above, we shall confine ourselves to citing here only two examples and then hurry on to the problems of the second epoch-making period. The following passages are selected from letters in "Labor and Industry" a union organ of the *Yūaikai*.

Example A:

"I want to and must become a 'human being.' I long to be given rights and freedom and be treated as a man with personality. But in fact I am allowed neither to have my own free will nor to secure the rights for existence. They treat me not as an individual but only as a machine for industry. Again I yell with pain: 'I want to be a human being!' "[18]

Example B:

"Capitalists are nothing else but equals with us. Therefore I only demand that they give us fair wages, i.e., due to our labour. We do not need anything like the special favours given by capitalists. . . . Awakening workers always prefer independence to the self-satisfied benevolence thrown on us by capitalists either in the form of entertainment, such as factory theater and sports meetings, or of welfare facilities, such as company houses, cooperative societies and sanitary

[18] *Rōdō oyobi sangyō*, March 1918.

provisions. We demand only our due and nothing else, for we are not beggars."[19]

The second epoch-making period in individuation came with the Great Earthquake of 1923, which had destroyed downtown Tokyo, the last repository of traditional Edo culture. We cannot stress too strongly the social significance of the changes which occurred in all aspects of life in Tokyo, the capital representing, in a compressed fashion, the modernization of Japan as a whole. People witnessed in amazement the transformations after the earthquake, especially the radical progress in mechanization. Yokomitsu Riichi describes the scene: "To an unbelievable extent the great city was reduced to burnt ruins that stretched as far as one could see. In this burnt-out field the incarnation of speed, i.e., automobiles, appeared to wander about the streets, soon followed by the monster of sound called radio; then the model of birds, the airplane, began to fly in the sky for practical use. All of these are embodiments of modern science, coming forth in Japan one by one immediately after the earthquake disaster. . . ."[20]

And it was Yokomitsu himself who, after the earthquake, became the champion of a new literary movement called *Shin-kankakuha* (school of new sensitivity), obviously stimulated by the rapid mechanization that surrounded him. To cite another example of response to the change in the mental climate of this period, Enomoto Ken-ichi (called Enoken), a famous comic actor who established himself in the gay quarters of Asakusa, recalled: "It is undeniable that the psychology of the audience has become modern and speedy since the phenomenal earthquake. . . . No longer could the quiet and composed comic opera appeal to the changing mental climate. Perceiving this, I wanted to stage comic drama that could stun the public."[21] Changes in the mode of living of

[19] *Ibid.*, July 1918.
[20] *Kaisetsu ni kaete*, in *Sandai meisaku zenshū*, vol. 4, 1941.
[21] *Kigeki hōdan*, 1952.

the people were revealed even in their way of eating. The well-known contemporary popular singer, Soeda Azenbō, called the period "the age of business-like eating and drinking."

"The new trend is that eating and drinking have become as speedy as lightning; restaurants in which we can enjoy pleasures of the table in tranquility and in a relaxed atmosphere have gone out of sight."[22]

The beginning of radio-broadcasting (1925); the proliferation of *baa* (bars), *kafuee* (cafés), *kissaten* (tea-rooms); the rapid growth of street buses and suburban railways; the beginning of the subway system (1927); the growth of department stores and modern business offices—all these were *après-la-sismique* phenomena. The *Chūo kōron*, in 1926, published a special issue entitled *Taishū bungei*. The name *taishū-bungei* (mass literature), coined around this period, soon replaced the former name *minshu bungei* (literature of the common people).[23] The fact that the first number of *King*, a popular monthly magazine first published in January 1925, sold out at once its 740,000 copies, and the fact that the *Yen-bon* (collections of famous novels, stories or poems priced at one yen each volume) came into vogue after 1926, told dramatically of the great success of mass advertising. The destruction of city areas was followed by the development of bedroom towns along suburban lines, symbolized by scattered *bunka-jūtaku* (cultured-residences) with red roofs and small gardens in which white-collar workers dreamed of enjoying "my happy, though cramped, home" (*semai nagaramo tanoshii wagaya*—a passage from a popular song); while *moga* and *mobo* (abbreviations for Modern Girls and Modern Boys) began to stroll the Ginza streets. In short, all events seemed to point to the full-fledged growth of "mass society" in a tiny, though central, part of the country.[24]

[22] *Asakusa teiryu ki*, in *Kaizō*, May 1928.

[23] The term *minshū bungei* had a "populist" tone which was succeeded, not by *taishū bungei,* but rather by the so-called proletarian literature.

[24] The Tokyo March, an outstanding song-hit in early Shōwa, is

The Great Earthquake marked also the turning point of political and social movements in modern Japan. The brutal slaughter of Ōsugi Sakae and prominent trade-union activists amidst the turmoil of the Earthquake disaster; the flare-up of the second "Defend-the-Constitution Movement"; the establishment of the Katō Cabinet (1924); the simultaneous enactment of the Universal Manhood Suffrage Act and of the Peace Preservation Act (1925); the formation of the various proletarian parties (1926); the drawing-up of the so-called 1927 Thesis by the Comintern; the prohibition of "social study groups" in many universities and colleges; and the well-known arrest of the communists and sympathizers, called the March Fifteen Incident (1928)—all were epoch-making events following one after the other the Great Earthquake, and all left their mark on future developments.

Here again we must confine ourselves to citing a few examples which indicate prevailing patterns of behavior, particularly among the younger generation, as observed through the eyes of contemporaries of that time.

There were two kinds of concerns preying on the minds of parents of college students, especially those from good families. One was that their sons and daughters might join in the *moga* and *mobo* craze, indulging themselves in the mood of *ero-gro-nonsense* (eroticism, grotesqueness, and absurdities). The other, of course, was the fear that their children might become infected with "dangerous thought." The situation appears very similar to that of the late Meiji when these two tendencies were lumped together as frivolous and subversive. This time, however, the extent of the infiltration of "dangerous thought" into the intellectuals and students was far greater and what was worse, those students who had been regarded as exemplary were found to be the transmitters of this dangerous thought. In the late Meiji, there existed some

---

interesting in that the text includes almost all symbols of mass culture present at that time: jazz, *rikyūrū* (liqueur), taxi-dancer, Marunouchi-building, office-girl, train rush-hour, subway and suburban line, bus conductress, film-theater, tea-room, department-store, etc.

common features between the two forms of "deviation" in terms of the personality types involved. In the post-earthquake era, however, everything labeled *modan* (modern), from *moga-mobo* to "modernism" in literature, was different from, and often in opposition to, *sakei* (leftist inclination). In a book published in 1930, with the title *Modan so to modan so* ("Modern Social Stratum and Modern Phenomenon"), Ōya Soichi, vividly describing the various aspects of "modern life," wrote, "There is no 'ideal' in modern life . . . maybe there is stimulus and sensation but nowhere can 'inspiration' be found. When sweetness is removed from what was once inspiring, there remains only stimulus." It was exactly this incessant pursuit of new stimulus that characterized mass culture of this period.

What about the so-called "thought problem"? Along with the *moga* and *mobo*, there were also the "Marx-boys" and "Engels-girls," terms of derision directed against the flippant pretensions displayed by those youths who considered Marxism fashionable. However, this was only a part of the story. An investigation made by the Ministry of Education on the personalities and family circumstances of the arrested leftist students revealed the unhappy and quite unexpected fact that 65.9 percent of those polled were found to be classified in the category of "good," such as "modest," "decent," "sober," or "diligent." Only 4.6 percent came under the heading of "bad," such as "hypochondriac," "weak will," "unrestrained," etc., with the remaining 29.5 percent occupying the "middle" position.[25]

Thus in "Leftist Thoughts and Movements in the Realm of Education," published in 1933, the Ministry of Education had to confess that "The prevailing assumption . . . that only those who have some personal deficiencies in family circumstance, health, or moral character are liable to lose the attitude of the golden mean and become susceptible to leftist tendencies, has not necessarily been confirmed by facts. According

[25] For details of this survey, see *"Sakei gakusei no shuki,"* vol. 1, Ministry of Education (1934). Also see Okada Tsunesuke's, *Shisō sakei no gen-in oyobi sono keiro* (1935).

to the survey of our Ministry, the greatest number of leftist students under investigation were modest and sound in character." In short, those youths were not so much the direct offspring of the "subversive" types in the late Meiji as the transformed figures of the *mahon seinen* (exemplary youths) of the Japanese Empire.

Where particularistic human relations, such as those found in the family, village community, or various sorts of *batsu* (clique) play a predominant role in determining the pattern of culture, it is in most cases by a strong commitment to a universalistic creed that a man can walk along the path of individual and autonomous decision-making. With the exception of Christianity in the early Meiji period, only Marxism could exert this kind of moral and intellectual influence on a considerable number of people from various strata in modern Japan. It should be remembered that Marxists in prewar Japan, both in the academic and non-academic spheres, were unique among their kind in the Asian countries in that they turned their backs almost completely on all traditional and nationalistic symbols.

Noteworthy in this respect is a distinction that existed between the highly anti-traditional attitude of Marxist youths in the early Shōwa period and the so-called cosmopolitanism of the early Taishō period, represented by the *Shirakaba-ha*, who also defied the traditional authorities. While the latter relied on personal feelings and emotions, the former was derived from commitment to a scientific "system" supposedly embodying the sole and ultimate truth. Thus, an earnest attempt to apply methodically and systematically this universal truth to every minute detail of society led the Marxist youths to a decisive break with particularistic ties at least, a break more drastic than that of their predecessors. What has been regarded as the incurable defects of Japanese Marxism —its highly "abstract" and "deductive" way of thinking and "mechanical" translation of theory into practice—was in fact, ironically, its merit as it revolutionized the daily behavior of the *individual*. The notorious Fukumoto-ism that came to dominate the movement rapidly after 1926 symbolizes both this merit and fault, with its principle of "separation prior to unification" accompanied by a vehement rejection of what was called *zuruzurubettari*, i.e., "slippery continuation of particular group relations, forced by inertia."[26]

Not that there did not prevail another kind of conformist attitude inside the Marxist movement,[27] particularly inside the organizational core of the movement. Nevertheless, for most of the former *mohan seinen* it was indeed an act of determination of a highly individualistic nature to expose themselves consciously to the radiation of "dangerous thought," even in the form of joining a small study group on Marxism. Besides being under constant threat of arrest and torture by the police, these youths, born and bred of good families, were in danger of being disowned by angry parents, and rejected by all their relatives. Thousands of families were plunged into an inexpressibly tragic situation overnight by the arrest of their beloved sons and daughters, while their other relatives had also to endure the cold eyes of those around them. No wonder that parents and even teachers, when pushed to the alternative, preferred that their sons and pupils become "pink," *momoiro*, which means indulgent in sexual pleasures, rather than "red," *aka*.

What the present writer is discussing here is only one aspect of the "red" problem in prewar Japan. The whole social unrest of the time, particularly after the onset of the Great Depression in 1929, and its impact on the attitudes of the people in general, are problems to be treated separately.

The depression brought forth a huge number of unem-

[26] There is an episode which reveals how extremely this principle of Fukumoto-ism was put into practice in its heyday; two intimate friends living in the same room came to be criticized by their comrades as keeping *zuruzurubettari* relation, and after hot discussions, it was decided that either of the two should move elsewhere!

[27] Here I deliberately use the expression "Marxist" movement instead of "communist" or "bolshevist" movement; in prewar Japan, the influence of Marxism as an ideology far surpassed that of the tiny and illegal Communist Party. It was not even a political movement narrowly defined, but rather an intellectual one, as was expressed symbolically by the term "thought problem."

ployed laborers, intellectuals and white collar workers, thereby accelerating the process of atomization to an extent unequaled before. Again, Ōya Soichi writes, in "Faces of 1930," "It is an obvious fact that families of the middle and lower classes are almost all on the brink of bankruptcy. Even an individual or a family who happens to obtain a job or to engage in an occupation is in constant danger of losing it. Furthermore, they have around themselves as 'satellites' the several unemployed individuals or sets of unemployed families to feed. Thus, both materially and psychologically, they have been pushed down to the same level as the unemployed. It is said that on every main street running from countryside to Tokyo, there is a continuous stream of unemployed workers who are going on foot 'to their native land' (*kikyō*). However these are none other than persons who had originally been driven out of their *Heimat*, and what is still worse, the *Heimat* themselves are now suffering even more than are the cities and towns at the bottom of this distress."[28]

The *déclassé* psychology of an unemployed white collar worker at the same period is well expressed in the following "confession." "Confronted with the furious storm of economic depression, my company, too, which has been under the patronage of the Morgan Company, the U.S. rich, threw out 400 factory workers and 30 office employees into a great sea of starvation. From that day on, I became unemployed. Workers stood up with weapons in their hands, i.e., they went on strike; but we white collar workers had no arms to fight with. I looked back in despair at my long life of slavery—oppressed, led by the nose, with neither rights nor freedom, yet I was the kind of man who could not have earned his livelihood any other way. . . . True, it was a life of shameful submission; but now even this has been lost. . . .

"A worm I must surely be. A worm that crawls around on the ground in a pitch-dark world, or gasps for breath, searching desperately for food. Unaware I have thrown away on the roadside the feeling that 'I am a human being.' Still I

[28] *Chūō kōron*, December 1930.

don't want to take regard of such a feeling, and I don't care about having again the lost human consciousness. All I want is to find something to eat . . . I don't know what to do: I have even stopped thinking. All I can do is to sit dumbly in a gloomy room, just like a piece of rubble."[29]

Even putting aside the problem of the heavy blows the depression dealt to the most traditional part of the country, such as the Tōhōku Districts, it is not too difficult for us to imagine what would happen were intellectual white collar workers as well as industrial laborers to turn into a massive group of tramps, not only materially but also psychologically. "My happy, though cramped home" was found to be too transient a dream to settle for; a shift, either from PRIVATIZATION or from DEMOCRATIZATION, to ATOMIZATION took place on a grand scale. Thus under various crusts of the society, amorphous radicalism smoldered, destined to cause successive explosions on the surface soon after 1930.

Whoever takes the trouble to examine the complicated score of the symphonic development of modern Japan, whose coda was the Second World War, will recognize the recurrence of certain characteristic figures. This is also true of the historical process which the present writer has called individuation on the attitudinal level. Whenever the phenomenon of individuation came to the surface and attracted the attention of the general public, the behavior patterns of either PRIVATIZATION or ATOMIZATION prevailed, usually outshining the faint flickering of INDIVIDUALIZATION and DEMOCRATIZATION. Of course it may be a feature common to the non-Western developing countries that INDIVIDUALIZATION and DEMOCRATIZATION lag behind technological growth. What is conspicuous in the case of Japan is the early appearance of the P A type, and especially the tendency to maximize PRIVATIZATION—a tendency which in the West did not prevail until the stage of "mass society," but which in Japan took place in the midst of a society still largely traditional in character. How is this

[29] "Hikari no nai sekai de," *Chūō kōron*, December 1930.

special characteristic reflected in the dynamics of Japan's political and social systems?

Of the four differentiated patterns of individuation, I and P represent the relatively stable elements; D and A, the unstable elements in modernization. Therefore we can infer that on the attitudinal level, PRIVATIZATION was the stabilizing factor and ATOMIZATION the dynamic factor in the course of the political history of Japan. Earlier I pointed out that the Individualization-Democratization behavior pattern was seen sometimes more clearly among the intellectual leaders of radical socialism than among the self-acclaimed, European-type individualists, who were in fact conformists. However, the source of energy of the radical movements was located in the atomized intellectuals and workers. Thus, during the period of rise of such movements, there takes place a shift of attitude from PRIVATIZATION to ATOMIZATION on a considerable scale, and in a lesser degree, either from INDIVIDUALIZATION or from ATOMIZATION to DEMOCRATIZATION. At this point the society as a whole approximates D A type. Whenever the movement declines, and the social climate becomes more tranquil, the atomized people move more or less toward PRIVATIZATION and the democratized persons move toward INDIVIDUALIZATION, or still further toward PRIVATIZATION. (See Paradigm E.) Hence the dynamics on the social level may be described as a pendulum movement between D A type and P A type, i.e., the prototype. This is not to say that exactly the same thing occurs each time when individuation appears conspicuously, for there is a ceaseless input into this configuration from the "traditional" sector which is outside the scope of our scheme.

It is important to notice the grave difference of this type of society from that which tends to move, say, between I P type and I D type. While in the latter case INDIVIDUALIZATION constitutes the common denominator, in the former case it is invariably the atomized individual who is the key to the shifting attitude, even though PRIVATIZATION outnumbers ATOMIZATION in a normal situation. As was shown above, the atomized type is characterized by his tendency to oscillate

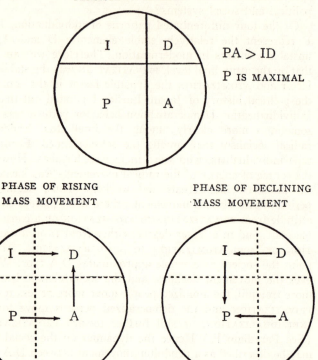

PERSISTENT PATTERN

PA > ID

P IS MAXIMAL

PHASE OF RISING
MASS MOVEMENT

PHASE OF DECLINING
MASS MOVEMENT

AD > IP
PA > ID

IP > AD
PA > ID

PARADIGM E

between over-politicalization and utter apathy, and he is most susceptible to authoritarian and charismatic leadership. No wonder, then, that in both periods discussed in this paper, the curves of the rise and fall of the radical movement were short and steep. Also, even if we disregard historical factors other than this, it is not surprising that, particularly in the 1930's, the heavy increase in atomization due to the Great Depression not so much favored the leftist movement as paved the way for ultra-nationalist tendencies.

However, it is one thing that the democratic or socialist movement in modern Japan lacked continuity and perseverance. It is quite another that the movement remained a ceaseless torment to the ruling elites. They did not consider the predominance of PRIVATIZATION to be a symptom of social stabilization, for they feared that privatization passes either into INDIVIDUALIZATION or ATOMIZATION and DEMOCRATIZA-TION.[30]

As a result, instead of encouraging certain selective patterns of individuation, the ruling class was inclined to see, in *any* sign of individuation, a symptom of political and social dis-integration. It was in this social context that the expression "individualism is a greenhouse for all radical ideas," came to be accepted. Thus, the other figure which recurs in our score of modern Japan's historical development is the over-sensitive response, on the part of the government, to every show of marked individuation, and the premature enforcement of pre-ventive measures against "subversive tendencies." That is to say, the response was not so much to actual disturbances as to their supposed or feared consequences in the future. So we see the enforcement of the Security Police Act of 1900, which

[30] Incidentally, one of the greatest changes brought by the postwar "democratic revolution" is that the attitude of *messhi-hōkō* (self-sacrificing service to the "whole") has been replaced by recognition of the *legitimacy* of privatized attitudes. Now the Conservative gov-ernment tries to attain long-range political stability by "containing" the people's attention to the enjoyment of daily life. That this policy has proved successful was admitted even by Sōhyō (The General Council of Japanese Labor Unions). "Our Course of Movement in 1960" reported that, "In spite of, or just because of the fact that there are so many unorganized workers and semi-employed who have bene-fitted very little from the progress of modernization, the union-worker is inclined to feel petite satisfaction in living in a ferro-concrete apart-ment or having an electrified home. Thus the tendency to be satisfied with happiness in an obscure nook is accompanied by the sentiment that 'we want a wage increase, but not any struggle for it.' Such a trend is bound to bring forth splits within the movement and weaken our fighting power. This is one of the reasons why the middle-class psychology of the workers has come to be discussed."

corresponds to the Peace Preservation Act of 1925; the promulgation of the *Boshin* Imperial Rescript of 1908, and of the Imperial Rescript for promoting the National Spirit in 1924; and finally the national standardization of the primary school textbook in 1903, which foreshadows the progression from the implementation of *Kōmin kyōiku* (civic education course) to *Shisō zendō kyōiku* (the education to guide thoughts to a good direction) in the late 1920's. It is symbolic that in the Imperial Rescript for Promoting the National Spirit, "frivolous radical tendencies" and "the habit of luxurious indulgence" are called the two prevalent patterns of the subversive way of life.

Just how neurotic was this concern of the power elite can be appreciated if we remember that the ruling oligarchy could not only count on the prevailing retreat of PRIVATIZA-TION, but could also perpetuate its own rule by encouraging the traditional conformism and the attitude of silent obedience. "You may as well contend against the authorities as reason with a crying child" was the attitude that prevailed especially in the rural sectors where the individuation process had not penetrated. That is to say, the prevalence of the P A type did not mean that the privatized and/or atomized individuals had become the majority in Japanese society. Furthermore, the behavior pattern fostered in the *ie* (family) or *buraku* (hamlets) continued to influence the people living in large cities.

It may be of use here to recall some of the economic characteristics of the Meiji era. As is well known, industrial labor·power was recruited from the strata of unmarried women in the case of the textile industry, and from the second and third sons of farm families in the case of heavy industries. The rapid recruitment was possible owing to the system of bringing migrant laborers from farming areas. The fact that the laborers were not formed into a social *class* in cities meant that they did not consider the city to be their permanent residence. Their life, therefore, was uncertain and lonely. Undeniably this is a factor contributing to the sporadic and disjointed character of the labor movement in modern

Japan. At the same time, however, because these workers could return to their homes if necessary (or at least they *believed* they could), the catastrophic process of atomization on the level of attitude was also checked. That urbanization, however extensive and precipitous it may have been, proceeded with ties still attached to agrarian sectors, could not help but influence the behavior patterns of these city workers.

Furthermore, the new situation that arose after the First World War prevented the intensification of atomization. With the rapid bureaucratization of enterprises during and after the war, the neglected problem of labor-management relations came to be placed on management's agenda. Concurrently factory workers in big firms, along with office workers, were now regarded as "respected" members of their firms, and they gained a new sense of belonging. Needless to say, such a policy was designed, negatively, to cut off the influence of the union movement, and positively, to raise productivity by fostering a feeling of loyalty to the firm. This is precisely what is implied in the famous principle of *kigyō-ikka* (firm-family) and *nenkō-joretsu-sei* (seniority system). The idea of familial paternalism in place of the fiction of lord-servant relationship, spread *in proportion to* the development of large-scale modernization. In short, urbanization in modern Japan, on the level of attitude as well, did not follow a one-way path from the agrarian to the urban. True, the return to the countryside of youths imbued with the "sinister influences of the city" may have constituted a real or imagined threat to the *junpū-bizoku* (pure mores and beautiful customs). But on the other hand, the great influx of people into big and small cities did spread the pattern of human relations based on the prototype of "family" and *buraku* into every corner of the private and public bureaucracies, thus counteracting the unstabilizing factor of individuation. This situation provided the *kotukai* (national polity) with a sociological basis, however ritualized it may have been as a belief system.

We must also take into account regional differences in the degree to which individuation penetrated. These differences were all the more colossal because of the rapid modernization in Japan. The premature appearance of aspects of "mass society" was geographically very limited. Yet it was precisely this limit which made these aspects so conspicuous. And particularly shocking was the metamorphosis of Tokyo, which represented everything that was "modern."

Tokyo's development and expansion was left almost entirely to its own "natural" momentum. There was no large-scale plan for the construction of streets, plazas, and parks, nor was there any architectural style. In short, no long-range measures existed to counter the population explosion. Tokyo has often been called a mammoth village. What was still worse, this "village" lacked its own norms and sanctions. Tokyo never created an urban pattern of living that would regulate the personality of its inhabitants. There was once the term *Edokko* (the typical man of Edo), but the *Edokko* was already a rarity by the late Meiji times. The expression "Tokyoko" never took root. Thus the inhabitants of Tokyo have until now failed to develop the slightest feeling of attachment or sense of belonging as "citizens of Tokyo," a situation almost incomparable with any traditional capital in the world. This is true in spite of the fact that *jōkyō* ("going to Tokyo") has always been the deep abiding desire of the agrarian youths since early Meiji. The boorish and topsy-turvy impression which the appearance of Tokyo conveys—an impression that has been intensified by the recurrence of large fires—together with the normlessness of Tokyo city life cannot but root in the minds of the people the fixed notion that city life or modernization in general *necessarily* means anomic confusion.

The term "free competition," current since late Meiji, has meant to the general public something far from the idea of a game in which the participants compete under accepted rules in the spirit of fair play. Rather, the use of the term conjures up scenes of train rush hours—the world of *yushō-reppai* (the survival of the fittest) that knows only the rule of the jungle. Such a fixed notion was bound to call forth violent reactions, particularly in time of social and national crisis.

To associate definitely and fatefully everything urban and modern with chaotic confusion would be tantamount to identifying the positive reaction to a tuberculin test with a serious case of consumption. There were many conditions in Japan that prompted men to make such hasty judgments. Hence not only the ruling elites and in-born conservatives were prone to identify one particular instance of individuation with *the* individuation and show neurotic reactions to it. Even in the minds of the Westernized intellectuals and urbanized workers, nostalgia remained for the traditional human relationship—the "undisturbed" relations supposedly existing in the family and *buraku*, virgin soil for any sign of individuation and the very world of the negative tuberculin reaction. There have been many cases of Japanese intellectuals who, once considered the ideological champions of individualism or international socialism, radically turned to traditionalism in such varied forms as "agrarianism" or "conquest of the modern world" in the face of national crisis. This does not necessarily mean that the indoctrination given to them in their primary schools was a success. Nor do political oppression or social pressures tell the whole story. As long as the ideologies of "individualism" or "democracy" are associated with what is urban, and as long as the reality of the mammoth city, represented by Tokyo, makes alien to the people the idea that there does also exist an ASSOCIATIVE form of individuation, then there will always be the psychological tendency to identify political and social chaos as well as lack of solidarity with individuation *per se*; the attraction to the "aseptic" will continue to frustrate efforts to strengthen, by exposure, the body's resistance to, or toleration of certain germs. This in spite of the fact that a negative reaction to a tuberculin test neither proves nor guarantees good health; sometimes it may even indicate greater susceptibility to severe infection in the future.

LIST OF CONTRIBUTORS

ROBERT N. BELLAH, formerly of Harvard University, is Professor of Sociology at the University of California, Berkeley. He has published many studies in the sociology of religion in Japan, including *Tokugawa Religion: The Values of Pre-Industrial Japan* (1957).

ALBERT M. CRAIG, Professor of History at Harvard University, is the author of *Chōshū in the Meiji Restoration* (1961) and co-author (with J. K. Fairbank and E. O. Reischauer) of *East Asia: The Modern Transformation* (1965).

R. P. DORE, Professor of Sociology with special reference to the Far East at the London School of Economics and Political Science, and the School of Oriental and African Studies, University of London, is the author of *City Life in Japan* (1958), *Land Reform in Japan* (1959), and *Education in Tokugawa Japan* (1964), and editor of *Aspects of Social Change in Modern Japan* (1967).

ROGER F. HACKETT, Professor of History at the University of Michigan, is former editor of the *Journal of Asian Studies*, co-author of *A Global History of Man*, of articles on the development of Japan's modern army, and author of *Yamagata Aritomo* (forthcoming).

JOHN W. HALL, formerly of the University of Michigan and now Alfred Whitney Griswold Professor of History at Yale University, is the author of *Tanuma Okitsugu (1719-1788), Forerunner of Modern Japan* (1955); *Japanese History, a Guide to Japanese Research and Reference Materials*; co-author (with R. E. Ward and R. K. Beardsley) of *Village Japan* (1959), and author of *Government and Local Power in Japan, 500-1700: A Study Based on Bizen Province* (1966).

STEPHEN N. HAY, formerly of the University of Chicago, is now at the East Asian Research Center, Harvard University.

He is the co-compiler of *Sources of Indian Tradition* (1958) and of *Southeast Asia, a Bibliographic Guide* (1963); editor of Rammohun Roy's *Dialogue Between a Theist and an Idolater* (1963), and author of *Asian Images of East and West: Tagore and His Critics in Japan, China and India* (forthcoming).

JOHN F. HOWES, Assistant Professor of Japanese History at the University of British Columbia, translated and adapted *Japanese Religion in the Meiji Era* by Kishimoto Hideo (1956) and has written many articles on Christianity in modern Japan. He has in preparation an interpretive study on the works of Japan's best known Christian, Uchimura Kanzō.

MARIUS B. JANSEN, formerly of the University of Washington and now Professor of History at Princeton University, is the author of *The Japanese and Sun Yat-sen* (1954), *Sakamoto Ryōma and the Meiji Restoration* (1961), and Associate Editor of the *Journal of Asian Studies*.

SHŪICHI KATŌ is Professor of Asian Studies at the University of British Columbia. He is co-editor of *Kindai Nihon shisō-shi kōza*, author of numerous books on Japanese literary, cultural and social history, and contributor to several symposia published in the United States.

MASAO MARUYAMA is Professor of Political Theory at Tokyo University and has taught at Harvard University and St. Anthony's College, Oxford, as Visiting Professor. In Japan he is known for his Studies in the History of Japanese Political Thought (*Nihon seiji shisō-shi kenkyū*; 1952 and seven subsequent impressions), his volumes of essays published as *Gendai seiji no shisō to kōdō*, 2 vols., 1956, and numerous shorter studies. A collection of his essays, edited by Ivan Morris, has been published in English under the same title as the Japanese set of 1956, *Thought and Behaviour in Modern Japanese Politics* (Oxford University Press, 1963).

HERBERT PASSIN is Professor of Sociology, East Asian Institute, Columbia University, and author of: *Education and Society in Japan* (1964); *In Search of Identity* (with J. W. Bennett and R. K. McKnight) (1958); *The Japanese Village in Transition* (with A. F. Raper and others) (1951), and *Africa—Dynamics of Change* (with K. A. B. Jones-Quartey) (1964).

DONALD H. SHIVELY, formerly of the University of California (Berkeley) and Stanford University, is Professor of Japanese History and Literature at Harvard University. A former editor of the *Journal of Asian Studies*, he is the author of many studies on theater and cultural history, including *The Love Suicide at Amijima* (1953), and of "Motoda Eifu: Confucian Lecturer to the Meiji Emperor" in *Confucianism in Action* (ed. D. S. Nivison and A. F. Wright, 1959).

HERSCHEL WEBB, Associate Professor of Japanese at Columbia University, is the author of *Research in Japanese Sources, a Guide* (1964) and *The Japanese Imperial Institution in the Tokugawa Period* (1968).

HELLMUT WILHELM is Professor of Chinese History in the Far Eastern and Russian Institute of the University of Washington. He is the author of numerous books and articles on Chinese history and literature, among them *Chinas Geschichte* (1942), *Gesellschaft und Staat in China* (1944 and 1960), several studies on the *Book of Changes*, and has in preparation a study of the intellectual history of the Ch'ing Dynasty.

INDEX

537

539